CRUSOE'S SECRET

by the same author

poetry

A STATE OF JUSTICE

THE STRANGE MUSEUM

LIBERTY TREE

FIVEMILETOWN

SELECTED POEMS 1972–1990

WALKING A LINE

THE WIND DOG

THE INVASION HANDBOOK

THE ROAD TO INVER

adaptations

THE RIOT ACT: A VERSION OF SOPHOCLES' *ANTIGONE*

SEIZE THE FIRE: A VERSION OF AESCHYLUS' *PROMETHEUS BOUND*

play

THE HILLSBOROUGH SCRIPT: A DRAMATIC SATIRE

anthologies

THE FABER BOOK OF POLITICAL VERSE

THE FABER BOOK OF VERNACULAR VERSE

WILLIAM HAZLITT: THE FIGHT AND OTHER WRITINGS
(WITH DAVID CHANDLER)

THOMAS HARDY (POET TO POET SERIES)

criticism

THOMAS HARDY: THE POETRY OF PERCEPTION

IRELAND AND THE ENGLISH CRISIS

MINOTAUR: POETRY AND NATION STATE

WRITING TO THE MOMENT: SELECTED CRITICAL ESSAYS 1980–1996

THE DAY-STAR OF LIBERTY: WILLIAM HAZLITT'S RADICAL STYLE

Crusoe's Secret

The Aesthetics of Dissent

TOM PAULIN

faber and faber

First published in 2005
by Faber and Faber Limited
3 Queen Square London WC1N 3AU
Published in the United States by Faber and Faber Inc.
an affiliate of Farrar, Straus and Giroux LLC, New York

Photoset by RefineCatch Limited, Bungay, Suffolk
Printed in England by Mackays of Chatham plc, Chatham, Kent

A CIP record for this book
is available from the British Library

ISBN 0-571-22115-7

2 4 6 8 10 9 7 5 3 1

For Mariam Said, and in memory of Edward Said

[illegible] there he [illegible]
Prefer, and piety to God, though [illegible]
To thee not visible, when I [illegible]
Seemed in thy world erroneous [illegible]
From all: my sect thou seest, [illegible]
How few sometimes may know, when thousands err.

John Milton, *Paradise* [illegible]

there be, who faith
Prefer, and piety to God, though then
To thee not visible, when I alone
Seemed in thy world erroneous to dissent
From all: my sect thou seest, now learn too late
How few sometimes may know, when thousands err.

John Milton, *Paradise Lost*, Book Six, ll. 143–8

Contents

Acknowledgements

I owe a great debt of gratitude to Christopher Whalen for his help and advice. For their help and assistance, I am also grateful to Joan Arthur, Roy Foster, Jenny Houlsby, Simon Humphries, Angie Johnson, Valerie Kemp, Laura Keynes, Jamie McKendrick, Andrew McNeillie, Jon Mee, Bernard O'Donoghue, Dan O'Hara, Lucy Reynolds, Christopher Ricks, Xon de Ros, Greta Rye, Marilee Scott, Stephanie West, Duncan Wu.

Versions of these essays were first published in the following: 'Shakespeare's Sonnets: The Key' in the *London Review of Books*, 22 January 1998, as 'In the Workshop'; 'Jangling Monarchy: John Milton' in the *London Review of Books*, 8 August 2002, as 'Jangling Monarchy'; 'The Limits of the New Historicism: Andrew Marvell' in the *London Review of Books*, 25 November 1999, as 'O brambles, chain me too'; 'The Jaw-Bone of an Ass Espied: John Bunyan' in the *London Review of Books*, 16 December 2004, as 'Holy Boldness'; 'Crusoe's Secret: Daniel Defoe' in the *London Review of Books*, 19 July 2001, as 'Fugitive Crusoe'; 'Outside In: Richard Brinsley Sheridan' in the *Independent on Sunday*, 26 October 1997, as 'In the Limelight'; 'The Shaggy, the Rude, the Awkard: John Clare' in the *London Review of Books*, 19 February 2004, as 'Gentlemen and ladies came to see the poet's cottage'; 'Gently and Pauseably: Christina Rossetti' in the *Times Literary Supplement*, 18 January 2002, as 'The cadence in the song'; 'An Indian Child: Rudyard Kipling' in the *Times Literary Supplement*, 8 March 2002, as 'The Imperial theme'; 'Synge and Irish History' in Nicholas Grene, ed., *Interpreting Synge: Essays from the Synge Summer School, 1991–2000* (Dublin: Lilliput Press, 2000), as

'*Riders to the Sea*: A Revisionist Tragedy?'; 'Pick, Pack, Pock, Puck: Joyce's Dislike of Aquacity' in the *Dublin Review*, 7 (Summer 2002), as 'Joyce and the noise of life'; '*The Waste Land*: A Keynsian Epic?' in the *Times Literary Supplement*, 29 November 2002, as 'Many cunning passages'; 'Crusoe Revisited: Elizabeth Bishop' as the Introduction to Elizabeth Bishop, *Complete Poems* (London: Chatto & Windus, 2004); 'Himself Alone: David Trimble' in 'Diary', the *London Review of Books*, 7 October 2004; 'The Critic as Artist: Edward Said' in the *Guardian*, 25 September 2004, as 'Writing to the moment'.

Introduction

In 1893, Henry James confided an idea for a new novel to his notebook:

I am putting my hand to the idea of the little story on the subject of the partagé child – of the divorced parents – as to which I have already made a note here. The little *donnée* will yield most, I think – most *ironic* effect, and this is the sort of thing mainly to try for in it – if I make the old parents, the original parents, *live*, not die, and transmit the little girl to the persons they each have married *en secondes noces*. This at least is what I ask myself.

James's term for what he elsewhere calls 'the virus of suggestion' was for a time part of what we now call critical discourse – Wilde, William James, T. S. Eliot and Auden all used the term *donnée*, and in doing so they imparted a certain Jamesian exquisiteness to the already sophisticated – because French – word for a revealing fact. The critical *donnée*, unlike the aesthetic, has never been a subject, but – on that balancing other hand – maybe it's worth discovering. It's less an obscure piece of knowledge than finding something hidden in the daylight, but that process is picky, at times obsessive, a matter of trusting hunches and intuitions, and weighing particular words that for reasons that aren't immediately apparent seem to stick. Wordsworth's 'mountain', as I shall explain, was one such word that took nearly thirty years to attain a particular obdurate density. This means that the explanation of this reading process has to move from a series of examples, rather than offer an overarching or categorical idea – though I would argue that the essential critical approach is formalist and historical.

Let me try to explain, and in making the attempt I'll take encouragement from a remark John Kerrigan made in a review of a book with a rather unprepossessing title, *Reading After Theory* (Valentine Cunningham, 2001): 'However open to abuse the autobiographical impulse may be, to set out the life circumstances that "situate" one's critical judgements can be virtuously self-analytical and helpful to the reader.' What we're often given as a governing idea – the critical *donnée* – is something that happens because a piece of knowledge which we already possess is activated by chance. I noticed this some years ago through the accident of being asked to teach a course in eighteenth-century literature, and in preparation re-reading a number of classic texts – *Robinson Crusoe*, Dryden's *Aeneid, Clarissa* – which I'd last taught back in the 1970s, when literary criticism still clung to the idea of the autonomous work of art, the well-wrought urn. I still think it should hold to that ideal, but only when practised by really intelligent scholars and critics – Helen Vendler's study of Shakespeare's sonnets (*The Art of Shakespeare's Sonnets*, 1997) is so completely and stringently dedicated to an ideal of close formal analysis that it ought to influence all studies of verse and prose that follow it.

Vendler shows how many sonnets have in each quatrain a key word, which then becomes what she terms a 'couplet tie'. In Sonnet 73, for example, the word 'leaues' in the second line – 'When yellow leaues, or none, or few doe hange' – is caught up in the couplet tie 'leaue', so that it is recalled in the closing couplet:

> This thou perceu'ft, which makes thy loue more ftrong,
> To loue that well, which thou muft leaue ere long.

Then something nags at me, as I remember an earlier seminal work, which I read in sixth form – Empson's *Seven Types of Ambiguity*. In one of his gruff, piercing asides Empson remarks of the bare, ruined choirs in Sonnet 73:

> To take a famous example, there is no pun, double syntax, or dubiety of feeling, in 'Bare ruined choirs, where late the sweet birds sang', but the comparison holds for many reasons; because ruined monastery choirs are places in which to sing, because they involve sitting in a row, because they are made of wood, are carved into knots and so forth, because they used to be surrounded by a sheltering building crystallised out of the likeness of a

forest, and coloured with stained glass and painting like flowers and leaves, because they are now abandoned by all but grey walls coloured like the skies of winter, because the cold and Narcissistic charm suggested by choir-boys suits well with Shakespeare's feeling for the object of the Sonnets, and for various sociological and historical reasons (the protestant destruction of monasteries; fear of puritanism), which it would be hard now to trace out in their proportions; these reasons, and many more relating the simile to its place in the Sonnet, must all combine to give the line its beauty, and there is a sort of ambiguity in not knowing which of them to hold most clearly in mind. Clearly this is involved in all such richness and heightening of effect, and the machinations of ambiguity are among the very roots of poetry.

The historical vision this remark opens up has stayed with me, and so, too, has the sense that historical knowledge complements aesthetic analysis (later the concept of Angst added another voice, or approach). Re-reading *Crusoe*, I noticed that the dates 1659–1687, which define Crusoe's sojourn on the island, are a version of 1660–1688: the entire term of the Stuart Restoration. If Defoe had used those dates, his message and political ideology would have been clear to his readers. Those on his side – the Whigs – would have applauded him, but he would have lost his Tory readers (he appeals to them in *Memoirs of a Cavalier*) and he would have made those in the middle uneasy that he had a quite palpable design on them. But he would also have lost that idea of a working, bonding, productive consensus, which his experience of Stuart repression and the Monmouth rebellion's bloody aftermath had taught him was a central, civic value.

Following through the significance of those dates, and helped by the work of the students I taught, I began to imagine a study of Defoe which would uncover his secret code. I dreamed of a book and settled for a long essay, an essay written for an audience that doesn't necessarily see a historic resonance in this sentence from Defoe's *Roxana*:

I could not be of one Opinion, and then pretend myself to be of another; nor could I go to Confession, who knew nothing of the Manner of it, and should betray myself to the Priest, to be a Hugonot, and then might come into Trouble; but in short, tho' I was a Whore, yet I was a Protestant Whore, and could not act as if I was Popish, upon any Account whatsoever.

Defoe is thinking of Nell Gwynne's famous remark to an angry London mob, when they mistook her for Charles II's unpopular, French, Catholic mistress, Louise Kerouaille, Duchess of Portsmouth. To the mob, Nell Gwynne shouted: 'I am the Protestant Whore.' A theme that is continued, when Roxana has a premonition of her husband's murder:

I star'd at him, as if I was frighted, for I thought all his Face look'd like a Death's-Head; and then, immediately, I thought I perceive'd his Head all Bloody; and then his Cloaths look'd Bloody too; and immediately it all went off; and he look'd as he really did; immediately I fell a-crying, and hung about him, My Dear *said I*, I am frighted to Death; you shall not go, depend upon it, some Mischief will befal you; I did not tell him how my vapourish Fancy had represented him to me, that I thought was not proper; besides he wou'd only have laugh'd at me, and wou'd have gone away with a Jest about it: But I press'd him seriously not to go that Day, or if he did, to promise me to come Home to *Paris* again by Day-light: He look'd a little graver then, than he did before; told me, he was not apprehensive of the least Danger; but if there was, he wou'd either take Care to come in the Day, or, as he had said before, wou'd stay all Night.

But all the Promises came to nothing; for he was set upon in the open Day, and robb'd, by three Men on Horseback, mask'd, as he went; and one of them, who, it seems, rifled him, while the rest stood to stop the Coach, stabb'd him into the Body with a Sword, so that he died immediately.

This is meant to remind Defoe's readers of the assassination of Henry of Navarre – Henry IV of France – the Huguenot King who, converting to Catholicism, said: 'Paris is worth a mass.' He was stabbed in his coach by Ravaillac. Defoe, who had Huguenot friends in London, would have held their history in his cultural memory, just as Hazlitt did during the White Terror, which followed the defeat of Napoleon. Burke's famous phrase for his tribal or family feelings for Irish Catholics – 'little platoon' – is also true of Dissenters.

History, I realize, is often anecdote, *petite histoire*, lodged in the memory. Defoe's readers would have recognized that he is designing a particular, Whiggish narrative. They would have known that he is ideologically driven. And so is Wordsworth, except in his political subconscious he is sceptical, even subversive, of what he – at least on the surface – thinks he believes. Looking at these lines

> The sounding cataract
> Haunted me like a passion: the tall rock,
> The mountain, and the deep and gloomy wood,

I began to think how Seamus Heaney's landscapes are seldom what they seem. I can see a milk churn on a wooden stand by a country road, the demesne wall under beech trees near Castle Dawson – they hide something, and carry a memory of an ambush. It was then that the heavily accented amphibrach – 'the móuntain' – took on a special force (it picks up the *ow* in 'sounding', the *nt* in 'Haunted' and the *t* in 'tall'). The weight of the phrase made me translate it into *La Montagne*, which was the name given in the French National Assembly to the sloping benches where the Jacobins sat, and which was applied to that group. I'm talking about this process of discovery because we read, not by paraphrasing, not by translating the words into concepts, but by realizing the individual texture and identity, the quiddity, of the words, phrases, lines or sentences that catch our eye and which we hear. These are the *données* that speak to us, and they are often thickened or inspissated by subliminal, fringe, or possible meanings that need to be delicately uncoded. And I recognize that my account of 'Tintern Abbey' may seem too thickly historical, at least for those who want those sportive lines of wood to belong simply to nature.

For many years I regarded Synge's *Riders to the Sea*, which I'd first studied at school, as a terse, great, naturalistic play about the lives of impoverished Aran islanders. Then, after reading a lot of Irish history as the Troubles in the North of Ireland took hold, I noticed something as I re-read the play for a class: Bartley enters the cottage kitchen and 'Speaking sadly and quietly', the stage direction says, asks: 'Where is the bit of new rope, Cathleen, was bought in Connemara?' His sister, Cathleen, says: 'it's on a nail by the white boards. I hung it up this morning, for the pig with the black feet was eating it.' Then his other sister, Nora, gives him the rope: 'Is that it, Bartley?' Margaret interjects: 'You'd do right to leave that rope, Bartley, hanging by the boards.' Bartley, the directions say, takes the rope, and 'beginning to work with the rope' says: 'I've no halter the way I can ride down on the mare.' In an effort to persuade him to stay Maurya says:

> It's a hard thing they'll be saying below if the body is washed up and there's no man in it to make the coffin, and I after giving a big price for the finest white boards you'd find in Connemara. [*She looks round at the boards.*]

Bartley continues working at the halter.

The halter and the new boards are linked, and they are repeatedly emphasized. It was the conjunction of rope and boards that brought into my memory an account of the execution of Robert Emmet – he stood on the loose, unnailed board over the drop, holding the handkerchief he was to drop when he was ready. The historian, Ian McBride, tells the story at the beginning of a review of two bicentenary studies of Emmet:

> Robert Emmet's last words – following a dispute with the hangman about the positioning of the rope about his neck – were 'not yet', or more precisely 'not y–'. Three times the executioner asked if he was ready, and each time Emmet delayed. On the third 'not . . .', according to an eyewitness account, the hangman kicked the single plank from under his feet, and Emmet 'was dangling like a dog, writhing in the agonies of the most revolting and degrading to humanity of all deaths'. Half an hour later the body was taken down and beheaded, as the sentence for high treason required. Under the scaffold dogs were seen lapping up Emmet's blood, and spectators rushed to dip their handkerchiefs in it, thus securing a relic of perhaps the greatest of all Ireland's republican martyrs.

And then McBride adds: 'At least we think that's what happened.' One story, I recall, has the hangman saying: 'Are you ready, sir?' and receiving no reply. The account I had read reminded me of the theme of hanging, which runs through *The Playboy of the Western World*, and eventually led me to see the historical theme that is subtly and almost invisibly embedded in *Riders to the Sea* (recently I've come to view Bartley putting on a new jacket in exchange for his old as a version of Emmet's splendid United Irish uniform, as well as a signal that he is shortly to be translated into the newness of eternity).

Again, the tin scoop in Seamus Heaney's 'Sunlight', which is sunk past its 'gleam' in the meal bin, reminds me of the gleam of arms in the *Aeneid*, or a famous phrase in George Dangerfield's study, *The Strange Death of Liberal England*, where he speaks of the 'sheen' of arms in Ulster. Many years before the term 'decommissioning' became a means of wrong-footing the peace process, Heaney's tense, monosyllabic, closing lines act as a prolepsis.

It's here I came up against the idea of borders and barriers. In *Literature, Partition and the Nation State*, a literary study of culture and conflict in Ireland, Israel and Palestine, Joe Cleary states that the subject of partition receives little attention in all the writing on nations and nationalism that has emerged over more than the past twenty years. The assumption has been that partition was inherited from the colonial states that preceded newly independent states. Benedict Anderson's *Imagined Communities* neither 'invites us to ask', Cleary states, nor provides us with the theoretical equipment to consider why 'territorial cleavages' of this kind should have happened in some colonies and not in others. The border between the state of Northern Ireland and the Irish Republic has disappeared from the landscape – I notice this on the road from Derry to Letterkenny, where a tall, grey, steel, fortified customs and army post with a watchtower used to cast an eerie vigilance over the surrounding, rather English demesne landscape that made me think I was in the Gloucestershire of Stevenson's *The Black Arrow*. But the border remains in the hearts and minds of everyone who belongs to the North of Ireland, and to many who grew up in the peaceful state south of its invisible shadow.

In the introduction to the *Encyclopaedia of Ireland*, a comprehensive work greatly influenced by the peace process, Brian Lalor states that individual contributors experienced considerable difficulty with the concept of being asked 'to write on a unitary island'. These contributors tended, in their separate scholarly disciplines, not to let their critical scrutiny extend either north or south 'beyond the opaque glass of the border'. The point I am making is that the critical positions from which these essays come involves the experience of border, tribe, community, and the histories that produced them.

In a characteristically subtle border poem, 'The Boundary Commission', Paul Muldoon glances at the public body that was supposed to redraw the border after the signing of the Anglo-Irish Treaty in 1921. The poem, though it does not say so, is set in Pettigo, a small town, partly in Donegal, partly in Fermanagh, where the border runs down the main street:

> *You remember that village where the border ran*
> *Down the middle of the street,*
> *With the butcher and baker in different states?*
> Today he remarked how a shower of rain
>
> Had stopped so cleanly across Golightly's lane
> It might have been a wall of glass
> That had toppled over. He stood there, for ages,
> To wonder which side, if any, he should be on.

Which side, if any, these essays are on, I leave it for the reader to decide.

These essays are largely about English Dissenting writers, or writers, such as Clare or Kipling, who were touched by Dissent – by Methodism in their cases – or about writers like Yeats and Joyce, who drew on Blake (and in Joyce's case also Defoe) to build their visions of the New Jerusalem. As Sharon Achinstein shows in her important study, *Literature and Dissent in Milton's England*, Dissenters were committed to 'publicity, openness, and generative dispute'. They naturally sought out controversy, and aimed to expand the culture of political knowledge. It was while reading what could be regarded as a Dissenting polemic – Keynes's *The Economic Consequences of the Peace* – that I realized that it was a major source for *The Waste Land*, where the repeated word 'violet' is a pun on 'violent', a memory of a war that ended in a brutal, punitive peace.

I've found again and again that it's an individual sound (that *uh* in 'Sunlight' or the same sound in Marvell that led me to guess that Cromwell's name must have been pronounced 'Crummle' by his contemporaries), or it has been a word or a cadence that has acted as the *donneé* for an essay. Re-reading Camus, whom I'd studied at school in Belfast in the 1960s, and then left behind, I became interested in the word 'buta', which occurs in the opening pages of the novel, where Dr Rieux 'sortit de son cabinet et buta sur un rat mort, au milieu du palier' ('left his office and stumbled against a dead rat in the middle of the landing'). I'd been drawn back to Camus because he chooses a quotation from Defoe's second sequel to *Robinson Crusoe* as epigraph to *La Peste*:

Il est aussi raisonnable de represénter une espèce d'emprisonnement par une autre que de représenter n'importe quelle chose qui existe réellement par quelque chose qui n'existe pas. (It is reasonable to represent one kind of imprisonment by another, as it is to represent anything that really exists by that which does not exist.)

Camus is signalling his intentions, but he doesn't appear to have stimulated critics of Defoe to interpret his work symbolically, and to see, for example, *A Journal of the Plague Year* as a political allegory of life under the Restoration.

That word 'buta', Rieux stumbling or tripping over a dead rat, began to reverberate for me as I read, though it doesn't occur again until halfway through the novel:

Pense un peu à toutes les combinaisons, les descentes et les passes qu'il faut faire avant de marquer un but. (Why, think of all the swerves and runs and passes you've got to make to score a goal.)

Two pages later, Rambert 'reprit cet air de réflexion buté qui lui était habituel et remonta sur son tabouret' ('The look of brooding obstinacy that Rambert so often had came back to his face, and he climbed on to his stool again'). About twenty pages later, we're told: 'Il n'avait plus qu'une patience sans avenir et une attente buttée' ('There was nothing more than a patience without a future, and a stubborn speculation'). Towards the end of the novel: 'Une sorte de panique les prenait à la pensée qu'ils pouvaient, si près du but, mourir peut-être, qu'ils ne reverraient pas l'être qu'ils chérissaient et que ces longues souffrances ne leur serraient pas payées' ('They were seized with a sort of panic at the thought that they might die so near the goal and never see the ones they loved again, and their long privation have no recompense').

These are the uses of 'but' and 'buter' and its variants that I can find. In English, 'stub' and 'stubborn' would be close, but 'end' and 'goal' are also its meanings (Camus was a gifted goalkeeper, so the word was close to his heart). It is a nodal word or cluster of cognate words and meanings – what Empson calls a 'complex' word, like 'honest' in *Othello*. Deep in Camus's subconscious, his political subconscious, he knows that 'buter' also means in gangster's slang 'to kill, to whack', and that 'butin' means 'booty'. There are guilts and anxieties attached to the word, as well as direction, teleology, ultimate destinations, which Camus, as a *pied noir* in an Algeria he regards as a permanent *département* of France, is deeply uneasy about. As he says at the end of the allegory, 'cette chronique ne pouvait pas être celle de la victoire définitive' ('this chronicle cannot be one of definitive victory').

When Rieux stubs his foot against the dead rat on the landing, he releases a series of words for 'stubborn': 'l'obstination aveugle' ('blind obstinacy'), 'le piétinement obstiné' ('obstinate shuffling'), which embody, in Ulster loyalist terms, the not-an-inch fixity of the settlers' position. The trap is that when Father Paneloux preaches on Exodus, the images of plague in the biblical book are symbols, I take it, of the various terrorist campaigns that the Israelites visited on the Egyptians while they endured exile and imprisonment under Pharaoh. The French Algerians are sleepwalkers, blind to the rest of the world, who experience 'un sentiment d'exil' ('a feeling of exile'), when they see smoke shuffling from the funnel of a railway train. But the *pieds noirs* are, in the priest's analogy, not the Israelites, but the Egyptians. The tiny, strategic mentions of Arabs – like blacks playing bit-parts in old movies – are threats to the whole fabric. Camus is covering himself when he brushes them in.

The 'fou qui tire sur la foule' ('the madman who fires on the crowd') is a French settler who has gone mad under the strain of being a colonizer, and his action is a prolepsis of the Battle of Algiers. What is also interesting is the treatment of time – 'ce piétinement énorme' ('this enormous marking of time') – in a city 'sans avenir' ('with no future'). The French Algerians have no future, and when Camus says 'la maladie abandonnait ses positions' ('the illness abandoned its positions'), the parallel with an urban guerrilla campaign is clear. The term 'séparation' significantly describes their experience, and I recall more than twenty years ago listening to a commentary by Ian Paisley on the Book of Exodus that was called 'Separation'.

When Camus says 'il fallait retrouver leur vraie patrie', he insists on their separation, loneliness and exile. From 'but' to 'butt' – rifle butt, butt as a target for arrows – the word expresses the twisted knot of conflicting emotions at the heart of Camus's imagination. He would have spotted that Defoe's *Journal of the Plague Year* was about the sufferings of the Dissenters under the Stuart Restoration. At school, we read *La Peste*, comfortably, as being about the Nazi occupation of France, which is how it has often been interpreted. But it was when I read Conor Cruise O'Brien's short study of Camus that the colonialist strategies of his writing became clear. As Edward Said shows in his discussion of Camus and French imperial experience in *Culture and Imperialism*, there is an 'elision and compression' in O'Brien's 'otherwise tough-minded analysis' of Camus, when he considers him as an individual artist 'anguished over difficult choices'. As Said shows, Camus's writing is informed by an 'extraordinarily belated, in some ways incapacitated colonial sensibility', which enacts an imperial gesture in a form – the realist novel – which was well past its greatest achievements in Europe. Camus declared that an Algerian nation never existed, yet he describes 'a community with nowhere to go'.

The pattern I look for is a pattern of repetition, or, in the case of Christina Rossetti, the structural principle of the pause, which derives from her reading of George Herbert, who wrote that the priest conducting a church service should speak 'gently and pause-ably'. The subject here is not political or historical – isn't connected with Dissent – and reminds me that aesthetic pleasure need not always be entangled with social issues. It is in Milton, though, and my argument that there is an allusion to the *Aeneid* at the beginning of *Paradise Lost* stems from an initial wish to find such an allusion. In order to make that connection I went from an English translation of Milton's *Second Defence of the English People* to the original Latin text, where the word 'gravis' caught my eye. I looked it up in the *Chambers Murray Latin-English Dictionary* which lists the uses of the Latin words in the classic Latin authors. Under the long entry for 'gravis' appears 'regina Marte gravis'. From there I went to the *Aeneid* and realized that Milton had encoded an allusion to the birth of the English Republic in his opening account of God's creation of the world.

Reading Bunyan and Clare, I realized that a nodal word for them is 'rude', and reflecting on it I began to see that a history of English poetry from Langland onwards could be constructed around the multiple meanings and the social and aesthetic anxieties which adhere to 'rude'. It is the acoustic adhesiveness of words and patterns of sound that fascinates me (*jingled jaunty jangled* is one of such a pattern in *Ulysses*) and these essays are attempts to examine and explore those patterns. They now seem to me belated, for just as I began to write about Edward Said's discussion of Camus, the news of his death reached me. The inspiration of that courageous man, whom I loved dearly, is behind all these essays.

Shakespeare's Sonnets: The Key

Recently I was teaching a poem by Yeats that has always reminded me of a stretched sonnet. 'In Memory of Eva Gore-Booth and Con Markiewicz' has an octave of 20 lines and a sestet of 12 lines, but as Yeats was not interested in the sonnet form (he wrote very few sonnets), the comparison is probably subjective. The poem begins:

> The light of evening, Lissadell,
> Great windows open to the south,
> Two girls in silk kimonos, both
> Beautiful, one a gazelle.

Eight lines later, Yeats gives a reprise of the opening:

> Many a time I think to seek
> One or the other out and speak
> Of that old Georgian mansion, mix
> Pictures of the mind, recall
> That table and the talk of youth,
> Two girls in silk kimonos, both
> Beautiful, one a gazelle.

Immediately after this, at the beginning of the elongated second section of the poem, Yeats writes:

> Dear shadows, now you know it all,
> All the folly of a fight
> With a common wrong or right.

That line 'Dear shadows, now you know it all' I have always found almost unbearably emotional, and standing in front of a class of undergraduates I again wondered why this was. Very early the next morning I woke with the answer: the line reproduces in a slightly different pattern the *o* sounds in *windows / open / south* in the second line. The two young women are shadows now, but in saying so Yeats brings back his earlier line which blazed its light behind their silky young bodies. Then in the very last line of the poem – 'Bid me strike a match and blow' – he softens its angry, cornered, very Protestant destructiveness by concluding the poem with a final *o* sound that takes us back to the heaven of that opening quatrain. It's like watching someone turn from blowing vigorously into a fire in order to breathe gently against a dandelion clock. Realizing the subtlety of Yeats's music, I began to imagine a critical account of his or any poet's work which would jettison all earnest explication of the text – meaning, paraphrasable content, social and historical situation – and concentrate entirely on sound, cadence, metre, rhyme, form. A critical study that would be true to Yeats's dictum 'Words alone are certain good.' And then I began to wonder where I could find such a book.

Helen Vendler's long study, *The Art of Shakespeare's Sonnets* (1997), is that purely aesthetic study of poetic language in action, and it begins appropriately with this statement: 'I assume that a poem is not an essay, and that its paraphrasable prepositional content is merely the jumping-off place for its real work . . . I do not regard as literary criticism any set of remarks about a poem which would be equally true of its paraphrasable content.' Taking issue with a recent editor of the *Sonnets*, John Kerrigan, she points to his lack of interest in the linguistic variation in Sonnet 129, and says he takes 'a single-minded expository view of the poem, as though it were a self-consistent sermon'. For Vendler, the verbal imagination's true intent is '*always to make a chain of interesting signifiers*, with the "message" tucked in as best the poet can'. And she says that because many readers prefer to think of the *Sonnets* as 'discursive prepositional statements', rather than as 'situationally motivated speech acts', we remain condemned to a 'static view of any given sonnet'. Gently criticizing Stephen Booth's account of the contrary pulls in Sonnet 146, she grants that his discussion is 'interesting', but finds it too preoccupied 'with meaning alone'. The editorial and critical accounts published over the last thirty years do not pay enough attention to the *Sonnets* as poems. Putting the intellectual and expository to one side, Vendler says that she is more concerned with the aesthetic experience we encounter 'temporally' as we read the sonnet.

We encounter that experience in a particularly structured way, because, as she marvellously shows, each sonnet has what she terms a 'couplet tie' – the words that appear in the body of the sonnet (lines 1–12) which are repeated in the couplet (13–14). By 'words', she means 'a word and its variants': for example, *lives, live* and *outlive* count as one word. Often Shakespeare uses a more complex form of repetition than the couplet tie. In Sonnet 7, the first quatrain (Q1) contains the word *looks*, Q2 the word *looks* again. Q3 the word *look* and the couplet the word *unlooked-on*. She calls the root word – in this case, *look* – a 'key word', and registers it at the end of her commentary on each sonnet. The couplet tie which she also prints at the end of each commentary, of course contains the key word. So far so necessarily technical, but let us see how it applies in practice in her discussion of Sonnet 15 which, as with every sonnet, she prints both in the original Quarto form and in her own modernized version:

When I confider euery thing that growes
Hold in perfection but a little moment.
That this huge ftage prefenteth nought but fhowes
Whereon the Stars in fecret influence comment.
When I perceiue that men as plants increafe,
Cheared and checkt euen by the felfe-fame skie:
Vaunt in their youthfull fap, at height decreafe,
And were their braue ftate out of memory.
Then the conceit of this inconftant ftay,
Sets you moft rich in youth before my fight,
Where waftfull time debateth with decay
To change your day of youth to fullied night,
And all in war with Time for loue of you.
As he takes from you, I ingraft you new.

When I consider every thing that grows
Holds in perfection but a little moment,
That this huge stage presenteth nought but shows
Whereon the stars in secret influence comment;
When I perceive that men as plants increase,
Cheerd and checked even by the selfsame sky,
Vaunt in their youthful sap, at height decrease,
And wear their brave state out of memory:
Then the conceit of this inconstant stay
Sets you most rich in youth before my sight,
Where wasteful Time debateth with Decay
To change your day of youth to sullied night,
And all in war with Time for love of you,
As he takes from you, I ingraft you new.

The last five lines, she points out, are 'sung under the sign of the sullying scythe' and they remain a hymn to the human 'love-syllable *you*', which is the 'conceit of impermanence':

Sets YOU most rich in YOUTH before my sight,
Where wasteful Time debateth with decay
To change YOUr day of YOUth to sullied night;
And all in war with Time for love of YOU,
As he takes from YOU, I ingraft YOU new.

The couplet rhyme, mimetically and phonetically additive to resemble 'ingrafting', is 'YOU' / 'YOU new'. Looking at the Quarto text, she remarks that she has no doubt that 'night', a noun that could be characterized by many possible adjectives, is '**sull**ied' because the young are youth**full** and time is waste**full**. And she further notes that in the Quarto spelling, the old-style *s* of *sull-* even resembles the *f* of *-full*. So this sonnet is bound together by one of those 'alliterative, assonantal and anagrammatic semantic strings' in which Shakespeare delights: 'On the **stage** influenced by **stars** is our mortal **state** making *incon***stant stay; waste d***eb***ates dec***a***y** to create *ch***ange** of a **day**.' By bringing out the acoustic texture of the sonnet, Vendler makes it sensuously alive, and I would only suggest that part of the linguistic fun of the opening three lines is the way in which Shakespeare duplicates the *o* in *grows*, in *Holds* and *moment* before allowing the pejorative sense of *shows* to burst the round sign's fragile perfection like a bubble. This crossing out of the sound is caught up ten lines later in 'most rich in youth' where it works to subvert the obvious sense of the phrase by placing it under a type of sonic erasure. This is an effect I only noticed because of Vendler's stringent close readings of each sonnet. She concludes her account of Sonnet 15 by pointing out: 'KEY WORD: YOU (it could be argued that this word is not present in Ql, but I suggest it is phonetically hiding in 'HUge', chosen precisely for its anticipation of YOU)'.

As is evident from the layout, this is a critical book which adopts the form of a handbook or reader's guide, and in her Introduction Vendler says that her Commentary is not intended to be read straight through: rather, it is intended as a work of 'writerly scrutiny' which those interested in the *Sonnets*, or students of the lyric, or 'poets hungry for resource', may want to browse in. She has included a recording of some of the *Sonnets* read aloud by herself, because the three other readings available are done by actors who, typically I would say, speak the lines with constant mis-emphases and ignore the inner antitheses and parallels. *The Art of Shakespeare's Sonnets* is therefore not a conventional critical book and though I read it straight through at a steady rate of a hundred pages a day, it is better dipped into, but dipped into by overlapping stages. Reading it is like being offered a huge plate of oysters, or doing a Spot-the-Ball competition, or playing obsessively with a Rubik's Cube that always comes out right after the effort of following a tight technical argument accompanied often by a detailed diagram. Because it does not offer an argument that develops chapter on chapter, any account of it must explicate the initial approach and then consider a number of moments out of a multitude where the critic directs her formidable mind to the game these sonnets play. It is Vendler's supreme critical virtue that she can write from inside a poem, as if she is in the workshop witnessing its making. Her manner of setting the Quarto next to the modernized text makes the experience of reading the

Sonnets a new and radical one: we read each poem twice and then we realize that actually Shakespeare wrote 154 sonnets, each of which has been rewritten by subsequent editors. Perhaps the closest analogy to this sense of never quite stepping into the same river twice is reading the first editions of John Clare's volumes and then reading the same poems in the unpunctuated original manuscript versions Eric Robinson and his fellow editors print in the big Oxford edition of Clare.

A good example is Sonnet 19:

Deuouring time blunt thou the Lyons pawes,
And make the earth deuoure her owne ſweet brood,
Plucke the keene teeth from the fierce Tygers yawes,
And burne the long liu'd Phænix in her blood,
Make glad and ſorry ſeaſons as thou fleet'ſt,
And do what ere thou wilt ſwift-footed time
To the wide world and all her fading ſweets:
But I forbid thee one moſt hainous crime,
O carue not with thy howers my loues faire brow,
Nor draw noe lines there with thine antique pen,
Him in thy courſe vntainted doe allow,
For beauties patterne to ſucceding men.
Yet doe thy worſt ould Time diſpight thy wrong,
My loue ſhall in my verſe euer liue young.

Devouring Time, blunt thou the lion's paws,
And make the earth devour her own sweet brood,
Pluck the keen teeth from the fierce tiger's jaws,
And burn the long-lived phoenix in her blood,
Make glad and sorry seasons as thou fleet'st,
And do whate'er thou wilt, swift-footed Time,
To the wide world and all her fading sweets:
But I forbid thee one most heinous crime,
O carve not with thy hours my love's fair brow,
Nor draw no lines there with thine antique pen;
Him in thy course untainted do allow
For beauty's pattern to succeeding men.

Yet do thy worst, old Time: despite thy wrong,
My love shall in my verse ever live young.

Reading the Quarto text with its furred type, I catch an accent which I once heard many years ago reproduced in a television documentary where John Barton coached members of the RSC in the 'correct' pronunciation of Shakespearean English: the accent sounded like a mixture of the Ambridge, Birmingham and Ulster accents. In 19, we hear not 'phoenix' but *Phaenix*, not 'heinous' but *hainous*, not 'old' but *ould*. Elsewhere there are other sounds still current in Ulster – *cowld* for 'cold', *hower* for 'hour' – and words such as *brave* for 'fine, good, bold, nonchalant', or *miching* for 'playing truant'. Hearing that deep guttural accent – an accent made deeper by the collied print of the Quarto text – I register the fourth line like this: 'And barn the lane-liv'd Phaynix in har bludd'.

Looking at the modernized equivalent beside it – 'And burn the long-lived Phoenix in her blood' – is rather like emerging onto a trim lawn where tea and cucumber sandwiches are being served. The Quarto text sounds like Stephen Rea, the modernized one like Gielgud or Prince Charles. The same or very similar modernized texts in Katherine Duncan-Jones's scholarly and accessible edition, *Shakespeare's Sonnets* (1997), seem perfectly presentable on their own, but in Vendler are often destabilized by their immediate adjacency to the Quarto texts. Duncan-Jones prints 'And burn the long-lived Phoenix in her blood;' and includes some of the Quarto spellings (not *Phaenix*, though) below her text. I agree with her punctuation of the line, but feel very strongly that Arden's general editorial policy ought to have been broadened to include the Quarto texts (an index of first lines would be a help too).

In her commentary on this sonnet, Vendler suggests that the 'murderous vitality' of the opening quatrain issues from the Shakespeare of the tragedies, while the rest of the poem with its mentions of 'swift-footed Time' and 'fading sweets' fits more equably in the elegiac mode. This type of comment is an essential part of what I can only call the dramatic experience of reading Vendler: a few pages earlier she takes Sonnet 18's famous opening line – 'Shall I compare thee to a summer's day?' – and in a lovely run of exact adjectives worthy of Hazlitt remarks that it is 'gentle, light, innocuous, dulcet'. Commenting on Sonnet 19, she notes that the imaginative effort is spent on 'the great hard words', with their frequent trochaic or spondaic emphasis: *blunt, paws, brood, pluck, keen, teeth, tiger's jaws, burn, blood*. And she then points out that 'Dev**our**ing Time . . . the earth dev**our** . . . with thy h**ours**' tolls the progression that turns devouring Time to *swift-footed* Time and then to *old* Time. The effect of this patterning is to jettison 'all values' except beauty's pattern, *young* in verse. Prompted by this highly sensitive analysis, I would add that in the last line the letter *v* is triumphantly asserted so that we get the idea of vitality expressed in an almost tactile fashion. Here, the modernized line – 'My love shall in my **v**erse e**v**er li**v**e young' – makes this almost sculpted effect visually more apparent.

It is a strong theme in Vendler's commentary that Shakespeare delights in anagrams, graphic or phonetic puns, and in what she calls 'graphic overlaps': *s***tars, astr***ology*, *con***stant** and **art**. In Sonnet 7, for example, the central image of the sun's *Car* generates 'anagramatically scrambled' cars elsewhere in **grac***ious*, *s***acr***ed* and *t***ract**. The ageing of the sun in the poem seems to generate *hom***age, age,** *g***old***en pilgrim***age**. The poem also suppresses the word *sun* until the closing word of the last line – 'Unlooked on diest unless thou get a son' – leaps off the page with complete inevitability. The *sun / son* theme runs throughout the sequence, nowhere more pervasively than in Sonnet 33:

> Fvll many a glorious morning haue I feene,
> Flatter the mountaine tops with foueraine eie,
> Kiffing with golden face the meddowes greene;
> Guilding pale ftreames with heauenly alcumy:
> Anon permit the bafeft cloudes to ride,
> With ougly rack on his celeftiall face,
> And from the forlorne world his vifage hide
> Stealing vnseene to weft with this difgrace:
> Euen fo my Sunne one early morne did fhine,
> With all triumphant fplendor on my brow,

But out alack, he was but one houre mine,
The region cloude hath mask'd him from me now.
Yet him for this, my loue no whit difdaineth,
Suns of the world may ftaine, whe heauens fun ftainteh.

Full many a glorious morning have I seen
Flatter the mountain tops with sovereign eye,
Kissing with golden face the meadows green,
Gilding pale streams with heavenly alchemy;
Anon permit the basest clouds to ride
With ugly rack on his celestial face,
And from the fórlorn world his visage hide,
Stealing unseen to west with this disgrace:
Even so my sun one early morn did shine
With all triumphant splendour on my brow;
But out alack, he was but one hour mine,
The region cloud hath masked him from me now.
Yet him for this my love no whit disdaineth,
Suns of the world may stain, when heaven's sun staineth.

Katherine Duncan-Jones's notes are as always helpful: glossing the word *ride*, she says in a rather Yeatsian manner that the clouds are 'upstart cavaliers, beggars on horseback; as they cross the sun's face they may also figure lines or wrinkles: cf. Fr. *se rider*, to become wrinkled'. She also notes that *rack* which is 'a mass of clouds driven before the wind in the upper air' is cognate with 'wrack' or 'wreck', suggesting an obstruction that is at once 'ruinous and fragile' (there's also the sexual connotation of *ride* exploited later in the sequence, where it is, once more, maritime – 'anchored in the bay where all men ride' in Sonnet 137; the same image pattern is present in Sonnet 80). And she notes the internal rhyme with *alack* in line 11. Elsewhere, she points out various numerological moments (the total of the 'dark lady' sonnets is 28, which reflects male disgust with the lunar, menstrual, cycle alluded to in their number, and I would guess that the number 33 is chosen as a trinal number which picks up the reference to 'heaven's sun' – i.e. Christ. Vendler demonstrates how this sonnet displays a 'progressive acceleration' of its narrative from eight to four lines to one line, and she includes a diagram to demonstrate this shrinking formal movement:

A. *Heaven's sun* clouded { [GOOD] 4 / [BAD] 4 }

B. *Sun of the World* clouded { [GOOD] 2 / [BAD] 2 }

Yet him for this my love no disdaineth:

[*suns/world* when *heaven's sun*]
[stain when staineth]

Although Vendler's diagrams aren't always helpful, this one does expose the technical playfulness of the form. Unlike Duncan-Jones, she tends not to make detailed links with Shakespeare's plays, but I believe it is necessary to set two passages from *Richard II* and *Henry IV*, *Part 1* next to this sonnet – which, as Vendler says, is the first to remark on 'a true flaw' in the friend.

In Act III of *Richard II*, Bolingbroke and his party confront Richard at Flint Castle in Wales:

> See, see, King Richard doth himself appear,
> As doth the blushing discontented sun
> From out the fiery portal of the East,
> When he perceives the envious clouds are bent
> To dim his glory, and to stain the track
> Of his bright passage to the Occident.

The Duke of York replies:

> Yet looks he like a king: behold his eye,
> As bright as is the eagle's, lightens forth
> Controlling majesty. Alack, alack for woe,
> That any harm should stain so fair a show.

The link between these speeches and Sonnet 33 seems clear: *track* and *alack, alack* point to the *rack / alack* internal rhyme, partly because 'track' contains 'rack'. This would mean that in the sonnet Shakespeare – the Jacobean Shakespeare, Duncan-Jones convincingly argues – is both remembering lines he wrote perhaps ten years earlier in the reign of Elizabeth, and also recalling performances by the actors who spoke his lines. He seems to be drawing on nature for his conceit, but equally he is drawing on the created nature of his own art. The young man is a flawed, brilliant royal actor, and he is also an actor playing that actor. A performance of the play was subsidized by the Essex conspirators on the eve of their rebellion in 1601. Essex, like Richard, had returned from a military campaign in Ireland, though from the conspirators' point of view what counted was the justified deposition of an anointed monarch. The other, I think important, and as I realize from Kerrigan's superb notes, often remarked, connection with the history plays is the way that cool, sly verb *permit* picks up Prince Hal's speech after he has been left alone by Falstaff and Poins:

> I know you all, and will awhile uphold
> The unyoked humour of your idleness.
> Yet herein will I imitate the sun,
> Who doth permit the base contagious clouds
> To smother up his beauty from the world.

The young man in the *Sonnets* is by implication as ruthless, manipulative and detached as Hal, and Shakespeare's complicated feelings for him are given a deliberately formulaic shape in the last couplet's apparently forgiving statement. But if we apply the *sun / son* pun and read 'heaven's sun' as Christ, then an abyss of contradictions is opened up, because Christ is stainless. Therefore sons of the world can never 'stain', a word that appears three times in *Richard II*, and three in *Henry IV, Part 1*. This is to argue the necessity of analysing the intertextuality of the *Sonnets*, but it is Vendler's ambition to concentrate on the complex dazzle of their linguistic surfaces. One of my favourite moments is her discussion of Sonnet 29.

When in disgrace with Fortune and men's eyes,
I all alone beweep my outcast state,
And trouble deaf heaven with my bootless cries,
And look upon myself and curse my fate,
Wishing me like to one more rich in hope,
Featured like him, like him with friends possessed,
Desiring this man's art, and that man's scope,
With what I most enjoy contented least;
Yet in these thoughts myself almost despising,
Haply I think on thee, and then my state
(Like to the lark at break of day arising
From sullen earth) sings hymns at heaven's gate,
For thy sweet love remembered such wealth brings
That then I scorn to change my state with kings.

The defective key word is *state* (missing in Q2, which describes 'the state of others, not his own'), and the couplet tie is *state* (2,10,14) and *sing* (-*s*) [-*sing*] (9,11,12). It's in her analysis of this last word or sound that Vendler's method produces a remarkable coup: she shows that in 'the most joyous play' of the poem, what she terms the 'disgruntled present participles' – *wishing, desiring*, with their 'wrong' arrangement of letters – suddenly give way to new present participles where the letters are arranged 'right'. That is, *despi***sing** and *ari***sing** appear and lead to *sing*. What we hear is *sing, sing, sing*: the poem 'fairly carols'. And she concludes her commentary by showing that even

> the first line of the couplet (in *b***rings** – 'rings!') makes the air resound; but at the end, in the scorned *kings*, the word *sing* lies scrambled again, as it did in *wishing* and *desiring*. As he integrates the world of kings with the world of nature, locates his superlative friend, and, as a lark, finds a listening heaven, the poet rediscovers an integrated mental state.

This analysis is wonderfully alive to the quick of the poem, to those subliminal tricks which sounds and signs play on the reader, and it shows Shakespeare's art triumphing over his despair at the 'art' and 'scope' of writers he was in competition with. This approach ought to be as common in literary criticism as the analysis of imagery and linguistic ambiguity, but what we are witnessing is a writerly responsiveness to sound and the sheer texture of words.

One example of Vendler's tactile sense of language is her account of the way in which the word *badges* in the closing couplet of Sonnet 44 – 'Receiving nought by elements so slow / But heavy tears, badges of either's woe' – picks up the *dj* sound in *in***j***urious* and **j***ump*, which appear earlier in the poem. Reading that last couplet, I was struck by how heavy *badges* sounded, and began to perceive how the acoustic adhesiveness certain words acquire resembles a form of memory. The *b* sounds in the couplet pick up earlier sounds (there are two previous uses of *but*) and pass them on to *badges*; so does another *dj* sound in *large*, and so do the several *ah* sounds. The result is that *badges* becomes like a particle of especially dense matter, as if concentrating in itself the weight of the whole poem. Vendler states that there is no couplet tie, and it therefore follows that there can be no key word or words, but a case could be made for looking at the sonnet like this:

> If the **du**ll substance of my flesh were thought,
> In**ju**rious **d**istance should not stop my way,
> For then **d**espite of space I woul**d** be brought,
> From limits far remote, where thou **d**ost stay.
> No matter then although my foot **did** stand
> Upon the farthest earth remove**d** from thee,
> For nimble thought can **ju**mp both sea and l**and**
> **A**s soon **a**s think the place where he woul**d** be.
> **B**ut **ah**, thought kills me that I am not thought,
> To leap lar**g**e lengths of miles when thou **a**rt gone,
> **B**ut that, so much of earth and water wrought,
> I must atten**d** time's leisure with my moan,
> Receiving naught **b**y elements so slow
> **B**ut heavy tears, **badges** of either's woe.

The *b, a, d, dj* and *uz* sounds that make up *badges* are spread over the preceding quatrains, so that the word acts like the vanishing-point in a perspectival drawing. This explains, I believe, the scaly weight of the word *badges* (I'm tempted to see a kind of venereal pun here – 'bad juice' – but that may be over-ambitious.

There is a similar effect in the phrase from Sonnet 40, 'lascivious grace', which Vendler calls one of those 'striking phrases', with which the sonnets are sprinkled: phrases that have 'a greater aesthetic effect than we can account for at first'. It occurs in the final couplet – 'Lascivious grace, in whom all ill well shows, / Kill me with spites yet we must not be foes' – and it 'skirts blasphemy' because the moral import of the words *ill* and *well* which immediately follow it brings 'religious *grace* into earshot'. The fallen state of the 'infatuated speaker' is shown by the way he has made the positive word *grace* the noun which 'conveys essence', while the condemnatory word *lascivious* remains only a modifying adjective. Where the phrase 'graceful lasciviousness' would show a speaker properly defining the relation between 'graceful show and lascivious substance', 'lascivious grace' presents a speaker 'helplessly enthralled by beauty'. The phrase is conspicuous because it contains the only sophisticated polysyllable in a couplet of monosyllables, but we need also to answer the question Vendler poses: why does *lascivious* fall on the ear like something expected? Here, we need to look at the phrase in context:

> Take all my loves, my love, yea take them all;
> What hast thou then more than thou hadst before?
> No love, my love, that thou mayst true love call,
> All mine was thine, before thou hadst this more.
> Then if for my love thou my love receivest,
> I cannot blame thee, for my love thou usest;
> But yet be blamed, if thou this self deceivest
> By wilful taste of what thy self refusest.
> I do forgive thy robb'ry, gentle thief,
> Although thou steal thee all my poverty;
> And yet love knows it is a greater grief
> To bear love's wrong than hate's known injury.
> Lascivious grace, in whom all ill well shows,
> Kill me with spites yet we must not be foes.

What happens is that *lascivious* echoes the 'trisyllables of evildoing' that make up the amphibrachic rhyme words *receivest* and *deceivest* of the second quatrain (an amphibrac is a trisyllabic foot: x / x). Thus the *us* sounds in *refusest* and *deceivest* and the *see-ves* in the latter anticipate the *siv-us* sounds in *lascivious*. As Vendler remarks, it is by such 'confirmatory coffin nails' that correspondences are hammered home. But as she points out, *grace* has some hooks of its own, not only in its initial consonants and vowels which remind us of the **gr***eater* **gr***ief* that **gr***ace* has caused, but also its possession of the same 'satanic hiss' that exists in *receive***st**, *use***st**, *deceive***st**, *refuse***st** and, inevitably, *la***sc***ivio***us**. For Vendler, the phrase 'lascivious grace' is the 'helpless unifying summary' of all the divisions which precede it.

What is so exciting about this approach to poetry is its manner of locking on to the way in which sound, as opposed to image, patterns work. And, of course, there is often a playful wit shaping these effects – as in the 'erotic' use of *p* sounds in Sonnet 98 which reach their 'phallic apogee' in Sonnet 151:

> My soul doth tell my body that he may
> Triumph in love; flesh stays no farther reason,
> But rising at thy name doth point out thee
> As his triumphant prize; proud of this pride,
> He is contented thy poor drudge to be,
> To stand in thy affairs, fall by thy side.

Noting that the 'unstoppability of orgasm' is imitated here, Vendler suggests that detumescence is represented not only by the 'semantic decline' from *proud* to *poor*, but also from *tr-iu-mph* to *dr-u-dge*, words whose initial double consonants, triple final letters and common *u* in the middle make them 'some sort of graphic cousins'. Again and again, I want to haul out examples of this supreme critical imagination at work, but it should be apparent that criticism of the *Sonnets*, and by extension, critical accounts of poetry, will never be the same again. This is an epic, innovatory study which ought to mark a new beginning for criticism.

In reading the *Sonnets* right through for the first time in many years, I became fascinated and puzzled by Shakespeare's obsessive use of the adjective *sweet*, a word which is only effective if it is used very sparingly. It is used frequently in both *Richard II* and the two parts of *Henry IV*, and Katherine Duncan-Jones notes a particularly interesting conjunction of sonnet and historical drama in 108, which begins:

> What's in the brain that ink may character
> Which hath not figured to thee my true spirit?
> What's new to speak, what new to register,
> That may express my love, or thy dear merit?
> Nothing, sweet boy . . .

This, the editor notes, is the only time the youth is so addressed, though the epithet 'sweet' has often been applied to him in other forms: 'thy sweet self' (1), 'thy sweet self' (4), 'sweet semblance' (13), 'sweetest bud' (35), 'Thine own sweet argument' (38). Noting that the phrase 'sweet boy' caused some earlier editors embarrassment (one altered it to 'sweet love', another to 'sweet joy'), she points out that in the last scene of *Henry IV, Part 2*, the phrase occurs again when Falstaff addresses the newly crowned Henry V:

FALSTAFF: God save thee, my sweet boy!
KING: My Lord Chief Justice, speak to that vain man.
CHIEF JUSTICE: Have you your wits? Know you what 'tis you speak?
FALSTAFF: My king! My Jove! I speak to thee, my heart!
KING: I know thee not, old man. Fall to thy prayers.

In Sonnet 108, immediately after the phrase 'sweet boy', Shakespeare says: 'but yet, like prayers divine, / I must each day say o'er the very same, / Counting no old thing old.' Like the rhymes on *alack* in Sonnet 33 and in its source in *Richard II*, the passage of dialogue from *Henry IV, Part 2* strengthens the associative link between Shakespeare and Falstaff, the young man and the newly crowned king. Shakespeare is dramatizing the abject nature of his love as foolish, ridiculous, self-pitying, Falstaffian, while the object of that love is totally ruthless, completely confident, his absolute superior in every way. The sun has broken free of its base contagious clouds.

Shakespeare tends to kick the word *sweet* around like an adjectival football, rather in the way we sometimes say someone is a very 'nice' person and mean that they have shallow, calculating, good manners. Duncan-Jones also glosses the phrase 'compound sweet' in Sonnet 125 in a particularly interesting way:

> Were't ought to me I bore the canopy,
> With my extern the outward honouring,
> Or laid great bases for eternity,
> Which proves more short than waste or ruining?
> Have I not seen dwellers on form and favour
> Lose all, and more, by paying too much rent,
> For compound sweet forgoing simple savour,
> Pitiful thrivers, in their gazing spent?
> No, let me be obsequious in thy heart,
> And take thou my oblation, poor but free,
> Which is not mixed with seconds, knows no art,
> But mutual render, only me for thee.
> Hence, thou suborned informer, a true soul
> When most impeached, stands least in thy control.

Shakespeare is contrasting the constancy of private love with the complex dangers of court favour, and Duncan-Jones suggests that the image of 'compound sweet' could most naturally be applied to Elizabeth's favourite, the Earl of Essex, who had been rewarded in 1590 with the 'farm of sweet wines' – the right to charge tax on all imported sweet wines. As well as suggesting a sweet aristocratic food, or medicine, the phrase 'compound sweet' may mean 'beguiling or attractive financial agreement', what we now term a 'sweetener'. The adjective therefore carries associations with political power, favouritism, corruption and danger – it is an apparently lyric term which has been given a negative public spin. It's here that I must express a reservation about a statement Vendler makes in her introduction:

> How are the *Sonnets* being written about nowadays? And why should I add another book to those already available? I want to do so because I admire the *Sonnets*, and wish to defend the high value I put on them, since

they are being written about these days with considerable jaundice. The spheres from which most of the current criticisms are generated are social and psychological ones. Contemporary emphasis on the participation of literature in a social matrix balks at acknowledging how lyric, though it may *refer to* the social, remains the genre that directs its *mimesis* toward the performance of the mind in *solitary* speech. Because lyric is intended to be voiceable by anyone reading it, in its normative form it deliberately strips away most social specification (age, regional location, sex, class, even race). A social reading is better directed at a novel or a play: the abstraction desired by the writer of, and the willing reader of, normative lyric frustrates the mind that wants social fictions or biographical revelations.

This needs to be said in order to clear the ground for Vendler's brilliantly focused way of reading the *Sonnets*, but these lyrics do not seek to shake off the dirt of the public world – often they wish they could, but the ugly dangerousness in the youth's personality and in some of his actions cannot be avoided and is in any case part of his attraction. I should add that I do not agree with Vendler's rejection of Andrew Motion's historicist view of Keats's poems, in her review of his biography of Keats (the *London Review of Books*, 16 October 1997), and believe that 'To Autumn' is on one level a great political poem which elegizes those who were massacred at Peterloo.

Among the many appealing features of Duncan-Jones's edition are the sudden epiphanic connections she makes with what we know of Shakespeare's life. Commenting on the line in Sonnet 62 where Shakespeare looks in his mirror and is shown 'me myself indeed, / Beated and chopped with tanned antiquity', she notes that in *Hamlet* the Gravedigger says that tanners' skins become toughened with their trade. Drawing on an earlier scholar, E. K. Chambers, she suggests that since Shakespeare's father was a 'whittawer', who prepared leather for gloves, he may well have believed that his own skin had been affected by this process. On the opening of Sonnet 71 – 'No longer mourn for me when I am dead / Than you shall hear the surly sullen bell / Give warning to the world that I am fled' – she notes that it would have been in the power of the dead speaker's heirs to commission a prolonged tolling of the bell, as Shakespeare appears to have done for the burial of his actor brother Edmund in

St Saviour's, Southwark on 31 December 1607, paying 20 shillings for 'a forenoone knell of the great bell'.

Such details help to anchor the lyrics empirically and, as Thomas Hardy endlessly shows, such random, discrete facts are essential to our need to imagine experience. Annotating Shakespeare's meditation in Sonnet 68 on ageing and the means used to disguise it, Duncan-Jones notes that wigs and false hair must often have been in his thoughts, both because he himself was a 'bald actor', and also because in 1604 he lodged in Silver Street, the centre of the wig trade. Falstaff, the Prince tells him, has a 'pitiful bald crown', so Shakespeare may also be thinking of this moment, which occurs at the beginning of the scene within a scene where Hal and Falstaff enact Hal's imminent meeting with his father (II.iv), and Falstaff pleads with Hal not to banish 'sweet Jack Falstaff'. Banish plump Jack, he says, and banish all the world. The future king playing his own father replies: 'I do, I will.'

When we're hurt or anxious in love or friendship, we tend to dramatize our feelings, to invent characters for them, and Shakespeare in love returns frequently to the friendship – the unequal exploitative matiness – between fat Jack and cold Hal. Their relationship involves role-playing, and because actors took on their parts, the allusiveness in the *Sonnets* is a multi-layered mix of fictionality and authentic emotion. Where does one end and the other begin?

One of the most authentic moments occurs in 94, a sonnet which Empson computed to have 4096 'possible movements of thought' (he was also a mathematician so he must be right). The poem could be addressed to the Machiavellian Prince Hal:

> They that have power to hurt, and will do none,
> That do not do the thing they most do show,
> Who, moving others, are themselves as stone,
> Unmoved, cold, and to temptation slow:
> They rightly do inherit heaven's graces,
> And husband nature's riches from expense;
> They are the lords and owners of their faces,
> Others, but stewards of their excellence.

> The summer's flower is to the summer sweet,
> Though to itself it only live and die,
> But if that flower with base infection meet,
> The basest weed outbraves his dignity:
> For sweetest things turn sourest by their deeds;
> Lilies that fester smell far worse than weeds.

As Duncan-Jones notes, *expense* plays on refraining from the emission of semen, a subject that occurs in other sonnets, and which here is a metaphor for a particular kind of highly controlled and controlling personality. The way *sweet* chimes with *weed, deeds, weeds* means that that adjective is tainted or stained in that final lethal couplet which speaks with a chill definitive contempt. Duncan-Jones points out that the last line occurs in what she terms an 'anonymous play', *The Reign of King Edward the Third*, which was first published in 1596. Some scholars have argued that this play was actually written by Shakespeare, and in 1996 Eric Sams published an edition in which he argues – convincingly, I think – that it is by Shakespeare.

In the second act of *Edward III*, the Earl of Warwick, totally against his will, but at the King's request, attempts to persuade his daughter, the Countess of Salisbury, to become the King's mistress and 'secret love'. She refuses and Warwick replies:

> A spacious field of reasons could I urge
> between his glory, daughter, and thy shame
> that poison shows worst in a golden cup
> dark night seems darker by the lightning flash
> lilies that fester smell far worse than weeds
> and every glory that inclines to sin
> the shame is treble by the opposite.

Duncan-Jones leaves the question of Shakespeare's authorship of *Edward III* open, but I think that in Sonnet 94 he is again recalling his own lines – lines which imagine evil and corruption in a king. He is redressing an unequal balance of power in his relationship with the young man by recalling this passage in a manner that sounds decisively damning, except that Edward, the 'lascivious King', as the Countess calls him, repents of his desire in a speech to the Countess which begins: 'Even by that power I swear that gives me now / the power to be ashamed, of myself.' That repeated noun *power* is another associative link with Sonnet 94, and points to the theme of personal and social power which runs through the *Sonnets*. The words *base* and *basest* pick up the 'base clouds' in Sonnet 34 and the 'base court' the sun of Richard II descends into, as well as the 'base contagious clouds' which Hal, sun-like, permits to smother his beauty from the world. Something intense, dangerous, complex and, from Shakespeare's point of view, awful and disgusting is going on, and in her account of the squeamish, overwhelmingly male accounts of the *Sonnets*, Duncan-Jones wryly quotes John Kerrigan, who in his edition speaks of 'the sonnets to the youth' as arising out of 'comradely affection in the literature of friendship'. Kerrigan goes on to dismiss what he terms 'innumerable crackpot theories' about the poet's life and love-life – 'fantasies', he says, in which the *Sonnets* have played a large part. It is Duncan-Jones's intention as scholar and critic to challenge the issue of sexuality which Kerrigan and other editors have consistently side-stepped, and to show how there are references in the poems to menstrual bleeding, semen, cunts, erections, detumescence, female flesh as a sexual commodity, syphilis and orgasms. She also points to the 'strongly mysogynistic bias' which is hinted at early on in the sequence, and which becomes dominant in the Dark Lady section. This is an edition which uniquely makes the *Sonnets* issue from the body's moods as well as from the mind's. This of course is a Cartesian distinction which I do not mean to uphold: rather, it is the ontological merging of spirit and body which she affirms in her approach, and she does so in the teeth of the preceding male editors.

Jangling Monarchy: John Milton

In 1936, with the Spanish Civil War begun and world war on the horizon, the distinguished Scottish scholar and editor of Donne, H. J. C. Grierson, gave a series of lectures on Milton and Wordsworth, which began by addressing the attacks on Milton that T. S. Eliot and his acolytes were mounting. The revival of interest in metaphysical poetry, which Grierson had done so much to stimulate, had prompted critics to discuss the connection between form and content in poetry: 'The favourite phrase is "unified sensibility". We are told a little pontifically that this unified sensibility was disturbed by the great influence of Milton, so that the natural medium of our thought has become exclusively prose.' Grierson must have smelt reaction in Eliot's royalist rejection of Milton's republican poetics.

The revival of interest in English republicanism in recent years might be thought to have stimulated interest in Milton, but here Thomas Corns, editor of *A Companion to Milton*, sounds a warning note. This collection of essays, he writes, appears at a time when Milton's standing with a wide readership appears 'altogether more insecure'. In the US students prefer to study contemporary literature, while in British universities modular curricula – an academically indefensible reform – make it possible to avoid studying Milton. But even if Milton is ignored by many students, the academic study of his verse and prose 'has never been healthier', according to Corns. The anxiety, however, must be that this great prophet of English liberty no longer speaks to a readership beyond the academy, and thus that Eliot's attempt to sideline Milton and the values he embodies has partly succeeded. And if Milton is ignored, so, too, are the classical foundations on which his republicanism stands. As Martin Dzelzainis argues in an essay on his republicanism in the *Companion*, he drew on Sallust and Roman law for his account of the ennobling effects of liberty. One phrase in Milton's *History of Britain* – 'from obscure and small to grow eminent and glorious commonwealths' – appears to be taken directly from Sallust's rendition of a speech by Cato in which he tells the Senate not to 'suppose that it was by arms that our forefathers raised our republic from obscurity to greatness'. Cato's message can be felt throughout Milton's writing, where the good angels are polemicists whose swords are symbolic of pens, printing presses, pamphlets.

It is perhaps difficult to read Milton's narrative in *Paradise Lost* in this way – we visualize the Archangel Michael's two-handed sword not as the double lever on a printing press, but simply as a sword, while we see 'chaos' and the 'abyss' physically, as part of outer space. Yet Milton, the adept student of Spenser, was designing a flexibly symbolic – rather than rigidly allegorical – system, a way of shaping history and politics that Defoe sought to popularize in his prose, and one which needs to be examined in the light of Milton's prose writings.

Take that word 'abyss', which appears near the beginning of *Paradise Lost*:

> And chiefly thou O Spirit, that dost prefer
> Before all temples th'upright heart and pure,
> Instruct me, for thou knowst; thou from the first
> Wast present, and with mighty wings outspread
> Dove-like sat'st brooding on the vast abyss
> And mad'st it pregnant.

At the beginning of his *Pro Populo Anglicano Defensio Secunda*, or *Second Defence of the English People*, Milton gives thanks to God chiefly for three reasons. The first, in George Burnett's 1809 translation, is

> that I was born in those times of my country, when the effulgent virtue of its citizens – when their magnanimity and steadiness, surpassing the highest praise of their ancestors, under the inspection of God first implored, and under his manifest guidance, setting examples and performing deeds

of valour, the greatest since the foundation of the world – delivered the Commonwealth from a grievous domination, and religion from a most debasing thraldom.

Burnett's translation of the phrase 'virtus eximia' as 'effulgent virtue', rather than 'outstanding' or 'extraordinary virtue', seems rather precious, but he was thinking, I would suggest, of light coming out of darkness at the Creation. Milton is remembering this passage when he begins *Paradise Lost* with an account of God creating the world, an account which he repeats twice later in the poem: in Book Three, 'Confusion heard his voice, and wild uproar / Stood ruled,' until at his second bidding 'darkness fled, / Light shone, and order from disorder sprung.' And in Book Seven, God is again shown dove-like on the abyss:

> His brooding wings the Spirit of God outspread,
> And vital virtue infused, and vital warmth
> Throughout the fluid mass, but downward purged
> The black tartareous cold infernal dregs
> Adverse to life: then founded, then conglobed
> Like things to like . . .

It is not only the foundation of the world that is referred to here, but the foundation of the English Commonwealth out of political chaos. The word 'abyss', which appears nineteen times in the poem, represents at one level the state described by the phrase 'gravi dominatione rempublicam' in *The Second Defence*. The word *gravis*, as well as meaning 'heavy', can also mean 'pregnant', so the abyss on which the dove of the Holy Spirit broods, making it 'pregnant', is analogous to the 'gravi dominatione' which the republic suffered. The word also occurs in Book One of the *Aeneid* – 'regina sacerdos Marte gravis' ('a princess of the royal blood pregnant by Mars') and Virgil goes on to say that one of the twins the priestess Ilia is pregnant with – Romulus – will found Rome.

Milton knew that the poem he was dictating to his amanuensis would be scrutinized by the recently restored monarch's Licenser of the Press, so he coded the English people's formation of a republic as the creation of the 'heavens and earth'. The idea passed the censor by, just as it has passed by many readers, but it was nonetheless Milton's founding intention in composing his epic. As David Norbrook shows in his seminal study *Writing the English Republic*, the language of chaos and creation briefly took on optimistic overtones during the Commonwealth, but with its disintegration the images became despairing. *The Grand Concernments of England Ensured*, an anonymous pamphlet which appeared in 1659, shows that the image of the Commonwealth as being created from a void was a current one: '*you have made* England, Scotland, Ireland, *A Chaos without form and void*, and I doubt your Omnipotency will never speak the word for such a creation, as any honest man shall say when he hath looked upon it, *that it is very good*.'

The authorities were concerned, though, by a related image in Book One which describes Satan's obscured glory:

> as when the sun new ris'n
> Looks through the horizontal misty air
> Shorn of his beams, or from behind the moon
> In dim eclipse disastrous twilight sheds
> On half the nations, and with fear of change
> Perplexes monarchs.

According to Milton's early biographer, the Irish republican John Toland, Charles II's Licenser for the Press regarded these lines as subversive, and wanted to suppress the whole poem.

Immediately after the passage in which he imagines God hatching the universe out of the abyss, Milton asks:

> what in me is dark
> Illumine, what is low raise and support;
> That to the height of this great argument
> I may assert eternal providence,
> And justify the ways of God to men.

This invocation mirrors the opening of *The Second Defence*, where he describes how he 'accepted, of those very deliverers of the country, and by general consent, the part spontaneously assigned me;

namely, to defend publicly (if anyone ever did) the cause of the people of England, and thus of liberty itself'. At the bedrock of Milton's imagination is a belief in God, and a certainty that republics are divinely ordained and that he has been sent to justify and vindicate them (the *t*'s in these lines of verse seem to vibrate with his certainty, like taut, plucked strings). In *Paradise Regained*, his shorter, much neglected, plain-style epic, Milton again addresses God, saying:

> Behold the kings of earth how they oppress
> Thy chosen, to what highth their power unjust
> They have exalted, and behind them cast
> All fear of thee, arise and vindicate
> Thy glory, free thy people from their yoke.

Milton uses the words 'justify' and 'vindicate' to refer to a desired state that is about to be reached. In *Samson Agonistes,* Manoa, Samson's beloved father, says that God will not long defer to 'vindicate the glory of his name'. In *The Life of John Milton: A Critical Biography*, Barbara Lewalski argues that in his early tracts Milton works out a poetics of satire that justifies invective as what he terms 'sanctified bitternesse'. He aligns it with biblical prophecy and gives the words 'justify' and 'vindicate' the additional sense of 'argue for this chosen art form (be it verse or prose)'. Rereading *Paradise Lost* recently, I felt that Milton's use of 'happy' and 'happiness', too, has another level of meaning, which is generally thought to have been added to the words in 1725, when Francis Hutcheson invented the phrase 'greatest happiness for the greatest numbers', later adapted by Bentham. The words, in Milton's usage, have a general, public application which speaks for his unrelenting social activism. They are touched or toughened by *Gesellschaft*.

As well as drawing into his poetry the vocabulary and images he uses in his polemics, Milton also moulds innumerable quotations from his vast reading in English and several other languages into verse that seems effortlessly self-sufficient and sublime – verse that appears to transcend sources, borrowings, allusions, other than the clearly biblical. Noting that no writer before Milton had fashioned himself 'quite so self-consciously' as an author, and also that he nowhere refers to his Catholic grandfather or more distant ancestors or seeks to trace a family tree, Lewalski points to the fact that he begins his story with his father, a Protestant 'self-made bourgeois scrivener'. Milton's verse, conceived in the high lonely tower of his visionary intellect, appears to have complete autonomy. Like Samson, he resembles 'that self-begotten bird', the phoenix, when in fact he is, as Hazlitt pointed out, 'a writer of centos, and yet in originality scarcely inferior to Homer'.

This patchwork-quilt effect or, to use a favourite image of Hazlitt's, this melting of scrap metal into statues, can be seen if we consider the repeated images of ugly, dissonant noise in Milton. In an account of the building of the Tower of Babel in the last book of *Paradise Lost*, the Archangel Michael describes how 'a jangling noise of words unknown' replaces the 'native language' of the denizens of the now fallen world. As Alistair Fowler's notes in the magnificent – if underhistoricized – Longman edition show, the phrase 'jangling noise' is taken from Sylvester's 1613 translation of the Huguenot poet Du Bartas's *The Divine Weeks and Works*: 'A jangling noise not much unlike the rumours [uproar] / Of Bacchus' swains amid their drunken humours'. This is the direct source of the phrase, but Milton is also drawing on a speech made by the Princess of France in *Love's Labours Lost*: 'Good wits will be jangling; but, gentles, agree / This civil war of wits were much better used / On Navarre'. The word 'jangling' is associated in Milton's imagination with civil war (the phrase 'jangling opinions' appears in his 1641 pamphlet *Animadversions*). A word closely associated with it is 'jarring', which he also uses several times, for example in *An Apology against a Pamphlet*, of 1642, where he remarks: 'And how to break off suddenly into three jarring notes, which this comforter hath set me, I must be wary, unlesse I can provide against offending the eare, as some musicians are wont skilfully to fall out of one key into another without breach of harmony.'

These lines from Book Two which describe the doors of Hell opening are both a musical transition from one key to another and an acoustic representation of cannonfire and the clash of arms:

> on a sudden open fly
> With impetuous recoil and jarring sound
> The infernal doors, and on their hinges grate
> Harsh thunder.

Milton is considering the aesthetic problem of how to shift style without breaking the harmony – or how to appear to break the harmony while really maintaining it. He hated what he called 'barbarous dissonance', which he linked with drunken Royalist revellers, just as he linked the 'flashy songs' which 'grate' on 'scrannel pipes' in *Lycidas* with Royalist bishops and priests. In *Samson Agonistes* the 'popular noise', 'hideous noise' and 'universal groan' are ways of encoding the London crowd's spontaneous groan at the executions of the regicides, and in Book Seven Milton imagines 'the barbarous dissonance / Of Bacchus and his revellers . . . the race / Of that wild rout that tore the Thracian bard / In Rhodopè'. Here he is remembering the regicides' executions (they were hung, drawn and quartered), and the period immediately after the Restoration when he was arrested and was himself in danger of execution. In March 1660, just two months before the Restoration, an anonymous pamphleteer linked Milton with the most notorious regicide traitors, and suggested that 'when he is condemned to travel to *Tyburn* in a Cart, he will petition for the favor to be the first man that ever was driven thither in a *Wheel-borrow*.'

Milton knew he was a marked man, but tried desperately through his pamphlets to persuade General Monck and other military and political leaders to maintain the republic. Laura Lunger Knoppers's essay in the *Companion* on Milton's late political prose offers a detailed and lively account of this period when, in Milton's symbolic code, England fell from being a happy republic into a jangling fallen monarchy. In late February 1660, Milton had published a pamphlet called *The Readie and Easie Way to establish a Free Commonwealth* in which he aimed to show 'with what ease we may now obtain a free Commonwealth, and by it with as much ease all the freedom, peace, justice, plentie that we desire'.

But by March that year Milton realized that the republican General Monck, who had addressed the restored Parliament and told them that bringing back the King would mean arbitrary power and the return of the prelacy, had now become a kingmaker. As Knoppers shows, political events in March 1660 did not move in the direction that Milton had hoped. Monck, as Commander-in-Chief of the Armed Forces, kept the remaining republican sympathizers in the Army under control, preventing any remonstrance by his officers against Charles Stuart, or 'any single-person rule', on the grounds that they should not meddle with civil authority. By mid-March, Monck appears to have bowed to the popular will to bring back the King; on 19 March, he accepted a letter from the King and was secretly giving advice that would lead to the Restoration. In a revised version of *The Readie and Easie Way*, which appeared early in April, Milton hoped to remind the General of his republican principles and so persuade him to save the state:

> A king must be ador'd like a Demigod, with a dissolute and haughtie court about him, of vast expence and luxurie, masks and revels, to the debaushing of our prime gentry both male and female . . . to the multiplying of a servile crew, not of servants only, but of nobility and gentry, bred up then to the hopes not of public, but of court offices, to be stewards, chamberlains, ushers, grooms, even of the close-stool . . . a single person . . . will have little els to do, but to bestow the eating and drinking of excessive dainties, to set a pompous face upon the superficial actings of State, to pageant himself up and down in progress among the perpetual bowings and cringings of an abject people, on either side deifying and adoring him.

Charles II entered London on 29 May 1660, in a triumphant parade led by three hundred cavalry in cloth of silver. This royal triumph, John Leonard notes in a clever essay on 'self-contradicting puns' in *Paradise Lost*, is evoked in Book Five:

> Meanwhile our primitive great sire, to meet
> His godlike guest, walks forth, without more train
> Accompanied than with his own complete
> Perfections, in himself was all his state,
> More solemn than the tedious pomp that waits
> On princes, when their rich retínue long

> Of horses led, and grooms besmeared with gold
> Dazzles the crowd, and sets them all agape.

There is a republican pun on 'state' here, and Leonard also notes that Milton, who was hiding in a friend's house in Bartholomew Close, would have heard the roar of cannons and the crowds shouting 'God Save the King!' How typical of Milton, Leonard says, to mock it all 'with one naked man'.

It is typical, too, of Milton to re-create the scene by remembering a passage from *Macbeth*, an echo scholars have missed. After murdering Duncan, Macbeth tells Lady Macbeth that his grooms woke up briefly and cried 'God bless us!' and 'Amen', as if they 'had seen me with these hangman's hands' – that is, hands bloody after disembowelling someone who is being executed for treason. Lady Macbeth then angrily asks Macbeth why he carried the daggers from the chamber, and tells him to take them back and 'smear / The sleepy grooms with blood'. He refuses, and she angrily says that she will do it:

> If he do bleed,
> I'll gild the faces of the grooms withal,
> For it must seem their guilt.

As she says this, Macduff and Lennox begin their drawn-out knocking on the castle gate.

Milton remembered this great dramatic moment, when, blind and vulnerable, he composed his epic under the new state. The passage in Book Five says that Charles will be, as his father was, a man of blood, and also remembers the fate of the regicides. As Lewalski points out, Cromwell's adviser Hugh Peters was executed as a regicide because he promoted 'regicide before the fact'. This was a dangerous precedent for Milton: he had written *The Tenure of Kings and Magistrates* after the execution of the King in 1649 to 'reconcile men's minds' by defending the general proposition that it is lawful to execute a tyrant. As Milton imagined those gilded grooms besmeared with blood, he would have been remembering the sufferings of his regicide friends on the scaffold. He would also have been remembering his experience of prison, and the decision by the Commons to select twenty notable non-regicides for rigorous punishment short of death. Milton's name was floated briefly on 18 June, but not seconded; several of his powerful friends, including Marvell and Sir William Davenant, whom Milton had saved from execution as a Royalist conspirator under the Commonwealth, helped to rescue him. The recollection of images from *Macbeth* might also contain a trace of subconscious regicide guilt.

Milton may have had the regicide executions in mind earlier in *Paradise Lost*, when in Book One he describes Moloch:

> horrid king besmeared with blood
> Of human sacrifice, and parents' tears,
> Though for the noise of drums and timbrels loud
> Their children's cries unheard.

Again Milton emphasizes noise, which he invariably associates with kings and their followers. The pamphlet he attacks in *The Second Defence of the People of England* was called *Regii sanguinis clamor ad coelum, adversus parricidas anglicanos*, or *The Clamour of the Royal Blood to Heaven against the English Parricides*, and this title is implicit in these lines from Book Six describing the war in heaven:

> now storming fury rose,
> And clamour such as heard in heaven till now
> Was never, arms on armour clashing brayed
> Horrible discord . . .

The *clamor ad coelum* becomes 'clamour such as heard in heaven' (and the internal rhyme on 'armour' places responsibility on the Royalists as rebels against Parliament): the noise is an evil intrusion.

Milton is fascinated by horrible discord: as well as appearing in *Paradise Lost*, the phrase 'barbarous dissonance' is used in the much earlier masque *Comus*, where the 'wonted roar' fills the air with 'barbarous dissonance' until there is 'an unusual stop of sudden silence'. Although Milton often sees dissonance as the expression of an uncivilized Royalism, the music of his verse from time to time requires a heavy-metal reverberation to be set against its soaring munificence. He must occasionally throw a spanner in the works and listen to its clatter as the wheels of his mighty style grind and falter. That is what happens in these lines from Book Two:

> so eagerly the fiend
> O'er bog or steep, through straight, rough, dense, or rare,
> With head, hands, wings, or feet pursues his way,
> And swims or sinks, or wades, or creeps, or flies.

The crammed, recalcitrant, jarring, heavy stresses express Satan's struggle, so that when the metre returns to normal iambics in the last line, the monosyllabic verbs and their rhythm seem clean and refreshed, tingling like the silence after loud noise or that 'unusual stop of sudden silence'. To achieve this effect, however, barbarous dissonance or 'clamour' is first necessary, and so Milton has to integrate Satan's evil and barbaric energy into his metre. In theological terms this strategy embodies the idea of good coming out of evil, while in classical republican ideology it represents a version of the Machiavellian idea that popular tumults give a republican constitution its animating spirit. Thus the devil's party has a place within an overall structure. There are times when Milton appears to represent Satan as his secret sharer, and, as Stephen Fallon argues in the *Companion*, he can hesitate between a heroic self-conception, 'as unparalleled spokesperson of God', and the fear that by over-reaching he has forfeited God's favour.

That fear and the anxiety that he is shadowing Satan's actions can be felt in the witty, tragic, elevated and personal verse paragraph 'Hail holy light', which opens Book Three of *Paradise Lost*. Here, Milton presents himself as having flown, like Satan, 'through utter and through middle darkness', and having climbed back up the 'dark descent . . . / Though hard and rare'. This echoes that impacted moment when Satan struggles through 'straight, rough, dense, or rare', and reascends 'though hard and rare'. But there is another, especially poignant Satanic echo in Book Two, where 'adventurous bands' of fallen angels 'With shuddering horror pale, and eyes aghast / Viewed first their lamentable lot, and found / No rest'.

In the image of eyes that find 'no rest', Milton anticipates the opening paragraph of Book Three, where, addressing 'holy light', he writes

> but thou
> Revisit'st not these eyes, that roll in vain
> To find thy piercing ray, and find no dawn.

Here, the Milton who was taught by the heavenly muse to 'venture down / The dark descent' is creating a shadowy parallel with the 'adventurous' fallen angels whose watchful eyes that find no rest are mirrored by Milton's sightless, rolling eyes that 'find no dawn'. The echoic language and cadence intensify the misery of his blindness, and communicate his fear that his over-reaching ambition has cut him off from God's favour and put him in Hell with the fallen angels. This tragic sense of isolation – 'wisdom at one entrance quite shut out' – is beautifully and ironically expressed by the adjective 'darkling', used of the nightingale's song: 'as the wakeful bird / Sings darkling'. Here the surface melody as well as the tender diminutive effect and the pun on 'darling' obscures the rage, barbarity and chaos of *King Lear*:

> For you know, nuncle,
> 'The hedge-sparrow fed the cuckoo so long
> That it had it head bit off by its young.'
> So out went the candle, and we were left darkling.

In picking up the Fool's lines, Milton is sending another coded message from his pitch-dark prison, as well as launching the word 'darkling' into poetic diction so successfully that its original tragic context has been all but erased. When Milton says that instead of the 'book of knowledge fair' his sightless eyes are presented with a 'universal blank / Of nature's works to me expunged and razed', he is thinking not just of a book with blank pages, but of the heath in *Lear*. He uses the phrase 'blasted heath' from *Macbeth* in Book One, and it's clear that Shakespeare's tragedies are embedded in his imagination and are used by him to represent his personal experience as hellish and desperate.

Recently, I've been pondering why Milton represents chaos in Book Three as 'ever-threatening storms . . . blustering round', and then immediately compares Satan to a vulture walking on 'this windy sea of land', where – lovely image – 'Chineses drive / With sails and wind their cany wagons light'. The answer, I think, can be found in *The Second Defence*, where Milton attacks his Royalist enemy Alexander More, supposed author of *The Clamour* [or *Cry*] *of the Royal Blood to Heaven against the English Parricides*. Answering this 'very effective polemic', as Lewalski describes it, Milton dismisses More as the 'barren windy egg' ('ovum hoc irritum & ventosum') from which issued 'that flatulent cry of the royal blood' ('ex quo tympanites iste clamor regii sanguinis prorupit'). These are the robust English phrases which the unnamed translator uses in the Bohn edition of the prose, though 'flatulent cry' is more literally 'tympany', which means 'swelling'. The image of Satan as vulture is an adaptation of *Eikonoklastes*, where Milton attacks Charles I for 'so greedily pursuing the six members into the house of commons', where he 'had not the forbearance to conceal how much it troubled him that the birds were flown. If some vulture in the mountains could have opened his beak intelligibly and spoke, what fitter words could he have uttered at the loss of his prey?'

The connections between the prose and the verse underline time and again what a relentlessly historical narrative *Paradise Lost* is, and point to the need for an edition of the epic which will detail the historical events it draws on and interprets, as well as mapping the historical geography of the poem: its antipathy to the North, associated with Charles raising his standard at Nottingham, with Scotland and with Strafford's Yorkshire. Satan's association with 'glistering spires' implies Royalist Oxford, and Pandemonium is the Divinity School in the Bodleian Library, where the Royalists held their parliament after fleeing London. When Milton describes Adam and Eve as 'Godlike erect, with native honour clad' he means by 'native' to present them as heroically English, and when he calls Eden the 'happy garden' he is echoing *Richard II*, set on the brink of an earlier civil war. In his famous speech, the dying John of Gaunt calls England

> This other Eden, demi-paradise,
> This fortress built by nature for herself
> Against infection and the hand of war,
> This happy breed of men . . .

Gaunt calls England 'this earth . . . this teeming womb of royal kings' and Milton echoes him in Book Seven when he says that earth's 'fertile womb teemed at a birth'. Milton substitutes 'Innumerous living creatures' for Shakespeare's kings, but draws on his patriotism to shape his own vision of a free England, also adapting one of Gaunt's images of 'insatiate' cormorants to describe one of Satan's disguises.

That vision is complicated by the way in which he moves immediately from the patriotic 'native honour clad' to an image of Adam that is troubled by history:

> His fair large front and eye sublime declared
> Absolute rule; and hyacinthine locks
> Round from his parted forelock manly hung
> Clustering.

The relatively rare parted forelock was worn by Milton and by Oliver Cromwell, whom Milton praised at first, but then failed to write an elegy for, so extending the silence about Cromwell he had maintained during the last months of the Protectorate. As Dzelzainis shows in the *Companion*, Milton was hostile to the rule of any single person, and reproved Venice and the Dutch Republic for failing to exorcize every vestige of a single person 'from their bodies politic'. That hostility can be felt in the emphatic, trochaic placing of 'Absolute' at the beginning of the line, and in the three strong stresses on the percussive monosyllables of 'fair large front'. Milton is reliving the anxieties he allowed to infiltrate his apparent panegyric of Cromwell in *The Second Defence*, where he enjoins Cromwell not to allow liberty 'to be violated by yourself, or in any one instance impaired by others'. Earlier in this passage, he praises Cromwell for rejecting those proud titles which are admired by the vulgar (this becomes the 'tedious pomp' that waits on princes in the 'grooms besmeared with gold' passage). He then goes on apparently to praise

Cromwell by stating 'What is a title but a certain definite mode of dignity? Your achievements surpass every degree even of admiration, and much more do they surpass even title; – they rise above the popular atmosphere of titles, as the tops of pyramids hide themselves in the clouds.' Continuing, he remarks that the title of king would be 'unworthy the transcendent majesty of your character'. This seems to be unambiguous praise, but the two mentions of pyramids in *Paradise Lost* both refer to Satan. In Book Two he springs upward 'like a pyramid of fire', and in Book Five he comes

> to his royal seat
> High on a hill, far blazing, as a mount
> Raised on a mount, with pyramids and towers
> From diamond quarries hewn.

The image of the pyramid associates Satan with 'impious Pharaoh', over whose realm – Milton means England – a 'pitchy cloud' of locusts are 'warping on the eastern wind'. The locusts, for Milton, must be symbols of royal favourites and courtiers, and his anxiety about Cromwell's rule and his increasing use of monarchical symbols towards the end of the Protectorate finds complex expression in the figure of Satan.

Milton remembered his injunction to Cromwell not to violate liberty when he composed the speech in which Samson laments that he is unable to serve his nation:

> these redundant locks
> Robustious to no purpose clustering down,
> Vain monument of strength.

The idea that his locks – now he is locked in prison – are 'redundant' places his power in the past. The Commonwealth, by the time Milton composed this passage, was also in the past: it had faltered when Richard Cromwell, who succeeded his father as Lord Protector, lost his nerve in April 1659. As Sharon Achinstein shrewdly notes in the *Companion*, the description of Samson's locks is prefigured in a passage in *Areopagitica*, where Milton imagines 'a noble and puissant Nation rousing herself like a strong man after sleep, and shaking her invincible locks'. As Achinstein suggests, Milton has mixed feelings about Samson, who is invoked in this image of postlapsarian sexual excess, as Adam wakes in shame:

> So rose the Danite Strong
> Hercúlean Samson from the harlot-lap
> Of Philistéan Dalilàh, and waked
> Shorn of his strength.

Adam and Eve are also, just before this, implicitly compared to Antony and Cleopatra (both pairs of lovers 'couch' on flowers) – this makes them equally strong, equally 'puissant'. Adam and Eve are both compared to Samson after he is shorn – 'they destitute and bare / Of all their virtue': it's another mutually martial, but defeated image, like that of Antony and Cleopatra after the battle of Actium, and like the image of the English nation in *Areopagitica*. The verb 'shorn' also picks up the image of Satan, who is like the eclipsed sun 'shorn of his beams'. In both cases the verb is placed emphatically at the beginning of the line in order to demonstrate the weakness of a certain kind of masculine power.

Milton is often perceived as a misogynist, but, as Achinstein shows, he argued in *Doctrine and Discipline of Divorce* for marriage as 'an apt and cheerfull conversation'. He advocated a spiritual, companionate relation between the sexes, and his views on marriage, Achinstein states, may be seen as representing a 'step forward' for women. It could be argued that the male / female image of the nation in *Areopagitica* represents this idea of mutually sustaining power, an idea implicit, as Fallon shows in the *Companion*, in the opening lines of *Paradise Lost*, where the spirit both broods on and impregnates the abyss, thus combining male and female roles. This is analogous, Fallon argues, to Milton's role as the author of the poem: he dictated it early in the morning to his amanuensis, complaining that he 'wanted to be milked'. He was thus mother and father of his text, 'the passive receptacle of inspiration and the active ancestor of eternal providence'.

The link between Samson's 'redundant' locks and the disintegration of the Commonwealth demands that we consider the role of

Richard Cromwell as well as that of General Monck. Richard's accession, Knoppers shows, was warmly received by a broad section of the gentry. He met various challenges, such as the republican backlash in Parliament in 1659, with combined tact and forcefulness, but faltered under a barrage of propaganda for the 'Good Old Cause' that temporarily united sectarians, republicans and politically active elements of the Army. Samson's locks are compared by his father Manoa to 'a nation armed', a 'camp' of faithful soldiers, but this ennobling, idealized image is offered just before Samson's death in the 'hideous noise' of the temple's destruction. In the earlier description of Samson's locks as robustious 'to no purpose', we glimpse the Army divided against itself as the country slides back towards monarchy.

Just over twenty lines after Manoa's remark, Samson says that his 'dark orbs' will yield 'to double darkness nigh at hand'. This alludes to the autobiographical passage at the start of Book Seven describing the dangers of Milton's life under the Restoration, where he is fallen on evil days and evil tongues, in 'darkness, and with dangers compassed round'. Both lines emphasize the proximity of a danger he can't see, its claustrophobic nearness. The double *d* sounds in 'double darkness' and 'darkness . . . dangers' are one example of the way Milton's ear is again and again drawn in fascinated repulsion to that hard dental. This is again apparent in Samson's long speech at the beginning of the drama, in which he rages against his blindness and captivity:

> Blind among enemies, O worse than chains,
> Dungeon, or beggary, or decrepit age!
> Light the prime work of God to me is extinct,
> And all her various objects of delight
> Annulled . . .
> . . . I dark in light exposed
> To daily fraud, contempt, abuse and wrong.

The *d*'s and *l*'s fight a battle for dominance here, while the name 'Dalila' (part symbol, as Cedric Brown has argued, of Catherine of Braganza, Charles II's wife) is implicitly ghosted in 'delight' and 'dark in light', which prepare for the great pentameter's crashing *d*'s: 'O dark, dark, dark, amid the blaze of noon' – where the clanging repeated adjective gives way to healing iambics. A few lines later the *l* in 'blaze' fights back – 'Let there be light, and light was over all' – then darkness and death become dominant again in the strong verbs 'confined', 'quenched', 'diffused', until in the last line of the speech there is near equilibrium, slightly biased to the *l* that signifies light – 'Their daily practice to afflict me more'. This uneasy equilibrium is evident in the opening line of *Samson Agonistes* – 'A little onward lend thy guiding hand' – where *d* dominates. But in the closing line – 'And calm of mind all passion spent' – *l* is dominant, and this allows, subliminally, for a hope that in the future a voice might again say 'Let there be light.' Also in the last line of *Paradise Lost* – 'Through Eden took their solitary way' – the consonant Milton prized above all others, the *l* in the centre of his name, stands out. The prophetic confidence evident in these endings imbued everything Milton wrote, and can be felt slightly earlier in *Paradise Lost* when the Archangel Michael surveys the experience of defeat, as Christopher Hill has described it, and says that those who have been conquered and enslaved by war shall 'with their freedom lost all virtue lose'. The garden of liberty seems irretrievably and emphatically lost at this point, until Michael prophesies that 'the one just man alive' will return and redeem the world:

> One man except, the only son of light
> In a dark age, against example good,
> Against allurement, custom, and a world
> Offended . . .

As we know, Milton did not believe in the rule of one man, so the one just man must be Christ at the Second Coming. But, as with Samson, it is difficult not to feel the pressure of Milton's identification with 'the only son of light' in a dark age of custom and temptation.

In Milton's verse and prose, the affirmation of unshakeable principle combines with what the Lady in *Comus* calls 'sacred vehemence'.

The invective he justified as 'sanctified bitterness' becomes the 'enormous bliss' which he sings in his verse – both rise out of that holy rage. It may be that post-imperial guilt makes many readers nowadays reluctant to participate in his soaring, architectonic genius, as he builds the nation and affirms its liberties:

> Encompassed by such countless multitudes, it seems to me that, from the columns of Hercules to the farthest borders of India, that throughout this vast expanse, I am bringing back, bringing home to every nation, liberty, so long driven out, so long an exile; and as is recorded of Triptolemus of old, that I am importing fruits for the nations, from my own city, but of a far nobler kind than those fruits of Ceres; that I am spreading abroad among the cities, the kingdoms, and nations, the restored culture of citizenship and freedom of life.

Triptolemus, or Trioptolemus, was sent by Demeter to teach humanity how to use agriculture. He was given a chariot drawn by dragons in which he rode through the air scattering seeds on the inhabited earth. It is this benign, organic idea of liberty, in which ideas are the seedcorn of the commonwealth, that Milton celebrates in his writing. This prose passage shows that nearly a decade before he began *Paradise Lost*, Milton was planting the garden of liberty with fruits for his and other nations. In the original Latin, the phrase translated as 'to the furthest borders of India' reads 'ad extremos Liberi Patris terminos' ('to the furthest borders of Father Liber'). Liber is the Italian god who makes all manner of seeds fertile. Milton is punning on 'liberty' here, and by using fruit, he chose a primary symbol so tactile it can mislead readers into a simple sensuous realism that defeats his intellectual purpose. This, perhaps, is the real dissociation of sensibility, one that takes place in the minds of those readers for whom liberty is an abstract concept, and an apple is simply an apple. However, these new studies of his life and work should make us all revisit Milton's verse and prose with bolder wing, in order to appreciate the heroic manner in which his unified sensibility affirms what he regarded as the ideal polity.

The Limits of the New Historicism: Andrew Marvell

In the great quilted cento that is *Moby-Dick*, there is a passage which might be interpreted as Melville's response to James Barry's 1776 engraving *The Phoenix or the Resurrection of Freedom*. In the engraving Andrew Marvell is depicted with Milton, Locke and Algernon Sidney among the mourners at the bier of Britain's traditional liberties. Across a pond the mourners can see a Neoclassical rotunda with an eagle-like phoenix raising its strong wings. Below the cupola the words LIBERT. AMERIC. are inscribed. It is a potent, and in England, where the Cork-born artist engraved it, a rare republican icon that celebrates the transplantation of radical English political ideology to the American shore. The engraving is reproduced on the dust-jacket of *Marvell and Liberty* (1999), a collection of essays edited by Warren Chernaik and Martin Dzelzanis, which, like David Norbrook's recent *Writing the English Republic*, chimes with the discontent that a significant percentage of British people now feels about the monarchy.

That sense of friendship, of a shared and living republican culture, is present in Melville's many allusions to Milton, as well as in these intriguing paragraphs which open Chapter 58, 'Brit':

> Steering north-eastward from the Crozetts, we fell in with vast meadows of brit, the minute, yellow substance, upon which the Right Whale largely feeds. For leagues and leagues it undulated round us, so that we seemed to be sailing through boundless fields of ripe and golden wheat.
>
> On the second day, numbers of Right Whales were seen, who, secure from the attack of a Sperm Whaler like the Pequod, with open jaws sluggishly swam through the brit, which, adhering to the fringing fibres of that wondrous Venetian blind in their mouths, was in that manner separated from the water that escaped at the lip. As morning mowers, who side by side slowly and seethingly advance their scythes through the long wet

grass of marshy meads; even so these monsters swam, making a strange, grassy, cutting sound; and leaving behind them endless swaths of blue upon the yellow sea.

Melville is alive to the future dangers which face the new republic, and he airs his anxiety by building these lines from Marvell into his prose:

For when the sun the grass hath vexed,
The tawny mowers enter next;
Who seem like Israelites to be,
Walking on foot in a green sea.
To them the grassy deeps divide,
And crowd a lane to either side.

With whistling scythe, and elbow strong,
Those massacre the grass along:
While one, unknowing, carves the rail,
Whose yet unfeathered quills her fail.

You can't make an omelette, Marvell may be hinting, without breaking eggs, though on the other hand – and there's usually another sleight of hand with him – he may be ironizing the English revolutionaries when he shows how the mower

The edge all bloody from its breast
He draws, and does his stroke detest,
Fearing the flesh untimely mowed
To him as black a fate forebode.

Melville knew Marvell's work: in his republican novella *Billy Budd*, he picks up the phrase 'starry Vere' from 'Upon Appleton House'. In these twinned republican imaginations, Leviathan, the state as whale, as monster of the deep, or the state as squad of bronzed soldiers, advances with a 'strange, grassy, cutting' or 'whistling' sound. And sound, the sonic resonance of action, event and metrical language, is one of Marvell's subjects in his phantasmagoric poem. His ear is attuned to what Mandelstam called 'the noise of time', and this means that readers must seek the political and the historical in the delicate acoustic texture of his work. Not only does he foreground sound as a subject in 'Upon Appleton House', he builds very subtle effects into the web of his language, employing a principle of spreading or kinetic assonance. Where Melville predicts the rise of the US as a sinister maritime republic with an all-powerful navy (Ahab is a fighting Quaker like Richard Nixon), Marvell hints at what the future may hold for a Commonwealth that has no institutional continuity. The theme of wounded male narcissism – the mower on a hot day mown, self-injured – may be one way of giving imaginative shape to what it feels like to live inside a new political bubble that's stretched to bursting point. But let us first address what is known about the life of *That Most Excellent Citizen and Uncorrupted Member of Parliament*, as his first biographer Edward Thompson described him in 1776, the year of James Barry's engraving.

Andrew Marvell, whose father was an Anglican clergyman, was born in the East Riding of Yorkshire in 1621, and entered Trinity College, Cambridge in 1633 at the age of twelve. He left Cambridge in 1641 without obtaining his MA, and soon left for the Continent, where he appears to have acted as tutor to a wealthy young man. (On the other hand he may have entered his brother-in-law Edmund Popple's trading-house.) When he returned to England in 1647 his political sympathies were apparently royalist. Though he was soon to change his views, the best readings of his poetry are sensitive, as Nicholas Murray points out, to the 'strangeness of his genius', and avoid tidy ideological categories. We need to attend to the 'uncanny tremor of implication' that makes the lucid surfaces of his poems 'shimmer with a sense of something undefined and undefinable beneath them'. This is apparent in the poems he wrote while living on Thomas, Lord Fairfax's estate in Yorkshire, where he was appointed tutor to Fairfax's daughter Mary some time after Fairfax resigned as Commander-in-Chief – or Lord General – of the Parliamentary forces. Fairfax resigned because he did not want to take military action against the Scots; he had also been opposed to the execution of Charles. Though Fairfax's outlook and his Horatian retirement from public life are reflected subtly in the poems, Marvell came to admire Cromwell in the years from 1653 to Cromwell's death in 1658 – he was the de facto laureate to the new state. He also became tutor to William Dutton, who was a member of Cromwell's household.

At this time Marvell was referred to as 'a notable English-Italo-Machiavellian' – for reasons that are mysterious he had the reputation of being a crafty and powerful figure. In 1657 he entered the public service as assistant to his friend Milton, who was Secretary of Foreign or Latin Tongues. He was now at the heart of the English government and a frequent visitor to Milton's house in Petty France. He first became one of the two MPs for Hull in 1659 and was re-elected in May 1660, a month after Charles II's triumphal return to London. He remained an MP until his death in 1678, and during his long parliamentary career was appointed to 120 committees, acted as teller in eight divisions and made fourteen speeches – a 'diligent enough' record, Murray says, for his day. He enjoyed political activity and lobbying, but was a bad speaker, a reserved, cautious, taciturn man who, John Aubrey noted, 'had not generall acquaintance'. He lived in meagre lodgings in central London, and appears to have had a close friendship with Prince Rupert which, according to an early Marvell editor, Thomas Cooke, meant that when it was unsafe for him to have it known where he lived 'for fear of losing his life by treachery, which was often the case, his royal friend would frequently renew his visits in the habit of a private person'.

Marvell was so often in danger, this editor says, that he was forced to have his letters directed to him under another name. An anonymous poet called him 'this Islands watchful Centinel', and his vigilant patriotic shade can be glimpsed behind these lines of Larkin's celebrating Hull, that remote city beloved of many poets, which stands like a lonely beacon on the North Sea:

> Isolate city spread alongside water,
> Posted with white towers, she keeps her face
> Half-turned to Europe, lonely northern daughter,
> Holding through centuries her separate place.

Although Hull's first poet is perhaps the most celebrated political poet in English, it seems as hard for posterity to place him as it was for his contemporaries. This supple, humorous, highly intelligent poet was also one of the foremost defenders of English liberty during the dark days of the Restoration, or it may be that he was posthumously re-created as a Whig hero. The monument raised to him in the Church of St Giles-in-the-Fields in London was either forbidden by the rector or destroyed, but this epitaph, thought to have been composed by his nephew Will Popple, celebrates his genius:

NEAR UNTO THIS PLACE LYETH THE BODY OF ANDREW MARVELL ESQUIRE, A MAN SO ENDOWED BY NATURE, SO IMPROVED BY EDUCATION, STUDY & TRAVELL, SO CONSUMMATED BY PRACTICE & EXPERIENCE; THAT BY JOINING THE MOST PECULIAR GRACES OF WIT & LEARNING WITH A SINGULAR PENETRATION, & STRENGTH OF JUDGEMENT, & EXERCISING ALL THESE IN THE WHOLE COURSE OF HIS LIFE, WITH AN UNALTERABLE STEADINESS IN THE WAYS OF VIRTUE, HE BECAME THE ORNAMENT & EXAMPLE OF HIS AGE; BELOVED BY GOOD MEN, FEAR'D BY BAD, ADMIR'D BY ALL, THO IMITATED ALASS BY FEW, & SCARCE FULLY PARALLELLED BY ANY, BUT A TOMB STONE CAN NEITHER CONTAIN HIS CHARACTER, NOR IS MARBLE NECESSARY TO TRANSMIT IT TO POSTERITY, IT WILL BE ALWAYS LEGIBLE IN HIS INIMITABLE WRITINGS, HE SERVED THE TOWN OF KINGSTON UPON HULL, ABOVE 20 YEARS SUCCESSIVELY IN PARLIAMENT, & THAT, WITH SUCH WISDOM, DEXTERITY, INTEGRITY & COURAGE AS BECOMES A TRUE PATRIOT, HE DYED THE 16. AUGUST 1678 IN THE 58TH YEAR OF HIS AGE,

SACRED

TO THE MEMORY OF ANDREW MARVELL ESQR AS A STRENUOUS ASSERTER OF THE CONSTITUTION, LAWS & LIBERTIES OF ENGLAND, AND OUT OF FAMILY AFFECTION & ADMIRATION OF THE UNCORRUPT PROBITY OF HIS LIFE & MANNERS

It is worth meditating on the ways in which Marvell the radical English patriot has slipped to the edges of cultural memory. The first comprehensive biography was written in French by Pierre Legouis and published in an edition of 500 copies in 1928. It appeared in English, abridged and lacking its rich footnotes, in 1965. Despite the enormous amount of critical commentary on the poems, a lot of it tedious and exasperating, no major biography has appeared since Legouis and no life, aside from Nicholas Murray's *World Enough and Time* (1999), is currently in print. Yet

Murray's brief biography can only be viewed as a prompt towards a full historical and critical study.

The problem here, as with many biographies, is that the general reader at whom biographies are directed is deemed to be nervous of any kind of sophisticated literary criticism which points to the sometimes bottomless, tantalizing nature of aesthetic experience. Murray is alive to such experience, as his comments on the shortcomings of a reductive New Historicist reading shows, but he has not sought to draw his readers into it. In an essay on Marvell's poetics of enclosure, reprinted in Healy's collection, one of Marvell's most interesting recent critics, Jonathan Crewe, shows how 'The Garden' exposes 'a widespread cultural fantasy of the supposedly autonomous, originary masculine subject'. This, though Crewe does not say so, is because Marvell's irony uses a form of camp to unsettle conventional categories and tantalize his readers. Crewe's commentary is particularly acute when he discusses the stanza that follows this one:

> Meanwhile the mind, from pleasure less,
> Withdraws into its happiness:
> The mind, that ocean where each kind
> Does straight its own resemblance find,
> Yet it creates, transcending these,
> Far other worlds, and other seas,
> Annihilating all that's made
> To a green thought in a green shade.

The word 'green' occurs nearly thirty times in Marvell's poems, and I can remember trying to puzzle out the simultaneously intellectual and tactile nature of these lines as an undergraduate on hot summer days in the flat green fields outside Hull. The element of camp can be found in the next stanza, as Marvell deploys with self-conscious confidence the obvious dualism of traditional Christian belief:

> Here at the fountain's sliding foot,
> Or at some fruit-tree's mossy root,

Casting the body's vest aside,
My soul into the boughs does glide:
There like a bird it sits, and sings,
Then whets, and combs its silver wings;
And, till prepared for longer flight,
Waves in its plumes the various light.

Crewe argues that the 'liberated' masculine soul in the poem is in fact 'an exotic figure of "feminine" narcissism' represented by the bird of paradise that 'whets and combs its silver wings'. For Crewe, this narcissistic figure follows logically from the great closing couplet of the previous stanza, which reduces the pastoral subject to a 'thought-possessed "shade" '. I would suggest that Marvell plays with the two sounds made by the letter *i*, both of them contained in the word 'sliding', which helps design a typically slippery image.

As the assonance spreads, Marvell appears to be almost obsessively underlining both the sound *i* and the concept *in*:

My soul into the boughs does glide:
There like a bird it sits and sings,
Then whets and combs its silver wings;
And, till prepared for longer flight,
Waves in its plumes the various light.

My hunch is that the *i* sound in 'flight' represents a disembodied Cartesian or Puritan idea of mind which he rejects in favour of in-ness, the interiority of the closing couplet of the last stanza:

Two paradises twere in one
To live in paradise alone.

Perhaps there is a form of dangerous pantheism here, which the adept politician is masking behind Christian piety and a jokey light-verse tone. What is significant, though, is the deliberately preening quality created by the repeated *i* sounds, so that 'flight' takes off into an empty disembodied heaven. What he prefers is 'in paradise', the two sounds hand in glove, like the mortalist's idea of embodied spirit.

One of my favourite examples of Marvell's stringent poetic ear is the way he exploits the name 'Cromwell', which was then given the rather less resonant pronunciation 'Crummle' – the effect is rather like a wall being pounded by a battering-ram. The future Lord Protector first appears in the early Royalist elegy Marvell wrote for Lord Francis Villiers, who was killed in 1648 in a skirmish with Parliamentary forces. The only surviving copy of this poem is in Worcester College, Oxford, and though it cannot be definitely proved to be by Marvell, George Clark, the early editor who discovered it, believed it was. In the poem, Marvell says:

> 'Tis always late
> To struggle with inevitable fate.
> Much rather though, I know, expect'st to tell
> How heavy Cromwell gnashed the earth and fell.

This sets up the pattern of *uh* sounds which runs through these lines from the famous 'Horatian Ode upon Cromwell's Return from Ireland':

> So restless Cromwell could not cease
> In the inglorious arts of peace,
> But through adventurous war
> Urgèd his active star.

The repetition of the *uh* sound validates the name 'Cromwell' or 'Crummle' and makes it overwhelming like fate – or a force of nature. On the other hand, we might argue that Marvell's memory of his earlier lines – if the Villiers elegy is his – complicates the effect of the *uh* sound and that this passage from the 'Horatian Ode' could be thought to mimic the slugging, thumping sounds of battle and disgust. This textured complication is present in the following lines from 'Upon the Hill and Grove at Bil-borow', which is dedicated to Fairfax:

> Here learn, ye mountains more unjust,
> Which to abrupter greatness thrust,
> That do with your hook-shouldered height
> The earth deform and heaven fright.

The same sounds are used as the major key in these lines from Marvell's poem celebrating 'The First Anniversary of the Government under His Highness the Lord Protector, 1655':

> Cromwell alone with greater vigour runs,
> (Sun-like) the stages of succeeding suns:
> And still the day which he doth next restore
> Is the just wonder of the day before.
> Cromwell alone doth with new lustre spring,
> And shines the jewel of the yearly ring.

The passage with its attendant kinetic assonance builds a majestic image of Cromwell while hinting at the problem of succession, but the next lines, which conclude with a deliberately dissonant, because forced or uprooted, stress, introduce a complication:

> 'Tis the force of scattered time contracts,
> And he in one year the forces of ages acts:
> While heavy monarchs make a wide return,
> Longer and more malignant than Saturn.

The thud of that last unexpected stress casts over the sun-like Cromwell the leaden gloom of heavy Saturn who was deposed by his son Jupiter, just as Cromwell the regicide may in time be deposed.

This, however, is over-schematic about an exercise in the sounds which time or history make within the present political moment: Marvell uses the Machiavellian injunction 'now' three times in the 'Horatian Ode', and it is the stretched moment, like thrumming canvas, that his delicate ear attempts to catch.

He knows that there is a chaotic void at the heart of political action which turns the world upside down and gives an image for it in his poem on the death of Cromwell:

> Thou in a pitch how far beyond the sphere
> Of human glory tower'st, and reigning there
> Despoiled of mortal robes, in seas of bliss,
> Plunging does bathe, and tread the bright abyss.

'Tread', that soldier's or even farmyard verb, is typically strong and concrete, while 'bright abyss' is both heavenly and hellish. It's almost as if Cromwell is treading grapes in a pastoral, which in a sense he is, because Marvell is remembering this extraordinary phantasmagoric moment from 'Upon Appleton House':

> And now to the abyss I pass
> Of that unfathomable grass,
> Where men like grasshoppers appear,
> But grasshoppers are giants there:
> They, in their squeaking laugh, contemn
> Us as we walk more low than them:
> And, from the precipices tall
> Of the green spires, to us do call.

Any decent edition of Marvell will detail the allusions here to grasshoppers in the Old Testament and to Marvell's Cavalier friend, Richard Lovelace's poem 'To a Grasshopper', but it is the reference to 'green spires' as 'precipices tall' that intrigues me. It may be that Milton was recalling this passage when he compared Satan to a scout who sees from a hill 'some renowned metropolis / With glistening spires and pinnacles adorned'. Milton repeats the image later in *Paradise Lost* when he describes Satan's head

> Crested aloft, and carbuncle his eyes;
> With burnished neck of verdant gold, erect
> Amidst his circling spires, that on the grass
> Floated redundant.

The spires here are partly Rome, partly Royalist Oxford's dreaming spires; they also recall the circling shape of the snake. Marvell relishes the squeaking laughter of the giant Royalist grasshoppers which are both belittled and ominously huge, as Charles's forces will be when Richard Cromwell fails to get very far along the 'rugged track' – that *uh* sound again – which Marvell imagines him beating down now his 'great parent' is dead.

It is a moment of surreal political premonition, like a passage from *Gulliver's Travels* or like this passage which imagines the hayfield as a sea:

> When after this 'tis piled in cocks,
> Like a calm sea it shows the rocks,
> We wondering in the river near
> How boats among them safely steer.
> Or, like the desert Memphis sand,
> Short pyramids of hay do stand.
> And such the Roman camps do rise
> In hills for soldiers' obsequies.

This is witty, gentle and accurate – haycocks do look like rocks in a calm sea – but the Egyptian and Roman imagery suddenly contradicts the native Englishness by introducing sharp geometrical shapes which belong to an imperial slave culture. In *The Reason of Church Government* Milton compares the rule of bishops to a 'pyramid' that aspires and 'sharpens' ambition, saying that it is 'the most dividing and schismatical form that geometricians know of'; and in his *Second Defence of the English People* he warns Cromwell not to 'invade that liberty which you have defended', arguing that Cromwell ought not to assume the title of king, because actions such as his are lost in clouds like 'the points of pyramids'. Later, Satan in *Paradise Lost* is shown raised on a mount 'with pyramids and towers'.

It may be that the connection with Milton is a coincidence, but I cannot think that the two poets, who were both friends and colleagues, failed to influence each other. And if I'm here pointing to an element of historical premonition, a deliberate unease within Marvell's affectionate pastoralism, this is because it is possible to perceive something other than the historical in this type of writing, something unforeseen, even unknowable. James Loxley's essay 'The Prospect of History: Marvell's Landscapes in Contemporary Criticism' is particularly interesting in this context because it seeks to unsettle the apparently solid Whig foundations on which New Historicist interpretation rests. Arguing against Louis Montrose's apparently famous chiasmic formulation 'the history of texts and the textuality of history', Loxley challenges the idea that history can be simply 'emptied into textuality'. He is concerned to unsettle the new critical settlement which emerged after the Theory Wars of the early eighties, and argues that Montrose's chiasmus 'ought not to be taken as the definition of a criticism that has absorbed and moved on from the moment of theory'. He wants a historicism which is 'less self-consciously new' to attend to 'an aporetic moment', a moment of doubt and perplexity that will be 'not the basis of a method but the beginning, yet once more, of its critique'.

Loxley properly insists that the critical spirit exists hand to mouth on sinking sands or trembling bogland, never on solid classical foundations, and reflecting on his essay I'm drawn through that Lycidasian cadence 'yet once more' to one of the most extraordinary stanzas in 'Upon Appleton House' – stanza 77, where Marvell indulges wittily in a fantasy involving bondage and auto-asphyxia. Earlier in the poem he mentions Cawood Castle, seat of the Archbishop of York, saying the sight – meaning his eyesight – plies its 'invisible artillery' on the proud castle: 'As if it quarrelled in the seat / The ambition of its prelate great'. Then he describes wandering into a grove:

> The oak leaves me embroider all,
> Between which caterpillars crawl:
> And ivy, with familiar trails,
> Me licks, and clasps, and curls, and hales.
> Under this antic cope I move
> Like some great prelate of the grove.

I can never read the last couplet without imagining how Frankie Howerd or Kenneth Williams would have delivered it – this is quite deliciously camp, and that word 'antic' is also theatrical, for it inescapably carries a memory of Hamlet's 'antic disposition'. However, as Elizabeth Story Donno points out in her edition of Marvell, Milton uses the word in his 1642 *An Apology for Smectymnus*: 'it has no rubric to be sung in an antic cope upon the stage of a high altar'. The phrase denotes a 'grotesque ecclesiastical vestment', and the spellings 'antic' and 'antique' were interchangeable, so there is a pun meaning 'grotesquely old-fashioned' at work here. But this is the lead-in to the next verses where he draws on Donne's 'The Ecstasy' to fuse sensually with the 'velvet moss' – another High Church vestment – before stanza 77's almost orgasmic scream:

> Bind me, ye woodbines, in your twines,
> Curl me about, ye gadding vines,
> And, oh, so close your circles lace,
> That I may never leave this place:
> But lest your fetters prove too weak,
> Ere I your silken bondage break,
> Do you, O brambles, chain me too,
> And, courteous briars, nail me through.

This passage is one of several – the stanza with the screaming grasshoppers is another – where the poem descends into unforeseen, but in a way perfectly logical insanity. It recalls, in addition to Milton and Shakespeare, Marvell's Royalist friend Richard Lovelace's 'To Althea':

> When I lie tangled in her hair,
> And fetter'd to her eye,
> The gods, that wanton in the air,
> Know no such liberty.

Marvell has tied himself in these conventional Cavalier knots before – 'the curlèd trammels of her hair' ('The Fair Singer'), and 'Black eyes, red lips, and curlèd hair' ('The Singer') – but this is a more typical ironic fantasy of solitary self-gratification which both mocks that selfish and painful pleasure, and glances at Puritanism: 'Cease, tempter. None can chain a mind / Whom this sweet chordage cannot bind'. This is the Soul's reply to the 'charming airs' Pleasure proposes in 'A Dialogue between the Resolved Soul and Created Pleasure', and we may savour the exquisite agony that is intimated in that phrase 'sweet chordage', as well as noting the mnemonic presence of the couplet in those triple binding internal rhymes in the first line of stanza 77. The circle which Marvell is attempting to square elsewhere in the poem and in the house's architecture is there in the third line's triple orgasmic *o* rhymes. (I'm reminded of Leopold Bloom's bondage fantasy, which wittily suggests that Ireland is tied up inside Egypt / Britain's house of bondage.)

Marvell the camp bishop – the poet in ecclesiastical drag – is taking Royalism and Anglicanism to the limit of absurdity. He is also recalling Archbishop Laud's execution (the Archbishop courteously suggested that the spectators underneath the scaffold should move from under the block, lest they be covered in his blood), and the 'royal actor' Charles on the scaffold. It might be too much to suggest that the *oo* rhymes in the last couplet recall Caesar's 'et tu Brute', but my point is that there is a deliberate too-muchness, a phantasmagoric, over-the-top quality in this stanza and elsewhere. Anyone who has seen Ian Paisley preaching in a darkened mission hut in Africa, or Gerry Adams walking up the steps of Stormont in an Armani suit, will appreciate that politics can go beyond itself into that almost transcendental grotesquerie that is the antic. As I write, Baroness Thatcher has just addressed the Tory Party Conference, head and body out of sync like a demented puppet. Politics isn't simply what Harold Macmillan described as 'events, dear boy', though he meant the unforeseen, the unpredictable, the utterly unexpected – it is the chaos those words attempt to represent.

To adapt an encouraging remark of Tom Stoppard's about an audience arriving at one of Howard Brenton's plays – 'a lot of denim' – I would suggest that there is a lot of silk in this poem. The military flowers Marvell terms 'silken signs', the dew-wet meadows are like 'green silks but newly washed', the vines catch him in their 'silken bondage', but Marvell also uses the words 'lick' and 'slick', which follow from the river's 'wanton harmless folds' to echo the word 'snake' and suggest the word 'silk'. He says 'No serpent new nor crocodile / Remains behind our little Nile' – a witty glance at the snake in the Garden of Eden, and at Cleopatra or the 'serpent of the old Nile', as well as at the escape from Egypt theme that he sternly represents in the Puritanical ascent of the resolved soul in the previous stanza, 78, which itself follows the bondage stanza:

> Here in the morning tie my chain,
> Where the two woods have made a lane,
> While, like a guard on either side,
> The tree before their Lord divide;
> This, like a long and equal thread,
> Betwixt two labyrinths does lead.
> But where the floods did lately drown,
> There at evening stake me down.

This is the exit from Egypt, the Minotaur's labyrinth and the Garden of Eden, and it seems to set the course for a 'long and equal' republic, except that, in another anticipation of Swift's Gulliver, he is tied down by the strings of political intrigue. The dislocation of scale in the poem is reminiscent of Lilliput and Brobdingnag, and it must be that Swift was influenced by this master of the octosyllabic couplet, a form Swift himself employs in a workmanlike manner, quite lacking Marvell's super-subtle deftness of touch.

My own hunch is that Marvell owes a lot to Spenser, and that the tawny mowers are a version of the 'yron man' Talus in *The Faerie Queene*, whom Spenser based on Talos, the Bronze Man who was guardian of Crete. If the bronzed, suntanned mowers can be associated with Talus, Marvell may have intended the ghost of Talus's relationship with Artegall, Knight of Justice, whom Spenser based on Lord Grey – Spenser served as his Secretary while Grey was Lord Deputy of Ireland and supported his violent measures. Marvell may, in other words, be making a link with Cromwell's policies in Ireland and with the Levellers who mutinied against being sent to Ireland (Fairfax helped to suppress the mutiny). Too arcane, perhaps, but Marvell is such a tantalizing poet that he effortlessly inspires the critical soul to whet its silver wings. I look forward to the annotated editions of his verse and prose which, at long last, are now in preparation. They may, among other things, determine whether this poet of 'liminal states' was gay, as a few scholars suggest. John Creaser is the only critic in these two recent collections of essays to attend to Marvell's finely modulated prosody, but the renewed interest in his work and his life which these three studies represent make me hopeful that a new generation of critics capable of appreciating the formal joys of verse may soon redefine New Historicism. Meanwhile, the real task for literary critics is to find a way of communicating with a general audience.

The Jaw-Bone of an Ass Espied: John Bunyan

John Bunyan was born in a cottage on the eastern border of Elstow, near the hamlet of Harrowden in Bedfordshire, in November 1628. His father was a brazier who may have sent his son to a grammar school for a time. As a child he suffered from nightmares that were subsequently to colour his 'tortured conversion experience', as Richard Greaves terms it in his biography, *Glimpses of Glory: John Bunyan and English Dissent* (2002). Bunyan was thirteen when the English Revolution – Civil War, Greaves terms it – broke out, and at sixteen he became a soldier in a regiment garrisoned at Newport Pagnell. During his army years Bunyan witnessed the struggle between Presbyterians who wanted to reform the Church of England and radical sectaries who wanted to separate from them. He had a religious awakening in 1650, the year his blind daughter Mary was born, and suffered from a series of nervous illnesses which Greaves unhelpfully approaches through modern psychiatric theory and William Styron's compelling account of his experience of severe depression. He preached to a Bedford congregation which a contemporary called 'Bunian his society'. Bunyan's preaching got him into trouble well before the Restoration of the monarchy and the traditional church in 1660. By this time he was reading Fox's *Book of Martyrs*, and as Greaves suggests was moved by the courage of those who had faced the rack, the gallows and the stake. Bunyan's legal torments began when he was invited to preach at the hamlet of Lower Samsell on 12 November 1660. When he arrived at Lower Samsell, a friend told him about a rumoured warrant for his arrest, but he decided to preach, not wanting to set a bad example to recent converts or to other Nonconformists by fleeing. He was arrested and would have been released if he had offered a humble apology and promised to follow his vocation instead of breaking the law. He refused and was put on trial and sentenced to three months in jail. He was kept in jail because he refused to admit he had wrongfully convened the group at Lower Samsell. His second wife Elizabeth, courageous and pious like his first wife, who died leaving him four children, presented a petition to secure his release. Angered by the callous attitude of one of the justices of the peace and by the mockery of several bystanders, she shed her deferential demeanour and denounced the proceedings for their perceived bias against commoners: 'Because he is a Tinker, and poor man; therefore he is despised, and cannot have justice.' Elizabeth had miscarried when she heard the news of Bunyan's arrest, and her experience is glimpsed in the second part of *Pilgrim's Progress*: 'A Dream I had of two ill-lookt ones, that I thought did Plot how to make me miscarry in my Journey, that hath troubled me much: Yea, it still runs in my mind, and makes me afraid of every one that I meet, lest they should meet me to do me a mischief, and to turn me out of the way.'

Bunyan described his imprisonment and dealings with magistrates in five pastoral letters, he also compared his first collection of verse, *Profitable Meditations*, published in 1661, and *I Will Pray With the Spirit*, which was 'almost certainly written' in 1662. He supported his family by making long tagged laces in jail, and was made miserable by thoughts of his family's sufferings. As Greaves shows, he wrote *Pilgrim's Progress*, which was published in 1678, not only as a guide to the Christian life, but as an attempt to shape the Restoration crisis of 1667–73 by setting liberty of conscience against the state's authority and the conformity of the rich, the corrupt, the careerist and the spineless.

Remarking that there is 'no escaping the fact' that *Pilgrim's Progress* is a 'profoundly political tract', Greaves fails to communicate the pressure of those times. He remarks that Louis XIV 'was no friend to his Huguenot subjects', but does not bother to notice the fact or the extent of Louis' persecutions. It's as though he wants to avoid confronting the suffering that Louis inflicted, and that this is part of a larger project to palliate historical conflict. Noting that

Jack Lindsay's statement that Bunyan's *The Holy War* is a commentary on 'absolutism against the liberties of the people', he asserts that this view 'cannot be sustained' without explaining why. Yet a Bunyan scholar whom he cites elsewhere, Sharon Achinstein, has convincingly argued that *The Holy War* is 'a veiled commentary on the political situation during England's Exclusion crises'. Greaves briefly mentions the distinguished educationist Charles Morton, who became vice-president of Harvard, and at whose academy Defoe was educated, but his sense of the dissenting culture that Morton and Bunyan belonged to is bland and uninformed. He shows that Bunyan was close to the Rye House plotters, who were tried in 1683 for conspiring to assassinate Charles II and his brother, James, Duke of York, but offers a rather quietistic figure who becomes 'gentler, more tolerant' with the years (this is not the view of Achinstein, who writes subtly about Bunyan's identification with Samson). He mentions that Benjamin and William Hewling were executed after Sedgemoor, but fails to note that they were friends of Defoe's at Morton's academy (they helped to inspire *Robinson Crusoe*). Greaves passes over the Bloody Assizes in a few sentences, merely noting that approximately 250 Sedgemoor rebels were executed. Without summoning Macaulay's anger at Judge Jeffreys' butchery, historical truth surely demands that the vicious suppression of the rebellion be at least acknowledged.

But Greaves's passionless comfortable prose composed in Florida sunshine betrays no sense of the Dissenters' experience during the Restoration. He notes that Bunyan could pack London meeting-houses to overflowing at a day's notice, and that the tenth and eleventh editions of *Pilgrim's Progress* in 1685 and 1688 made Bunyan a celebrity. He adds that his printed sermons 'suggest he was at times a powerful orator', but nowhere does he try to analyse and appreciate the power which 'Bishop Bunyan' created. He reduces one of the most powerful and influential writers and preachers of his age to a dull worthy figure, instead of one of the avatars of the British national conscience. Both Michael Greaves and Davies in his recent critical study, *Graceful Reading: Theology and Narrative in the Works of John Bunyan* (2002), appear to accept, even collude with, Bunyan's diminished presence in contemporary British culture, though this was not the case in earlier generations: E. P. Thompson states that Paine's *The Rights of Man* and Bunyan's *Pilgrim's Progress* are the two foundation texts of the English working-class movement. Thomas Cooper, the Chartist, called *The Pilgrim's Progress* the 'book of books'. It has been translated into more than two hundred languages and is especially popular in the Third World. It permeates Dickens's work, as well as Hardy's, and of course supplied the title of Thackeray's great novel *Vanity Fair*.

Bunyan remains an enduring presence in the cultural memory of Ulster Protestantism. In a lecture on Bunyan, given many years ago and released on tape, Ian Paisley praises this 'dreamer and penman' for his 'strong doctrinal preaching', his opposition to the civil and ecclesiastical authorities, the enormous crowds he drew, and for his prose style. This 'poor unschooled tinker' became, Paisley argues, 'the most prominent man of letters as far as English literature is concerned'. He had 'the tinker's power of reaching the heart'. Bunyan the rebel lives in Paisley's preaching and fuels his opposition to liberal theology, Catholicism and political change. Bunyan the commonwealth man and soldier in the parliamentary army has become one of the early manifestations of the most reactionary and negative forms of Ulster Unionism, a Unionism that paradoxically carries a creative energy that looks forward, not backward.

Bunyan's courage and integrity, his timeless communicativeness, speak directly to anyone who feels they are in the power of Mr Worldly-Wiseman, 'my Lord Turn-about, my Lord Time-server, my Lord Fair-speech'. Bunyan, through the character of By-ends, adds 'Mr Smooth-man, Mr Facing-bothways, Mr Any-thing, and the parson of our parish, Mr Two-tongues'. These visionary caricatures remind us that underneath the social and institutional surfaces where we work with and encounter other people – friends, acquaintances, colleagues, enemies and those in between these categories – beneath this surface exist certain forces for good and evil, and certain irrefrangible principles. However much we try to dip, dodge and jerk in our social and professional lives, there are moments when we fall into what can feel like a bottomless pit. Bunyan, like

Milton and Blake, is one of the guides we may summon when we find ourselves making that plunge.

Perhaps it is unfair for anyone living in present-day England to expect a critic to identify with Bunyan's dream of truth, but Michael Davies's lengthy study is remarkable for its failure to empathize with Bunyan's heroic political battles. Davies tries in his introduction to argue, though in fact he only states, that 'non-doctrinal readings' of Bunyan can sometimes be 'inappropriate (if not pernicious, on occasion)' because they frequently issue from 'distinct historical and polemical' motives. Though Davies properly calls attention to Bunyan's doctrine of grace, he separates the politics of the period from Bunyan's dissenting faith and dismisses those critics he disagrees with as 'the likes of Davie,' or Greaves, Fowler, Parker, Hobbes, Sherman, Leavis. They are sinners who have failed to see the light of true doctrine, which states that Bunyan is always keen to point any metaphor or analogy 'towards the spiritual and away from the political when discussing salvation'. When Bunyan describes grace as setting 'open the prison doors' and letting the prisoners go free, he is 'not necessarily advocating a politicized experience'.

For Davies, Bunyan is 'simply discussing grace as offering the only possible liberty from a range of spiritually perilous factors'. Behind Bunyan's doctrine of grace there is a language that, 'despite its surface radicalism', is centred in a desire to assure and comfort the burdened sinner. Writing in a gungy, parlando style, Davies is concerned to deny the reasons that drew Bunyan's contemporaries to him, and which have made his dream vision available in almost every written language.

In a sermon 'The Greatness of the Soul and the Unspeakableness of the Loss Thereof', Bunyan says:

> No suit of apparel is by God thought good enough for the soul, but that which is made by God himself, and that is that curious thing the body. But oh! how little is this considered – namely, the greatness of the soul.

Bunyan instils confidence in their own spiritual greatness and power in his largely disenfranchised audience: like Antigone confronting

Creon, he challenges the class structure and the institutions of the period. In 'Justification by an Imputed Righteousness; or, No Way to Heaven but by Jesus Christ', he states:

> Living by faith begets in the heart a son-like boldness and confidence to Godward in all our gospel duties, under all our weaknesses, and under all our temptations. It is a blessed thing to be privileged with a holy boldness and confidence Godward, that he is on our side, that he taketh part with us, and that he will plead our cause 'with them that rise up against us'.

It is this quality of holy boldness that Bunyan's writing communicates, and it moved and uplifted his audiences deeply, instilling into them – or, rather, drawing out of them – a confidence that each and every one was the equal of the next person, and need not be intimidated by those who held power in the land. As Christopher Hill shows in his biography of Bunyan, John Owen, a former vice-chancellor of Oxford, told Charles II he would gladly exchange his learning for the 'tinker's power in the pulpit'. Owen, who was a millenarian, often invited Bunyan to preach to his Moorfields Congregation.

The confidence, the holy boldness that Bunyan asserts, is not a simple, armoured, spiritual front – his emotional openness and frankness leads him to admit feelings of anxiety and fear at what his enemies have in store for him. In 'The Greatness of the Soul' he anticipates Crusoe's fate when he imagines a man 'be taken by them of Algiers, and there made a slave of, and there be hunger-bit, and beaten till his bones are broken'. The repeated *b* sounds, the mainly monosyllabic words, give a physical texture to Bunyan's language, as well as encoding his experience of seventeen years in a Stuart jail. The solitariness of the Puritan soul at times gives way to that sense of being abandoned which Crusoe feels in his darkest moments. Where Milton designs a magnificent, climbing cadence in the lonely tower passage in *Il Penseroso*, Bunyan offers an image which is both homely, and to a seventeenth-century audience, slightly foreign and unusual:

> But this man has provided for things; like the tortoise, he has got a shell on his back, so strong and sound that he fears not to suffer a loaden cart

to go over him. The Lord is his rock, his defence, his refuge, his high tower, unto which he doth continually resort.

In folklore, the tortoise symbolizes slowness, determination and long life – here the little land turtle lovingly evoked in 'Christ a Complete Saviour' is like someone low down the social scale whose faith is a high visionary stone tower which protects and encircles the soul. From 'tortoise' to 'resort' the run of *t* and *o* and *r* sounds pattern and cadence the statement. Where his Cavalier near-contemporary, Lovelace, chooses the grasshopper as a symbol of his precarious identity, Bunyan the Roundhead identifies with a shy creature with a horny shell.

In 'Baby Tortoise', Lawrence makes the tortoise into a Roman legionnaire, then a *testudo*, the siege engine made of shields:

Nay, tiny shell-bird,
What a huge vast inanimate it is, that you must row against,
What an incalculable inertia.

Challenger,
Little Ulysses, fore-runner,
No bigger than my thumb-nail,
Buon viaggio.

All animate creation on your shoulder,
Set forth, little Titan, under your battle-shield.
The ponderous, preponderate, inanimate universe;
And you are slowly moving, pioneer, you alone.

After the vernacular first line, Lawrence deliberately employs a series of Latinate polysyllables, then in the next poem 'Tortoise Shell' he sees the shell as a Christian symbol, exclaiming 'The Cross, the Cross'. For Lawrence, too, the tortoise is a symbol of the free individual conscience on the social margins. And like Bunyan, he speaks with a demotic tenderness, calling it a 'wee mite', a 'sprottling insect'. In one of the few passages which show an appreciation of Bunyan's almost animist response to the natural world, Greaves notes that Bunyan also mentions asps, adders, frogs, toads, grasshoppers, locusts, bees, hornets, butterflies, moths, flies, fleas, ants, spiders, scorpions, as well as worms, maggots, snails, eagles, hawks, robins, nightingales, crows, owls, swallows, cuckoos, wrens, vultures. He also mentions partridges, pelicans, storks, ostriches and peacocks, but seems to have had little interest in fish.

In 'The Resurrection of the Dead, and Eternal Judgement', where Bunyan uses a cadaver as a similar symbol, he says:

> The body ariseth, as to the nature of it, the self-same nature; but as to the manner of it; how far transcendent is it! There is a poor, dry, wrinkled kernel cast into the ground, and there it lieth, and swelleth, breaketh, and, one would think, perisheth; but behold, it receiveth life, it chitteth, it putteth forth a blade, and groweth into a stalk, there also appeareth an ear; it also sweetly blossoms, with a full kernel in the ear: it is the same wheat, yet behold how the form and fashion of that which now ariseth, doth differ from that which then was sown, is no glory, when compared with that in which it riseth.

Here, what I take to be Bunyan's mortalism is expressed in an organic metaphor that takes authority from the dialect verb 'chitteth' ('provincial and almost obsolete', his devoted Victorian editor, George Offor, wrongly notes). The verb 'chit' is commonly used by gardeners to mean 'to sprout, to shoot at the end of the grain', and there is also a suggestion of another meaning – to 'chirp' – which gives a new-hatched quality, added to the diminutive, sometimes slightly derogatory 'little child', 'little slip of a thing'. At the same time, there is an identification being made between Bunyan and his audience and the 'poor, dry, wrinkled kernel' which has been 'cast' into the ground. Like the figure of the castaway, to which he returns, the buried human body is a symbol of what it feels like to be at the mercy of powerful political forces.

The promise of resurrection becomes a figure for political emancipation: 'I have a dream,' Bunyan is saying with Martin Luther King, 'a dream we can all make true'. In bringing imagination to the explanation of religious doctrine and the fight for justice, Bunyan aligns himself with 'the learned Herbert', quoting his couplet from 'The Temple' in his verse preface to *Scriptural Poems* – 'A verse may find him, who a sermon flies / And turn delight into a sacrifice.' In 'The History of Samson', the most powerful of those poems, he makes Samson into the figure of the fearless preacher who uses his jaw to defeat his enemies:

> The Philistines against him gave a shout:
> And mightily the Spirit of the Lord
> Came on him, and like burning flax each cord
> That was upon his arms became; the bands
> Were likewise separated from his hands.
> And he the jaw-bone of an ass espied,
> And took and smote them till a thousand died.
> Then said he, with an ass's jaw-bone I
> Have made mine enemies in heaps to be.
> Behold I have destroyed a thousand men
> With this same worthless ass's jaw.

As Hill points out, *Pilgrim's Progress* was written in jail at almost exactly the same time as Milton, 'imprisoned by blindness', was composing *Paradise Lost*, *Paradise Regained*, and *Samson Agonistes*. Bunyan was, Hill notes, the first major English writer who was neither London-based, nor university educated, and he must, like Bottom, have recognized in the ass a figure for his lowly position in the class structure, and a compensating symbol of boundless imagination and power. The ass's jawbone is, as I've suggested, a figure for the preacher's boundless flow of words, the power of those words, but also their flimsy, opinionated vulnerability. Samson is both a heroic freedom fighter and blind helpless prisoner.

In 'Christian Behaviour', Bunyan offers another symbol for the doctrine he is preaching:

> The doctrine of the gospel is like the dew and the small rain that distilleth upon the tender grass, wherewith it doth flourish, and is kept green. Christians are like the several flowers in a garden that have upon each of them the dew of heaven, which being shaken with the wind, they let fall their dew at each other's roots, whereby they are jointly nourished, and become nourishers of one another.

The small rain seems to rise out of one of the most famous medieval lyrics:

Westron wynde when wyll thow blow
the smalle rayne downe can rayne–
Cryst yf my love wer in my armys
and I in my bed agayne!

The small rain comes out of the common tongue and is a figure, again, for the diminutive social position of Bunyan and his audience, many of whom once belonged to a victorious army that sang psalms before it charged into battle. The tender grass, like Whitman's leaves of grass, represents the democratic energy of the popular will. In despair in 'The Flitting', one of Bunyan's admirers, John Clare, cries out: 'still the grass eternal springs / Where castles stood & grandeur died.' The dew distilled on the grass is also an image of mutual support, the communal faith which sustains puritan congregations – what the Unitarians called 'sociality'. Bunyan develops this idea in the next sentence where he says: 'For Christians to commune savourly of God's matters one with another, it is as if they opened to each other's nostrils boxes of perfume.' Bunyan stresses not only the 'inward man', but the sustaining warmth of togetherness, of company.

It is Bunyan's observation of small things, like the 'dish of milk well crumbed' in the second part of *The Pilgrim's Progress* that makes – or made – his work so popular and accessible. Earlier in the second part, Christiana and Mercy are asked to observe a hen and chickens in the House of the Interpreter:

So they gave heed, and perceived that the hen did walk in a fourfold method towards her chickens. 1. She had a common call, and that she hath all day long. 2. She had a special call, and that she had but sometimes. 3. She had a brooding note. And 4. She had an outcry.

Then the Interpreter compares the hen to God, whom he calls 'your King'. The homely comparison speaks to ordinary experience, as does this paragraph in *Grace Abounding*:

But God did not utterly leave me, but followed me still, not now with convictions, but judgements, yet such as were mixed with mercy. For once I fell into a creek of the sea, and hardly escaped drowning: another time I fell out of a boat into Bedford river, but mercy yet preserved me alive: besides, another time being in the field, with one of my companions, it chanced that an adder passed over the highway, so I having a stick in mine hand, struck her over the back; and having stounded her, I forced open her mouth with my stick, and plucked her sting out with my fingers, by which act had not God been merciful to me, I might by my desperateness have brought myself to mine end.

He then relates how during a siege in the Civil War, one of his company took his place 'and coming to the siege, as he stood sentinel, he was shot in the head with a musket ball and died'. This sense of being one of the elect is an unattractive feature of puritan individualism, but it must have made many members of his audiences feel special, feel what we now term 'empowered'.

For Davies, the aim of *Grace Abounding* is 'strictly and wholly pastoral and doctrinal'. Bunyan always aims to inspire 'faithful not social revolution' in his readers – an assertion which frees Davies from giving any consideration to the cadences of Bunyan's prose, or to its language and imagery. Although he tells us that he has adopted 'the vocabulary of a post-modern poetics', it is impossible to discern what that poetics is. His critical method has no connection with aesthetics and merely represents a *mentalité* that is blank, weightless, wholly unable to sympathize with Bunyan's battle against the Stuart state.

By his use of ordinary detail, Bunyan proves the Word on the common pulse of shared experience. He tells us that now he could evoke from himself to God, 'and should reckon that all those graces of God that now were green in me, were yet but like those cracked groats and four-pence-halfpennies that rich men carry in their purses, when their gold is in their trunks at home'.

The graceful confidence of Bunyan's language has a physical texture which convinces by its homely simplicity: 'Physicians get neither name nor fame by pricking of wheals, or picking out thistles, or by laying of plasters to the scratch of a pin; every old woman can do this. But if they would have a name and a fame, if they will have it quickly, they must, as I said, do some great and desperate cures.' Bunyan repeats the phrasal rhyme name / fame, but he also gives 'quickly' a significant emphasis because it draws into itself 'pricking', 'picking', 'thistles', 'pin' and 'this'. The word doesn't simply mean 'speedily', as we realize when he begins the next sentence: 'Let them fetch one to life that was dead.' The quick and the dead are foreshadowed in 'quickly', which as well as meaning 'quick' in the sense of 'living', also carries a reminiscence of the fleshy quick pricked and scratched by pins.

Later in this sermon which is titled 'The Jerusalem Sinner Saved; or, Good News for the Vilest of Men', so Bunyan refers to the 'buffetings of Satan'. Then he offers another homely illustration, saying first that great sinners 'are like dry wood, or like great candles, which burn best and shine with biggest light'. Then he discusses sinners and grace before saying:

> Candles that burn not bright, we like not; wood that is green will rather smother, and sputter, and smoke, and crack, and flounce, than cast a brave light and a pleasant heat.

Here he uses 'brave' in the old Elizabethan sense still current in the North of Ireland: it means 'good, magnificent, fine'.

Bunyan's language has a tactile quality: 'jiggs and tricks and quicks'; 'the sore, grieved, wounded, and fretted place, which is the conscience'; 'there was not a pin, nor a loop, nor a tack in the tabernacle'; 'God is fixed as a nail in a sure place.' In 'The Greatness of the Soul', he says 'yet we can but lie in hell till we are burnt out, as the log doth at the back of the fire.' In 'Christ a Complete Saviour', he tells us that we shall see Christ 'in his robes, in his priestly robes, and with his golden girdle about his paps'. Later in this sermon, Bunyan says:

> The hardest or worst part of the work of thy Saviour is over; his bloody work, his bearing of thy sin and curse, his loss of the light of his Father's face for a time; his dying upon the cursed tree, that was the worst, the sorest, the hardest, and most difficult part of the work of redemption; and yet this he did willingly, cheerfully, and without thy desires; yea, this he did, as considering those for whom he did it in a state of rebellion and enmity to him.

There is a cragginess in the prose at first – those repeated *uh* sounds in 'hardest', 'worst', 'work', 'curse', 'cursed', 'sorest', 'difficult'. Then with 'redemption', 'willingly, cheerfully' the tone shifts into a climbing confidence, so that when we reach 'rebellion' the memory of 'redemption' turns the word up and back till the passage becomes a kind of poem which contradicts or complicates its surface meaning. Bunyan represents what he called 'the bustle and cumber of the world' in his verse and prose. Again and again, he employs dialect words which give body and authority to his writing: 'how brag and crank are our poor wantons and wicked ones in this day of forbearance!' Here, 'brag' means 'spirited, brisk, lively' and is used by Auden in *The Age of Anxiety*: 'how brag and crank were the birds'. 'Crank' means 'brisk, jolly, lusty, spiritful, buxom' and is used by Milton in *L' Allegro*: 'Jest and youthful Jollity, / Quips and cranks, and wanton wiles, / Nods, and becks, and wreathed smiles.'

The rough and tumble of Bunyan's monosyllables has the tactile intimacy of direct speech:

CHRISTIAN: Just here, said Christian, did I sit down to rest me; but being overcome with sleep I there lost this roll out of my bosom.
FAITHFUL: But good brother, hear me out: so soon as the man overtook me, he was but a word and a blow: for down he knocked me and laid me for dead. But when I was a little come to myself again, I asked him wherefore he served me so. He said, 'Because of my secret inclining to Adam the First'; and with that he struck me another deadly blow on the breast, and beat me down backward; so I lay at his foot as dead as before. So when I came to myself again, I cried him mercy; but he said, 'I know not how to show mercy', and with that knocked me down again. He had doubtless made an end of me, but that one came by and bid him forbear.
CHRISTIAN: Who was that, that made him forbear?
FAITHFUL: I did not know him at first, but as he went by, I perceived the holes in his hands, and his side; then I concluded that he was our Lord. So I went up the Hill.

Christian then explains that the man who overtook him was Moses, 'he spareth none, neither knoweth he how to show mercy to those that transgress his law.' Simultaneously, Bunyan makes Moses and the limitations of Mosaic law robustly, immediately present to his readers. Davies comments on this passage, and suggests that the burden of guilt is made heavier by 'the oppressiveness of religious legalism', but he fails to notice how the holes in Christ's hands are made physically present in an almost casually realistic manner, like the pricking pins in the passage I quoted earlier. Under the guise of remembering early Christian and later protestant martyrs, Bunyan offers a vision of Restoration England in the Valley of the Shadow of Death where 'the way was all along set so full of snares, traps, gins, and nets here, and so full of pits, pitfalls, deep holes and shelvings down there, that had it now been dark, as it was when he came the first part of the way, had he been a thousand souls, they had in reason been cast away.' Now he sees that at the end of the Valley 'lay blood, bones, ashes and mangled bodies of men, even of pilgrims'. A little before him he spies a cave 'where two giants, Pope and Pagan, dwelt in old time'. Both Greaves and Davies appear unable to see the symbolic political code that Bunyan is employing.

That code, which was designed to put Charles's Licenser of the Press off the track, becomes apparent if we consider 'old time' is a piece of deliberate naivety, because Bunyan would have been thinking of Charles II and his closeness to the Catholic Louis XIV, as well as of Charles's Catholic brother, James. He would also have had in mind certain recent martyrs to the Whig cause: Algernon Sidney and William Russell, as well as the 'Protestant joiner', Stephen College. Bunyan's printer had published a ballad by College, 'The Raree Show', which attacked the King and the Duke. College was an apprentice of Smith's, and was brought to Oxford, sentenced to death and hanged for sedition. The struggles and deaths which formed the Exclusion Crisis in the 1680s are part of the historical vision of *The Pilgrim's Progress*, just as they are part of Dryden's attack on Monmouth, Shaftesbury and the Exclusionists in *Absalom and Achitophel*. Smith was committed to Newgate in 1681 and charged with treason. Between 1661 and 1678 Smith printed nearly all Bunyan's books, but in 1678, when Smith was in permanent trouble and deeply involved in politics, Bunyan, Hill shows, moved to another radical printer, Benjamin Harris, who between July 1679 and January 1680 printed the Whig Exclusionist *Domestick Intelligence* (Nathaniel Ponder, however, published *The Pilgrim's Progress*). Harris was always in trouble with the authorities. He was pilloried and fined £500, a huge amount. Bunyan's career is therefore linked with two heroes of the struggle for press freedom, and we must recognize that Bunyan's voice takes its life partly from his knowledge that by speaking aloud and then publishing his words, he is challenging the authority of Judge Jeffreys and Lord Chief Justice Scroggs. When Bunyan says that Vanity Fair 'is an ancient thing, of long standing, and a very great Fair', he is thinking of those concepts of tradition and cultural heritage which weigh on so many English institutions. There is a turn in his voice here which gives to 'ancient' the sense of 'ancient as sin'. The phrase 'long standing' consorts oddly with the flimsiness of a fair's temporary buildings, but Bunyan means that Vanity Fair is London, with its parliament, palaces and law courts. It is important that critics working on Bunyan make firm connections with the politics of the period, and don't push them into the background.

When we read the famous opening paragraph of *The Pilgrim's Progress*, we can see that this isn't simply a religious allegory of sin and redemption:

> As I walked through the wilderness of this world, I lighted on a certain place, where was a den; and I laid me down in that place to sleep: and as I slept I dreamed a dream. I dreamed, and behold I saw a man clothed with rags, standing in a certain place, with his face from his own house, a book in his hand, and a great burden upon his back. I looked, and saw him open the book, and read therein; and as he read, he wept and trembled: and not being able longer to contain, he brake out with a lamentable cry; saying, 'What shall I do?'

The rags of sin, the burden of sin and individual conscience are clearly figured here. The anapaestic movement of the prose – 'As I walked through the wilderness of this world' – is lulling. We have just opened Bunyan's book to find a familiar Protestant image of the Bible translated. Perhaps we remember the martyr William Tyndale who translated the Bible so the 'meanest plough-boy' could read it. Then we begin to see that the 'great burden' on the man's back is the tinker's pack Bunyan must have carried down muddy lanes and roads in Bedfordshire. He is both inside and outside his own book, just as we are. But the burden is more than a pack of tools, more than a symbol of guilt and sin. The weight of the state, its cruel and biased judicial system, is on his back. As we read, the words *back, book, brake* echo each other, and we catch the Lutheran emotionalism that is such a feature of Bunyan's prose. The repeated *i* sounds in the paragraph produce a lonely lyric, tight with grief and suffering. In the next paragraph, Christian tells his wife and children, 'I am for certain informed that this our city will be burned with fire from Heaven.' Here, Bunyan is recalling the Great Fire of London, eleven years earlier, as well as his profound emotional and spiritual struggles. There is a psychological, as well as a religious and political, dimension to his writing, which has a genuine, often moving emotional integrity.

The most affecting, most powerful moment is this passage from *Grace Abounding*, where Bunyan describes having left his wife and children to go to jail:

> the parting with my wife and poor children hath oft been to me in this place, as the pulling my flesh from my bones; and that not only because I am somewhat too fond of these great mercies, but also because I should have often brought to my mind the many hardships, miseries and wants that my poor family was like to meet with, should I be taken from them, especially my poor blind child, who lay nearer my heart than all I had besides; O the thoughts of the hardship I thought my blind one might go under, would break my heart to pieces.

In the next heartfelt, dramatic paragraph, he exclaims in grief:

> Poor child! thought I, what sorrow art thou like to have for thy portion in this world? Thou must be beaten, must beg, suffer hunger, cold, nakedness, and a thousand calamities, though I cannot now endure the wind should blow upon thee: but yet recalling myself, thought I, I must venture you all with God, though it goeth to the quick to leave you: O I saw in this condition I was as a man who was pulling down his house upon the head of his wife and children; yet thought, I must do it; I must do it; and now I thought of those *two milch kine that were to carry the ark of God into another country, and to leave their calves behind them* (1 Sam. 6:10–12).

This paragraph is the prose equivalent of Yeats's 'The Cold Heaven', where love is sent out naked on the roads for punishment, except that Bunyan's prose has paternal love, instead of erotic and amatory despair at its quick. The citation from Samuel is a coded political statement: in this chapter the ark of the Lord is in the country of the Philistines for seven months. They call for the priests and diviners, asking 'What shall we do to the ark of the Lord? Tell us wherewith we shall send it to his place.' They are advised to 'send it not empty', but to return God 'a trespass offering'. They attach two milch kine to the cart, and a coffer with 'the mice of gold and the images of their emerods'. The lords of the Philistines follow the cart to the border of Beth-shemesh. Later, God smites the men of Beth-shemesh because 'they had looked into the ark of the Lord'.

In the next chapter, Samuel speaks to all the house of Israel, saying:

> If ye do return unto the Lord with all your hearts, then put away the strange gods and Ashtaroth from among you, and prepare your hearts unto the Lord, and serve him only: and he will deliver you out of the hand of the Philistines.

Bunyan leaving his home and family to serve a prison sentence for preaching, feels he is on a journey from the land of the Philistines to his own land, but that homeland is one which worships strange gods, will be punished and then return as the children of Israel, hearkening to Samuel's words, will put away Boalim and Ashtaroth, and serve 'the Lord only'.

The biblical quotation serves to allay his guilt that he is pulling down his house 'upon the head of his wife and children'. He is facing the consequences of his revolutionary commitment to Christian doctrine, and he is confronting the personal, domestic consequences that follow from his political stance. He is grieving at sticking to his uncompromising principles, and we may compare his stern courage with the conduct of the Whig Lord and Rye House conspirator, William Russell (one of Bertrand Russell's ancestors), who, some years later, 'refused to purchase', G. M. Trevelyan writes, 'the life that was so sweet to him by a declaration that subjects may not resist their sovereign'. He chose death, rather than deny 'the principles of freedom'.

Bunyan, too, feared 'that my imprisonment might end at the gallows', and a few paragraphs after recounting how he felt leaving his wife and children he says:

> . . . it was a great trouble to me: for I thought with myself, that in the condition I now was in, I was not fit to die, neither did I think I could if I should be called to it: besides, I thought with myself, if I should make a scrabbling shift to climb up the ladder, yet I should either with quaking or other symptoms of faintings, give occasion to the enemy to reproach the way of God and his people, for their timorousness: this therefore lay with great trouble upon me, for methought I was ashamed to die with a pale face, and tottering knees, for such a cause as this.

Bunyan hopes he will have the courage to die nobly like a martyr, and as condemned prisoners do he often has what the Czech Communist Artur London, who was nearly hanged with Slansky, terms 'that dream' (the nightmare of being led to the scaffold). Bunyan says, 'I was also at this time so really possessed with the thought of death, that oft I was as if I was on the ladder, with the rope about my neck.' He derives a bleak comfort from the thought that he might have an opportunity 'to speak my last words to a multitude' that had come to see him die. He thinks that 'if God will but convert one soul by my very last words, I shall not count my life thrown away, nor lost.'

In one of his most beautiful, most tragic and passionate paragraphs, he delivers this dramatic speech:

> I thought also, that God might choose whether he would give me comfort now, or at the hour of death; but I might not therefore choose whether I would hold my profession or no: I was bound, but he was free: yea, 'twas my duty to stand to his Word, whether he would ever look upon me or no, or save me at the last: wherefore, thought I, the point being thus, I am for going on, and venturing my eternal state with Christ, whether I have comfort here or no; if God doth not come in, thought I, I will leap off the ladder even blindfolded into eternity, sink or swim, come heaven, come hell; Lord Jesus, if thou wilt catch me, do, if not, I will venture for thy name.

The direct, unflinching vernacular rhythm voices Bunyan's courage and integrity: 'wherefore, thought I, the point being thus, I am for going on, and venturing my eternal state with Christ.'

The terse phrases build the repeated '*i*' sounds to culminate in 'Christ'. There is a similarly inflected moment in the preface to *Grace Abounding*, where Bunyan asks 'Have you never a hill Mizar to remember? Have you forgot the close, the milk-house, the stable, the barn, and the like, where God did visit your soul?' The assonance of *close, house, soul*, binds the phrases together and gives them both physical presence and a visionary uplift.

Bunyan's use of the verb 'scrabbling' in his account of his fear of being hanged, runs with similar words that evoke work, discomfort, danger. Towards the end of the second part of *The Pilgrim's Progress*, he says 'The way also was here very wearisome, through dirt and slabbiness.' In 'A Treatise on the Fear of God', he says 'we so often lie grabbling under the black and amazing thoughts that are engendered in our hearts by unbelief.' In 'The Law and Grace Unfolded' he says that in the sad condition we are in it is 'by grace . . . a beginning to scrabble out of it'. To read Bunyan is to notice his relish of local vernacular phrases. In 'The Heavenly Footman' he mentions the 'soul-entangling flatteries' of what he terms 'sink-souls'. George Offor, Bunyan's Victorian editor, says this is one of his 'strong Saxonisms, full of meaning'. Offor frequently points to Bunyan's 'Saxonisms', and this must be connected to that particular Nordic cultural formation which Carlyle extends and celebrates in *Heroes and Hero-Worship*. Carlyle states that Burns is gaining a certain recognition 'over all quarters of our wide Saxon world: wheresoever a Saxon dialect is spoken, it begins to be understood, by personal inspection of this and the other, that one of the most considerable Saxon men of the eighteenth century was an Ayrshire peasant named Robert Burns. Yes, I will say, here too was a piece of the right Saxon stuff: strong as the Harz-rock, rooted in the depths of the world.' When Bunyan says 'will not Christ be shuff and shy', Offor notes that 'shuff' is from the old Saxon word *schufan*, though he is mistaken – it is a dialectal pronunciation of 'shy'. When Bunyan remarks that Careless has left the door 'a little achare', he notes that the word is from 'to chare, to turn about or backwards and forwards'. Bunyan's phrase 'gleads of promise', Offor says, is 'from Saxon *glow*, anything heated or hot', though

Bunyan is using the noun 'gleed', which means a 'hot coal'. When he speaks of how the warmth of Christ's wings overshadowing the face of the soul 'gives thee as it were a gload upon thy spirit', Offor glosses 'gload' as 'a warm, eager, passionate saying'. He calls 'fish-whole' a 'very striking and expressive term', and says that 'whole' is from the Saxon, 'which language abounded in Bunyan's native country of Bedford'. It appears in *The Wars of Alexander* as 'fish-hale'. The words 'tines', 'ceiled', 'sad', 'trepan', 'thodes', and the expression 'will they, nill they', he identifies as Saxon.

In 'The Author's Apology for his Book', with which he prefaces *The Pilgrim's Progress*, Bunyan moves intuitively from the image of his fancies sticking 'like burrs' to state that his book is 'writ in such a dialect / As may the minds of listless men affect'. Twice using the word 'rude' – an obsessive term in his admirer Clare – he justifies his art in a deliberately naive, vernacular style: 'Be not too forward therefore to conclude / That I want solidness, that I am rude.' And he denies he is 'rude' in handling 'figure, or similitude'. Here, he is alluding to *A Discourse of Ecclesiastical Politie*, a pamphlet published in 1670 by Samuel Parker, the Bishop of Oxford, who dismissed the adherents of 'Schismatical Non-conformity' as the worst and most dangerous enemies to 'the Security of Government' and as 'the rudest and most barbarous people in the world'. Bunyan's uses of 'rude' glance at Parker's attack, an attack which also called for an Act of Parliament to 'abridge Preachers use of fulsome and lushious Metaphors'. Bunyan's *Scriptural Poems* show a confident, precise grasp of the rhyming couplet, but in his verse apology for *The Pilgrim's Progress* he aims to appear both wondering and slightly uncertain of his gift and of the reception of his book by his congregation who, like the Bishop of Oxford, are unsympathetic to images, metaphors, artistic effects:

> When at the first I took my pen in hand,
> Thus for to write, I did not understand
> That I at all should make a little book
> In such a mode . . .

His confidence in his use of vernacular cadences shows in the sudden elucidatory parenthesis in this passage:

> Am I afraid to say that Holy Writ,
> Which for its style and phrase puts down all wit,
> Is everywhere so full of all these things,
> (Dark figures, allegories), yet there springs
> From that same book that lustre and those rays
> Of light that turns our darkest nights to days.

The way his voice drops in an afterthought as he adds the particular explanation 'Dark figures, allegories' changes the rhythm of the lines before that rhythm returns with a leap in the verb 'springs'. The change of tone and cadence also softens and makes more subtle the *things / springs* rhyme. In this earlier couplet: 'Fell suddenly into an allegory / About their journey, and the way to glory', the greater stress on 'glory' pushes back on to 'allegory' to fuse the two words into the subliminal pun 'alleglory'. Had the rhymes been reversed 'allegory' would have taken on a bloody and a clumsy tinge as the shifted stress on the second syllable – 'alle*gory*' – would suggest 'gory'. Davies calls the verse preface a 'sophisticatedly constructed verse apology' – a clunking phrase typical of his critical prose (he tells us that Bunyan's *The Holy War* 'ends dissatisfactorily').

Davies is unable to see, for example, that Bunyan took the figure of Apollyon from Revelation because this angel, who is king of the bottomless pit, carries 'lion' in his name. Apollyon rebukes Christian for being almost persuaded to turn back 'at the sight of the lions'. The republican puritan, Christian, has allowed this symbol of the British monarchy to frighten him, and it may be that on one of his trips to London Bunyan, like the young Defoe, heard the lions roaring at the Tower. When he describes how Apollyon 'stroddled quite over the whole breadth of the way', we may be sure that Charles II, his brother, and many powerful public figures weighed on his choice of that rude, ungainly word 'stroddled' – a word that denies Appolyon's Greek, and therefore classic and sophisticated name. The hobgoblins, satyrs and dragons of the pit, the 'very deep ditch' and the 'very dangerous quag' into which King David, slayer of the giant Goliath, once fell, are all symbols of Stuart England, where there is heard 'a continual howling and yelling, as of a people under unutterable misery who there sat bound in affliction and irons'. The Valley of the Shadow of Death in which they suffer 'is every whit dreadful, being utterly without order'. That last word flies in the face of the arguments of the monarchist political philosophy of Filmer, who tried to justify absolutism and whom Algernon Sidney opposed.

Bunyan's first readers and those who followed them for many generations will have perceived the historical struggle his narrative describes. As he lifts his pen to start his author's apology, I see Joe Gargery choosing a pen from the pen-tray 'as if it were a chest of large tools'. Of course, Bunyan is a highly assured writer, here only reassuring his audience with a display of anxious modesty, but the oral culture he embodies, like Joe's, carries – 'savours of' he would say – such human kindness and communal bonds that it is impossible to read him without being awed by his resolute genius. He is a 'good limner', the author of one of the very greatest English hymns:

Who would true valour see
Let him come hither;
One there will constant be,
Come wind, come weather.
There's no discouragement,
Shall make him once relent,
His first avowed intent,
To be a pilgrim.

Who so beset him round,
With dismal stories,
Do but themselves confound;
His strength the more is.
No lion can him fright
He'll with a giant fight,

But he will have a right,
To be a pilgrim.

Hobgoblin, nor foul fiend,
Can daunt his spirit:
He knows, he at the end,
Shall life inherit.
Then fancies fly away,
He'll fear not what men say,
He'll labour night and day,
To be a pilgrim.

Prompted by Amiens' song in *As You Like It*, Bunyan changes the *abab* rhyme scheme to resolute triplets before introducing the unrhymed refrain, which concentrates in its two *ih* sounds the *ih* sounds in the previous lines. In more polite or standard English, he might have written 'He knows that at the end', but he rejected the clacky middle rhyme to create a more spoken, more uplifting line that catches the cadence of 'Come wind, come weather'. He is also echoing *Lear* in 'hobgoblin, nor foul fiend'. To stand by his tomb in Bunhill Fields is to muse on the way his name rhymes with the graveyard's name – and it is to remember all those often anxious, but steady and fearless Dissenters whom Bunyan inspired. Bunyan the wandering tinker who became the convinced pilgrim fought the lion and the giant.

Crusoe's Secret: Daniel Defoe

In 1830, a few months before he died in a Soho rooming-house, Hazlitt published a lengthy essay on a new biography of Daniel Defoe in the *Edinburgh Review*, where he remarked that in *Robinson Crusoe* Defoe abandoned the political and religious subjects he addressed in his pamphlets, and confined himself to 'unsophisticated views of nature and the human heart'. Hazlitt's misreading is not uncommon. The novel is seen as the archetypal Puritan adventure story, a self-sufficient fiction which transcends the controversies Defoe addresses in his journalism. This is rather like saying that TV programmes such as *Castaway* and *Big Brother* tell us nothing about the social moments that created them. Although some recent scholars have noticed that Crusoe's rhetoric of absolutism and submission 'places the right and might of sovereignty in the office of the monarch', as Manuel Schonhorn puts it in *Defoe's Politics* (1991), his rather lopsided, overly monarchist study, critics tend to link the novel only intermittently to the historical period it covers, and have not succeeded in offering a critical view of the text as a historical allegory or parable. If Hazlitt – one of Defoe's heirs and like him nourished in Dissenting culture – missed the point, it is not surprising that later readers have also failed to grasp that *Robinson Crusoe* is an epic account of the experience of the English Dissenters under the Restoration.

Defoe was born on about 30 September 1660, a few streets from where Milton lived in St Giles Cripplegate. In the course of his career, he often quoted Milton, and though he was careful to criticize the Commonwealth and Protectorate – a necessary journalistic strategy – he emerges in *Daniel Defoe: Master of Fictions* (2001), Maximilian Novak's powerful account of his life and career, as a principled radical whose seemingly protean changes of direction and allegiance were always in the service of the polity founded by the Glorious Revolution. He boasted of wearing a mourning ring that had been given at the funeral of Christopher Love, a Presbyterian minister beheaded in 1653 for his part in a plot to overthrow Cromwell. Defoe mentions Love in his 1704 pamphlet *The Dissenters Answer to the High-Church Challenge* – it is reprinted in W. R. Owens and P. N. Furbank's excellent eight-volume edition *Political and Economic Writings of Daniel Defoe* (2000). With cleverly recessive irony Defoe says that Love was beheaded 'for the horrid fanatic plot, contrived for the bringing in, *as they then called him, Charles Stuart*, and the restoring of monarchy'. This remark functions mainly as an alibi for his loyalty to the post-Protectorate political structure, and is intended to shield him from the charge of being a closet republican, or a classical republican like John Toland. He believes in a 'legal limited monarchy', and has a humane idea of consensus and national unity within such an arrangement. He is an active, adept pragmatist, a revolutionary moderate.

In *Robinson Crusoe*, Defoe speaks of Crusoe's 'life of anxiety' after he sees the footprint on the beach, and although Novak doesn't draw this parallel, the atmosphere of anxiety which suffuses the novel can be traced to the 'feeling of conspiracy' which dominated Dissenters' thinking during the Restoration – G. M. Trevelyan calls the years 1678–85 'the reigns of terror'. As Defoe noted in his remarkable periodical, the *Review*, there was a moment early in the reign of Charles II when London Dissenters feared they would be forced into the Catholic Church and have their Bibles confiscated. They decided to copy the Bible in shorthand, and though he was only a boy, Defoe 'worked like a horse, till I wrote out the whole Pentateuch, and then was so tired I was willing to run the risk of the rest.' As Novak shows, these feelings of anxiety went well beyond the Dissenting community – Catholics were supposed to have started the Fire of London, and there was a justified suspicion that there was a secret clause in the Treaty of Dover, which Charles made with Louis XIV in 1670, agreeing to restore

Catholicism to England. Dissenters were also suspicious of Charles's Declaration of Indulgence, which in 1672 suspended the penal laws against both Catholics and Dissenters. Many Dissenters preferred the risk of prison to state toleration of Catholicism, which they regarded as the real enemy. Defoe, however, though a firm Trinitarian Protestant, was committed to religious toleration, and in *Crusoe* his hero establishes 'liberty of conscience' in his island kingdom – Catholic, Protestant and pagan are all tolerated.

Defoe, who claimed a knowledge of five languages, was educated at Charles Morton's Dissenting Academy in Newington Green. Morton was a distinguished teacher and educationalist who was incessantly harassed by the Anglican Church till he left England for North America, where he became Vice-President of Harvard. The American connection can be sensed in *Crusoe*, and it is wittily glanced at by Mark Twain as he rewrites the novel with a tender and mischievous irony (Huck's account of the contents of the catfish's stomach – a brass button, a round ball 'and lots of rubbage' – is pure Defoe).

At Morton's Academy, students were taught science and other subjects in English, not in Greek or Latin, a radical idea at the time, and they were also instructed in the art of writing good English prose, an enduring subject in the curricula of Dissenting academies (Hazlitt also studied prose composition). Defoe's emphasis in his journalism and pamphlets on 'easy, plain and familiar language' is the direct result of Morton's inspired teaching. Defoe praises Morton's Academy in his 1712 pamphlet *The Present State of the parties in Great Britain*:

There was, some years ago, a private Academy of the *Dissenters* not far from *London*, the master or tutor of which read all his lectures, gave all his systems, whether of *philosophy* or *divinity*, in English; had all his declaimings, and dissertations in the *English* tongue. And tho' the scholars from that place were not destitute in the languages, yet it is observ'd of them, they were by this made masters of the *English* tongue, and more of them excelled in that particular than of any school at that time. Here were produced of ministers, Mr *Timothy Cruso*, Mr *Hannot* of Yarmouth, Mr *Nathaniel Taylor*, Mr *Owen* and several others; and of another kind, poets Sam. Wesley, Daniel De Foe, and two or three of your *Western* martyrs that, had they liv'd, would have been extraordinary men of that kind, *viz. Kitt. Battersby*, young *Jenkins, Hewlin*, and many more.

The mention of Timothy Cruso and the 'Western martyrs' is, as I hope to show, central to the novel Defoe was to write five years later.

In his first full-length work, *An Essay Upon Projects*, which was published in 1697, Defoe asserted that there is a 'direct signification of words, or a *cadence in expression*, which we call speaking sense; this, like truth, is sullen and the same' (here 'sullen' means 'stubborn'). When Crusoe tells us that 'accordingly I victualled my ship for the voyage, putting in two dozen of my loaves (cakes I should rather call them) of barley bread, an earthen pot full of parched rice', we can see that Defoe the conscious stylist has pitched in that explanatory parenthesis in order to give another turn to the vernacular cadence of his prose – we can hear and believe the quick authenticating drop in Crusoe's voice. Praising Morton's genius as a teacher, Defoe said his pupils were taught to write in a style 'all equally free and plain, without foolish flourishes and ridiculous flights of jingling bombast' – the implication being that they were not taught what he called 'Oxford modern dialect'. This Puritan aesthetic and egalitarian ideology – plain style – can be felt in Defoe's every sentence. Morton also contributed a paper to the *Philosophical Transactions* of the Royal Society on the use of sea sand containing organic compounds for fertilizer. The essay includes a 'project' for the increased use of such sand and, as Novak points out, is very much in Defoe's projecting mode.

There was an anti-monarchical bias in most Dissenting academies, and the struggle between Puritans and the Stuart state resulted, according to Defoe's figures, in eight thousand Dissenters, captured at illegal religious meetings, dying in filthy prisons. Defoe was particularly upset by the death in jail of Thomas Delaune, his wife and two children, and he blamed his community for not supporting them.

When the Duke of Monmouth landed at Lyme Regis on 11 June 1685, to begin his rebellion against his uncle, the new Catholic monarch, James II, Defoe left his young wife, Mary, whom he had married eighteen months before, to join the rebels. Novak notes that some of his former schoolmates at Morton's Academy lost their lives in the rebellion, but he does not name them. This is a pity, because as I've recently discovered, a source other than Alexander Selkirk's narrative stirred Defoe's imagination, and points to the crucial effect which the Battle of Sedgemoor (6 July 1685) had on Defoe and on what is effectively his coded spiritual autobiography, *Robinson Crusoe*. In a book called *The Western Martyrology*, published in 1705, the Whig writer John Tutchin – a former rebel and friendly pamphleteering rival of Defoe's – described how two brothers, William and Benjamin Hewling, who had fought at Sedgemoor, fled by sea but 'were driven back again, and with the hazard of their lives got on shore (over dangerous rocks), where they saw the country filled with soldiers, and they being unwilling to fall into the hands of the rabble, and no way of defence or escape remaining to them, they surrendered themselves prisoners'.

William Hewling, who was nineteen years old, was hanged at Lyme Regis on 12 September 1685, and Benjamin Hewling, aged about twenty-two, was hanged on 30 September – he is probably the 'Hewlin' Defoe remembers as one of the Western martyrs in the passage I quoted from *The Present State of the parties*. Both were former pupils at Morton's Academy, and their deaths must have been in Defoe's mind as he described Crusoe's miraculous escape from drowning:

> I was now landed, and safe on shore, and began to look up and thank God that my life was sav'd in a case wherein there was some minutes before scarce any room to hope. I believe it is impossible to express to the life what ecstasies and transports of the soul are, when it is so sav'd, as I may say, out of the very grave; and I do not wonder now at that custom, *viz.* That when a malefactor who has the halter about his neck, is tied up, and just going to be turn'd off, and has a reprieve brought to him: I say, I do not wonder that they bring a surgeon with it, to let him blood that very moment they tell him of it, that the surprise may not drive the animal spirits from the heart, and overwhelm him: *For sudden joys, like griefs, confound at first.*

Crusoe lands on the island like a reprieved convict, and he keeps the date of his landfall as a sacred anniversary, inscribing it on a post: '*I came on shore here on the 30th of Sept. 1659.*' The date is mentioned a total of six times in the novel, and it stands both as a commemoration of Benjamin Hewling's death day, possibly of Defoe's birthday and of his miraculous survival of the slaughter and the notorious Bloody Assizes which followed the battle.

Eking out his ink, Crusoe remarks that 'by casting up times past: I remember that there was a strange concurrence of dates, in the various Providences which befel me; and which, if I had been superstitiously inclin'd to observe days as fatal or fortunate, I might have had reason to have look'd upon with a great deal of curiosity.' This tells us that the dates in the novel are to be attended to closely, and the dates of the execution of the Duke of Monmouth (15 July 1685) and his fellow rebel the Duke of Argyll (30 June 1685) are both silently memorialized – the days of the month, not the years – in Crusoe's journal. On 7 May 1660, the House of Lords proclaimed Charles king, and so signalled the end of England's republican state, and on 7 May Crusoe records in his journal: 'Went to the wreck again, but with an intent not to work, but found the weight of the wreck had broke itself down, the beams being cut, that several pieces of the ship seemed to lie loose, and the inside of the hold lay so open, that I could see into it, but almost full of water and sand.' A ship is a traditional symbol of the state, and I think, too, that the Spanish wreck may be associated with the wrecks of the Armada which, Milton says, 'larded our seas'.

In her meticulously detailed biography of Defoe, which was published in 1989, Paula Backscheider says that at least four of his schoolmates from Morton's Academy were executed in the wake of the rebellion. They were Kitt Battersby, William Jenkyns and the Hewling brothers. Another former schoolmate, John Shower, was pardoned on 5 November 1686. He would have gone through the same legal processes as Defoe, who was also pardoned a few months later, on 31 May 1687. (Crusoe's name is based on that of another pupil – Timothy Cruso – who became a Dissenting minister and whom Defoe mentions next to the Western martyrs.) Backscheider states that Defoe's luck in remaining uncaptured after the battle 'was simply amazing, at best a one-in-fifteen chance'. Defoe had a relative who ran a free school at Martock, fifteen miles from Sedgemoor, and he may have hidden there. His lucky escape haunted him for the rest of his life – the shadow of the gallows, images of executions and, as in the case of Moll Flanders, sometimes of reprieves, fall across all his writings. Like his maker, Crusoe is a deeply anxious as well as courageous personality, describing at one point how he feels in 'great perplexity and anxiety of mind', at another mentioning what he terms, in a significant phrase I quoted earlier, 'the life of anxiety'. It is a constant and deepening theme in the novel, and it has to be connected with what I can only call survivor's guilt, an ontological condition which kept Defoe in permanent proximity to the scaffolds on which his courageous schoolmates perished (over a hundred Falklands veterans have committed suicide because of post-traumatic stress disorder, and the very high incidence of suicide among Vietnam veterans is well known – there is no reason to think earlier generations did not endure similar mental suffering).

A leading figure in the rise of the publishing industry, Defoe emerges at the age of fifty-nine, with the publication of *Robinson Crusoe* in 1719, as the first great novelist in English, and a hugely popular author in Europe. He is such a master realist that critics and scholars have been slow to take seriously his remark in the preface to its immediate sequel, *The Further Adventures of Robinson Crusoe*, about the story being a 'parable'. He emphasizes his aesthetic intention in the next sequel, *Serious Reflections . . . of Robinson Crusoe*, where he insists that 'the story, though allegorical, is also historical'. I recently came across an article published in the journal *History* in 1925 by one George Parker MD which argues that *Crusoe* is a detailed, logically worked-out allegory, but because Parker does not believe that Defoe fought at Sedgemoor his reading is badly skewed, though he makes the interesting point that Crusoe and Friday's fight with the bear and wolves symbolizes Harley's trial and acquittal (Defoe uses the image of bear and wolves in the *Review* ironically to symbolize the Dissenters). But really we need to abandon the one-for-one schema demanded by allegory in favour of shifting symbols, and associative or subliminal links, because – to stay with this example – on an another level the ability of the wolves to move in lines 'as regularly as an army drawn up by experienced officers' must be connected with the Jacobites, who four years earlier had attempted to overthrow George I's Whig state. The wolves may also, perhaps primarily, be a shifting symbol representing Louis XIV's armies, which Marlborough defeated.

Although critics and biographers have made sporadic links between Crusoe and Defoe, so far as I can tell none has thought the novel and his other works to be crucially defined by a type of Dissenting anxiety rooted in Stuart persecution, and particularly in Sedgemoor and the Bloody Assizes, which were presided over by the notorious Judge Jeffreys, who was to die in the Tower after William of Orange landed.

In *The Plague* Camus perceived and employed the allegorical structure of *A Journal of the Plague Year*, though that novel is usually regarded as an early example of uncomplicated literary realism. Camus's epigraph is taken from *Serious Reflections . . . of Robinson Crusoe*: 'It is as reasonable to represent one kind of imprisonment by another, as it is to represent anything that really exists, by that which exists not!' For example, we can see allegory in Crusoe's resolution to move his tent from 'the place where it stood, which was just under the hanging precipice of the hill, and which, if it should be shaken again' – by an earthquake – 'would certainly fall upon my tent' is both actual and symbolic of his social anxieties. The hanging precipice in poetry, Christopher Ricks has shown, is an image of civil war, and it has a similar significance in Defoe's prose. Here he is also alluding to Hosea: 'they shall say to the mountains, Cover us; and to the hills, Fall on us' (10.8). The chapter insists on Israel's 'sin', and this is part of the fabric of Defoe's anxiety. He is, as the Irish phrase has it, always 'nationally minded'. He makes a grim joke of those anxieties three paragraphs later when he remarks: 'And though I had a grindstone, I could not turn it and grind my tools too, this cost me as much thought as a statesman would have bestow'd upon a grand point of politics, or a judge upon the life and death of a man.' Defoe, who saw writing as the production of saleable commodities, is ironically creating an image for the writing of his pamphlets – he grinds innumerable axes in them. Commenting on a passage where he talks of '*we Writing Manufacturers*', Novak suggests that he was aware of the materials of the writer's craft 'as no other writer of his time' – and Crusoe is here symbolically imaging those materials and that dogged deployment of technical skill. He is also brooding on Sedgemoor again, because after constructing the grindstone Crusoe kills three birds and 'as we serve notorious criminals in England' hangs them 'in chains for a terror to others'. The public world of law and politics is always in Defoe's consciousness, and his descriptions of Crusoe working with tools captures both what Heidegger terms the 'transparency' of equipment in use, and the active participation of his journalism in the public sphere – Judge Jeffreys's cruelty haunts both these passages.

As Crusoe and the ship's crew row towards the island, they work the oars 'with heavy hearts, like men going to execution'. Defoe is imaginatively gripped by his memories of the Monmouth rebellion and by a fealty to his dead comrades. Earlier in the novel, when he is recounting his first experience of sea travel, Crusoe twice uses the casually revealing word 'hurry' to describe his thoughts and the first storm he encounters. He speaks of 'the hurry of my thoughts', and two paragraphs later says that during the 'first hurries' of the storm, he lay still and 'stupid' in his cabin. The word 'hurry', in the seventeenth and eighteenth centuries, had a meaning beyond 'speed and commotion' – it meant 'social or political disturbance, tumult'. In *The Present State of the parties in Great Britain* he speaks of 'war, and the various hurries of the time'. This is the sense of the term in *Coriolanus* (the populace are 'in wild hurry'), while in Ireland the 1798 Rebellion was colloquially called 'the hurry'. Defoe wants his readers to make a subliminal connection with rebellion, and he again uses the hanging metaphor – closely connected with it – in the sixth year of Crusoe's 'reign', when he undertakes a difficult journey in his canoe and is carried back to the island on an eddy. 'They who know what it is to have a reprieve brought to them upon the ladder' may guess his 'present surprise of joy', Crusoe tells us.

But while Defoe wants to align Crusoe with the anti-Stuart rebels, he adds a complicating, deliberately distracting detail to Crusoe's first landfall on the island, which would have been familiar to his readers, particularly his Tory readers. Crusoe is scared that the island contains 'ravenous beasts', so he spends his first night in 'a thick bushy tree like a fir, but thorny'. Another rebel, Charles Stuart, is famously supposed to have hidden in an oak tree to evade his pursuers after the Battle of Worcester, and Defoe the devoted builder of consensus politics wants to draw both parties of readers into his narrative. The same consensual outlook is cunningly expressed in *Memoirs of a Cavalier*, where the benign monarchist narrator disinterestedly praises Fairfax, the commander of the Parliamentary army (and political moderate), as 'a complete general, strict in his discipline, wary in conduct, fearless in action ... of a modest, noble, generous disposition'. The narrator also frequently praises Defoe's hero, Gustavus Adolphus, who is meant by association to remind the reader of his supreme hero, William of Orange. As Novak points out, Defoe noted several times that Gustavus Adolphus would promote common soldiers to officers on the battlefield. Defoe's egalitarianism is expressed succinctly in what we would now call his anti-racist – and hugely popular – poem *The True-Born Englishman*: 'Fame of families is all a cheat / 'Tis personal virtue only makes us great.' Though he points to the allegorizing of national unity – another term for consensus – in *Further Adventures of Robinson Crusoe*, Novak does not argue that the original novel is an autobiographical and historical epic, but he does seek to refute those scholars who doubt whether Defoe fought at Sedgemoor. He adduces a passage in Defoe's short biography of the Duke of Marlborough, where he writes of the miseries of a soldier's life: 'in a rainy season, when the whole country about them is trod into a chaos, and in such intolerable marches, men and horses dying and dead together, and the best of them glad of a bundle of straw to lay down their wet and weary limbs.'

'He was there,' Novak tersely insists. Describing soldiers in the rain in this short biography, Defoe speaks of 'the ugly sights, the stinks of mortality, the grass all withered and black with the smoke of powder'. The last detail is unusual and authentic, and as Defoe remarks earlier in the *Life of Marlborough*, 'matters of fact are the best arguments'. This assertion might stand for his realist or concrete aesthetic – no ideas but in things, as another generous puritan pragmatist stated. Reading Defoe's idealized portrait of the temperate, sober, careful, courageous, politic, skilful, courteous, mild, affable, humble Marlborough, one also sees the heroic figure of Crusoe emerge from the common man by dint of his own innate, solitary talents. Defoe hopes to shape opinion by eulogizing the Duke, and in the novel he is also keen to show a rebellious, wayward son metamorphose into a military engineer, inventor, farmer, soldier, governor, country squire and admiral. This can-do philosophy is North American in its energy, although it lacks that distinctive North American confidence: there is an underlying sense of trauma in Crusoe's narrative, both wary and serious, because Defoe is trying to settle accounts with his experience of war, fear, prison, bankruptcy and persecution. He wants to represent the darkness and the chaos he came through as the survivor of a terrible battlefield and a hanging assizes, but part of him is wedded to secrecy, so he cannot, or will not, talk directly to his readers. The *dei inferni*, the gods of kinship and tribal solidarity, speak in his fiction, while in his journalism the daylight gods, as Hegel called them, of free, self-conscious, social life speak spryly of reform and progress. But the anxious pull of piety and the enduring aftershock of the rebel defeat cannot be ignored.

Monmouth's campaign was undertaken in the heavy rain which fell on the West of England in June and July 1685, and when Crusoe complains that the rain which fell on his island in July was 'much more dangerous' than the rain that fell in September and October, Defoe must have been thinking of that doomed rebellion in the lashing summer rain thirty-four years earlier. The July rain theme – another 'concurrence of days' – also evokes his experience in the pillory, to which he was sentenced for publishing *The Shortest Way with the Dissenters* in 1702. An entry in Evelyn's diary for July 1703, which Novak cites, records 'great and long continual rain' for the month when Defoe stood three times in the pillory: men could die in the pillory when stones were thrown at them, but Defoe was fêted, so popular were his writings.

One of Crusoe's favourite emphatic words is 'deliverance', and William of Orange's landing at Torbay on 5 November 1688 was to

Defoe a miraculous and – another favourite word – 'glorious' event, which he celebrated directly in his journalism, and more obliquely in his fiction. (The sudden south wind which brought William and his fleet, it was thought miraculously, into Torbay, is mentioned approvingly in *Crusoe*.) The word was also used by Benjamin and William Hewling in prison, as reported by their sister: 'We know He is able to deliver . . . Oh, God is a strong refuge.'

On 29 October 1692, Defoe found himself in Fleet Prison after two business schemes failed. He had invested in a diving-engine to search for treasure from wrecks (Crusoe has more luck here), and also in a civet cat farm to make perfume. His debts totalled £17,000, and he had already lost the dowry of £3700 that his wife Mary Tuffley brought on their marriage on 1 January 1684 – less than three weeks after the execution of his hero Algernon Sidney for his alleged part in the Rye House Plot. Defoe's life after his imprisonment for debt in 1692 must have been uncomfortable, Novak suggests. He speculates that the 'secret kind of life' he had to live in order to evade arrest for debt may have 'introduced him to various other forms of secrecy'. He was to become a government spy when Robert Harley was Lord High Treasurer (effectively Prime Minister) and he uses the word 'secret' obsessively in *Crusoe* (it occurs five times on one page). Novak sees his experience of prison and the survival strategies to which it led as crucial to his personality, commenting that he was to be imprisoned several more times during his life but 'it never ceased to be the nightmare that haunted his soul'. Crusoe's remark, 'I was a prisoner, locked up with the eternal bars and bolts of the ocean, in an uninhabited wilderness', obviously expresses this nightmare, as well as reflecting the Dissenters' experience of oppression and internal exile under the Stuarts. The Exodus theme in *Crusoe* is a version of this exile, and there is an allusion here to the long and weighty Psalm 78, which Crusoe has quoted earlier: 'Can God furnish a table in the wilderness?'

Psalm 78, which praises God who 'brought in the south wind' and celebrates the Israelites' escape from Egyptian bondage, is one of English Puritanism's master tropes, and Defoe must have drawn a particular inspiration from its opening verses:

Give ear, O my people, to my law: incline your ears to the words of my mouth.
I will open my mouth in a parable: I will utter dark sayings of old.

Crusoe is a dark parable or 'allegoric history' (a phrase from the preface to the second sequel which Camus quotes) which catches the existential risks of business and political life, or what Defoe in his journalism calls 'the unbounded ocean of business', or 'amphibious politics'. One of the high points in his life was 29 October 1689, when he rode in the Lord Mayor's Show to which William III had been invited. The troop of volunteer cavalry, made up of eminent citizens, was led by Monmouth's son, and Defoe must have tasted victory in this Whig civic pageant. Crusoe's occasional moments of exhilarating power and authority – feeling that he is 'prince and lord of the whole island' – reflect Defoe's sense of liberation and his intimacy with state power, first acquired in William's reign.

Crusoe is particularly ebullient after he establishes what he terms 'my country-house' on the western side of the island. At one level, he is rewriting the country-house poem in democratic prose (his enemy Pope, who nevertheless admired *Crusoe*, also revises the genre in his 'Epistle to Burlington'), but on another level Defoe is again thinking of Andrew Marvell:

I descended a little on the side of that delicious vale, surveying it with a secret kind of pleasure (tho' mixt with my other afflicting thoughts) to think that this was all my own, that I was king and lord of all this country indefeasibly, and had a right of possession; and if I could convey it, I might have it in inheritance as completely as any lord of the manor in England.

This is a moment of significantly bourgeois, not aristocratic joy (note the legal term 'convey'), and it returns to a moment in Defoe's 1713 pamphlet *An Answer to a Question That No Body thinks of, VIZ But what if the QUEEN should die?*:

The Queen raises no money without act of Parliament, keeps up no standing army in time of *Peace*, dis-seizes no man of his property, or estate, but every man sits in safety under his vine, and his fig-tree; and we doubt not but we shall do as long as her majesty lives. *BUT what if the Queen should die?*

Defoe would have associated the vine with a verse in Psalm 80, whose Exodus theme is close to that of Psalm 78: 'Thou hast brought a vine out of Egypt; thou hast cast out the heathen, and planted it.' But this association would have been added on to the primary allusion to a verse in 1 Kings: 'And Judah and Israel dwelt safely, every man under his vine and under his fig tree, from Dan even to Beer-sheba, all the days of Solomon' (4.25). P. N. Furbank's notes to this pamphlet are helpful and detailed, but he misses this biblical allusion and its link to Crusoe on his fruitful island.

In the *Review* Defoe provocatively remarks that Queen Anne has 'no more title to the crown than my lord mayor's horse' – a strategic reduction of the power of monarchy in order to develop the argument for national autonomy, popular sovereignty, property rights and freedom under the law which his sensuous images of fruitful gardens embody. As well as drawing on the struggles of the Israelites to achieve freedom, he is also alluding to Marvell's country-house poems and to 'Bermudas' – really a poem about England – where God

> hangs in shades the orange bright
> Like golden lamps in a green night,
> And does in the pom'granates close
> Jewels more rich than Ormus shows.
> He makes the figs our mouths to meet,
> And throws the melons at our feet,
> But apples plants of such a price,
> No tree could ever bear them twice.

Marvell's puritan mariners are safe, like Crusoe, 'from the storms, and prelate's rage', and I am sure that Marvell's verse is deeply embedded in Defoe's imagination.

Crusoe's country-house joke also opens up a parallel between Crusoe, the gifted soldier and general, as he becomes, and Fairfax, on whose estate in Yorkshire Marvell wrote some of his finest poetry, and whom Defoe, as I've noted, compared in adulatory terms to another hero, Gustavus Adolphus. Echoing Marvell, he describes how the 'delicious vale' contains an abundance of cocoa trees, orange and lemon, and citron trees; but all wild, and very few bearing any fruit, at least not then: However, the green limes that I gathered were not only pleasant to eat, but very wholesome; and I mix'd their juice afterwards with water, which made it very wholesome, and very cool, and refreshing.

Both Defoe and Marvell express the ideas of individual liberty, property rights and equal citizenship through the imagery of fruit and gardens. The abundant clusters of grapes in *Crusoe* – often eaten dried – must partly symbolize the enjoyment of freehold. Defoe must also be thinking of the manna or 'angels' food' which the Psalmist says God rained on the Israelites in the desert.

Some biographers have noted that Defoe is so politically insistent and argumentative that he must have been the real force behind William of Orange's public utterances, writing speeches for him and orchestrating propaganda for the monarchy. My feeling is that his friendship with William and with Robert Harley, who like him was educated in a Dissenting academy, and who came of a Presbyterian family, is reflected at moments in Friday's relationship to Crusoe. Harley dominated the government of Queen Anne and directed the War of the Spanish Succession. He was outmanoeuvred by his dangerous rival, the Jacobite sympathizer Henry St John, Viscount Bolingbroke, and dismissed from office by Anne on 27 July 1714, five days before her death. On George I's accession he was imprisoned, and acquitted only in July 1717. Just as Crusoe rescues Friday from cannibals, Harley effectively rescued Defoe from prison to give him a social position as a leading government propagandist. As Novak shows, throughout the eighteenth century the Whigs lived in 'continual fear' of a successful counter-revolution by the Jacobites, and Crusoe's fear of the cannibals must reflect that pervasive social anxiety. Defoe's language in the novel is Hobbesian: 'I was reduced to a mere state of nature,' Crusoe tells us, while the twice-used adjective 'brutish' echoes the famous state of nature passage in *Leviathan*.

Crusoe is either anxious and fearful or exultantly confident, just as Defoe is one moment in prison with men destined for the gallows or else prospering from the brick factory he established in Essex. In a letter to Harley, he says of this wealthy period: 'I began to live, took a good house, bought me coach and horses a second time.' He speaks of William's 'bounty' and is proud, like Friday, to call him 'master'. William needed a strong standing army to back up the central aim of his foreign policy, which was to prevent France and Spain being joined as a single nation, and Defoe disagreed with republicans like Toland over this issue, running against a principle that is deeply embedded in English political culture. As Novak shows, everything Defoe wrote in 1701 was directed towards involving England in what was to be called the War of the Spanish Succession. This was the year he published *The True-Born Englishman*, his first popular success and the most frequently reprinted poem of the reign of Queen Anne. The evidence for the mixture of nationalities in England is revealed, Novak suggests, in the syntax, vocabulary and grammar of the poem:

> From this amphibious ill-born mob began
> *That vain ill-natur'd thing, an* Englishman.
> The customs, sirnames, languages, manners,
> Of all these nations are their own explainers:
> Whose relics are so lasting and so strong,
> They ha' left a *Shibboleth* upon our tongue;
> By which with easy search you may distinguish
> Your *Roman-Saxon-Danish-Norman* English.

His attack on English insularity, xenophobia and 'absurd pride in purity of descent' was part of a larger scheme to make the English see not only that their national affairs were tied to those of Europe but that they were 'connected to the Continent by a historic pattern of immigration'.

When Crusoe tells us that his father was 'a foreigner of Bremen', he is reminding his readers of Defoe's robustly furious attack on the idea of racial purity. Defoe chose Bremen, I would guess, because it was an independent city-state, a Hanseatic free town with ancient legal privileges, and he is probably implying that Crusoe's father was a refugee from the Thirty Years War. Crusoe's original name, Robinson Kreutznaer, reminds us also of England's historic connections with European Protestantism, and perhaps in 'Crusoe' we are also meant to discern the word 'crusader' clipped and attached to the last two syllables of Defoe's name (the 'crusadoe' coin, mentioned in the text, is also relevant). Crusoe's inventor most definitely was a crusader – he is as copiously opinionated as Shaw, but intellectually more flexible and less self-promoting. Crusoe's father left Bremen for Hull, and it is from Hull that Crusoe sets off on his first voyage. Hull is an unexpected city for a London-born writer to choose – why, as a famous story has it, should he or anyone take a ticket to Hull? The reason, I would guess, is that Defoe associated Hull with its famous radical MP Andrew Marvell, who may have been poisoned by his political enemies in 1678, when Defoe was eighteen. Hull is therefore the embodiment of quasi-republican principle and also of a heroic maritime adventurousness. Somewhere in British or English culture, Hull occupies a special, if seldom visited position, as a gateway to Holland and Protestant Europe, as well as to the high seas. Or in Larkin's version of Yeats's version of Milton, Hull is a lonely tower, vigilant and visionary. Defoe, it must be recognized, is one of the most influential architects of the British national consciousness.

Novak shrewdly points to a Hobbesian current in Defoe's political thinking. The state dissolves into the 'promiscuous crowd', which comprises all members of society, and the revolution that occurs uses the mob as its agent, though in England the people who possess property will become the heirs of the revolution (Crusoe steering his canoe over dangerous eddies is a metaphor of crowd theory and political manipulation). Defoe is the prose laureate of classic bourgeois revolution, and in the chaos of Crusoe's landfall he is representing that revolution, rather as Blok seeks to give images of the Russian Revolution in 'The Twelve'. In 1702, when he published his great polemic *The Shortest Way with the Dissenters*, Defoe was forced to go into hiding. By adopting the persona of a fanatical Tory High Churchman, he scuppered the passage of a Bill outlawing occasional conformity. The government was angry at Defoe, who in Novak's phrase 'slipped over the edge of the abyss', and it announced a reward of £50 for the apprehension of 'Daniel de Fooe', the author of a 'scandalous and seditious' pamphlet:

He is a middle-sized spare man about 40 years old, of a brown complexion, and dark brown coloured hair wears a wig, a hooked nose, a sharp chin, grey eyes, and a large mould near his mouth, was born in *London*, and for many years was a hose factor in Freeman's-yard, in Corn hill, and now is owner of the brick and pantile works near *Tilbury-fort in Essex*.

He may have gone to Holland, but remained for the most part in London, aided by the radical Whig underground of tradesmen and craftsmen. His pamphlet was burned by the common hangman in New Palace Yard, and after several months on the run he was captured at the home of a French weaver named Sammen in Spitalfields (it was an appropriate hideout: Defoe was devoted to the cause of the Huguenots and argued strongly in favour of their rights as asylum seekers). He was sent to Newgate prison, where he was examined by the Earl of Nottingham, who was Secretary of State for the southern region. When Defoe was sentenced to stand in the pillory for three days in July 1703, the government intended him to suffer a 'memorable humiliation' – his enemies never let him forget it – but he turned it into a public triumph. A contemporary painting shows him being toasted and surrounded by flowers on a bright, not a rainy, day. It shows, in Pope's phrase, 'unabashed Defoe'.

Defoe is a risk-taker, an opportunist, a hired pen, a showman, an at times dubious businessman who cheated his mother-in-law and believed in the slave trade, but he is *au fond* the journalist as civic hero, the master polemicist of his age. To be fair, Novak argues that Defoe believed that slaves should become indentured servants, but in his pamphlets he lists 'negroes' along with other commodities like tobacco, copper, almonds, wax. He is a master list-maker, but these catalogues are unsettling in their narrow businesslike confidence. He nonetheless has Crusoe's power over Friday evolve into a relationship of equals – then again he is careful to point out that Friday is not a 'negro'. His dark skin perhaps alludes to Defoe's 'brown complexion', but he is ideally handsome in ways the wedge-chinned Defoe with the 'mould' near his mouth was not.

Harley kept Defoe in jail for many months in order to wear down his resistance to working for him. His affairs were now, Novak says, 'as thoroughly wrecked as Crusoe's ship', but on his release he expressed a Friday-like devotion and obligation to Harley as his 'so generous and so bountiful' benefactor. He was to work very closely with Harley – both men viewed the Bills against occasional conformity as attempts to diminish or destroy the political influence of the Dissenters; both were intent on bringing about a Union between England and Scotland, and both enjoyed secrecy. Crusoe's pride in what he terms 'the whole island' reflects Defoe's Unionism, as well as his deeply topographical historical imagination, which finds its fullest expression in his prose equivalent of Drayton's *Polyolbion*, that benignly patriotic travel narrative *A Tour through the Whole Island of Great Britain*. Defoe the brick and pantile manufacturer has a sense of place, of earth, clay, light, locality and atmosphere – a radical chthonic nativism similar to Cobbett's. Always in haste, he was characterized as 'the briskest and most scurrying genius in the annals of English literature'. In his characteristically firm handwriting he could compose a pamphlet a day. Writing to Harley, he compares himself to a man lost at sea who found the distance to the shore too great for him to manage. This Crusoe-like metaphor makes one realize again that his sense of the sea, his admiration for what he calls 'the beautiful useful form of a ship', made him one of the great avatars of the British imagination. When Churchill said that the British people during the Second World War were as 'sound as the salt in the sea', he was using that type of patriotic maritime metaphor at which Defoe excelled.

Defoe convinced Harley of the importance of 'a scheme of general intelligence', a system of spies and agents who would relay a constant supply of information to the Secretary of State. Sent to Scotland by Harley, he risked his life to report on Scottish opinion about the Union, which, in a poem he published in the *Review*, he called 'Nature's strong cement; / The life of *power*, and *soul of government*.' Though he established a factory for weaving linen in

Edinburgh, he felt isolated in Scotland, which he found a 'remote country'. Crusoe-like, he felt 'forgotten' there, and referred to his situation as a form of 'torture'. While in Scotland, he learned of his daughter Martha's death, and it is one of Novak's gifts as a biographer that he lets us see Defoe the devoted husband and father, the puritan who believed in 'companionate marriage' and female education, the journalist who also wrote the early equivalent of agony columns, and who discussed sexual relationships in his journalism. His devotion to private and public happiness made him argue more than a century before University College was established that London needed a university open to everyone. He also argued for the establishment of old people's homes, a national system of improved roads, and a whole series of political, social and economic reforms. He influenced the system of cabinet government and helped shape the office of prime minister. Defoe led a dangerous life, and he would have reflected on the violence that pamphleteering could provoke when he eulogized John Tutchin. Defoe called Tutchin a 'very valuable person' and praised his 'zeal against tyranny'. Though it was Tutchin's poem *The Foreigners* which provoked Defoe to write *The True-Born Englishman*, he admired him deeply and must have been influenced by his *Western Martyrology*, which was published fourteen years before *Crusoe*. After Sedgemoor Tutchin was sentenced by Judge Jeffreys to be whipped regularly through every market town in Dorsetshire once a year for seven years. He petitioned James II to be hanged instead, but neither sentence was carried out. He was eventually so badly beaten up by political opponents that he died of his injuries. Where Tutchin had stressed his participation in Monmouth's rebellion, Defoe mentioned the event sparingly, never admitting he took part, which is why some have doubted he fought in the Battle of Sedgemoor.

On 12 July 1715, Defoe was tried for libel along with two printers. He was found guilty, fined heavily, and sentenced to be whipped from Newgate to Charing Cross, and to be imprisoned for two years. He was, as Novak writes, singled out as a person of vicious character and a danger to the state, but he did not come up for sentencing. Once again, he had struck a deal with the government, an event which he regarded as close to miraculous and which he describes in *Serious Reflections . . . of Robinson Crusoe.* Defoe had become such an influential journalist that in 1717 he was accused of being 'Corrector General' of the press. He was legendary for his subversive journalistic methods, and wrote for both Whig and Tory journals, as a way of combating Jacobitism.

The Pretender was crowned at Perth on 23 January 1716, but sailed back to France less than a fortnight later. Defoe predicted a new age of moderation, and perhaps following his advice the government acted cautiously. There were few executions of rebels, and eighteen months later a general amnesty was issued. Clemency is an important theme in *Crusoe* and elsewhere in Defoe's writings. Remembering that the Williamite Revolution was bloodless, and recalling Monmouth's earlier clemency to Scottish rebels after the Battle of Bothwell Brig during Charles II's reign, he emphasizes the values of mercy and humanity. This is reflected in Crusoe's remark about the cannibals' 'cruel bloody entertainment', a coded reference to Judge Jeffreys's mocking and vindictive conduct at the Bloody Assizes, which Crusoe's phrase 'so outrageous an execution' also glances at. Crusoe is compassionate towards the cannibals and also learns not to be an absolutist governor of his island – this is again directed at James II, who believed in the divine right of kings, and, as Marlborough pointed out, was as hard as stone.

With Defoe's consistent belief in tolerance and forgiveness goes an enduring interest in military science that makes him resemble Sterne's Uncle Toby. He was an expert on all kinds of building and the science of fortification, and argued for the establishment of a military academy. Like Uncle Toby, he is at times a military bore, and appears almost to parody this interest when Crusoe's deepening anxiety about the cannibals leads him obsessively to improve his fortifications (the 'living hedge' of his fort also symbolizes the British Constitution). Always engaged, always busy and committed, he seems to embrace all possible positions, as if tirelessly reinventing and then extending the public sphere every time he puts pen to paper. Like Cadmus, he sows the earth with innumerable dragon's teeth in order to found Thebes. There is, at the same time, a pride in identifying himself as a professional writer, that species of writing manufacturer who labours over his pamphlets like Crusoe constructing his chair and table, or turning his grindstone.

Defoe loved a good fight, and his family life, as Novak shows, must have been turbulent, affectionate and often chaotic. His son-in-law, the gifted educationalist Henry Baker, married to his favourite daughter, Sophia, remarked that 'ruin and wild destruction sport around him', and he died in great pain in 1731 while in hiding from a persistent creditor. He was buried in Bunhill Fields on 26 April 1731 and, as Novak points out, 'his grave may be found among the great Dissenting Englishmen of his century, not far from those of John Bunyan, Isaac Watts and William Blake.'

As I've suggested, Defoe is Milton's heir, and I like to think that one of the most apparently straightforward passages in *Crusoe* contains an allusion to a poem by Milton which Defoe would have known and admired. Crusoe escapes from Morocco with a great lump of beeswax wrapped in sailcloth, which he later recalls when he makes candles from goats' fat on the island. Defoe's father, James, was a successful tallow chandler, so Defoe is writing with a professional eye when he says of the beeswax:

> I had none of that now; the only remedy I had was that when I killed a goat, I sav'd the tallow, and with a little dish made of clay, which I baked in the sun, to which I added a wick of some oakum, I made me a lamp; and this gave me light, though not a clear steady light like a candle.

Though this is an example of his exacting verisimilitude, it also picks up symbolically on a remark of Charles Morton's which compares the understanding to 'a candle . . . to search and find out by its exercise, all those inward acts and inclinations which would otherwise lie hidden and undiscovered'. Deeper than this traditional image lies a central passage in *Il Penseroso*:

> Or let my lamp at midnight hour
> Be seen in some high lonely tower,
> Where I may oft outwatch the Bear,
> With thrice great Hermes, or unsphere
> The spirit of Plato . . .

Crusoe is a lonely Protestant visionary intellectual studying sacred texts by the light of the free individual conscience, and at one point he refers to 'the great lamp of instruction, the Spirit of God'.

There are other moments in *Crusoe* that demand a symbolic interpretation, and here the new Pickering & Chatto edition of Defoe's pamphlets and journalism is essential reading (so, too, are the same publisher's recent editions of Hazlitt and De Quincey, which have taken their places in libraries unsung and largely unreviewed). Take for example the passage where Crusoe shakes out a bag that appears to hold nothing but 'husks and dust'. In fact, it contains a few seeds of what Crusoe terms 'our *English* barley'. Thanks to God's 'Providence', the barley grows and after four years Crusoe has sufficient quantities to bake some of it into bread. I've long seen this as a parable of investment (the green shoots of economic growth is a cliché we all know, and in the *Review* Defoe remarks that credit comes upon a man or a nation insensibly 'as dust upon the cloths'). This symbolism is confirmed by a telling moment in *An Essay upon Public Credit* where Defoe says that it is 'the effect of a substance, not the substance, 'tis the *sunshine* not the sun; the quickning SOMETHING, *call it what you will*, that gives life to *trade*.' He then remarks in *An Essay upon Loans* that loans without credit are like a ploughman tilling 'barren soil'. Again and again, his genius for metaphor and soundbite takes us back to the obsessions and imaginative strategies that shape his fiction. As well as hanging, he is obsessed with ditches – a drainage ditch was crucial to the Sedgemoor defeat, Monmouth was captured hiding in a Hampshire ditch, William of Orange spoke of fighting to the 'last ditch', a phrase that still reverberates in the cultural memory of Ulster Unionism.

There is another allusion to Milton when Crusoe describes the beginning of his ill-fated voyage to the island – 'I went on board in an evil hour, the first of September 1659, being the same day eight year that I went from my father and mother at *Hull*, in order to act the rebel to their authority, and the fool to my own interest.' In *Paradise Lost*, at the crucial moment when Eve eats the apple (an act that symbolizes the Stuart Restoration and the wreck of the Commonwealth), Milton says:

> her rash hand in evil hour
> Forth reaching to the fruit, she plucked, she ate:
> Earth felt the wound, and nature from her seat
> Sighing through all her works gave signs of woe,
> That all was lost.

Famously Milton rhymes 'ate' with 'seat' ('sate') to produce what is sometimes wrongly described as the only couplet, the only moment of Restoration verse style, in the epic. Defoe is echoing this moment of rebellion against God's republican state, but he is also shading in his own rebellion against a Stuart monarch, as well as the fraught relationship with his father, which Novak convincingly intuits. One of the interesting things about Defoe is that he is a psychological as well as a political novelist – consciousness, emotion, states of mind, guilt, being-in-the-world are his subjects too.

Defoe's prose is nimbler, more easy and graceful in the journalism and pamphlets than it is in the graver, more concentrated cadences of *Crusoe*, and it always has the crowded energy of London's streets and markets, as well as a wide historical range and a celebrative eagerness and human tenderness quite different from Swift's deliberately rebarbative and uncomfortable style – a style that obsessively targets Defoe and which Defoe scorned, attacking Swift's *Examiner* with its 'unintelligible jingle, fine-spun emptiness, and long-winded repetition, without truth, and without evidence, without meaning'. In his journalism, as in *Crusoe*, Defoe is fond of imagining pilots shooting up their 'watery hill', and his many maritime moments culminate in a tribute to sailors: '*Les Enfans Perdue, the Forlorn hope of the world*; they are fellows that bid defiance to terror, and maintain a constant war with the elements; who by the magic of their art, trade in the very confines of death, and are always posted within shot, as I may say, of the grave.' A 'forlorn hope' is a vanguard sent into battle, and here Defoe the great survivor and escape artist is designing an image of what inspires his multifarious writings. He begins one article by saying: 'Upon my first launching out into the vast ocean of fluid matter, which is to be the subject of this paper' – he is a

Crusoe of the pen, a death-defying sailor who craves risk and danger always.

There is rumoured to be only one graduate student working on Defoe in Britain at present, but Novak's compelling biography and the new Pickering & Chatto edition should help redeem the critical neglect his work has suffered. It is interesting that one of his greatest admirers, James Joyce, should have seen *Crusoe* as 'the English *Ulysses*' – Joyce recognized that it was a national epic which, like his own, is closely entangled with a historical narrative that has become myth, and which is originally set out in the Book of Exodus. In their art, Defoe and Joyce point the way out of Egyptian bondage, a censored press and a guarded speech. But *Crusoe* must also be understood as a survival narrative, like the account of another Monmouth rebel called John Coad which is entitled *A Memorandum of the Wonderful Providence of God to a poor unworthy Creature during the time of the Duke of Monmouth's Rebellion and to the Revolution of 1688*. In it Coad speaks of the 'great rain' and recounts how he was condemned to be hung, drawn and quartered as a deserter and a rebel. Luckily, he was able to take the place of a man called Jo Haker who was unwilling to be transported. He stayed for five years in Jamaica before returning to England in 1690, where he found his wife and three sons alive 'but in a very poor condition'. Like Crusoe, he compares his captivity to 'the Jewish captivity in Egypt', and like Crusoe, he draws on the Psalms to describe his experience: 'Thus *the Lord sent from above*; he took me, *he drew me* out of many waters, *he delivered* me from my *strong enemies*, and from them *that hated* me, for they were too *strong for* me.' Coad's narrative, which was praised by Macaulay, was published in 1849. It adds vitally to our understanding of Defoe, who gives complex fictional form to his experience of the Stuarts in *Crusoe, A Journal of the Plague Year* and his other novels. There is still no historically annotated edition of *Paradise Lost*, and editions of Defoe similarly betray that historical amnesia which, despite the new historicism, is still a persistent feature of literary studies in this country. It is one of the curious effects of consensus politics that this enemy of Jacobitism and fiery advocate of national unity should be so consistently neglected.

Clarissa: Dissenting Epic

Clarissa and *Ulysses*, both epic poems in prose, are the two greatest novels in English. *Ulysses* is the object of innumerable books, essays, conferences and celebrations, while *Clarissa* is rarely visited and admired. To discuss Richardson's genius is to whistle in the dark – almost no one reads him or studies him, though *Clarissa* is one of the finest expressions of English puritanism, a historical and political novel, which is also a profound psychological study. Richardson's father, a London joiner, was a Sedgemoor rebel who returned to his native Derbyshire, where Richardson was born in 1689. Derbyshire is central to the Industrial Revolution – Richard Arkwright was born there in 1732, in Cromford, and the founder of the American industrial revolution, Samuel Slater, was born in Belper in 1768. Slater memorized the details of machinery made by Arkwright, Hargreaves and Crompton, and emigrated secretly in 1789 (the emigration of textile workers or the export of drawings of textile machinery was forbidden). In *Clarissa*, there is a persistent theme of emigration to North America, a theme which expresses the frustration of English puritans at their treatment by the government and the court.

Richardson, like Arkwright and Slater, was largely self-educated, and knew the classics only in translation, but in his masterpiece *Clarissa* he sought to reclaim the *Aeneid* in particular from court culture. Milton originally published *Paradise Lost* in ten books, as he did not wish to appear to be imitating the *Aeneid*, because royalists had appropriated the Virgilian heroic mode before and after the Restoration. Charles was celebrated as a new Augustus, the Restoration was portrayed as a Golden Age restored. By 1674, when Milton produced an edition of *Paradise Lost* in twelve books, Virgil was no longer an obvious signifier of Royalism, and Milton could now reclaim that central epic tradition from the court. Dryden claimed it back with his translation of the *Aeneid*, which was published in 1697 and is a major English epic that carries a Jacobite meaning, in which the wandering Aeneas of the first six books is meant to remind readers of James II. Dryden's translation is topical, particularly in its preference for words such as 'exil'd' and 'restor'd'.

As the son of an associate of Monmouth and Shaftesbury, Richardson feared a Stuart Restoration – Bonnie Prince Charlie, the Stuart Pretender, briefly occupied the city of Derby in 1745, a few miles from where he was born in the village of Mickleover. (There is some doubt about Richardson's claim that his father knew Monmouth and Shaftesbury, but it is significant that he claimed a connection with them.) In his work as a printer in London, he had met many Jacobites, printed their journals and observed their high-handed, insouciant manners – that camp witty nihilism that so offends the puritan conscience. He also understood the attractions of aristocracy and of the theatre which was restored after 1660. His characterization of his epistolary art – 'writing to the moment' – is derived from his own villain Lovelace's description of the theatrical nature of his letters. The *mentalité* survives, as we can see in the popular esteem accorded to Alan Clark's diaries. Richardson did not love a lord, but he knew that almost everyone else did.

Towards the end of his epic, he alludes to the *Aeneid*, when Belford describes the dying procuress Sinclair:

> The other seven seemed to have been but just up, risen perhaps from their customers in the fore-house, and their nocturnal orgies, with faces, three or four of them, that had run, the paint lying in streaky seams not half blowzed off, discovering coarse wrinkled skins: the hair of some of them of divers colours; obliged to the blacklead comb where black was affected; the artificial jet, however, yielding apace to the natural brindle: that of others plaistered with oil and powder; the oil predominating: but every one's hanging about her ears and neck in broken curls, or ragged ends; and each at my entrance taken with one motion, stroking their matted locks with both hands under their coifs, mobs, or pinners, every one of which was awry. They were all slipshod; stockingless some; only under-petticoated all; their gowns, made to cover straddling hoops, hanging trollopy, and dangling about their heels; but hastily wrapped round them as soon as I

came upstairs. And half of them (unpadded, shoulder-bent, pallid-lipped, feeble-jointed wretches) appearing from a blooming nineteen or twenty perhaps overnight, haggard well-worn strumpets of thirty-eight or forty.

I am the more particular in describing to thee the appearance these creatures made in my eyes when I came into the room, because I believe thou never sawest any of them, much less a group of them, thus unprepared for being seen. I, for my part, never did before; nor had I now but upon this occasion been thus *favoured*. If thou *hadst*, I believe thou wouldst hate a profligate woman as one of Swift's Yahoos, or Virgil's obscene Harpies squirting their ordure upon the Trojan trenchers; since the persons of such in their retirements are as filthy as their minds – Hate them as much as I do; and as much as I admire and next to adore a truly virtuous and elegant woman: for to me it is evident that as a neat and clean woman must be an angel of a creature, so a sluttish one is the impurest animal in nature.

In a note, Richardson directs us to Swift's 'A Lady's Dressing Room', and in citing the poem and *Gulliver's Travels* he is aligning Swift, the enemy of the Dissenters, with everything that Lovelace represents. Richardson will also have been thinking of Book Three of the *Aeneid*, where in Dryden's translation Virgil describes the harpies who 'snatch the Meat; defiling all they find: / And parting leave a loathsome Stench behind'. Like Defoe, who is also reworking the *Aeneid* in *Robinson Crusoe*, Richardson wants to reclaim Virgil's poem, and to associate the harpies with the court party. He also, late in the novel, plays a complicated game with the *Aeneid*, when he makes Lovelace compare himself to '*pius* Aeneas', who was 'an ungrateful varlet' to the '*hospitable* princess', Dido. This in effect puts the *Aeneid* back in the royalist or Jacobite camp, and reminds readers that Aeneas is not as heroic and worthy a figure as he elsewhere appears. It's here we can see that the name 'Clarissa Harlowe' is intended to carry negative meanings – meanings which represent England's recent history under the Stuarts (Defoe is doing something similar in *Roxana*). 'Clarissa' means 'most clear', and Richardson intends us to see her as the sun – early in the novel Anna Howe, whose name echoes *Clarissa Harlowe*, compares her to the sun, adding that Clarissa's brother's and sister's eyes 'ache to look up at you'. In *Paradise Lost*, Milton calls the sun 'great palace now of light', and Richardson wants to identify his heroine with this republican symbol of divine truth and reason. The harlots, a noun dangerously close to 'Harlowe', represent the darkness, ugliness and irrationality that are part of the historical burden that the English nation carries. Just as the madam's name, 'Sinclair', carries 'sin', so 'Harlowe' carries both 'halo' and 'low'. Richardson has created a name which, from a certain perspective, functions like an oxymoron: it carries opposites. He wants her to embody the soul of the nation, and he needs to represent that soul as trapped in all that is represented by Mrs Sinclair's 'huge quaggy carcase'. Clarissa, imprisoned in the brothel, is a symbol of the English nation as the Israelites in Egyptian – i.e. Stuart – bondage. Through a series of allusions to *Paradise Lost*, Richardson quietly insists that this is the next epic, after *Crusoe*'s development of Milton's historical narrative, to embody the experience of the English people in their struggles against proud and unjust rulers. Using the ship-of-state symbol, which Defoe so naturalistically employs, Clarissa says whatever course

> I shall be permitted or be forced to steer, I must be considered as a person out of her own direction. Tossed to and fro by the high winds of passionate control, and, as I think, unreasonable severity, I behold the desired port, the *single state*, which I would fain steer into; but kept off by the foaming billows of a brother's and sister's envy; and by the raging winds of a supposed invaded authority; while I see in Lovelace, the rocks on the one hand, and in Solmes, the sands on the other; and tremble lest I should split upon the former, or strike upon the latter.

The allegory is forced, but it makes the connection with *Crusoe* and it also sets up the association of the word 'state' with the ship Clarissa is comparing herself to.

In letter 16, Clarissa describes the 'odious Solmes sitting asquat between my mamma and sister'. This picks up the famous moment when Satan is found 'Squat like a toad, close at the ear of Eve', a line which is also echoed by Lovelace, when he describes to Belford how 'I poured my whole soul into her attentive ear'. A moment later in letter 16, the squat Solmes 'must needs rise and stalk towards a chair'. This echoes the moment when Satan becomes a lion and 'stalks with fiery glare'. Perhaps the central Miltonic value in the novel can be felt when Clarissa in a letter to her father says, 'You know, sir, my open, free, communicative temper'. This ethic of communication is celebrated by Milton who argues that education would spread much more 'knowledge and civilitie, yea religion' through all parts of England

> by communicating the natural heat of government and culture more distributively to all extreme parts, which now lie numb and neglected, would soon make the whole nation more industrious, more ingenuous at home, more potent, more honorable abroad. To this a free Commonwealth will easily assent; (nay the Parlament hath had already some such thing in designe) for of all governments a Commonwealth aims most to make the people flourishing, virtuous, noble and high spirited.

In Hazlitt's prose, this ethic of communication, and its accompanying insistence on education, is a pervasive theme. It flies in the face of a culture of secrecy and official manipulation of the truth.

But the strongest and most persistent allusion to Milton occurs in these moments:

> Many a one have I taught to dress, and helped to undress. But there is such a native elegance in this lady that she surpasses all that I could imagine surpassing.

> That *native dignity*, that *heroism* I will call it . . .

> A sweet auburn beauty is Miss Howe. A first beauty among beauties, when her sweeter friend (with such a commixture of serene gracefulness, of natural elegance, of native sweetness, yet conscious, though not arrogant, dignity, every feature glowing with intelligence) is not in company.

> This *native dignity*, as I may call it, induced some superficial persons who knew not how to account for the reverence which involuntarily filled their hearts on her appearance to impute pride to her.

These passages echo Milton's many uses of 'native', and especially Satan's first sight of Adam and Eve:

> Two of far nobler shape erect and tall,
> Godlike erect, with native honour clad
> In naked majesty seemed lords of all.

Richardson's prose and Milton's verse employ the word 'native' to embody a primordial English patriotism and republicanism, threatened by monarchical evil. Richardson, like Defoe, covers his tracks by making a slighting reference to Cromwell, when Lovelace remarks, 'as Cromwell said, it must be my head or the king's'. This is followed by a paragraph which shows the conscious epic artist at work:

> How it swells my pride to have been able to outwit such a vigilant charmer! – I am taller by half a yard, in my imagination, than I was! I look *down* upon everybody now! – Last night I was still more extravagant. I took off my hat, as I walked, to see if the lace were not scorched, supposing it had brushed down a star; and, before I put it on again, in mere wantonness and heart's-ease, I was for buffeting the moon.

We are meant to associate 'hat' with 'head', and so remember the execution of Charles I, and we are also meant to remember:

> From morn
> To noon he fell, from noon to dewy eve,
> A summer's day; and with the setting sun
> Dropped from the zenith like a falling star.

Milton is echoing Howes's description of Hephaistos's fall in the *Iliad*, and he would have known that both Pope and Dryden translated this passage.

Richardson carefully says that Lovelace's hat 'brushed down a star', not 'brushed against', because he wants us to see an image of a falling star against the heavens, and to identify Lovelace with it. He returns to this epic moment towards the end of the novel, when Lovelace in his characteristically kitschy manner relates how in a dream he

> ascended with her to the region of seraphims; and instantly, the opening ceiling closing, I lost sight of *her*, and of the *bright form* together, and found wrapped in my arms her azure robe (all stuck thick with stars of embossed silver), which I had caught hold of in hopes of detaining her; but was all that was left me of my beloved Miss Harlowe. And then (horrid to relate!) the floor sinking under *me*, as the ceiling had opened for *her*, I dropped into a hole more frightful than that of Elden and tumbling over and over down it, without view of a bottom, I awaked in a panic . . .

Elden is a deep pothole in the Peak District, and it conveniently brings Eden and therefore Milton's epic to mind.

Richardson aims to identify Lovelace with both Satan and Charles I. Lovelace at one point falls into what he terms 'the old dismal thirtieth of January strain' – he is remembering the execution of Charles on that day. Lovelace's servant Joseph Leman, dictating a letter to his master, hopes that Lovelace will 'not be hanged like as a common man; but only have his head cut off or so'. Richardson does not wish us to miss the parallel, and he also draws it with Charles II when Lovelace quotes the passage in *Absalom and Achitophel*, where Charles is compared to 'a lion slumb'ring'. Lovelace says he has a view to act the part of Dryden's lion.

Richardson also compares Lovelace to Tarquin and to Caesar, most interestingly in the letter where Lovelace commiserates with Belford, who has been thrown from his horse. He remarks that 'a rake's neck is always in danger, if not from the hangman, from his own horse', and then develops the association:

> Caesar never knew what it was to be *hypped*, I will call it, till he came to be what Pompey was; that is to say, till he arrived at the height of his ambition: nor did thy Lovelace know what it was to be gloomy, till he had completed his wishes upon the charmingest creature in the world, as the other did his upon the most potent republic that ever existed.

The parallel between Clarissa and the English republic is obvious here, and it is made again when Lovelace explains that his imagination has been stimulated by court love poetry: 'I must have a Cynthia, a Stella, a Sacharissa.' By beginning the list with Ralegh's name for Elizabeth I, Richardson rules out a monarchical parallel, as well as offering a critique of the language and values shared by poets like Ralegh, Sidney and the Cavaliers. Richardson has many targets – Henry VIII, the 'Tyrant Tudor', is on the list, as is Rochester, the Jacobite Thomas Wharton, and another Jacobite, Pope's friend, Henry St John, Viscount Bolingbroke, whose betrayal of the Catalans in the Treaty of Utrecht is mentioned.

Richardson's devout puritanism can be felt in this cunning allusion to *Paradise Lost*:

> But oh! Jack, What was Sixtus the Vth's artful depression of his natural powers to mine, when, as the half-dead Montalto, he gaped for the pretendedly unsought Pontificate, and, the moment he was chosen, leapt upon the prancing beast, which it was thought by the amazed conclave he was not able to mount without the help of chairs and men?

Here Richardson is thinking of Milton's pun, when Satan and his daughter Sin gaze at 'this new wondrous pontifice' (the new noun combines 'bridge' and 'pontiff', meaning Pope). The adverb 'pretendedly' also works to summon the Pretender to mind, because Richardson's anxiety about the permanence of the Hanoverian Succession is always present. When James Harlowe, Clarissa's brother, travels to Edinburgh, this was meant to remind contemporary readers of Charles Edward, the Young Pretender's occupation of Edinburgh, where he was crowned and held court. Similarly, the fact that Lovelace dates one of his last letters 14–18 September is also significant: he tells Belford 'I am preparing to leave this kingdom', and it was on 20 September 1746 that Charles Edward left Scotland. As critics have noted, the duel between Morden and Lovelace in 'a little lone valley' is meant to reproduce the Duke of Cumberland's defeat of the Jacobites at Culloden in 1746. Richardson has Lovelace's second, De La Tour, say that he found Colonel Morden 'was too well used to the bloody work', and in this remark he conveys both his distaste for duelling and his concern at Cumberland's ruthlessness: he was nicknamed 'Butcher Cumberland'.

On the symbolic level, Morden functions as the 'one just man alive', who Milton prophesies will come to earth to redeem mankind, but in the narrative he is a fallible and flawed human being, whose absence from England makes Clarissa vulnerable. Her family home, Harlowe Place, is shown to be a dangerous and compromised building; when it is compared to Versailles: 'like Versailles,' Lovelace says, 'it is sprung up from a dunghill within every elderly person's remembrance.' The fact that it has a 'Dutch-taste' garden is meant to signal both the Harlowes' loyalty to the Hanoverian Succession, which followed the Williamite Settlement, and to point to a rottenness within the political culture of the period. The summerhouse, where Clarissa meets Lovelace, is meant to remind us, I think, of 'a certain summerhouse in the garden', where Portia was seduced by Alexander More, according to Milton in the *Second Defence of the English People*. Clarissa's repeated exclamation 'What am I about to do!' is a way of dramatizing a historical calamity analogous to the actual Restoration or the Restoration of the Young Pretender.

Richardson's great ambition is to overthrow an aristocratic honour or shame culture, and replace it by a middle-class morality that can be termed a conscience or guilt culture. Sir Charles Grandison's assertion that reputation and conscience are the same thing represents this ambition, as does his complete indifference to the damage to his reputation which his refusal to accept a challenge to a duel will cause. Lovelace recognizes Clarissa's unyielding principle, and refusal to be influenced by other people's opinions: 'What can be done with a woman who is above flattery, and despises all praise but that which flows from the approbation of her own heart?' Rather like a conduct book, Richardson is telling his female readers how they ought to behave – the idea of the free individual conscience, which Lovelace recognizes here, flies in the face of the aristocratic idea of honour and society.

This concept of reputation – a kind of moral *bella figura* – is offered in one of the great passages of dialogue, Anna Howe's argument with her mother, who has just received a marriage proposal from Clarissa's 'nasty' Uncle Anthony:

D. You'll be so good as to forgive me, Madam – But I thought everybody (he among the rest) knew that you had always declared against a second marriage.

M. And so I have. But then it was in the mind I was in. Things may offer– I stared.

M. Nay, don't be surprised! – I don't intend – I don't intend–

D. Not, perhaps, in *the mind you are in*, Madam.

M. Pert creature! – (*rising again!*) – We shall quarrel, I see! – There's no–

D. Once more, dear Madam, I beg your excuse. I will attend in silence – Pray, Madam, sit down again – Pray do – (she sat down) – May I see the letter?

No; there are some things in it, you won't like – Your temper is known, I find, to be unhappy – But nothing *bad* against you; intimations, on the contrary, that you shall be the better for him, if you oblige him.

Not a living soul but the Harlowes, I said, thought me ill-tempered: and I was contented that *they* should, who could do as they had done by the most universally acknowledged sweetness in the world.

Here we broke out a little; but, at last, she read me some of the passages in it – But not the *most mightily* ridiculous; yet I could hardly keep my countenance neither. And when she had done:

M. Well now, Nancy, tell me what you think of it?
D. Nay, pray, Madam, tell me what *you* think of it?

That phrase 'the most universally acknowledged sweetness in the world' represents both Clarissa's inner strength of conscience and a divine recognition of it that is expressed as a form of social acknowledgement. It unites guilt culture with shame or honour culture. The phrase has an arresting, expansive clarity, which rises above the furiously cross-hatched dialogue between mother and daughter, whose style in turn challenges the melodious exchanges which characterize Restoration comedy. The weight, the energy and noise of the quarrel belong also to epic, for it is Richardson's great achievement to centre its momentousness in ordinary, domestic life. The toad-like Solmes is not aggrandized by the glance at Satan – rather evil is made banal, so that it sits on an armchair or under a cabinet.

Outside In: Richard Brinsley Sheridan

In a rather queasy poem about Irish political failure, 'Parnell's Funeral', Yeats elegizes the tragic leader:

> Through Jonathan Swift's dark grove he passed, and there
> Plucked bitter wisdom that enriched his blood.

In *A Traitor's Kiss: The Life of Richard Brinsley Sheridan* (1997), Fintan O'Toole's dazzling biography of the extraordinary man who was both the greatest dramatist of his time and one of its most significant politicians and orators, we see how Sheridan was brushed by the wings of Swift's tortured and subversive imagination. He passed through Swift's dark grove, but he did so without bitterness, without being scarred by the passage from Protestant Ireland to political life in Britain. That sunny middle name, Brinsley – a family name of his godfather, Lord Lanesborough – prepares us for the eloquence and grace of the famous surname.

He was born on the then fashionable north side of Dublin in 1751. His mother Frances was a gifted writer and novelist, his father one of the leading actors in the country, as well as an influential educationalist and teacher of elocution. In 1759, the family moved to London – Sheridan never set foot in Ireland again, though late in his career he nearly succeeded in being elected for an Irish constituency. He regarded himself as Irish, and, as O'Toole shows, his identification with Ireland was central to the construction of his public persona. While penetrating into the heart of the British political elite, a part of him always belonged incorruptibly to the outside. He was educated at Harrow, like Byron, who just after leaving school noted that the great orators were Demosthenes, Cicero, Quintilian, Sheridan. Though he was tormented as a poor player's son at school, he made some important aristocratic friends there and learnt to ride, speak and wield a sword like a gentleman.

As Sheridan's father, Thomas, argued in a book on British education published in 1756, the ancient republics of Greece and Rome were founded on oratory: 'Their end was liberty; liberty could not subsist without virtue, nor be maintained without wisdom and knowledge; and wisdom and knowledge unless communicated with force and perspicuity, were useless to the state.' As playwright, theatre manager, prominent Whig politician and orator, Sheridan's aim was liberty for Britain and Ireland. The story of his life, as O'Toole tells it, is epic in its scope – this man was so important that when he upset Napoleon by criticizing him in a speech to the House of Commons, the French ambassador tried to win back his support for the French republic by inviting Sheridan to a six-hour dinner at which he and his close friend the Prince of Wales consumed huge amounts of food and wine. And this for a speech in which Sheridan had tempered his criticisms of Napoleon's occupation of Switzerland with the remark that he was 'a great philosopher and philanthropist'.

Sheridan's grandfather, Dr Thomas Sheridan, was a close friend of Swift, who was attracted by his anarchic use of language, his 'promiscuous and sometimes surreal punning', and his knowledge of Gaelic (the Gaelic-speaking O'Sheridans were converted to Protestantism in the seventeenth century by a notably liberal Church of Ireland bishop, the English-born William Bedell, whose mission and the respect in which the native Irish held him are touchingly described in an opening chapter which is subtly keyed to the possible outcome of the Irish peace talks of autumn 1997). Dr Sheridan helped Swift weave the ambiguous themes of loyalty and treason in *The Drapier's Letters*, and his son – Swift's godson and Sheridan's father – became obsessed with language and speech, an obsession which was to mould the young playwright's radical, classically republican imagination. Sheridan learned to exploit words, master the tongue, turn the slippery ambiguity of language into a weapon and reinforce its power by speaking from behind the mask of an assumed persona. He always knew that a speech could make or break a career, because his grandfather, grabbing a sermon at random to deliver on the aniversary of the accession of George I, destroyed his career when an enemy told Dublin Castle that the text – 'Sufficient unto the day is the evil therof' – made the sermon a coded attack on the King. So complete was Sheridan's mastery of speech that in the early 1800s, he nearly persuaded George III to send him and the Prince of Wales to govern Ireland (the Prince would be Lord-Lieutenant and together they would bring about Catholic emancipation). Hazlitt, who placed him alongside Swiftand Goldsmith in his personal pantheon of Irish writers, said that even in his decline no one could pass him in the street without 'beingstruck with him as one of the brightest and bravest of men'. The light in his super-intelligent eyes captivated Hazlitt and Coleridge, as well as many of his contemporaries.

O'Toole tells the story of his boozy, rackety, supremely eloquent life with the fast-paced rhythm of an extended essay's permanent sense of unfolding discovery, so that we follow Sheridan through a series of adventures that the playwright-politician appears always to have designed to be made into 'ballads and paragraphs, and the devil knows what', as Sir Peter Teasle terms eighteenth-century PR in *The School for Scandal.* At the age of twenty, in a very public manner, he eloped from Bath with a famous and beautiful singer, Elizabeth Linley, fought two duels with an army officer who was in love with her, and in 1775 took London by storm with the production of two plays, *St Patrick's Day* and *The Rivals*, and a comic opera, *The Duenna*. The following year, like a film star buying the studio, he acquired Garrick's share in the Drury Lane Theatre, which he managed until it burnt down in 1809. At the age of twenty-five, he was part owner and effective controller of one of Europe's great theatres, with 2,300 seats. From here, he moved into the heart of the aristocracy, and at the age of twenty-nine he was elected MP for Stafford, even though he had refused to pander to the anti-Catholic prejudices of a powerful section of the electorate. Within three years of taking his seat, he had affirmed an independent line on Ireland, established himself as an ally, rather than a mere follower, of the revered Whig leader Charles James Fox, and begun to overtake Burke in parliamentary eminence. He also held office twice in those years.

Perhaps his greatest moment was when he attacked Warren Hastings, the governor-general of the East India Company, for his cruelty and corruption (an analogy with British rule in Ireland is implicit in his account of an India laid waste by war and famine). In a devastating speech lasting five and a half hours, he demolished Hastings's defence and exposed him as a 'traitor and a trickster'. Addressing the assembled MPs not as factional politicians, but as eighteenth-century men of sensibility, he concluded by calling for Hastings's impeachment. When he sat down, the whole House, for the first time in its history, 'erupted in a tumult of cheering and applause'. As O'Toole cleverly notes, having brought the house down with the famous screen scene in *The School for Scandal*, Sheridan now brought the House down with his oratorical genius. This was a decisive moment in the history of international law because the ideas on which Sheridan relied – the universal nature of human rights and responsibilities – would not be fully elaborated until the twentieth century. His enemy William Pitt said that he had 'a very high idea' of Sheridan and thought him a far greater man than Fox.

With typical Irish subtlety or opportunism, he knew how to appeal to monarchist conservatives and to democratic radicals, and in 1799 rebuilt his political reputation by staging *Pizarro*, an adaptation of a play by Kotzebue, which George III attended (Sheridan wrote an extra verse for 'God Save the King' for the occasion, which was particularly appropriate as someone had fired a shot at the King when he entered the royal box). The play combines covert support for Irish republicanism with British patriotism and advanced Whig ideas about limited monarchy. The previous year Sheridan had run huge risks to help several members of the United Irishmen, the revolutionary body which led an uprising that summer which was bloodily suppressed and whose bicentenary in 1998 was given a muted commemoration. Friendly with conspirators against the British state, he was talked about as a future Chancellor of the Exchequer and Prime Minister. No wonder Hazlitt, who was close to Sheridan's friend, the United Irish revolutionary and journalist, Peter Finnerty, said that he had a nose and mouth like Cromwell's.

As we follow Sheridan through the love affairs, the drinking bouts, dinners, plays, debts, friendships, his second marriage – to Esther Ogle, the daughter of the Dean of Winchester – the sense of danger and Wildean extremity becomes almost overwhelming; there are several stage or film dramas just waiting to be made here. One moment he could have been put in the Tower on a charge of treason, the next he might have been running the country, as he briefly did during one of George III's bouts of madness. Both a friend of the Prince of Wales and a friend of the people, both an insider at the heart of the Whig aristocracy and a priceless outsider, he managed to ride so many contradictions. In 1816, friends calling to see him on his deathbed had to push past bailiffs in the hall of his dirty, furnitureless house, but his coffin was carried to Westminster Abbey by the Duke of Bedford, the Earl of Lauderdale, Earl Mulgrave, the Lord Bishop of London, Lord Holland and Lord Spencer. Noting that last Whig aristocrat makes me realize that this biography is perfectly shaped for the new age of sensibility which Princess Diana's death and Tony Blair's response to it ('the People's Princess') have inaugurated. But primarily, and right from the first moving chapter, it also argues for a new Irish identity – Gaelic like the O'Sheridan ancestors, republican like the United Irishmen, and British – i.e. Orange – like the radical flank of the Whig party that Sheridan belonged to.

In his conservative phase, William Cobbett complained that it was impossible to determine 'on which side he spoke', a remark that shows the enduring influence of Swift's treasonously loyal ironies and ambiguities, as it also shows the way in which Sheridan turned the disadvantages of his ungentlemanly theatrical background and contradictory identities into exceptional political theatre (this mercurial undecidability is an enduring feature of Irish writing). Through his friendship with the Prince of Wales, he attempted to undermine the royal prerogative from within, while at the same time saving the British state from constitutional crisis by making a perfectly pitched speech in the Commons defending the Prince's relationship with Mrs Fitzherbert, the Catholic he had secretly married (the speech is shot through with contradictions but it did the trick).

Byron admired Sheridan and planned to write his life. In a letter to Tom Moore, Sheridan's first biographer, he advised him like this:

> Were his intrigues more notorious than those of all his contemporaries? And is his memory to be blasted, and theirs respected? Don't let yourself be led away by clamour, but compare him with the coalitioner Fox, and the pensioner Burke, as a man of principle, and with ten hundred thousand in personal views, and with none in talent, for he beat them all *out* and *out*. Without means, without connexion, without character, (which might be false at first, and make him mad afterwards from desperation,) he beat them all, in all he ever attempted. But alas, poor human nature! good night or rather, morning. It is four, and the dawn gleams over the Grand Canal, and unshadows the Rialto.

Linda Kelly quotes Byron at the end of her fluent and scholarly, if less impassioned biography, *Richard Brinsley Sheridan: A Life* (1997), but in a moving and effective moment O'Toole shows the unexpectedly pious William Godwin returning to the Abbey after Sheridan's lavish funeral.

> In the coming week he went again and again to the silent abbey to sit in front of the plain stone that marked the resting place of a man who had been one of his heroes. He remembered a man to whom he had written an open letter calling for a revolution in England. He remembered a man who had done all in his power to create a Britain that valued freedom over conquest and an Ireland that was stultified neither by Catholic tribalism nor by Protestant claims to ascendancy. He recalled to mind an evening over sixteen years before at his own house when Sheridan had sat up talking with two fellow-Irishmen, the revolutionary Arthur O'Connor and the lawyer and orator John Philpot Curran, who had coined a famous phrase about the price of freedom being eternal vigilance. Sitting there, Godwin remembered how the conversation that night had 'a most animated turn, and the subject was Love'.

It is impossible not to love Sheridan, and impossible not to rejoice in the way O'Toole honours his memory. Though his account is at times too compressed, it points to the urgent need for a study that grounds Sheridan more completely in the intricacies of British and Irish politics in the period. Meanwhile, Fintan O'Toole should be showered with garlands and loaded with prizes.

The Deep Heart's Core: Yeats and Blake

On 7 May 1889, W. B. Yeats wrote to this friend the old Fenian John O'Leary:

> I have been busy with Blake . . . You complain about the mysticism. It has enabled me to make out Blake's prophetic books at any rate. My book on him will I believe clear up that riddle for ever. No one will call him mad again. I have evidence by the way to show that he was of Irish extraction – his grandfather was an O'Neal who changed his name for political reasons. Ireland takes a most important place in his mystical system.

Yeats apparently drew this idea from C. Carter Blake, whom he mentions in a note to his *Book of Irish Verse*, published in 1895. Writing on 23 August 1889 to Douglas Hyde, Yeats said that Blake's grandfather 'was a Cornelious O'Neal', and on 2 September 1889 he told Father Matthew Russell that Blake's grandfather took the name Blake 'to dodge his creditors. So we may almost claim Blake as an Irish poet.' He told William Linnell on 28 October 1894, 'I feel that the getting Blake as adequately before the world as possible in this age of artistic materialism is something of a sacred charge. One never knows what mind he may awaken, what imagination he may quicken.' Earlier he has called Blake 'one of the great mystics of the world and after reading our book no one at any rate will ever again say that he was mad' (to Charles Elkin Mathews, spring 1890). Here, he is referring to the great three-volume study of Blake, which he wrote and edited with Edwin Ellis. Later, he linked Blake with Nietzsche, who 'modernises the doctrine that I learned from Blake' (to John Quinn, 6 February 1903).

In the introduction to the three-volume study, Yeats says:

James Blake, or, as he was called in childhood, James O'Neil, the father of the poet was of Irish extraction. A certain John O'Neil, James's father, had got into debt and difficulties in his own country. He married Ellen Blake, keeper of a *shebeen* house, at Rathmines, Dublin, and took her name. His young son, James, whose mother is unknown, but who was not the fruit of this union, began at the same time to use the name of Blake. But if the old O'Neil origin was hidden, the wild O'Neil blood showed itself strongly in the next generation. William Blake, as we call him, was, before all things an O'Neil. His descent from a stock who had seldom lacked their attendant banshee, even when hard destiny had brought low their estate, and hidden it under the smoke-blackened rafters of some poor cabin, may well have had much to do with his visionary gift. The rebellious political imagination of his grandfather came out in the young poet also. It was a dangerous freak then to wear a red Phyrgian cap in the streets of London, but he did this openly to show his republican sympathies in the days before the Reign of Terror had belied the early promise of the French Revolution. The constant and reckless generosity in money matters, and the intense shrinking from being paid, which were noticed in Blake, who would even 'turn pale when money was offered to him', strongly recall poor John O'Neil, who was reduced by worldly imprudence to the shift of concealing his good name under that of a woman who, however honest and prosperous, was socially inferior to him.

According to John Kelly, Yeats confessed in May 1900 that 'there was a good deal' in his 1893 edition of Blake, and in the work he and Edwin Ellis produced 'with which I am not in agreement'. Blake becomes significantly less Irish in the 1905 version of Yeats's introduction to his selection of Blake.

In the *Daily Express* (20 January 1895), Yeats refers to 'what Blake has called "minute appropriate words" ', and he repeats the phrase again in his *Book of Irish Verse*, when he says that William Allingham is 'a master of minute appropriate words'.

Yeats reinvents Blake's English Dissenting imagination as Irish, heroic, aristocratic and republican, the last a position Blake unflinchingly maintained throughout his life. Joyce, who read Yeats's distinguished selection of Blake, which was first published in 1893 and reprinted in 1905, also drew centrally on the Dissenting energies, which shape Blake's verse – Joyce's Blake is a working-class democrat, left-wing republican and domestic visionary.

If we look at Blake's 'The Smile', which Yeats includes mid-way in his selection, we can see that a phrase in that lyric helped to shape Yeats's most famous poem:

I will arise and go now, and go to Innisfree,
And a small cabin build there, of clay and wattles made:
Nine bean-rows will I have there, a hive for the honey-bee,
And live alone in the bee-loud glade.

And I shall have some peace there, for peace comes dropping
slow,
Dropping from the veils of the morning to where the cricket sings;
There midnight's all a glimmer, and noon a purple glow,
And evening full of the linnet's wings.

I will arise and go now, for always night and day
I hear lake water lapping with low sounds by the shore;
While I stand on the roadway, or on the pavements grey,
I hear it in the deep heart's core.

Yeats's ear was caught by the variation in the metre of 'Smile and Frown' between a smoothly conventional iambic movement, and a bunching of stresses – three strong stresses together – which is termed a 'molossus':

There is a Smile of Love
And there is a Smile of Deceit
And there is a Smile of Smiles
In which these two Smiles meet

And there is a Frown of Hate
And there is a Frown of disdain
And there is a Frown of Frowns
Which you strive to forget in vain

For it sticks in the Hearts deep Core
And it sticks in the deep Back bone
And no Smile ever was smild
But only one Smile alone

That betwixt the Cradle & Grave
It only once Smild can be
But when it once is Smild
Theres an end to all Misery.

The first line's 'There ís a Smíle of Lóve' is challenged by 'In which these twó Smíles méet'. Yeats heard that triple rhythm again at the beginning of the third stanza:

For it sticks in the Héarts déep Córe
And it sticks in the déep Báck bóne.

This was 1890, in London, where Yeats wrote 'The Lake Isle of Innisfree', a poem which he said was 'my first lyric with anything of my own music in it. I had begun to loosen rhythm as an escape from rhetoric and from that emotion of the crowd which rhetoric brings.' There is no mention of Blake here – Yeats is hiding his tracks. And indeed it has long been thought that that phrase in 'The Lake Isle of Innisfree' – 'I hear it in the deep heart's core' – was perhaps an echo of Shelley's *Adonais*:

'Wake thou', cried Misery, 'childless Mother, rise
Out of thy sleep, and shake, in thy heart's core,
A wound more fierce than his with tears and sighs.'

But Shelley's elegy for Keats does not help to inspire Yeats – rather the rhythm and the phrase 'Hearts deep Core' move from Blake's sinister, Gothic lyric into his youthful imagination. Yeats's impacted phrases: 'Nine bean-rows', 'bee-loud glade', 'deep heart's core', bring Blake's insistent rhythm into the poem and help to charge it with resolute certainty.

There is another link between Yeats's poem and Blake. In *The Four Zoas*, which Yeats discovered in manuscript, this passage occurs:

For Los & Enitharmon walkd forth on the dewy Earth
Contracting and expanding their all flexible senses
At will to murmur in the flowers small as the honey bee
At will to stretch across the heavens & step from star to star.

This paradisal moment brings its honey bee into Yeats's poem, where, following Blake's reverence for the small and the minute, he lists the contents of his island utopia. Joyce, who revered in addition to Blake that great Dissenting writer, Daniel Defoe, would also have detected the master's realism in those nine bean rows on the island.

If Blake leads us to a poem written early in Yeats's career, he also is present by anticipation in a number of poems which Yeats would write at the end of his life. He concludes the long essay he wrote as an introduction to his selection of Blake with this sentence and truncated quotation:

> Reengraved Time after Time
> Ever in their Youthful prime
> My Designs unchanged remain
> Time may rage by rage in vain
> For above Time's troubled Fountains
> On the Great Atlantic Mountains
> In my Golden House on high
> There they Shine Eternally.

Blake's phrase 'the Great Atlantic Mountains' spoke to Yeats, who would have recognized that it also appears in 'The French Revolution', where the war-like 'ancient peer', the Duke of Burgundy, asks:

> Shall this marble built heaven become a clay cottage, this earth an oak stool, and these mowers
> From the Atlantic mountains, mow down all this great starry harvest of six thousand years?

The Atlantic mountains are symbols of American republicanism – the mowers have emigrated from Marvell's England – and Yeats carefully crops his quotation from the Blake fragment he quotes at the end of his introduction:

> The Caverns of the Grave Ive seen
> And these I shewd to Englands Queen

But now the Caves of Hell I view
Who shall I dare to shew them to
What mighty Soul in Beautys form
Shall dauntless View the Infernal Storm
Egremonts Countess can controll
The flames of Hell that round me roll
If she refuse I still go on
Till the Heavens & Earth are gone
Still admired by Noble minds
Followed by Envy on the winds
Reengraved Time after Time
Ever in their Youthful prime
My Designs unchanged remain
Time may rage but rage in vain
For above Times troubled Fountains
On the Great Atlantic Mountains
In my Golden House on high
There they Shine Eternally

Blake is referring to his designs for Blair's poem, 'The Grave', which was dedicated to the Queen. Yeats strips away the reference, as he does the lines about the aristocratic Egremonts.

As a nationalist and republican Yeats would have puzzled his readers if he had included the lines about England's Queen and Egremont's Countess – by dropping them, he places the rest of the fragment in an Irish context. No one reading the lines can fail to place them in Sligo – for Irish readers the 'Great Atlantic Mountains' have to be Ben Bulben. We are beginning to glimpse late – very late – Yeats, because here, at the age of twenty-eight, in some deep, locked basement of his imaginative subconscious he is at work on his epitaph.

Yeats completed 'Under Ben Bulben' in September 1938. A year earlier he wrote 'An Acre of Grass':

Picture and book remain,
An acre of green grass
For air and exercise,

Now strength of body goes;
Midnight, an old house
Where nothing stirs but a mouse.

My temptation is quiet.
Here at life's end
Neither loose imagination,
Nor the mill of the mind
Consuming its rag and bone,
Can make the truth known.

Grant me an old man's frenzy,
Myself must I remake
Till I am Timon and Lear
Or that William Blake
Who beat upon the wall
Till Truth obeyed his call;

A mind Michael Angelo knew
That can pierce the clouds,
Or inspired by frenzy
Shake the dead in their shrouds;
Forgotten else by mankind,
An old man's eagle mind.

Blake seems to be Yeats's constant companion in the closing years of his life. The great Atlantic mountains are both republican symbols, and they are a transcendental symbol which Yeats explains in the edition of Blake he and Edwin Ellis published. In it they say that the mountains are eternally present for Blake partly because they are 'a symbolic place where imaginative creatures elude the washing of the sea of time and space, and the flood of the five senses'. This must be part of the meaning which that great Atlantic mountain, Ben Bulben, has for Yeats.

One day, perhaps, a scholar will comb the three-volume edition of Yeats to sift out his contributions from Ellis's. This sentence on Blake's early verse seems to me to be pure Yeats: 'the movements of his early verse are like the gambollings of some very powerful animal, still in its fluffy-footed and tottering babyhood.' The last two concatenated adjectives and the two *oo* sounds have a distinctively Yeatsian cadence.

The theme of time in Yeats – time and form – owes much to his reading of Blake. He quotes earlier in his 1893 introduction to Blake these lines of *The Book of Urizen* which describe the making of Enitharmon:

> Wonder, awe, fear, astonishment,
> Petrify the eternal myriads;
> At the first female form now separate
> They call'd her Pity, and fled.

'Pity' – Yeats defines as 'the vegetable mortal wife of Los', while Los 'though he is time', Yeats says, 'and more than one other great abstract thing is also Blake himself'. Blake's lines and Yeats's comments may be somewhere adjacent to Yeats's 'Peace':

> Ah, that Time could touch a form
> That could show what Homer's age
> Bred to be a hero's wage.
> 'Were not all her life but storm,
> Would not painters paint a form
> Of such noble lines,' I said,
> 'Such a delicate high head,
> All that sweetness amid charm,
> All that sweetness amid strength?'
> Ah, but peace that comes at length,
> Came when Time had touched her form.

Blake's insistence on form – on 'the more distinct, sharp, and wirey founding line, the more perfect the work of art' – that insistence reverberates in Yeats's use of the words 'form', 'line' and 'discipline'.

When he says of Robert Gregory: 'that stern colour and that delicate line / That are our secret discipline', Yeats is drawing on Blake:

We dreamed that a great painter had been born
To cold Clare rock and Galway rock and thorn,
To that stern colour and that delicate line
That are our secret discipline
Wherein the gazing heart doubles her might.
Soldier, scholar, horseman, he,
And yet he had the intensity
To have published all to be a world's delight.

He is also drawing on Blake's insistence on the importance of 'minute particulars', when he insists on the value of 'small things' in his poems: from the brown mice bobbing round and round the oatmeal chest in 'The Stolen Child' to the moorhens in 'Easter 1916', he is minutely particularizing details in order to locate vision.

Blake's word 'lineaments' is taken up by Yeats: 'ancient lineaments are blotted out' ('The Gyres'), 'Ireland's history in their lineaments trace' ('The Municipal Gallery Revisited'). He would have noted that Ireland and Sligo figure in Blake's visionary topography in *Jerusalem*:

And the Thirty-two Counties of the Four Provinces of
Ireland
Are thus divided: The Four Counties are in the Four Camps
Munster South in Reubens Gate, Connaut West in Josephs
Gate
Ulster North in Dans Gate, Leinster East in Judahs Gate . . .

And the names of the Thirty-two Counties of Ireland are
these
Under Judah & Issachar & Zebulun are Louth Longford
Eastmeath Westmeath Dublin Kildare Kings County
Queens County Wicklow Catherloh Wexford Kilkenny
And those under Reuben & Simeon & Levi are these
Waterford Tipperary Cork Limerick Kerry Clare
And those under Ephraim Manasseh & Benjamin are these
Galway Roscommon Mayo Sligo Leitrim

> And those under Dan Asher & Napthali are these
> Donegal Antrim Tyrone Fermanagh Armagh Londonderry
> Down Monaghan Cavan. These are the land of Erin
> (Chapter 3, *Jerusalem, Emanation of the Great Albion*)

Yeats argues in his introduction that Blake was a Gaelic aristocrat brought low. Yeats states:

> The very manner of Blake's writing has an Irish flavour, a lofty extravagance of invention and epithet, recalling the *Tain (Bo Cuilane)* and other old Irish epics and his mythology often brings to mind the tumultuous vastness of the ancient tales of god and demon that have come to us from the dawn of mystic tradition in what may fairly be called his fatherland.

The word 'lofty', which Yeats will later apply to John O'Leary, Lady Gregory and Maud Gonne, here webs Blake into what Yeats in the introduction calls 'ancestral turbulence' – an aesthetic and political energy, which he says showed again in Blake's brother, John, whom he compares to Shaun O'Neill – he means Shane O'Neill, the Gaelic aristocrat and rebel leader. And so Blake is behind the presentation of the old Fenian, John O'Leary:

> Beautiful lofty things: O'Leary's noble head;
> My father upon the Abbey stage, before him a raging crowd;
> 'This Land of Saints,' and then as the applause died out,
> 'Of plaster Saints'; his beautiful mischievous head thrown back.
> Standish O'Grady supporting himself between the tables
> Speaking to a drunken audience high nonsensical words;
> Augusta Gregory seated at her great ormolu table,
> Her eightieth winter approaching: 'Yesterday he threatened my life,
> I told him that nightly from six to seven I sat at this table,
> The blinds drawn up'; Maud Gonne at Howth station waiting a train,
> Pallas Athena in that straight back and arrogant head:
> All the Olympians; a thing never known again.

Yeats uses the adjective 'lofty' elsewhere in his verse – Constance Markiewicz, for example, is compared to a seagull 'When first it sprang out of the nest / Upon some lofty rock to stare' ('On a Political Prisoner').

When Yeats remarks that Blake 'is one of the great artificers of God who uttered great truths to a little clan', he is beginning the quest for the 'artifice of eternity' in 'Sailing to Byzantium' – a quest he is also preparing for when he remarks in the same introduction that Blake said 'Israel delivered from Egypt is art delivered from nature and imitation'. The Yeats who is later to write 'gather me / Into the artifice of eternity' is beginning his journey towards that supreme poem.

The Egyptian theme in Irish and English writing is almost always a republican trope, and Yeats describes Blake's work as 'republican art' – every one of his parts has, he says, a 'separate individuality and separate rights as in a republic'.

We can see this theme in 'Sailing to Byzantium':

I

That is no country for old men. The young
In one another's arms, birds in the trees,
– Those dying generations – at their song,
The salmon-falls, the mackerel-crowed seas,
Fish, flesh, or fowl, commend all summer long
Whatever is begotten, born, and dies.
Caught in that sensual music all neglect
Monuments of unageing intellect.

II

An aged man is but a paltry thing,
A tattered coat upon a stick, unless
Soul clap its hands, and sing, and louder sing
For every tatter in its mortal dress,
Nor is there singing school but studying
Monuments of its own magnificence;
And therefore I have sailed the seas and come
To the holy city of Byzantium.

III

O sages standing in God's holy fire
As in the gold mosaic of a wall,
Come from the holy fire, perne in a gyre,
And be the singing-masters of my soul.
Consume my heart away; sick with desire
And fastened to a dying animal
It knows not what it is, and gather me
Into the artifice of eternity.

IV

Once out of nature I shall never take
My bodily form from any natural thing,
But such a form as Grecian goldsmiths make
Of hammered gold and gold enamelling
To keep a drowsy Emperor awake;
Or set upon a golden bough to sing
To lords and ladies of Byzantium
Of what is past, or passing, or to come.

Yeats is remembering Blake as an old man, but he is also drawing on an anxiety about his own art – his traditional, metric art, which is now beginning to look archaic as free verse, or what Lawrence terms 'the poetry of the present', begins to consolidate Whitman's challenge to rhyme and metre. Whitman – and I think Lawrence – are in his mind here, as he remembers a question J. A. Symons asked in his study of Whitman, which was published in 1893: 'Is art destined to subside lower and lower into a kind of Byzantine decrepitude, as the toy of a so-called cultivated minority?' This anxiety about poetry's elite, minority status informs the poem, and is allayed only at the last minute where the poet, transformed into a golden toy, sings a temporal music that expresses the rhythms of nature.

Though it hasn't been noticed, Yeats is taking a risk in the poem by rhyming 'come' with 'Byzantium' – the ear enforces the rhyme strongly so that the 'um' at the end of the word reverberates dully. It is almost literally a bum rhyme – what Ted Hughes calls a 'deadlock rhyme', like the 'neglect / intellect' rhyme at the end of the first stanza, which is made even heavier by the word 'Monuments'. The 'me / eternity' rhyme at the end of the third stanza, which ghosts that classical word, is both facile and portentous. Yeats decides to have another go at the 'come / Byzantium' rhyme in the final couplet, where he reverses the rhyme order and introduces the cadences of the speaking voice, as well as picking up on the cadence of 'Fish, flesh, or fowl', and 'Whatever is begotten, born, and dies'. The final line redeems and transforms the previous, overdone rhyme, rather in the way that Lawrence in 'Bare Fig-Trees' rejects the over-adjectival lines he's just begun the poem with, and especially the adjective 'untarnished', in the line 'I say untarnished, but I mean opaque'.

James Joyce, who must have read Yeats's selection, also portrays Blake as a republican artist, stating that even among the members of the circle that included Wollstonecraft and Tom Paine 'Blake was the only one with the courage to wear the red cap in the street, emblem of the new age'. He took it off, Joyce says, after the September Massacres. Joyce points out that Blake 'continually insists on the importance of the pure, clear line that evokes and creates the image against the background of the uncreated void'. And Joyce, like Yeats, is pointing to lineation in Blake as an essentially republican aesthetic. Joyce's many allusions to Blake, his profound admiration for the poet, still await a definitive study – the nets of nationality, language, religion, come from *The Book of Urizen*; Stephen Dedalus's idea of the 'smithy of my soul', where he will forge the uncreated conscience of his race, derives from *The Book of Los* and *Milton*. Stephen's 'Am I walking into eternity along Sandymount strand?' derives from *The Book of Los*.

Perhaps most wonderfully and tenderly, this passage from Joyce's Trieste lecture on Blake (which I have quoted elsewhere; see p. 297) lets us see Bloom beginning to form deep in Joyce's imaginative subconscious:

Ought we to be amazed that the symbolic beings Los, Urizen, Vala, Tiriel, and Enitharmon and the shades of Homer and Milton should come from their ideal world to a poor room in London, or that no incense that greeted their coming was the smell of Indian tea and eggs fried in lard? Would this be the first time in the history of the world that the Eternal One has spoken through the mouth of the humble?

It is difficult to read this deeply democratic sentence and not see Bloom making breakfast, indeed see the whole structure and conception of Joyce's masterpiece beginning to unfold.

In *Milton*, Blake says 'A Moment equals a pulsation of the artery' and then says:

> Every Time less than a pulsation of the artery
> Is equal in its period & value to Six Thousand Years.

A few lines later he says 'Within a Moment: a Pulsation of the Artery'. The noun 'pulsation' does not lend itself to poetry, but Yeats was taken by the repeated phrase 'pulsation of the artery', and adapted it in 'A Meditation in Time of War':

> For one throb of the artery,
> While on that old grey stone I sat
> Under the old wind-broken tree,
> I knew that One is animate,
> Mankind inanimate phantasy.

I can't find that my heart returns an echo to this sentiment, but the link to Blake – even to Wordsworth in the cadence of 'that old grey stone' – suggests that Yeats is placing himself as the latest Romantic poet to confront war in a single pulse of subjectivity.

Blake's prophecies are acts of witness, which is how Van Morrison (in 'Let the Slave', *A Sense of Wonder*) delivers these lines from *America* and *Vala, or The Four Zoas*:

> Let the slave grinding at the mill run, out into the field:
> Let him look up into the heavens & laugh in the bright air;
> Let the inchained soul shut up in darkness and in sighing,
> Whose face has never seen a smile in thirty weary years;
> Rise and look out, his chains are loose, his dungeon doors
> are open.
> And let his wife and children return from the oppressor's scourge;
> They look behind at every step & believe it is a dream.

Singing. The Sun has left his blackness, & has found a fresher
 morning
And the fair Moon rejoices in the clear & cloudless night;
For Empire is no more, and now the Lion & Wolf shall cease.

What is the price of Experience do men buy it for a song
Or wisdom for a dance in the street? No it is bought with
 the price
Of all that a man hath his house his wife his children
Wisdom is sold in the desolate market where none come to buy
And in the witherd field where the farmer plows for bread
 in vain

It is an easy thing to triumph in the summers sun
And in the vintage & to sing on the wagon loaded with corn
It is an easy thing to talk of patience to the afflicted
To speak the laws of prudence to the houseless wanderer
To listen to the hungry ravens' cry in wintry season
When the red blood is filld with wine & with the marrow
 of lambs

It is an easy thing to laugh at wrathful elements
To hear the dog howl at the wintry door, the ox in the
 slaughter house moan
To see a god on every wind & a blessing on every blast
To hear sounds of love in the thunder storm that destroys
 our enemies house
To rejoice in the blight that covers his field, & the sickness
 that cuts off his children
While our olive & vine sing & laugh round our door & our
 children bring fruits & flowers

Then the groan & the dolor are quite forgotten & the slave
 grinding at the mill
And the captive in chains & the poor in the prison, & the
 soldier in the field
When the shattered bone hath laid him groaning among the
 happier dead.

Blake writes 'Empire is no more' in the opening passage from *America*, while Morrison adds 'the' to make it a specific reference to the British Empire, which is Yeats's point in 'The Valley of the Black Pig':

> The dews drop slowly and dreams gather: unknown spears
> Suddenly hurtle before my dream-awakened eyes,
> And then the clash of fallen horsemen and the cries
> Of unknown perishing armies beat about my ears.
> We who still labour by the cromlech on the shore,
> The grey cairn on the hill, when day sinks drowned in dew,
> Being weary of the world's empires, bow down to you,
> Master of the still stars and of the flaming door.

Set in the North of Ireland, near Crossmaglen, where the Black Pig's Dyke formed an ancient Ulster frontier, the poem draws on Blake to prophesy the end of empire. In the last line, Yeats takes another aesthetic risk by including 'of' twice – the soft *f* sounds play against the hard dentals and the repeated, stabbing *st* sounds.

Blake's phantasmagoric poem, 'London', is behind 'Easter 1916':

> I wander thro' the each charter'd street,
> Near where the charter'd Thames does flow.
> And mark in every face I meet
> Marks of weakness, marks of woe.
>
> In every cry of every Man,
> In every Infants cry of fear,
> In every voice: in every ban,
> The mind-forg'd manacles I hear
>
> How the Chimney-sweepers cry
> Every blackening Church appalls,
> And the hapless Soldiers sigh
> Runs in blood down Palace walls
>
> But most thro' midnight streets I hear
> How the youthful Harlots curse

> Blasts the new-born Infant's tear
> And blights with plagues the marriage hearse.

Yeats draws on this poem's vision of the urban crowd, when he describes the republican activists in the Dublin crowds, as they leave work:

> I have met them at close of day
> Coming with vivid faces
> From counter or desk among grey
> Eighteenth-century houses.

The Georgian houses carry a memory of Blake's late eighteenth-century lyrics, and his image of palace walls spattered with the blood of executed soldiers acts as a prolepsis for the executions in Kilmainham Gaol. River, city, crowd – both poems confront them, while the *deibdhe* rhyme 'faces' makes the opening lines a softened triplet, which has the effect of adding more stress and prominence to the line-break on 'grey', and so adds even more authority to the eighteenth-century houses, which are paradoxically destabilized by that hanging adjective and by the imminent revolution forming in the crowds (in fact, as we know, the Dublin crowd was angered by the Uprising).

But what drew Yeats and also Van Morrison to Blake was that strain of visionary Protestant radicalism – at times head-banging, obsessive, obscure and relentless in its search for secret codes and meanings, at others capable of a natural simplicity and boundless wonder above and beyond institutional ways of thinking. It was this quality or energy that spoke to the eternally anti-institutional Joyce. One day perhaps a study of this imagination will be written – for the moment we need to read Blake through Yeats, and Yeats through Blake.

A Republican Cento: 'Tintern Abbey'

Wordsworth's poem – a kind of irregular ode – announces itself through its rambling title as the work of a returning tourist: 'Lines written a few miles above Tintern Abbey, on revisiting the banks of the Wye during a tour, July 13, 1798'. Its date – 13 July 1798 – strikes no chords now for an English reader, but for a French or an Irish reader the date is resonant. In the summer of 1798, Irish republicans, overwhelmingly Catholic and Presbyterian, rose up against the Dublin government and tried to establish a republic on the French model. Wolfe Tone, one of the United Irish leaders, was captured on board a French warship in Lough Swilly off the coast of Donegal, brought to Dublin, tried and sentenced to death.

For the French reader, 13 July is the eve of Bastille Day. On 14 July 1789 – the last two digits are reversed by Wordworth's date, 1798 – a Parisian revolutionary crowd attacked the Bastille and destroyed it. But the date has another meaning: on 13 July 1793, Charlotte Corday assassinated Jean-Paul Marat, the hero of the Paris mob (Marat's death in his bath is commemorated in David's famous painting, which was presented to the Convention of the Republic in November 1793). On that day, as Kenneth Johnston points out, Wordsworth's former landlord in Orléans was executed with eight others after a political trial. Annette Vallon's brother, Paul, had been implicated in a 'trumped-up assassination charge' made by Léonard Bourdon, the Convention's representative in Orléans. Bourdon was a particularly harsh Jacobin, and the case was frequently discussed in the British press as an example of revolutionary terror.

Wordsworth's five years takes us back to that event, to Marat's assassination and to Charlotte Corday's execution which took place, not at the usual site the Place de Grève, where the Pompidou Centre now stands, but on the Place de la Révolution, where Louis XVI and Marie Antoinette were executed. Corday was executed by the same blade that clumsily decapitated Louis XVI.

All this was in Wordsworth's mind as he numbered the years that had passed since his last visit. He had visited France for the first time in 1790 (and was in Calais on 14 July 1790, when all the bells rang out at 11.30 in the morning) in the excitement of the new revolution. As Wordsworth and his companion Robert Jones made their way through France, they each carried a small bundle of 'needments' on their heads in peasant fashion. He made a second visit in November 1791, when he visited Paris, where he was close to the Girondins, who were the sentimentalists among the Revolutionaries and are often seen as moderate revolutionaries. Wordsworth also visited the National Assembly and the Jacobin Club. Then he moved to Orléans, where he had an affair with a young royalist, Annette Vallon, or married her secretly as Michael Baldwin argues. She gave birth to their daughter Caroline in December 1792 (by this time Wordsworth had returned to England). He became friendly in Orléans with Michel Beaupuy, a republican army officer, whose revolutionary spirit he commemorates in *The Prelude*, and who died fighting royalist insurgents. He also was in Paris when the September massacres took place (egged on by Marat the Parisian mob murdered over a thousand jailed priests and aristocrats).

Some Wordsworth scholars believe that Wordsworth made a third visit to Paris in October 1793. He told Thomas Carlyle that he had witnessed the execution of a French politician called Antoine-Joseph Gorsas, and in an edition of Burke Wordsworth owned he wrote next to Gorsas's name, 'I knew this man!'

In the poem, Wordsworth codes his personal guilts and political anxieties – he had abandoned Annette Vallon – through a series of allusions to Milton. The opening lines are elegiac, slightly weary and dispirited:

> Five years have passed; five summers, with the length
> Of five long winters!

Here Wordsworth is partly echoing the opening lines of Milton's *Lycidas*, his elegy for Edward King:

> Yet once more O ye laurels, and once more
> Ye myrtles brown, with ivy never sere.

He is also echoing, partly through the use of repetition, partly through the closeness of 'five' to 'evil', these lines from *Paradise Lost*:

> More safe I sing with mortal voice unchanged
> To hoarse or mute, though fallen on evil days,
> On evil days though fallen, and evil tongues.

The presence of these lines behind Wordsworth's establishes a gruelling, embattled tone, which shifts as he hears the murmur of the waters.

By stating that he can 'again hear / These waters rolling from their mountain springs / With a sweet inland murmur', Wordsworth implicitly notices that at this point on the Solent, the river isn't affected by the tides – tides that carry the British fleet. The river is pure at this point, its source is in the mountains, which signify wisdom, prophecy, authority, solitude. Wordsworth again echoes Milton, who writes:

> Whence Adam soon repealed
> The doubts that in his heart arose: and now
> Led on, yet sinless, with desire to know
> What nearer might concern him, how this world
> Of Heaven and Earth conspicuous first began;
> When, and whereof created, for what cause;
> What within Eden, or without was done
> Before his memory; as one whose drouth
> Yet scarce allayed still eyes the current stream,
> Whose liquid murmur heard new thirst excites,
> Proceeded thus to ask his heav'nly guest.

Perhaps the long *ee* at the beginning of 'Eden' stayed in Wordsworth's ear, because as well as the 'sweet' murmur of the water, he in the next line describes the 'steep and lofty cliffs', then the 'wild secluded scene', which impresses thoughts 'of more deep seclusion'. The sound is caught up a few lines later by 'season' and the repeated word 'green'.

The scene in the Wye Valley is Edenic and sinless, though Adam's repeated doubts have a political texture, as does the stream's 'murmur' in both passages – this could be the murmur of a revolutionary crowd, something both poets knew about. Also in the Bible 'murmur' is used for rebellion against God and Moses. In the next line, we meet 'these steep and lofty cliffs', a moment which prepares us for the imaginative centre of the poem:

> The sounding cataract
> Haunted me like a passion: the tall rock,
> The mountain, and the deep and gloomy wood.

– where the long *ee* sound in 'me' is dropped into 'deep', and so loses any sense of the Edenic. It loses it also, because this is Wordsworth's way of naturalizing within the landscape the Tarpeian Rock from which traitors were flung in classical Rome – here it works by association with the guillotine which, as I've suggested, is silently referred to in the poem's date. The word 'cliffs' concatenates with 'rock' and 'cataract'. The mountain is *La Montagne*, the raised seats in the French National Assembly where Robespierre and the Jacobins congregated, while the gloomy wood is the malevolent cunning of history, as well as the force of Burkean counter-revolutionary pessimism (Burke had been a Member of Parliament for Bristol). Carlyle, in his account of his conversation with Wordsworth about the Girondin Gorsas, says that Wordsworth 'witnessed the struggle of Girondin and Mountain'. The wood may also be a recollection of the 'selva selvaggia e aspra e forte' in the opening lines of the *Inferno*. Dante, in the next line, says of the wood 'che nel pensier rinova la paura!' ('the thought of which renews my fear'), and it is more than a childhood fear which Wordsworth is recollecting.

The word 'lofty' in the opening lines also picks up *Paradise Lost*:

That spot, to which I point, is Paradise,
Adam's abode; those lofty shades, his bower.
Thy way thou canst not miss, me mine requires.

'Lofty' is used twice more in Milton's republican epic:

So spake the fiend and with necessity,
The tyrant's plea, excused his devilish deeds.
Then from his lofty stand on that high tree
Down he alights among the sportful Herd.

The word 'lofty' can be both Adamic – embowered – and Satanic, taking an absolute position like Charles I raising his standard to begin the Civil War in 1642. Psychologically, Wordsworth wants to design a type of personal and political oxymoron, where absolute opposites are combined, like ice and fire in a love poem. He wants to merge his internal hell with the external paradisal landscape, to make opposites anxiously suffuse each other, as they do constantly in Seamus Heaney's poetry, where the natural world often carries ominous smells, textures, sounds.

Far off, Wordsworth's 'waters, rolling from their mountain springs' allude to Milton's 'eyes, that roll in vain', while the epic journey in *Paradise Lost* down to, then up out of the underworld – the theme of darkness and blindness – is reflected in the way in which Wordsworth's 'more deep seclusion' echoes Milton's 'dim suffusion veiled', a figure for his blindness. Wordsworth's ear is running with guttural *k* sounds: *cliffs, secluded, seclusion, connect, quiet, come*, and these sounds are abetted by the reiterated 'again' to underline and give greater force to 'this dark sycamore', which as well as carrying a concealed pun on 'sick' anticipates the counter-revolutionary 'deep and gloomy wood'. Because there is a significant allusion to *Othello* later in the poem, I think that Desdemona's willow song is behind the sycamore. It is a song that was sung by Desdemona's mother's maid, Barbary, who was forsaken by her lover, and who died singing it. Desdemona, who will shortly be murdered, sings it:

The poor soul sat singing by a sycamore tree,
  Sing all a green willow;

Her hand on her bosom, her head on her knee,
Sing willow, willow, willow.
The fresh streams ran by her and murmured her moans;
Sing willow, willow, willow.
Her salt tears fell from her, and soft'ned the stones –
Lay by these.

Subliminally, there is a political texture to 'plots' in 'orchard plots', and it's hard not to ghost 'corpses' in 'copses', as 'unripe' in the previous line carries the *r* to touch 'copses':

their unripe fruits,
Among the woods and copses lose themselves,
Nor, with their green and simple hue, disturb
The wild green landscape.

These lines Wordsworth changed to:

their unripe fruits,
Are clad in one green hue, and lose themselves
'Mid groves and copses.

In the revised lines the *r* and *o* in 'groves' passes over to 'copses'.

The word 'wild', which Wordsworth uses five times in the poem, was often used by the government to describe Jacobin activity (there is a faint echo of this in *Pride and Prejudice*, where Elizabeth is described as 'wild' by her mother, and where Lydia has a 'wild volatility'). The word 'green' is also used four times, and here Wordsworth wants to remind his readers of the English greenwood, a place deeply embedded in the cultural memory and mythology, where Robin Hood and his men forever fight against the Norman yoke. That phrase 'unripe fruits' looks forward to the 'coarser pleasures of my boyish days' – there is both an eroticism here, and an innocent denial of it. These are untouched breasts, which want neither to be stroked or looked at. But the phrase is close to 'fruit unripe' in the Player King's speech in *Hamlet*, where, after the Player Queen asserts that she will never marry again after his death, he replies:

> I do believe you think what now you speak,
> But what we do determine of we break.
> Purpose is but the slave of memory,
> Of violent birth, but poor validity,
> Which now like fruit unripe sticks on the tree,
> But fall unshaken when they mellow be.

The idea of sexual betrayal is part of the image of unripe fruit.

The hedgerows he describes I read as symbols of enclosed private property, as Enclosure began to remodel the landscape, taking over common land, and moving agriculture away from the medieval open-field system. Wordsworth softens and palliates the hedgerows into 'hardly hedge-rows, little lines / Of sportive wood run wild'. The wreaths of smoke ('these pastoral farms, / Green to the very door, and wreathes of smoke / Sent up, in silence, from the trees!') are subliminally a memory of gun smoke, and here Wordsworth is echoing his friend Coleridge's 'Frost at Midnight', which was written during the winter of the same year:

> Therefore all seasons shall be sweet to thee,
> Whether the summer clothe the general earth
> With greenness, or the redbreast sit and sing
> Bitwixt the tufts of snow on the bare branch
> Of mossy apple-tree, while the nigh thatch
> Smokes in the sun-thaw; whether the eave-drops fall
> Heard only in the trances of the blast.
> Or if the secret ministry of frost
> Shall hang them up in the silent icicles,
> Quietly shining to the quiet moon.

Wordsworth's phrase 'the quiet of the sky' echoes Coleridge's repeated use of 'quiet', but he is also remembering the smoking thatch, and the political, the ominous, phrase 'secret ministry', as well as the blunt 'hang them up'. That redbreast, too, carries an association with blood or with military uniforms. The word 'wreathes' is also ominous, suggesting a death or deaths are being commemorated.

A few lines earlier, he has used the political word 'disturb' just after the political adjective 'simple':

> Nor with their green and simple hue, disturb
> The wild green landscape.

His point is they both do and don't disturb the wild green landscape (after the 1798 Uprising in Ireland, the phrase could signify another, displaced politics, which may be why he dropped the line). The verb 'disturb' occurs six times in *Paradise Lost*, and is always associated with actions undertaken by the fallen angels: Adam tells Eve that Satan aims to 'disturb / Conjugal love'. Echoing this moment, Wordsworth has simultaneously introduced and denied the idea of a disturbance, as well as letting a pause build after 'hue'. This palliative strategy is developed in the 'hardly hedge-rows' moment – ever so slightly military this, crossed with lines of verse – where the 'little lines / Of sportive wood run wild' are like the kind of celebrating revolutionary crowds Wordsworth encountered on his first visit to France, crowds whose enthusiasm fused with his own. The hedgerows are festive, as if nature is taking part in one of the many civic festivals that took place in revolutionary France, and which Wordsworth witnessed. They also suggest a type of merry, communal pastoral verse, rather different from the kind composed by Wordsworth, who has airbrushed out a derelict pastoral on the banks of the Wye. The 'sportive wood' has 'run wild' – again that Jacobin adjective – and makes 'these pastoral farms / Green to the very door'. Once more, this is a crowd image of a green sea gently massing at the doorways of private property.

Then follows a curious moment: the wreaths of smoke are

> Sent up, in silence from among the trees,
> With some uncertain notice, as might seem,
> Of vagrant dwellers in the houseless woods,
> Or of some hermit's cave, where by his fire
> The hermit sits alone.

The 'uncertain notice' is partly a figure for Wordsworth's oblique recognition that the woods and the abbey were at that time full of itinerant, impoverished metal workers who lived in little huts among the ruins of the monastery. A contemporary traveller observed 'the poverty and wretchedness of the inhabitants are remarkable'. A contemporary poem noted 'Black forges, smoke and noisy hammers beat'. As Marjorie Levinson suggests in a seminal essay, Wordsworth's 'pastoral prospect is a fragile affair, artfully assembled by acts of exclusion'.

The destruction of the French Church, which had been the instrument of a corrupt ruling class, is obviously analogous to the English dissolution of the monasteries under Henry VIII: perhaps there is a trace of Protestant guilt and anxiety in the poem; or perhaps those emotions are allayed by the ruins absorbed into the landscape. A lot is being edited out, for as Levinson shows, Tintern was an ironworking village, the river was a thoroughfare for barges carrying coal from local mines, and the area was unusually active because there was a war on. The forests were populated by vagrants, who were casualties of a failing economy. Charcoal furnaces were dotted along the riverbank.

Levinson also notes that wealthy landowners would sometimes hire a man to live in a picturesque hut and grow a picturesque beard: Wordsworth's hermit sounds more natural, but in using that figure to represent the 'sole self' – a type of Protestant individualism – Levinson suggests that Wordsworth betrays 'something of the anxiety' which he must have felt at the time, something of his own self-disgust.

Levinson's essay is stringent, finely intelligent, historically and socially alert, but she misses the allusion to *King Lear* in the phrase 'houseless woods':

> Poor naked wretches, wheresoe'er you are,
> That bide the pelting of this pitiless storm,
> How shall your houseless heads and unfed sides,
> Your loop'd and window'd raggedness, defend you
> From seasons such as these?

By a type of allusive code, the forest dwellers enter the poem through that adjective 'houseless'. They are ragged, hungry figures exposed to the storm of history and economics. But he is shutting them out, partly because they embody his guilty conscience.

The word 'houseless' is also used by Oliver Goldsmith at the beginning of 'The Traveller':

> Remote, unfriended, melancholy, slow,
> Or by the lazy Scheld, or wandering Po;
> Or onward, where the rude Carinthian boor
> Against the houseless stranger shuts the door.

In a sense, Wordsworth is both opening and shutting a door in these lines. As Geoffrey Hartmann observes, an object in the poem does not materialize before it is effaced and smudged; a thought does not find full articulation before it is qualified or deconstructed; a point of view is not established before it dissolves into a series of impressions.

This layered, evasive, allusive method is partly a response to state censorship, and to the legal penalties for criticising the government. This can be observed in line 25, where Wordsworth says that in his long absence these 'forms of beauty have not been to me, / As is a landscape to a blind man's eye'. The repeated *i* sounds figure the first person pronoun here, and there are five other uses of the word 'eye' in the poem. The blind man is a figure for Milton, who in his blindness dictated his republican epic to an amanuensis during the early years of the restored monarchy in the 1660s. In *Samson Agonistes*, he says:

> So fond are mortal men
> Fall'n into wrath divine,
> As their own ruin on themselves to invite,
> Insensate left, or to sense reprobate
> And with blindness internal struck.

A series of *i* sounds foreground both 'blind' and implicitly the first person pronoun, as happens in the answering chorus:

> But he, though blind of sight,
> Despised and thought extinguished quite,
> With inward eyes illuminated,

> His fiery virtue roused
> From under ashes into sudden flame.

Milton is the major influence on Wordsworth's style and imagination, and Milton as Samson – as the blind English prophet trapped inside the restored Stuart state – is a figure for Wordsworth in a state at war with revolutionary France. And Wordsworth carries within him the survivor's guilt of someone who has been close to the September massacres, as well as the guilt of someone who has betrayed a lover and abandoned their child.

Milton is invoked again in the next line: 'But oft in lonely rooms, and mid the din / Of towns and cities'. In *Paradise Lost*, Satan declares war:

> He spake; and to confirm his words, out flew
> Millions of flaming swords, drawn from the thighs
> Of mighty cherubim; the sudden blaze
> Far round illumined hell; highly they raged
> Against the highest, and fierce with grasped arms
> Clashed on their sounding shields the din of war,
> Hurling defiance toward the vault of Heaven.

The word 'din' is used five times by Milton of infernal noise:

> dreadful was the din
> Of hissing through the hall, thick swarming now
> With complicated monsters.

Noise in Milton is always a figure for royalism and war – war caused by royalist ideology – and in Wordsworth the word 'din' picks this up, as well as his experience of noisy, political Paris. Also, he displaces the noise of the smiths and the metalworkers in and around the abbey on to far-off towns and cities.

At this point, the cadence of Wordsworth's verse takes the *wee* sound in 'hours of weariness' and passes it like a baton to 'sensations sweet' and to 'passing even into my purer mind' (he means his puritan mind, like Milton's). I'll allow for the moment the subliminal political possibilities of the phrase that follows – 'tranquil restoration' – but a curious thing happens immediately after it, when Wordsworth says in a hesitant manner

> such, perhaps,
> As may have had no trivial influence
> On that best portion of a good man's life;
> His little, nameless, unremembered acts
> Of kindness and of love.

There is a note of special pleading, of guilt, here, and its source, in literary terms, is in Milton's preface to a pamphlet called *The Judgement of Martin Bucer Concerning Divorce*: 'imprudent Canons; whereby good men in the best portion of their lives . . . are compell'd to civil Indignities, which by the Law of Moses bad Men were not compelled to.' Effectively, Wordsworth has divorced Annette Vallon, and is trying to settle terms with his guilty feelings. He is remembering Milton's unhappy first marriage to a royalist, and his divorce pamphlets.

Then Wordsworth begins to cheer himself up:

> Nor less, I trust,
> To them I may have owed another gift,
> Of aspect more sublime.

The term 'sublime' belongs to a republican aesthetic, while the term 'beautiful' belongs to a royalist aesthetic. Wordsworth is here signalling his political allegiances, and he is reinforcing them by another allusion to Milton, a passage late in *Paradise Lost*, where Adam says:

> Eve, thy contempt of life and pleasure seems
> To argue in thee something more sublime
> And excellent than what thy mind contemns.

This begins the curious doubling of Adam and Eve by Wordsworth and his sister, Dorothy. This passage is joyful as 'that blessed mood' lifts the 'weary weight / Of all this unintelligible world', and the power of harmony and the deep power of joy allow us to 'see into the life of things'.

Wordsworth appears to have reached an elevated and serene conclusion, but immediately he falls back into despair:

> If this
> Be but a vain belief, yet, oh! how oft,
> In darkness, and amid the many shapes
> Of joyless day-light; when the fretful stir
> Unprofitable, and the fever of the world,
> Have hung upon the beatings of my heart.

Two Shakespearean tragedies are in Wordsworth's mind at this point in the poem: the moment early in *Hamlet* where Hamlet says 'How weary, stale, flat, and unprofitable / Seem to me all the uses of this world', and the moment in *Macbeth* when Lady Macbeth says of Duncan: 'After life's fitful fever he sleeps well.'

The end of Shakespeare's tragedy is also present in the next passage, where Wordsworth is really turning the 'sylvan Wye' into the question 'why?' He speaks of 'gleams of half-extinguish'd thought', which picks up the semichorus in *Samson Agonistes*: 'But he, though blind of sight, / Despised and thought extinguished quite'. Then in the next line, when Wordsworth speaks of 'many recognitions faint', he is picking up the phrase 'dim suffusion veiled,' which Milton uses at the opening of Book Three of *Paradise Lost* to describe his blindness. Blindness, we must recognize, is a metaphor for being trapped in an oppressive political state: the German artist Max Beckmann has a small bronze statue he cast in Germany in 1934 called *Man in the Dark*. It is clearly a comment on Hitler's seizure of power the previous year.

Again Wordsworth invokes Milton in the line 'And somewhat of a sad perplexity', remembering the 'perplexities' of 'wand'ring thought' in *Samson Agonistes*. But then a curious change of mood occurs, as Wordsworth remembers his boyhood, 'when like a roe / I bounded o'er the mountains'. This is a memory of the last verse of *The Song of Solomon*, where the bride is singing to her bridegroom about their anticipated sexual union: 'Make haste, my beloved, and be thou like to a roe or to a young hart upon the mountains of spices.'

Wordsworth has displaced memories of Annette Vallon on to his innocent solitary boyhood – here she is calling him to her bed. But he is also designing a tortured gothic moment and probably recalling a passage in *Caleb Williams*, Godwin's classic political novel, published in 1794. Caleb escapes from prison where he was held on a trumped-up charge made by his malevolent aristocratic patron, Falkland, who is partly modelled on Edmund Burke. He exclaims:

> Ah, this is indeed to be a man!
>
> These wrists were lately galled with fetters, all my motions, whether I rose or sat down, were echoed to with the clanking of chains; I was tied down like a wild beast, and could not move but in a circle of a few feet in a circumference. Now I can run, fleet as a greyhound; and leap like a young roe upon the mountains . . . Sacred and indescribable moment, when a man regains his rights!

This allusion helps to explain the curious comparison 'more like a man / Flying from something that he dreads, than one / Who sought the thing he loved'. He is like Caleb Williams, a fugitive from corrupt justice, but he is also an absconding lover, who has fled the murderous politics of republican France. A memory of his affair with Annette Vallon is being projected on to this memory of his boyhood in the woods:

> For nature then
> (The coarser pleasures of my boyish days
> And their glad animal movements all gone by,)
> To me was all in all.

It's as if adult sex and adolescent masturbation are being merged, and then placed back in time to make them innocent and harmless. But there is a deeper allusion.

Othello at the beginning of the play describes to the Duke how he met Desdemona:

> Her father loved me; oft invited me;
> Still questioned me the story of my life
> From year to year, the battles, sieges, fortune
> That I have passed.

I ran it through, even from my boyish days
To th' very moment that he bade me tell it.
Wherein I spoke of most disastrous chances,
Of moving accidents by flood and field,
Of hairbreadth scapes i' th' imminent deadly breach,
Of being taken by the insolent foe
And sold to slavery, of my redemption thence
And portance in my travel's history,
Wherein of anters vast and deserts idle,
Rough quarries, rocks, and hills whose heads touch heaven,
It was my hint to speak.

Othello speaks as a survivor of many battles and disasters, and his image of the rough quarries, rocks and hills 'whose heads touch heaven', is somewhere in Wordsworth's memory, as he looks at the sounding cataract and summons rough textures, abrasions, perhaps coarser pleasures. His love affair wasn't tragic, like Othello's, but it was clearly painful.

In his unpublished republican polemic, *A Letter to the Bishop of Llandaff*, written in 1793, Wordsworth used similar imagery:

Appearing as I do the advocate of republicanism, let me not be misunderstood. I am well aware from the abuse of the executive power in states that there is no single European nation but what affords a melancholy proof that if at this moment the original authority of the people should be restored, all that could be expected from such restoration would in the end be but a change of tyranny.

We remember that the word 'restoration' appears in 'Tintern Abbey', and we may note that in the pamphlet Wordsworth uses it not of a restored monarchy but of popular sovereignty – Rousseau's central political idea. But there is a closer connection:

Considering the nature of a republic in reference to the present condition of Europe, your Lordship stops here: but a philosopher will extend his views much farther; having dried up the source from which flows the corruption of the public opinion, he will be sensible that the stream will go on gradually refining itself. I must also add that the coercive power is of the necessity so strong in all the old governments that a people could not but at first make an abuse of that liberty which a legitimate republic supposes.

It's then that Wordsworth employs an image of a republic maturing into legitimacy that is reprised in the lines I quoted from 'Tintern Abbey': 'The animal just released from its stall will exhaust the overflow of its spirits in a round of wanton vagaries, but it will soon return to itself and enjoy its freedom in moderate and regular delight.' The sexual imagery is softened into the metaphor of a disciplined consumption of alcohol. The coarser pleasures of his boyish days, now gone by like their glad animal movements, is a version of this idea of acquired temperance.

The phrase 'all in all', in the poem, by a circuitous route returns us to the image of a murdered king. Jonathan Bate in his study *Shakespeare and the English Romantic Imagination*, has pointed to an allusion to *Hamlet* in these lines. It's when Horatio tells Hamlet that his father was a 'goodly king', and Hamlet replies: 'A was a man, take him for all in all, / I shall not look upon his like again.' Hamlet, haunted by the ghost of a murdered father and King, is evoked by Wordsworth, who is haunted by a love affair with a courageous royalist, and we must assume by a form of regicide guilt. No wonder, then, that he softens these extremely uncomfortable memories by saying: 'The sounding cataract / Haunted me like a passion.' An innocent waterfall, we assume, but the problem is that 'cataract' is an uncomfortable, guttural, gothic word. It is a figure for the roar of history, and it is a cry of pain which anticipates 'the still sad music of humanity'. The word comes into Wordsworth's verse from *King Lear* and *Paradise Lost*:

> Blow, winds, and crack your cheeks! rage! blow!
> You cataracts and hurricanoes, spout
> Till you have drench'd our steeples, drown'd the cocks!
> You sulphurous and thought-executing fires.
> Vaunt-couriers of oak-cleaving thunderbolts,
> Singe my white head! And thou, all-shaking thunder,
> Smite flat the thick rotundity o' th' world!
> Crack nature's moulds, all germens spill at once,
> That make ungrateful man!

In Shakespeare's lines, 'cataracts' is stretched and pulled by *hurricanoes, crack, cheeks, rage, cocks, executing, couriers, oak-cleaving, all-shaking, thick, crack, ungrateful*. This is to highlight the *k* sounds, the gutturals, but the *t*'s, the dentals, in 'cataract' bounce around in *spout, till, steeples, thought-executing, vaunt, thunderbolts, white, flat, rotunditiy, nature's, that, ungrateful*. The nodal word 'cataract' lodged itself in Milton's imagination:

> but of God observed
> The one just man alive; by his command
> Shall build a wondrous ark, as thou beheld'st,
> To save himself, and household from amidst
> A world devote to universal wrack.
> No sooner he with them of man and beast
> Select for life shall in the ark be lodged,
> And sheltered round, but all the cataracts
> Of heav'n set open on the earth shall pour
> Rain day and night, all fountains of the deep,
> Broke up, shall heave the ocean to usurp
> Beyond all bounds . . .

The cataracts of heaven, the Archangel Michael says, will move the paradisal mountain down the 'great river to the opening gulf'. Here, Milton is underlining 'cataracts' with *ark, wrack, broke, great, gulf*, and he is remembering his account of hell at the beginning of the poem:

> what if all
> Her stores were opened, and this firmament
> Of hell should spout her cataracts of fire,
> Impendent horrors, threatening hideous fall
> One day upon our heads; while we perhaps,
> Designing or exhorting glorious war,
> Caught in a fiery tempest shall be hurled,
> Each on his own rock transfixed, the sport or prey
> Of racking whirlwinds, or for ever sunk
> Under yon boiling ocean, wrapt in chains,

> There to converse with everlasting groans,
> Unrespited, unpitied, unreprieved,
> Ages of hopeless end.

Off of 'cataracts' Milton bounces *rock, racking, sunk, groans, ages*, and Wordsworth remembers this passage as he evokes 'the tall rock, / The mountain, and the deep and gloomy wood'. Inside 'cataract' there is 'rack' – almost a pun 'tall rack' draws this out, stretches the word. And of course the blind man's eye is present here. We are in the dark again, as the deep and gloomy wood tells us. Samson's cry: 'O dark, dark, dark, amid the blaze of noon', is present too. So, I have already suggested, is the Jacobin *La Montagne*, which overlooked the *plaine* where the Girondins sat in the French National Assembly.

Here, Wordsworth appears to be putting his boyhood safely in the category of past physical, unreflective, non-intellectual experience, but his insistence on its sensuous thoughtlessness shades over into sensual language:

> That time is past,
> And all its aching joys are now no more,
> And all its dizzy raptures.

This is the language of sensual passion, with just the faint texture of 'cataract' in 'aching'. Hell and heaven are close in love's oxymorons, where we freeze in fire or burn and be but the more ice, as Yeats puts it.

Now Wordsworth takes over one of Milton's hoisting, yet-not-the-more cadences:

> Not for this
> Faint I, nor mourn nor murmur: other gifts
> Have followed.

The Bible is also in his mind here, because 'murmur' is how the speech of those who opposed God is characterized. As Mary Herrington-Perry, who notes this, shows, Wordsworth's statement 'For I have learned' also picks up: 'Not that I speak in respect of want: for I have learned in whatever state I am therewith to be content' (Philippians 4.11). Wordsworth is trying to find happiness after a period of nightmares, anxiety and guilt. His personal and his social conscience are troubling him, and out of the Book of Kings he adapts the famous phrase 'still small voice'. In chapter nineteen of the first book, the angel of the Lord visits Elijah:

> And he came thither unto a cave, and lodged there; and, behold, the word of the Lord came to him, and he said unto him, What doest thou here, Elijah?
>
> And he said, I have been very jealous for the Lord God of Hosts: for the children of Israel have forsaken thy covenant, thrown down thine altars, and slain thy prophets with the sword; and I, even I only, am left; and they seek my life, to take it away.
>
> And he said, Go forth, and stand upon the mount before the Lord. And, behold, the Lord passed by, and a great and strong wind rent the mountains, and brake in pieces the rocks before the Lord; but the Lord was not in the wind: and after the wind an earthquake; but the Lord was not in the earthquake:
>
> And after the earthquake a fire; but the Lord was not in the fire: and after the fire a still small voice.

The biblical passage helps to show how Wordsworth is ambitious of becoming a prophet, that he is also asking himself the question 'What am I doing here?' because the French people have in his vision thrown down the altars and slain their prophets with the sword. He says that the still, sad music of humanity is 'Not harsh nor grating', but by introducing those words he's bringing that grating noun 'cataract' back into the poem's sometimes dissonant music: we hear politics – the word itself here – and we hear the noise of popular tumult and suffering, perhaps the noise of the metal workers in the woods. This, like the movement of the River Wye, is an image of the revolutionary crowd, the common people, but disguised as a humanist inflection, which is how it is always read.

It's then that Wordsworth moves into the sublime passage in the poem:

And I have felt
A presence that disturbs me with the joy
Of elevated thoughts; a sense sublime
Of something far more deeply interfused,
Whose dwelling is the light of setting suns,
And the round ocean, and the living air,
And the blue sky, and in the mind of man,
A motion and a spirit that impels
All thinking things, all objects of all thought,
And rolls through all things.

This appears happy, resolved, exalted, but inside it there is a disturbing allusion to *Paradise Lost*:

From heaven, they fabled, thrown by angry Jove
Sheer o'er the crystal battlements: from morn
To noon he fell, from noon to dewy eve,
A summer's day; and with the setting sun
Dropped from the zenith like a falling star.

This, the most famous moment in *Paradise Lost*, evokes the fall of Haephestus in the *Iliad*. It is an epic moment, which reverberates through western literature, and by invoking it Wordsworth is signalling his epic ambitions (he was already at work on *The Prelude* at this period, and in the card-playing scene in the first book he has the 'sooty knaves' thrown down 'like Vulcan out of heaven'). He is also drawing on contemporary science, particularly on the theories and electrical experiments of Joseph Priestley. So that this apparently pastoral passage is more than it appears.

The science he is drawing on here he gained immediate access to through a sermon given by a Unitarian clergyman, the Reverend Joseph Fawcett, who in 1795 preached to a congregation in the Old Jewry meeting-house in London on 'Reflections Drawn from the Consideration that God is our Creator'. He told the congregation, which included Wordsworth, that the Creator:

is the great spring and impulse that actuates all things. He is in himself the attracting power that holds the particles of all bodies together, and combines all bodies into the beautiful systems we see them compose. He is himself the living soul that inhabits and animates every living thing; that propels every drop through every vein; that produces every pulsation of every artery, every motion of every limb, every action of every organ, throughout the whole animal kingdom. Every operating principle, through the ample compass of things, is God, that moment willing, God, that moment acting. He is the life of the world: at once the maker, the inspector, and the mover, of all things. Water we call the element of one animal; air, we say, is the element of another: the vital presence of God himself is the universal element, in which all living creatures 'live and move and have their being'.

This rhapsody to motion caught Wordsworth's imagination, and in 'Tintern Abbey' he celebrates the combined motion of consciousness and natural objects. The collocation of *thinking, things, thought, through, things* makes the Priestleyan identification of matter and spirit assonantly forceful. The special force which Wordsworth gives to the verb 'roll' here and in a line from a poem written the following year – 'Rolled round in the earth's diurnal course' – makes it clear that inert matter is not the subject.

This idea influenced Hazlitt, who was a friend of Fawcett's, and who in a letter on philosophy published in the *Monthly Magazine* in 1809, argued that we need to consider the existence of an 'entirely unknown and undefined principle, which may be called spirit as well as matter'. (Hazlitt frequently quotes and alludes to 'Tintern Abbey'.) Coleridge was also influenced by Priestley's new concept of matter interfused with spirit, and was for a few years a Unitarian. In his 1794 poem 'Religious Musings', he says:

> And ye of plastic power, that interfused
> Roll through the grosser and material mass
> In organizing surge!

Drawing on Coleridge, Wordsworth's lines develop the 'process theology' of Unitarianism, a sophisticated form of Protestant dissent which Wordsworth was close to at this time (he had a cousin who was a Unitarian, and he mixed socially with Unitarians).

The other allusions which he makes in the last section of the poem all work to reinforce its religious affirmations. Its opening lines:

> Nor, perchance,
> If I were not thus taught, should I the more
> Suffer my genial spirits to decay

fuse Milton's lines in *Paradise Lost*:

> Yet not the more
> Cease I to wander where the Muses haunt.

and in *Samson Agonistes*:

> But yield to double darkness nigh at hand;
> So much I feel my genial spirits droop,
> My hopes all flat.

Samson is here speaking of yielding to 'double darkness' – a phrase Hazlitt was to apply to the British government in the period after Napoleon's defeat – and Wordsworth is doubling darkness and blindness in his twin allusions.

Picking up Psalm 23 – 'He maketh me to lie down in green pastures: he leadeth me beside the still waters . . . Yea, though I walk through the valley of the shadow of death, I will fear no evil: for thou art with me' – he turns to his sister Dorothy and says: 'For thou art with me, here, upon the banks / Of this fair river.' A few lines later, he says: 'Oh! yet a little while / May I behold in thee what I was once', which picks up Christ telling the Apostles: 'I will not leave you comfortless: I will come to you. Yet a little while, and the world seeth me no more; but ye see me: because I live, ye shall live also' (John 14.18–19).

Dorothy is both God and Christ at this point in the poem. But there is something over-determined, even yukky, about the lines that follow: 'thou, my dearest Friend / My dear, dear Friend'. It's as if he needs to insist that his sister is no more than a friend. Here, I don't want to raise the idea of an incestuous relationship, rather to puzzle at the lines which immediately follow: 'and in thy voice I catch / The language of my former heart, and read / My former pleasures in the shooting lights / Of thy wild eyes.' It's as if Dorothy has been transformed into Annette Vallon, an idea that is emphasized by the phrase 'my former pleasures'. I catch the female form in 'former', partly because he says Dorothy's mind 'Shall be a mansion for all lovely forms'. Earlier, he has said of the landscape: 'these forms of beauty have not been to me, / As is a landscape to a blind man's eye.' There's something fleshy in his platonism here.

But it is the image of those pleasures 'in the shooting lights / Of thy wild eyes' that is curious. The shooting lights have to be a version of shooting stars, which call back Satan as a falling star, the image behind the setting suns passage. And that Jacobin adjective 'wild' casts its own light here. In Marlowe's translation of Lucan's republican epic *Pharsalia*, 'rings of fire / Fly in the air, and dreadful bearded stars, / And comets that presage the fall of kingdoms'. The light in Dorothy's eyes is ominous.

The fall of the French monarchy, Wordsworth's own fall into sexual knowledge, is there in those shooting lights, and it is hard to exclude the sexual sense of that adjective 'wild'. The Satanic associations of 'lofty' I've already covered, but there is a Miltonic cadence in 'that neither evil tongues, / Rash judgments, nor the sneers of selfish men'. Here Wordsworth is remembering

> Standing on earth, not rapt above the pole,
> More safe I sing with mortal voice, unchanged
> To hoarse or mute, though fall'n on evil days,
> On evil days though fall'n and evil tongues.

But this is not the first time Wordsworth has evoked the cadence of these fearless lines. His opening lines:

> Five years have passed; five summers, with the length
> Of five long winters!

Evil and five, repeated three times, mean not just that Wordsworth's simple accurate number is impregnated by the word 'evil', as I've suggested earlier, but that Milton's heroic resolution is being summoned to stiffen Wordsworth's republican resolve. Or is it his resolve to escape love, sex and politics that he is bringing to the surface of his consciousness? At the end of the poem, he is drawing his subject to a close by remembering its beginning – not just the opening lines, but that political verb 'disturb' which first occurs in 'disturb / The wild green landscape'. Now Wordsworth asserts that various evil things will not 'disturb / Our chearful faith'.

He is now in the frame of mind which involves departure, leaving behind something which was once good, then turned bad – or which he spoiled. So Dorothy's 'solitary walk' picks up the end of *Paradise Lost*: 'Through Eden took their solitary way.' The end of *Paradise Lost* is also evoked in these lines:

> Nor, perchance,
> If I should be, where I no more can hear
> Thy voice, nor catch from thy wild eyes these gleams
> Of past existence, wilt thou then forget
> That on the banks of this delightful stream
> We stood together.

At the end of *Paradise Lost*, Adam and Eve are led 'down the cliff as fast / To the subjected plain' by the Archangel Michael. That adjective 'subjected' carries a powerful sense of occupation, of being the victims of imperial power. Then Milton begins the final paragraph of his epic:

> They looking back, all th'eastern side beheld
> Of Paradise, so late their happy seat,
> Waved over by that flaming brand, the gate
> With dreadful faces thronged and fiery arms:
> Some natural tears they dropped, but wiped them soon;
> The world was all before them, where to choose
> Their place of rest, and Providence their guide:
> They hand in hand with wand'ring steps and slow,
> Through Eden took their solitary way.

This passage reprises an earlier, happier moment:

> Thus talking, hand in hand alone they passed
> On to their blissful bower; it was a place
> Chosen by the sovran Planter, when he framed
> All things to man's delightful use.

This may help explain Wordsworth's (to a modern ear) uneasy phrase 'delightful stream', because he is drawing on this and Milton's three other uses of 'delightful' in *Paradise Lost*: 'delightful task', 'delightful land', 'delightful land'.

In the first of these examples, Adam speaks; in the next two Eve – Dorothy has become Eve to Wordsworth's Adam in the closing section of 'Tintern Abbey'. But there is a final twist in the last line: 'More dear, both for themselves, and for thy sake'. As Mary Herrington-Parry, that devoted scholar of what she terms 'the spiritual presence of things', has shown, this is an allusion to Genesis: 'Say, I pray thee, thou art my sister: that it may be well with me for thy sake; and my soul shall live because of thee' (12.13). Here, Abram is asking his wife Sarai to say that she is his sister, in order to avoid being killed.

At some level, Wordsworth is saying that Annette represents danger, potential death, while Dorothy represents survival. This is the coded conclusion of Wordsworth's exploration of survivor guilt. He is remembering too much, and he wants to be able to forget. Perhaps on one level of his mind the double *ee*'s in 'delightful stream' mean Lethe, the river of forgetting. On another, it is the English Channel he is staring across at the burning garden, with its gate of dreadful faces and fiery arms. The eyes he mentions are sometimes blind, sometimes sighted, wild, fiery, but they are also figures for the tears Annette Vallon must have shed, and Wordsworth too, we may assume.

If 'Tintern Abbey' is in effect a cento of quotations vigorously assembled, it also draws on a weak poem, 'The Convict', which immediately precedes it in *Lyrical Ballads*. There Wordsworth stands at evening on the slopes of a mountain before repairing to the prison cell and describing the convict's sufferings:

> While the jail-mastiff howls at the dull clanking chain,
> From the roots of his hair there shall start
> A thousand sharp punctures of cold-sweating pain,
> And terror shall leap at his heart.

This gothic moment, the sound of the clanking chain, is reprised in the 'sounding cataract' passage. It infiltrates the rhythms and cadences of the lines and helps make a 'din', or helps bring the din of an urban prison into the landscape. The noisy industrial city of

Birmingham, where Joseph Priestley's house, chapel and laboratory were burnt to the ground by a Church-and-King mob on 14 July 1791, is part of the geography and fabric of his poem (Birmingham is about fifty miles from the Wye Valley), and the nearby city of Bristol, where the republicans Coleridge and Southey were lecturing and publishing, is also part of its social geography. London and Paris are there too, and Wordsworth may have remembered that the previous year a French warship had landed not far away on the coast of Monmouthshire. He observed British warships anchored downstream in the Solent, and the sound of war, as well as the anxieties it causes, are part of the acoustic texture of this uneven, but compelling poem, the anguished and exalted testimony of a committed republican, who is moving towards the deep and gloomy wood.

British Eloquence: Hazlitt and Liberty

Hazlitt's works, for the most part, are not available in cheap or accessible editions. Some of his books have never been reprinted, and it is hard to imagine that his third book, *The Eloquence of the British Senate*, will ever be republished. It was published in two volumes by J. Murray, J. Harding and A. Constable in 1807 when Hazlitt was twenty-nine years old, and was reissued, using the same sheets but different title pages, in 1808 and 1812. It was reissued in 1812 in New York in a single volume. It is subtitled *A Selection of the Best Speeches of the Most Distinguished Parliamentary Speakers from the beginning of the reign of Charles I to the Present Time*. In over a thousand pages, Hazlitt anthologizes mainly distinguished and powerful speeches, with some curiosities and duds included for variety. Hazlitt contributes a series of headnotes, footnotes and short essays in a style which has the spontaneity he esteems in many of the orators he includes. To read his short notes especially is to feel in direct communication with him, as he talks directly to us in the unbuttoned style he admired. At one point, he interrupts Burke's 1774 speech on the characters of Lord Chatham and Mr C. Townshend to say:

> [The following arguments towards the conclusion of this speech are so sensible, so moderate, so wise and beautiful, that I cannot resist the temptation of copying them out, though I did not at first intend it. Burke's speeches are to me, in this my parliamentary progress, what the Duke's castle was to Sancho: I could be content to stay there longer than I am able. I have no inclination to leave the stately palaces, the verdant lawns, the sumptuous entertainments, the grave discourse, and pleasing sounds of music, to sally forth in search of bad roads, meagre fare, and barren adventures. Charles Fox is indeed to come; but he is but the knight of the Green Surtout. Pitt is the brazen head, that delivers mysterious answers; and Sheridan, Master Peter with his puppet-show. *Mais allons*.–]

This may be self-indulgent, but its *parlando* style takes us directly into his imagination, before the speech resumes. It's as though Hazlitt is in dialogue with every speaker, and wants to share his delight or annoyance with us.

It's clear from his headnotes that he read widely from what he terms 'the crude undigested mass of the records of parliament' where, he says, there is such a 'tedious monotony, such a dreary vacuity of thought, such an eternal self-complacent repetition of the same worn-out topics'. He approaches the subject of the boring mass of oratory he has selected from in the 'advertizement' – what we would term an introduction – at the beginning of the first volume where, echoing Hamlet, he says: 'I was uneasy till I had made the monumental pile of octavos and folios, "wherein I saw them quietly inured, open its ponderous and marble jaws," and "set the imprisoned wranglers free again."' Like the ghost of Hamlet's father, the voices contained in his selection are, as he is suggesting, mainly our noble ancestors whose words rebuke both society and our standards of eloquence. The word 'ancestors', like the word 'ancient', reverberates in many of the speeches. Sir John Elliott in 1628 compares 'our ancient English virtue' to 'the old Spartan valour', Sir John Knight in 1694 speaks of 'the old English spirit', and Lord Belhaven in 1706 asks 'Should not the memory of our noble predecessors' valour and constancy rouse up our drooping spirits? Are our noble predecessor's souls got so far into the English cabbage-stalk, and cauliflowers, that we should shew the least inclination that way?' In a note on Sir John St Aubin's 1733 speech on the Triennial Bill, Hazlitt says that 'men's minds were never so truly English as they were at this period'. This collection, then, is an attempt to represent what Hazlitt terms the 'old English intellect', and it is significant that it was from his essay on an exemplar of that undivided intellect, Bulstrode Whitlock, that T. S. Eliot stole the idea of the dissociated sensibility which, in his view, was caused by the English Civil War.

If Hazlitt's aim is to represent certain heroic orators such as Chatham, Burke and Fox, he also wants to represent the ordinary country gentleman speaking earnestly, plainly, directly on an important political issue. Thus Sir John Wray, who was a member for

Lincolnshire in 1641, delivers a speech which, Hazlitt says, is 'chiefly remarkable for the *great* simplicity of the style, and as an instance of the manner in which an honest country gentleman, without much wit or eloquence, but with some pretensions to both, might be supposed to express himself at this period.' Sir John, at the opening of his very short speech, says that 'this great council' has been sitting for 'a longer time than any parliament hath done these many years'. He then develops a curious metaphor that must have appealed to Hazlitt:

> Mr. Speaker, we have had thus long, under our fathers, many ostrich eggs, which, as some observe, are longest in hatching, but once hatched, can digest iron; and we have many irons in the fire, and have hammered some upon the anvil of justice into nails; but we have not struck one stroke with the right hammer, nor riveted one nail to the head.

Hazlitt must have remembered Sir John's illustration when he praised Burke in the long essay on his oratory in the middle of the second volume. Stating that Burke is one of the '*severest* writers we have', he says that he didn't make 'fine colours with phosphorus', as chemists do, but 'by the eagerness of his blows struck fire from the flint, and melted the hardest substances in the furnace of his imagination'. This anticipates Hazlitt's account of Milton as a writer of centos: the power of his mind is 'stamped on every line. The flavour of his imagination melts down and renders malleable, as in a furnace, the most contradictory materials.'

Sir John is probably drawing on Lyly's remark in *Euphues* – 'The *Estrich* digesteth harde yron to preserue his healthe' – which becomes the title of one of Marianne Moore's most famous poems, 'He "Digesteth Harde Yron" '. Moore is designing a fable of the imagination, and she ends by saying 'This one remaining rebel/ is the sparrow-camel.' Like Sir John, she is interested in ways of empowering the spirit to oppose power.

Sir John's image of the ostrich's fabled ability to digest iron is present in the figure for Burke's style – the chamois – which Hazlitt offers in his seminal essay 'On the Prose-Style of Poets': 'all the while, instead of soaring through the air, it stands upon a rocky cliff, clambers up by abrupt and intricate ways, and browses on the roughest bark, or crops the tender flower'. This image of the prose writer as digesting both beautiful rhetorical tropes and objects as rebarbative and recalcitrant as oak bark or old bakelite plugs is drawn from Caesar's speech in *Antony and Cleopatra*, where he urges Antony to leave his 'lascivious wassails' and reminisces about retreat from Modena:

> . . . Thou didst drink
> The stale of horses, and the gilded puddle
> Which beasts would cough at. Thy palate then did deign
> The roughest berry on the rudest hedge.
> Yea, like the stag when snow the pasture sheets,
> The barks of trees thou browsed. On the Alps
> It is reported thou didst eat strange flesh,
> Which some did die to look on.

It could be argued that there is a consistent line in Hazlitt's thinking about prose style that stretches from his inclusion of Sir John's brief and insignificant speech to his essay nearly twenty years later: the prose writer, he insists, has a difficult way to go over rugged mountain tracks, his food boiled dog or worse, his style sinewy, at times martial, but also delicate and severe.

In designing what is in fact an advanced cultural primer and collection of source materials which exemplify the national mind and spirit – its fundamental belief in free speech and liberty – Hazlitt holds to the central Dissenting concept of disinterestedness. This he exemplifies in his remark that for him it has always been a test of the 'sense and candour' of anyone belonging to the party opposed to Burke, 'whether he allowed Burke to be a great man'. He also in his brief note on Sir John St Aubin shows how Tory principles safeguarded liberty, when he states that St Aubin was 'one of that phalanx of ability and energy, that regularly withstood the insidious encroachments, and undermining influence of Walpole's administration'. Asserting, in a sentence I quoted earlier, that men's minds were never 'so truly English' as they were at this period, Hazlitt suggests that even 'the leaven of Jacobitism, which was mingled up with the sentiments of many of the party, must have contributed to add a zest, a poignancy, a bitterness of indignation to their opposition to that overbearing influence, and despotic sway.' He concludes by praising St Aubin's speech as 'one of the most elegant and able compositions to be found in the records of the house of commons'. In his speech, which he delivered in 1733, St Aubin says:

> This is a season of virtue and public spirit. Let us take advantage of it, to repeal those laws which infringe on our liberties, and introduce such as may restore the vigour of our ancient constitution.

Liberty, Hazlitt shows his readers, needs constantly to assert itself against whatever party is in power. Though Hazlitt is wholly on the side of the Williamite Revolution and the Protestant succession, he is not a diehard or a *parti pris* radical, and is aware of the limitations of philosophic radicalism. Burke, Hazlitt argues, thought that the 'wants and happiness' of humanity were not to be provided for as we provide for a herd of cattle, 'merely by attending to their physical necessities'. Burke thought more nobly of his fellows: he knew that 'man had affections and passions and powers of imagination, as well as hunger and thirst and the sense of heat and cold'. This is similar to his later criticism of Percy Shelley in an almost unknown essay 'People of Sense', where he characterizes him as a rhapsodic sophist, and images the philosophic radicals' social ideas as 'bare walls and skeletons of houses'. With *The Eloquence of the British Senate*, Hazlitt begins his project to educate the left and to prise the imaginative faculty from the claws of monarchy and aristocracy.

Hazlitt, the devoted reader of Sir Walter Scott, praises the 'leaven of Jacobitism' in opposition to the first two Georges, but he makes his commitment to the Whig idea of liberty absolutely clear. In a speech delivered in 1680 on the bill to exclude James Duke of York from the succession to the crown, Colonel Birch states:

> we must either suppress popery, or be suppressed by it. For although that interest do not look so big as that of the protestants, yet I plainly see that it hath wrought like a mole under ground for a long time, and that it hath eaten into our bowels, and will soon come to the vital parts of the protestant religion, and destroy it too, if great care be not taken, and that speedily.

A few pages later, in a note to a speech by Lord William Russell who was executed as a conspirator in the Rye House Plot, Hazlitt remarks that he is 'generally looked upon as one of the great martyrs of English liberty'. And two pages later he characterizes Anthony Ashley Cooper, Lord Shaftesbury, as 'a man of fiery passions, turbulent, violent, and self-willed'. The expression of liberty as chaotic movement is reiterated by Sheridan, who said 'more witty things than ever were said by any one man in the house of commons' and who in a debate on employing the military in the suppression of riots argued against 'a dead and slavish quiet', a 'passive calm and submission' under the police. In Britain, there should be 'as much good order as was consistent with the active, busy, and bustling genius of liberty'.

Introducing this argument, Sheridan states that in 'a constitution of liberty, like that of England', it is the 'duty and the object of the people to prefer the essentials of freedom to the comforts of ease'. Here, as Hazlitt would have recognized, Sheridan is echoing these lines from *Samson Agonistes*:

> But what more oft in nations grown corrupt,
> And by their vices brought to servitude,
> Than to love bondage more than liberty,
> Bondage with ease than strenuous liberty.

Similarly, Sheridan's detestation of 'a dead and slavish quiet' echoes the 'fugitive and cloistered virtue' Milton rejects in *Areopagitica*.

Yet Hazlitt is building the heroic, principled, direct, unflinching voice or voices of the national culture – a unified voice which is without any accidence or personal fuss, and beyond both party and the various individuals it speaks through. The modern, necessarily fudgy term 'consensus' is implicit in his epic effort, but it sounds weak in comparison to the effect of these assembled voices which bustle and jar and build – liberty is noisy like a building site.

As a disinterested radical, Hazlitt wants to draw everyone into the family circle. He praises for its 'good sense and logical acuteness' a speech by Robert Rich, in the reign of James I, on the right of the Crown to imprison the subject without any reason being shown. He praises Thomas Wentworth, Earl of Strafford, who was executed by parliament in 1641, calling him a man of 'a fine understanding, and an heroic spirit and undoubtedly a great man'. Charles II, he notes, 'is justly celebrated for his understanding and wit', but there is 'nothing remarkable' in his speeches to Parliament. Mr Shippen, Member for Saltash, whose 1731 speech on the Address he includes, was

> one of the most vehement and vigorous opposers of the measures of government through the whole of [George II's] reign; and, no doubt, had imbibed a very strong tincture of Jacobitism. But he was a man of great firmness and independence of mind, a manly, vigorous, and correct speaker; and whatever his personal motives or sentiments might have been, the principles which he uniformly avowed and maintained, were sound and constitutional.

The adjective 'vehement', which Hazlitt often uses, derives from one of his favourite phrases in Milton, 'sacred vehemence'. It occurs in a speech the Lady addresses to Comus late in the masque:

> Enjoy your dear wit, and gay rhetoric
> That hath so well been taught her dazzling fence,
> Thou art not fit to hear thyself convinced;
> Yet should I try, the uncontrolled worth
> Of this pure cause would kindle my rapt spirits
> To such a flame of sacred vehemence,
> That dumb things would be moved to sympathize,
> And the brute Earth would lend her nerves, and shake,
> Till all thy magic structures reared so high,
> Were shattered into heaps o'er thy false head.

Sacred vehemence and gay rhetoric's dazzling fence might be reconstructed as a type of Puritan *hwyl* opposed to a fluent, but superficial, cavalier brilliance with language. Comus, the Lady tells him, has neither the 'ear', nor the 'soul', to apprehend:

> The sublime notion, and high mystery
> That must be uttered to unfold the sage
> And serious doctrine of virginity.

It's here that we might discern in sacred vehemence the expression of the national soul, but where Milton sees the Lady and Comus as polar opposites, with the Cavalier Comus an essentially marginal and unserious figure, Hazlitt does not see vehemence as the sole property or distinguishing feature of Puritans and Dissenters.

In a note to a speech made by Samuel Sandys in 1733, Hazlitt says that he was

> one of the most frequent and able speakers of this period. What his principles were I do not know: for the side which any person took at this time, was a very equivocal test of his real sentiments; toryism, through this and the preceding reign, generally assuming the shape of resistance to the encroachments of the prerogative, and attachment to the liberties of the people.

'Balance', like 'consensus' is an inadequate term to describe Hazlitt's treatment of British oratory – we need to see these voices as energies in a force field whose action never ceases. This is the 'active, busy, and bustling genius of liberty' which Sheridan praises.

One of those energies can be felt in the frequent interventions which Hazlitt makes. On the same page as the note on Samuel Sandys, there appears the final paragraph of a speech by Mr Campbell, Member for Pembrokeshire, against a bill to prevent officers of government from sitting in Parliament:

> but as I am convinced that a man's being in an office, does not in the least influence his way of thinking, or his manner of acting in this house; I therefore think we have no occasion for contriving any such remedies at present, and far less for such an extraordinary remedy as is proposed by the bill now before us; for which reason I am against committing it.

Hazlitt adds an asterisk to 'house', and exclaims: 'This is an entirely new view of human nature, different from any that has been hitherto commonly received!' As so often in the anthology, we share the illusion of listening to Hazlitt speaking – it's almost like happening upon a record of his familiar conversation. Here, Hazlitt laughs at Campbell's interested stupidity, but again and again it is the concept of disinterestedness he affirms. In a brief note on Frederick, Lord North, the Tory First Lord of the Treasury – i.e. Prime Minister – Hazlitt says: 'His speeches are in general, like the following, short, shrewd, and lively, and quite free from the affectation of oratory.' This is a different distinction between vehemence and rhetoric, one which allows common sense, practical wit to surpass oratorical art.

Hazlitt continues: 'He spoke like a gentleman, like a man of sense and business, who had to explain himself on certain points of moment to the country, and who in doing this did not think that his first object was to shew how well he could play the orator by the hour.' Hazlitt then quotes from what he terms Burke's 'masterly character' of North, which praises his 'mind most perfectly disinterested'. Even Canning, a Tory politician whom Hazlitt loathed, has 'a degree of elegance and brilliancy, and a certain ambitious tip-toe elevation in his speeches'. But Hazlitt, adds, 'they want manliness, force, and dignity'.

Hazlitt's deepest loathing is directed at William Pitt, whose oratory he characterizes as having 'a kind of faultless regularity', with 'nothing puerile, nothing far-fetched or abrupt in his speeches'. The whole force of Pitt's mind consisted 'solely in this evasive dexterity and perplexing formality.' He has left nothing behind him, not a 'single memorable saying – not one profound maxim'. Pitt is a Lockean orator: 'every subject presented to him nothing more than a *tabula rasa*, on which he was at liberty to lay whatever colouring of language he pleased'. The portrait is damning: Pitt had 'no general principles, no comprehensive view of things, no moral habits of thinking, no system of action'.

Yet Pitt was a supremely gifted and successful politician, as Hazlitt's closing sentence recognizes. Pitt was able to 'baffle opposition, not from strength or firmness, but from the evasive ambiguity and impalpable nature of his resistance'. Hazlitt says, 'no force could bind the loose phantom, and his mind soon rose unhurt from defeat: "And in its liquid texture mortal wound / Receiv'd no more than can the blind air".'

Here, Hazlitt adapts Milton's lines on the impalpable nature of the fallen angels – lines he would have known that Milton drew out of Ariel's speech in *The Tempest*:

> . . . the elements
> Of whom your swords are tempered may as well
> Wound the loud winds, or with bemocked-at stabs
> Kill the still-closing waters, as diminish

One dowl that's in my plume. My fellow ministers
Are like invulnerable.

Milton's lines, informed by Shakespeare's, close this hostile essay in a manner which bestows an invulnerable, if malign, spirituality and strength of mind on Pitt. Here, we perceive politics as a version of the war in heaven (which was of course Milton's vision of civil war politics). We may also note that Hazlitt introduced the Milton quotation with a line and a half from earlier in the same passage in *Paradise Lost*: 'not matchless, and his pride humbled by such rebuke'. This reminds us that Hazlitt, typically, is summoning the whole passage when he quotes from parts of it. The passage concludes:

All heart they live, all head, all eye, all ear,
All intellect, all sense, and as they please,
They limb themselves, and colour, shape or size
Assume, as likes them best, condense or rare.

Milton's admiration for the angels (of whose party he was not) and his ecstatic joy in the reach of his own poetic intellect, carries over into Hazlitt's conclusion to place imagination at the heart of political struggle. Strategically boring as Pitt's oratory is, he becomes a visionary creature at the end. That phrase 'all intellect', invisibly present in the two quotations from the passage, redeems Pitt's Lockean mind and gives it an active force.

It is in the examples Hazlitt includes of Burke's oratory that we find a resonant, vehement, witty, intellectually robust and confident style that speaks with a dramatic *éclat*, authority and sense of danger:

How comes this Junius to have broke through the cobweb of the law, and to range uncontrolled, unpunished, through the land? The myrmidons of the court have been long, and are still pursuing him in vain. They will not spend their time upon you or me. No; they disdain such vermin, when the mighty boar of the forest has broke through all their toils – is before them. But what will their efforts avail? No sooner has he wounded one than he lays another dead at his feet.

As I've tried to show elsewhere, this passage describes political prose – Junius's pamphlets – intervening decisively in public affairs. Hazlitt draws in his pamphlet *Free Thoughts on Public Affairs* on a term from hawking which Burke employs a few sentences later when he describes Janius 'still rising higher, and coming down souse upon both houses of parliament'. In Hazlitt's 1806 pamphlet Napoleon is going to 'come down *souse* upon our possessions in India'.

Here, we can see the young Hazlitt finding inspiration and epic certainty in Burke's imagery, vocabulary, and ability to make Junius's merely efficient prose sound sublimely powerful, feral and severe. Junius, he says, has the 'strut of a petit-maître', while Burke has the, possibly less dignified, 'stalk of a giant'. Here, Hazlitt is thinking of the passage in *Paradise Lost* where the invisible Satan spies on Adam and Eve, and 'about them round / A lion now he stalks with fiery glare'. Both uses of 'stalk' are implicit in this sentence from the great opening paragraph of 'A Landscape of Nicolas Poussin': 'He stalks along, a giant upon earth, and reels and falters in his gait, as if just awaked out of sleep, or uncertain of his way; – you see his blindness, though his back is turned.'

This essay, I've suggested elsewhere, is an elegy for Hazlitt's hero, Napoleon, and if we consider the sentence where Orion 'stalks' like a blind man, we can note that Samson and Milton are also present, as is Burke who has 'the stalk of a giant'. Blake, who characterizes himself as communicating with the spirits of Isaiah, Homer, and Milton, obviously felt, as Dante did towards Virgil, that he was in both a spiritual and physical proximity to their shades, their immortal intellects. Lacking Blake's visionary Puritan faith, Hazlitt employs allusive language, association and symbolism to express a similar concept of vatic communication. The Orion, who 'reels and falters in his gait', is like the nineteen-year-old Hazlitt uncertain of his mission, purpose, or gift. Or he is like the nineteen-year-old Hazlitt walking the road from Wen to Shrewsbury in the January darkness to hear Coleridge preach.

When we consider Hazlitt's use of the verb 'reels', we may perceive a reminiscence of this passage from his essay on Fox:

> Every thing shewed the agitation of his mind. His tongue faltered, his voice became almost suffocated, and his face was bathed in tears. He was lost in the magnitude of his subject. He reeled and staggered under the load of feeling which oppressed him.

In using 'stalks' and 'reels' of Orion, Hazlitt is remembering his own intellectual journey, and the inspiration that Burke and Fox were for him then and evermore.

What inspired him was both orators' vehemence on behalf of the oppressed, and in his inclusion of Burke's 1780 speech 'on presenting a Plan for the better security of the Independence of Parliament, and the economical Reformation of the civil and other Establishments', he would have wanted his readers to notice that when Burke spoke of Wales he was also thinking of Ireland:

That nation is brave and full of spirit. Since the invasion of king Edward, and the massacre of the bards, there was such tumult, and alarm, and uproar, through the region of *Prestatyn. Snowdon* shook to its base; *Cadre Edris* was loosened from its foundations. The fury of litigious war blew her horn on the mountains. The rocks poured down their goatherds, and the deep caverns vomited out their miners. Every thing above ground, and every thing under ground, was in arms.

Burke in the next sentence addresses the Speaker of the Commons: 'In short, sir, to alight from my Welsh Pegasus, and to come to level ground' – an image which would have spoken to the young Hazlitt, who was later to draw distinctions – notably in his essay on *Coriolanus* – between the imagination or 'principle of poetry', which he terms 'a very anti-levelling principle', and the understanding which is a levelling or equalizing 'republican faculty'. It's the *hwyl*, the passionate intensity, or sacred vehemence which informs Burke's prose and lifts it into the unstable, 'monopolizing faculty' of the imagination, that enraptures Hazlitt. At moments, Burke has an almost Shakespearean or Yeatsian intensity – later in the same speech he says:

There is nothing that God has judged good for us, that he has not given us the means to accomplish, both in the natural and moral world. If we cry, like children for the moon, like children we must cry on.

Here, Burke's lonely voice, the voice of what he elsewhere terms, the 'naked, shivering self', speaks out hopelessly, without power or institutional validity.

Burke is also a very witty orator, and in a 1774 speech on the characters of Lord Chatham and Mr C. Townshend he first praises Chatham's greatness, 'merited rank, his superior eloquence, his splendid qualities, his eminent services', and then turns to the administration Chatham formed in July 1766 from all sections of both houses. In a famous passage, Burke says he made an administration

> so chequered and speckled; he put together a piece of joinery, so crossly indented and whimsically dovetailed; a cabinet so variously inlaid; such a piece of diversified mosaic; such a tessellated pavement without cement, here a bit of black stone and there a bit of white; patriots and courtiers, king's friends and republicans; whigs and tories; treacherous friends and open enemies; that it was indeed a very curious show; but utterly unsafe to touch and unsure to stand on.

This might be an example of what became a favourite and ambivalent critical term of Hazlitt's – the cento – and I wonder if at moments, when he was completing an essay dovetailed and chequered out of favourite and new quotations, he remembered Burke's speech and felt anxious.

Hazlitt criticizes the famous Irish politician, Henry Grattan's 'double facings, and splicings and clenches in style', but he praises the Irish lawyer Edmund Curran's speeches which are free from 'that affectation, or false glitter, which is the vice of Irish eloquence'. We can consider *The Eloquence of the British Senate* as a portrait of the critic as a young man – like Stephen Dedalus he is assembling a series of styles in order to discover his own imaginative direction. His twinned themes are liberty and style, and like Joyce he aims to discover and design the national conscience.

One central image here occurs at the end of Mr Lenthall's 1657 speech on the inauguration of Cromwell as Lord Protector:

> When you have all these together, what a comely and glorious sight it is to behold a lord protector, in a purple robe, with a sceptre in his hand, a sword of justice girt about him, and his eyes fixed upon the bible! Long may you prosperously enjoy them all, to your own comfort, and the comfort of the people of these three nations.

This passage from the first volume is echoed in one of Wilkes's speeches in the second volume, where Wilkes says

The journals of Cromwell's parliaments prove, that a more equal representation was settled, and carried by him into execution. That wonderful, comprehensive mind embraced the whole of this powerful empire.

Earlier, Hazlitt in a brief headnote praises Wilkes, who takes the 'same ground', and often uses the same words as Junius, 'but I think he establishes his point more satisfactorily'. Junius – Philip Francis's alias – is important for Hazlitt as a polemical precursor, but he is often concerned with the limitations of his style, in order I would guess to keep the dash and wildness of Burke's style in full view. He goes on to say that Wilkes was a 'clear, correct, able, and eloquent speaker. His conversational talents were very brilliant. He was a very ugly and a very debauched man, but a great favourite with the women, whom he accordingly satirized without mercy.' Hazlitt, who frequented prostitutes, and for whom the term 'feminine' was a pejorative, must have identified with Wilkes.

The anthology also contains an important speech by Wilberforce against the slave trade, and most movingly a lacerating attack 'on frequent executions', delivered in 1777 by Sir W. Meredith, with 'heartfelt simplicity, before which wit, and elegance, and acuteness, and the pomp of words, sink into insignificance'.

Early in his speech, Meredith says:

By this nickname of treason, however, there lies at this moment in Newgate, under sentence to be burnt alive, a girl just turned of fourteen; at her master's bidding, she hid some white-washed farthings behind her stays, on which the jury found her guilty, as an accomplice with her master in the treason. The master was hanged last Wednesday; and the faggots all lay ready – no reprieve came till just as the cart was setting out, and the girl would have been burnt alive on the same day, had it not been for the humane but casual interference of lord Weymouth. Good God! sir, are we taught to execrate the fires of Smithfield, and are we lighting them now to burn a poor harmless child for hiding a whitewashing farthing!

Meredith's compassionate anger speaks for Hazlitt's detestation of capital punishment, and in this, the most terrifying passage in his speech, Meredith turns to a case prosecuted under a shoplifting act which was designed to protect bankers' and silversmiths' shops, and other shops which stocked valuable goods, but which goes 'so far as to make it death to lift any thing off a counter with intent to steal':

> Under this act, one Mary Jones was executed, whose case I shall just mention: it was at the time when press warrants were issued on the alarm about Falkland Islands. The woman's husband was pressed, their goods seized for some debts of his, and she, with two small children, turned into the streets a-begging. 'Tis a circumstance not to be forgotten, that she was very young, (under nineteen) and most remarkably handsome. She went to a linen-draper's shop, took some coarse linen off the counter, and slipped it under her cloak; the shopman saw her, and she laid it down: for this she was hanged. Her defence was (I have the trial in my pocket), "that she had lived in credit, and wanted for nothing till a press-gang came and stole her husband from her; but, since then, she had no bed to lie on; nothing to give her children to eat; and they were almost naked; and perhaps she might have done something wrong, for she hardly knew what she did." The parish officers testified the truth of this story; but it seems, there had been a good deal of shop-lifting about Ludgate; an example was thought necessary; and this woman was hanged for the comfort and satisfaction of some shopkeepers in Ludgate-street. When brought to receive sentence, she behaved in such a frantic manner, as proved her mind to be in a distracted and desponding state; and the child was sucking at her breast when she set out for Tyburn.

Asserting his belief that a fouler murder was never committed against law, than 'the murder of this woman by law', Meredith indicts his fellow MPs as the true hangmen. His speech illustrates the cruelty of the criminal law, and appears to come straight out of Defoe.

The Eloquence of the British Senate is one of Hazlitt's most occluded, most inaccessible publications, which means that any account of it has to quote copiously from the speeches it contains and from Hazlitt's essays, headnotes and interjections. It's neither a dated nor a sterile work, rather it is like a benign version of Milton's Pandemonium in which we can discern the depth, resilience and complexity of the British idea of liberty.

I Am a Traveller, Not a Reformer: William Hazlitt

Any serious writer who takes on the task of writing a travel book knows that the form – if it can be called a form – has serious problems. He or she is designing a consumer article – perhaps on a warm beach, at dusk, to the shush of the surf and the distant, naff strains of the soundtrack to *Captain Correlli's Mandolin*. Byron faces the problem on a beach on a Greek island in that supreme travel book, *Don Juan*:

> And the small ripple spilt upon the beach
> Scarcely o'erpassed the cream of your champagne,
> When o'er the brim the sparkling bumpers reach.

OK, this is tourist verse, pleasurable junk, Byron says, and by wittily confessing it gets away from the problem. Here, in Hazlitt's phrase, he is a traveller, not a reformer.

As Hazlitt presents it, the traveller's eye is drawn to a chaotic series of sense impressions that hit him, really out of Locke's philosophy, in order to argue that there is no other way of perceiving the world. This, as he calls it, 'jumble' of 'little teazing, fantastical, disagreeable, chaotic sensations' is a subject he returns to often in his *Notes of a Journey through France and Italy*, and it is embodied in the image pattern of froth which runs through the book. From the squeeze of lemon juice which his barber at Dieppe adds to the shaving lather, to his remark in Chapter 20 that French dramatic dialogue is 'frothy verbiage', there is a consistent, even obsessive, focus on the French attraction to 'immediate, sensible impressions', as he terms it. 'A Frenchman's imagination,' he insists, 'is always at the call of his senses.'

The problem for Hazlitt is that his own imagination must deliver what in journalism is termed a 'colour piece' to his readers, and as a former painter he is naturally drawn to visual images. He scolds himself and his readers by remarking that the eye is 'the vain or voluptuous part of our constitution', and in a description of the habit of the women in Parma of staring out of windows he states that in 'Hogarth, you perceive some symptoms of the same prurience of the optic nerve, and willingness to take in knowledge at the entrance of the eyes'. (This is similar to Wordsworth's and Coleridge's criticism of what they term 'the despotism of the eye'.) In an exasperated moment in the Alps late in the work, he remarks that the English abroad 'turn out of their way to see every pettifogging, huckstering object that they could see better at home, and are as *fussy* and fidgetty, with their smoke-jacks and mechanical inventions among the Alps, as if they had brought Manchester and Sheffield in their pockets!' Hazlitt's target here is the 'hard, dry, mechanical, husky' nature of the English understanding, its '*matter-of-factness*'.

This is a philosophical subject, and Hazlitt underlines his epistemological interest by suggesting that a 'metaphysician might say, that the English perceive objects chiefly by their mere material qualities of solidity, inertness, and impenetrability, or by their own muscular resistance to them'. They 'do not care about the colour, taste, smell, the sense of luxury or pleasure'.

Hazlitt – to use a once popular critical term – tends to offer a series of binary opposites, and the philosophical and aesthetic problem he addresses is similar to the distinction Yeats makes in a famous passage from the general introduction to his work between the mind of the poet as he writes and the mind of the poet who sits down to breakfast, his mind cluttered with what Yeats calls 'accidence' – chance bits and pieces, like the fragments of broken eggshell and toast crumbs he'll soon leave on his plate:

A poet writes always of his personal life, in his finest work out of its tragedy, whatever it be, remorse, lost love, or mere loneliness; he never speaks directly as to someone at the breakfast table, there is always a phantasmagoria. Dante and Milton had mythologies, Shakespeare the characters of English history or of traditional romance; even when the poet seems most himself, when he is Raleigh and gives potentates the lie, or Shelley 'a nerve o'er which do creep the else unfelt oppressions of this earth', or Byron when 'the soul wears out the breast' as 'the sword outwears its sheath', he is never the bundle of accident and incoherence that sits down to breakfast; he has been reborn as an idea, something intended, complete. A novelist might describe his accidence, his incoherence, he must not; he is more type than man, more passion than type.

I cite Yeats because Hazlitt's subject is imagination and intellect. As Uttara Natarajan has so persuasively shown in *Hazlitt and the Reach of Sense: Criticism, Morals and the Metaphysics of Power* (1998), he belongs to a school of British idealists, and he supports that philosophical position in essays such as 'Why Distant Objects Please'. He glances at this subject when he notes that he has twice lived in houses occupied by celebrated men (he's referring to Salvator Rosa and Milton), and that he finds to his mortification that 'imagination, is entirely a *thing imaginary*, and has nothing to do with matter of fact, history, or the senses. To see an object of thought or fancy is just as impossible as to feel a sound or hear a smell'.

This view of the imagination, which is distinctly un-Hobbesian, un-Lockean, is developed throughout *Notes of a Journey through France and Italy*, which is a particularly neglected work of Hazlitt's, and needs to be read as a short epic of the critical imagination founded upon his conjoined political and philosophical idealism.

It begins in Brighton, where Hazlitt and his second wife Isabella Bridgewater set off by steam-packet to Dieppe. Before he sketches Brighton, Hazlitt meditates on the sea:

There is something in being near the sea, like the confines of eternity. It is a new element, a pure abstraction. The mind loves to hover on that which is endless, and forever the same. People wonder at a steam-boat, the invention of man, managed by man, that makes its liquid path like an iron railway through the sea – I wonder at the sea itself, that vast Leviathan, rolled round the earth, smiling in its sleep, waked into fury, fathomless, boundless, a huge world of water-drops – Whence it is, whither goes it, is it of eternity or of nothing?

That slightly odd but obvious phrase 'a huge world of water-drops' leads us by association to his remark in his portrait of Horne Tooke in the recently published *The Spirit of the Age* that Tooke's eloquence is a 'succession of drops, not a stream'. Here, as I've argued elsewhere, Hazlitt is echoing his critique of Locke's epistemology when he compares evanescent sensations, impressions and thoughts to always separate bubbles 'that rise and disappear on the water'.

In a sentence he dropped from *The Morning Chronicle* where this and the other chapters subsequently appeared, he wrote after 'forever the same': 'the sea at present puts me in mind of Lord Byron – it is restless, glittering, dangerous, exhaustless, like his style.' Byron, like Wordsworth, Shelley and Keats – Tom Moore too – is part of the fabric of his imagination, as he turns in his prose and knows that, being poets, they are perceived to be his superiors.

This sense of occlusion or exclusion as a prose writer is behind this moment from his account of his and his wife's return through the Simplon Pass: 'Monteroso ascended to the right, shrouded in cloud and mist, at a height inaccessible even to the eye. This mountain is only a few hundred feet lower than Mont-Blanc, yet its name is hardly known. So a difference of a hair's breadth in talent often makes all the difference between total obscurity and endless renown!' This is a self-reflexive moment and it follows his account of their ascent, where he says 'The eagle screams over-head, and the chamois looks startled round'. The chamois is his symbol of prose style in the Alpine passage in 'On the Prose Style of Poets':

> It has always appeared to me that the most perfect prose-style, the most powerful, the most dazzling, the most daring, that which went the nearest to the verge of poetry, and yet never fell over, was Burke's. It has the solidity, and sparkling effect of the diamond: all other *fine writing* is like French paste or Bristol-stones in the comparison. Burke's style is airy, flighty, adventurous, but it never loses sight of the subject; nay, is always in contact with, and derives its increased or varying impulse from it. It may be said to pass yawning gulfs 'on the unstedfast footing of a spear': still it has an actual resting-place and tangible support under it – it is not suspended on nothing. It differs from poetry, as I conceive, like the chamois from the eagle: it climbs to an almost equal height, touches upon a cloud, overlooks a precipice, is picturesque, sublime – but all the while, instead of soaring through the air, it stands upon a rocky cliff, clambers up by abrupt and intricate ways, and browzes on the roughest bark, or crops the tender flower.

The sentence in *Notes of a Journey* where he mentions the eagle and chamois is preceded by the fir trees' 'star-ypointing pyramids'. This is a quotation from Milton's poem 'On Shakespear', where the phrase 'Star-ypointing Pyramid' and 'live-long Monument' occur. Though Milton says that Shakespeare has no need of a pyramid, he contrasts those phrases with 'th' shame of slow-endeavouring art'. In their slow ascent of the Simplon Pass, Hazlitt's allusive imagination is meditating on prose style. In Browning's phrase, he's conscious of being a 'dull-clothed, decent prose man', but on the other hand he knows he's the greatest prose writer of his age. There's an understandable artistic hang-up being expressed here, and part of Hazlitt's sense of failure can be discerned in his assertion that he is not prejudiced in favour of either Mount Cenis or the Simplon Pass because 'the road over each was raised by the same masterhand'. He is thinking of his hero Napoleon, whose 'iron glaive', as he terms it, smote these mountains. This idea of republican power and intellect is also reflected in his remark that the inn at Mount Cenis is where Rousseau stopped on his way to Paris 'to overturn the French Monarchy by the force of style'.

Before this, during their stay in Paris, Hazlitt's grief at Napoleon's defeat has been reawakened, but in his comments on the Alpine roads he is touching on the theme of stone which runs throughout this work. He wants to show rock and stone mastered by the human mind. This is part of his philosophic and aesthetic theme, and it culminates in his prose poem to Mont Blanc near the end of *Notes of a Journey*. There he calls the mountain 'a huge dumb heap of matter', and then states:

There is an end here of vanity and littleness, and all transitory jarring interests. You stand, as it were, in the presence of the Spirit of the Universe, before the majesty of Nature, with her chief elements about you; cloud and air, and rock, and stream, and mountain are brought into immediate contact with primeval Chaos and the great First Cause. The mind hovers over mysteries deeper than the abysses at our feet; its speculations soar to a height beyond the visible forms it sees around it.

On our left, a precipice of dark brown rocks of various shapes rose abruptly at our side, or hung threatening over the road, into which some of their huge fragments, loosened by the winter's flaw, had fallen, and which men and mules were employed in removing – (the thundering crash had hardly yet subsided, as you looked up and saw the fleecy clouds sailing among the shattered cliffs, while another giant-mass seemed ready to quit its station in the sky) – and as the road wound along to the other extremity of this noble pass, between the beetling rocks and dark sloping pine-forests, frowning defiance at each other, you caught the azure sky, the snowy ridges of the mountains, and the peaked tops of the Grand Chartreuse, waving to the right in solitary state and air-clad brightness. – It was a scene dazzling, enchanting, and that stamped the long-cherished dreams of the imagination upon the senses. Between those four crystal peaks stood the ancient monastery of that name, hid from the sight, revealed to thought, half-way between earth and heaven, enshrined in its cerulean atmosphere, lifting the soul to its native home, and purifying it from mortal grossness. I cannot wonder at the pilgrimages that are made to it, its calm repose, its vows monastic. Life must there seem a noiseless dream; – Death a near translation to the skies!

The power of the mind is asserted here, as Hazlitt remembers Shelley's 'Mont Blanc' perhaps Wordsworth's account of crossing the Alps. He also alludes to one of his favourite poems by Wordsworth, 'Tintern Abbey', when a few sentences later he says that they might have fancied themselves 'inclosed in a vast tomb, but for the sounding cataracts and the light clouds that flitted over our heads'. The 'sounding cataracts' are taken from a complex republican moment in 'Tintern Abbey':

> The sounding cataract
> Haunted me like a passion: the tall rock,
> The mountain, and the deep and gloomy wood.

The tall rock, as I've explained earlier, I take to be a figure for the Tarpeian Rock from which traitors and murderers were thrown in Ancient Rome – it's a figure for the guillotine, while the mountain is *Montagne*, the Jacobins in the National Assembly. In the sentence just before the one in which he uses 'sounding cataracts', he says that as the day closed in 'and was followed by the moonlight, the mountains on our right hung over us like a dark pall, and the glaciers gleamed like gigantic shrouds opposite'.

This is intended not just as description – rather Hazlitt is mourning Napoleon's defeat in these images. He follows Napoleon's path through what he calls, in another allusion to 'Tintern Abbey', the 'mighty world of landscape and history' ('the mighty world of eye and ear' is Wordsworth's phrase). Wordsworth is his difficult, imaginary companion as he follows Napoleon across the Alps and says in a bravura passage in Chapter 14 that he was 'drinking the empyrean'. Drawing on Milton's account of hell, and 'Tintern Abbey', he says

> you caught the azure sky, the snowy ridges of the mountains, and the peaked tops of the Grande Chartreuse, waving to the right in solitary state and air-clad brightness. – It was a scene dazzling, enchanting, and that stamped the long-cherished dreams of the imagination upon the senses.

This is a Wordsworthian spot of time, which by its refusal to vanish like a bubble or like snow melting in its fall – his image for Locke's epistemology – exists permanently in the active mind. The ancient monastery is significantly 'hid from the sight, revealed to thought'. Here the merely sensual optic nerve has been defeated by the intellect.

In the second chapter, Hazlitt sketches out the opposition between the seen, the visible universe of sense impressions and the unseen intellect when he remarks that entering Rouen Cathedral 'after the bustle and confusion of the streets' is like entering 'a vault – a tomb of worldly thoughts and pleasures, pointing to the skies'. He then makes a contrast between 'the infinite number of paltry, rush-bottomed chairs, huddled together in the aisle' like rubbish, and the 'great bell' of the Cathedral. The chairs are infinite like the discrete drops of water – i.e. sense impressions – in the ocean of Locke's idea of the mind. They are Yeatsian accidence, while the 'deep-mouthed' bell is the active intellect and imagination. Significantly, Hazlitt quotes from *Il Penseroso* when he describes the bell as 'swinging low with sullen roar'. Just after this line, Milton offers a few small things – glowing embers, cricket on the hearth, 'belmans drowsy charm' – before moving from their accidence to the great, central, visionary passage in the poem:

> Or let my lamp at midnight hour
> Be seen in some high lonely tower,
> Where I may oft outwatch the Bear,
> With thrice great Hermes or unsphear
> The spirit of Plato to unfold
> What worlds, or what vast regions hold
> Th'immortal mind that hath forsook
> Her mansion in the fleshly nook.

This, as it were, subliminal or implied quotation embedded in Hazlitt's reference to the bell, is anti-empirical. Like his prose, it sets the 'immortal mind' against the purely physical. My point here is that Hazlitt's memory holds whole passages, from which he selects phrases or lines. Thus in his account of Poussin's *Adam and Eve in Paradise* in the Louvre, he says it is a scene of 'sweetness and seclusion "to cure all sadness but despair." ' This is from *Paradise Lost*, 4.156, where Satan is approaching Paradise. A few sentences later, he says: 'If the "verdurous wall of Paradise" had upreared itself behind our first parents, it would have closed them in more completely.' This is also a quotation from *Paradise Lost*, but an earlier part of the same passage.

Hazlitt remembers Milton's visit to Italy, when he remarks that he believes it was in Italy that Milton had the 'spirit and buoyancy of imagination' to write his Latin sonnet on the Platonic idea of the archetype of the world, where he describes the shadowy cave in which 'dwelt Eternity' (*otiosa eternitas*), and ridicules the apprehension that Nature could ever grow old, or 'shake her starry head with palsy'. Once again the distinction between spirit and flesh is being made.

What Hazlitt wants is for his prose to communicate a buoyancy of imagination, which asserts the vitality of the radical critical spirit. Just as Yeats must put together small things – moorhens, longlegged flies – with stones and silence, he must set rushbottomed chairs against the great bell. He sets bell against chairs, true, but he wants them to play against each other like balls bouncing off a great wall.

My favourite example of this has the writer again at breakfast:

After waiting some time, we at last breakfasted in a sort of kitchen or out-house upstairs, where we had very excellent but homely fare, and where we were amused with the furniture – a dove-house, a kid, half-skinned, hanging on the walls; a loose heap of macaroni and vegetables in one corner, plenty of smoke, a Madonna carved and painted, and a map of Constantinople. The pigeons on the floor were busy with their murmuring plaints, and often fluttered their wings as if to fly. So, thought I, the nations of the earth clap their wings, and strive in vain to be free!

This is a domestic interior, not quite a still life, for Hazlitt puts his central critical value motion into it, and this leads to the sonorous, bell-like exclamation – an exclamation which for Irish republicans has a certain resonance:

I have but one request to make at my departure from this world. It is the charity of silence. Let no man write my epitaph. When my country shall have taken her place among the nations of the earth, then and not till then, let my epitaph be written.

This is Robert Emmet's speech from the dock. As it happens, Southey quoted another version of Emmet's speech in an 1803 poem entitled 'Written Immediately after Reading the speech of Robert Emmet, on his Trial and Conviction for High Treason'. This version of the speech does not contain the phrase 'nations of the earth', which was most probably added later, as patriotic prints of Emmet and copies of his speech circulated in Ireland, but I have no doubt that Ireland was one of the countries Hazlitt is thinking about here – Hazlitt, we know, was half-Irish.

This passage is followed a few sentences later by one of those sentences where the prose falters into routine travelogue, as he describes herds of 'slate-coloured oxen . . . browzing luxuriously. The broom floated above them, their covering and their food, with its flexible silken branches of light green, and presented an eastern scene, extensive, soft, and wild.' The too-insistent rhyme *green / scene*, and the closing adjectival triplet sink this sentence. But in these sentences on David's paintings, we see a much more subtle effect: 'I do not wonder David does not like Rubens, for he has none of the Fleming's bold, sweeping outline. He finishes the details very prettily and skilfully, but has no idea of giving magnitude or motion to the whole.'

Those adverbs 'prettily' and 'skilfully' are fluttery butterfly words for Hazlitt, and belong to those 'disagreeable, chaotic sensations' which he describes as typically French. Among the various assonantal runs, the *o* in 'bold' is picked up by 'no', 'motion' and the last word 'whole' to give the sentence the unity of vocal shades and texture which Hazlitt termed 'keeping'. If 'prettily' and 'skilfully' are rushbottomed chairs or fluttering, crooning pigeons, those repeated *o* sounds are the deep-tongued bell. The adverbs are superficial movement, not the core energy or gusto Hazlitt admires.

It's here I want to look at the stone theme in *Notes of a Journey* which I glanced at earlier. At the very beginning, in the fourth paragraph, Hazlitt remarks that the Brighton Pavilion is like 'a collection of stone pumpkins and pepper-boxes'. In the next paragraph, he glances at superficial motion – people at a watering-place 'may be compared to the flies of a summer' (a favourite quotation from Burke's *Reflections*). 'The only idea you gain is,' Hazlitt remarks, 'of finery and motion.' There are many moments later on where he suggests that French painting is like sculpture, or asserts that the finest sculpture in the world can only resemble 'a man turned to stone'.

I have argued elsewhere that stone is an image of the prose writer's anxieties in Hazlitt. He fears and dislikes the petrific, yet he fears that prose turns nature to stone. His solution is to make statues move. This he does in the extremely long footnote on the Elgin Marbles at the end of Chapter 11. There he concludes that the Apollo

> and other antiques are not equally simple and severe. The limbs have too much an appearance of being cased in marble, of making a display of every recondite beauty, and of balancing and answering to one another like the rhymes in verse. The Elgin Marbles are harmonious, flowing, varied prose. In a word, they are like casts after the finest nature.

Here he puts poetry on the back foot, and redeems prose by, curiously, using it to praise sculpture. His anxiety about prose is closely involved with his criticism of the English imagination as too solid, too hard and matter-of-fact, too wooden:

A metaphysician might say, that the English perceive objects chiefly by their mere material qualities of solidity, inertness, and impenetrability, or by their own muscular resistance to them; that they do not care about the colour, taste, smell, the sense of luxury or pleasure: – they require the heavy, hard, and tangible only, something for them to grapple with and resist, to try their strength and their unimpressibility upon. They do not like to smell to a rose, or to taste of made-dishes, or to listen to soft music, or to look at fine pictures, or to make or hear fine speeches, or to enjoy themselves or amuse others; but they will knock any man down who tells them so, and their sole delight is to be as uncomfortable and disagreeable as possible. To them the greatest labour is to be pleased: they hate to have nothing to find fault with: to expect them to smile or to converse on equal terms, is the heaviest tax you can levy on their want of animal spirits or intellectual resources. A drop of pleasure is the most difficult thing to extract from their hard, dry, mechanical, husky frame; a civil word or look is the last thing they can part with. Hence the *matter-of-factness* of their understandings, their tenaciousness of reason or prejudice, their slowness to distinguish, their backwardness to yield, their mechanical improvements, their industry, their courage, their blunt honesty, their dislike to the frivolous and florid, their love of liberty out of hatred to oppression, and their love of virtue from their antipathy to vice.

He complains that French painters affect the qualities of sculpture, and in a terse footnote he says this of Parisian houses:

The fronts of the houses and many of the finest buildings seem (so to speak) to have been composed in mud, and translated into stone – so little projection, relief, or airiness have they. They have a look of being *stuck* together.

Praising Burke's style, Hazlitt calls it 'airy, flighty, adventurous' ('On the Prose Style of Poets'). The term 'projection' is a version of Hazlitt's favourite Shakespearean image – 'pendent bed and procreant cradle' – which he also uses to describe the 'jutty' texture of Burke's prose.

What we see, then, is that *Notes of a Journey* is a narrative of aesthetic judgements, perceptions, arguments – a series of epiphanic moments or thoughtful jottings of the kind that we find in writers' notebooks, commonplace books and letters. James Joyce constructed a great novel – *A Portrait of the Artist as a Young Man* – out of such moments, and we should see Hazlitt's travel journalism as a narrative of his critical consciousness in an always energetic and communicative process. He is concerned with the transformed power of aesthetic and critical perception, as when he offers this dramatic reading of Raphael's *Fornarina*:

Raphael's Fornarina (which is also in this highly-embellished cabinet of art) faces the Venus, and is a downright, point-blank contrast to it. Assuredly no charge can be brought against it of *mimmini-piminee* affectation or shrinking delicacy. It is robust, full to bursting, coarse, luxurious, hardened, but wrought up to an infinite degree of exactness and beauty in the details. It is the perfection of vulgarity and refinement together. The Fornarina is a bouncing, buxom, sullen, saucy baker's daughter – but painted, idolized, immortalized by Raphael! Nothing can be more homely and repulsive than the original; you see her bosom swelling like the dough rising in the oven; the tightness of her skin puts you in mind of Trim's story of the sausage-maker's wife – nothing can be much more enchanting than the picture – than the care and delight with which the artist has seized the lurk-ing glances of the eye, curved the corners of the mouth, smoothed the forehead, dimpled the chin, rounded the neck, till by innumerable delicate touches, and the 'labour of love,' he has converted a coarse, rude mass into a miracle of art.

Near the end, as I've mentioned, another object of 'swelling proportions' – Mont Blanc – is described as 'a huge dumb heap of matter', and Hazlitt then moves to assert that his mind 'hovers over mysteries deeper than the abysses at our feet'. But his mind has already made a picture of Mont Blanc for us. A moving picture because they are travelling through a landscape which, significantly, has 'jagged pine-trees' and 'projecting rocks and stumps of trees'. Projection is a distinctive critical value for Hazlitt, and the landscape he moves through becomes his aesthetic, his style. He is painting pictures of it, or of interiors as when he describes being attended in the Hotel des Courriers, in Lyons,

by a brown, greasy, dark-haired, good-humoured, awkward gypsey of a wench from the south of France, who seemed just caught; stared and laughed, and forgot every thing she went for; could not help exclaiming every moment – '*Que Madame a la peau blanche!*' from the contrast to her own dingy complexion and dirty skin, took a large brass-pan of scalding milk, came and sat down by me on a bundle of wood, and drank it; said she had had no supper, for her head ached, and declared the English were *braves gens*, and that the Bourbons were *bons enfants*, started up to look through the key-hole, and whispered through her broad strong-set teeth, that a fine Madam was descending the staircase, who had been to dine with a great gentleman, offered to take away the supper things, left them, and called us the next morning with her head and senses in a state of even greater confusion than they were over-night.

This is almost the only glimpse we get of Hazlitt's second wife, and her *peau blanche* contrasts beautifully with this animated picture of the servant girl.

Hazlitt's use of the word 'greasy' is particularly interesting, because it signals both aesthetic disgust and its opposite, an erotic aesthetic attraction. Speaking through the English interlocutor in the critical dialogue, in Chapter 6, Hazlitt praises the 'unctuous' freedom of the artist's brushwork. In the essay 'Hot and Cold', which is one of the products of this tour, he praises the 'dirty, dingy, greasy, sun-burnt complexion of an Italian peasant or beggar, whose body seems alive all over with a sort of tingling, oily sensation'. For Hazlitt, this effect is linked to Titian's handling of oil paint, because in a passage he undoubtedly contributed to Northcote's *Life of Titian* praise is given to the 'heavy, dingy, slimy effect of various oils and megilps'.

In *Notes of a Journey*, he describes how the pit of a theatre in the Paris Opéra is almost half-full of men, 'in their black, dingy *sticky-looking* dresses'. He italicizes 'sticky-looking', so that we feel his sensuous relishing of the colour's texture, almost as though he is working oil and turps with a brush. A few sentences later, he speaks of 'a dark and pitchy cloud', and this echoes his opening description of Brighton:

Brighton stands facing the sea, on the bare cliffs, with glazed windows to reflect the glaring sun, and black pitchy bricks shining like the scales of fishes. The town is however gay with the influx of London visitors – happy as the conscious abode of its sovereign! Every thing here appears in motion – coming or going. People at a watering-place may be compared to the flies of a summer; or to fashionable dresses, or suits of clothes walking about the streets. The only idea you gain is, of finery and motion.

The *ih* sound in 'pitchy' runs through this sentence (it picks up 'Pavilion' in the previous paragraph) and gives it keeping. I see this sentence as a tiny Magritte painting, sinister in look and texture.

In Chapter 19, Hazlitt describes the 'dingy, melancholy flat fronts of modern-built houses', and in the same chapter he notes the 'greasy oil-skin cloaks' worn by pilgrims in Rome. Though he calls the pilgrims 'a dirty, disgusting set', his eye is drawn to their greasy oilskins that have the unctuous sheen of wet paint. This is true, too, of this passage: 'There is nothing unpleasant in a French theatre but a certain infusion of *soupe-maigre* into the composition of the air, (so that one inhales a kind of thin pottage,) and an oily dinginess in the complexions both of the men and women, which shews more by lamp-light.' He then praises the 'rich pulpy texture of the flesh' in Raphael, and for Hazlitt oiliness, art, and the living, healthy body are intimately related. Discussing French painting, the English interlocutor in Chapter 6 praises 'animated flesh, not coloured stone', one of Hazlitt's many dismissive remarks about sculpture.

If we take his remark about the Paris houses being composed in mud and translated into stone, we can see how this analogy between literary composition and architecture is developed in his great description of Venice, where he says that a city 'built in the air would be something still more wonderful; but any other must yield the palm to this for singularity and imposing effort'. Venice becomes a city of air and sea as Hazlitt evokes it before debating the differences in the genius of Titian and Giorgione.

He succeeds in making stone airy, and he does so again in the closing return through the Simplon Pass:

Crags, of which we could only before discern the jutting tops, gradually reared their full stature at our side; and icy masses, one by one, came in sight, emerging from their lofty recesses, like clouds floating in mid-air. All this while a green valley kept us company by the road-side, watered with gushing rills, interspersed with cottages and well-stocked farms: fine elms and ash grew on the sides of the hills.

Meditating on the Alpine landscape, Hazlitt turns to a favourite theme – the limitations of French culture. English culture has a material strength, which the French lacks:

> The words *charming, indescribable,* excite the same lively emotions in their minds as the most vivid representations of what is said to be so; and hence verbiage and the cant of sentiment fill the place, and stop the road to genius – a vague, flaccid, enervated rhetoric being too often substituted for the pith and marrow of truth and nature. The greatest facility to feel or to comprehend will not produce the most intense passion, or the most electrical expression of it. There must be a resistance in the matter to do this – a collision, an obstacle to overcome. The torrent rushes with fury from being impeded in its course: the lightning splits the gnarled oak. There is no malice in this statement; but I should think they may themselves allow it to be an English version of the truth, containing a great deal that is favourable to them, with a saving clause for our own use. The long (and to us tiresome) speeches in French tragedy consist of a string of emphatic and well-balanced lines, announcing general maxims and indefinite sentiments applicable to human life. The poet seldom commits any excesses by giving way to his own imagination, or identifying himself with individual situations and sufferings. We are not now raised to the height of passion, now plunged into its lowest depth; the whole finds its level, like water, in the liquid, yielding susceptibility of the French character, and in the unembarrassed scope of the French intellect.

This is the prose writer's internal landscape, the 'jutting' tops of the crags are certainly real crags, but they also figure the 'jutty frieze' in Duncan's praise of Macbeth's castle, by which Hazlitt communicates the texture of Burke's prose.

This passage is similar to Hazlitt's remark in 'On the Prose Style of Poets' that Burke's execution 'savours of the texture of what he describes, and his pen slides or drags over the ground of his subject, like the painter's pencil'. In the essay, he also remarks that in Burke's prose there is 'a resistance in the matter to the illustration applied to it'. Both the essay and Notes of a Journey were published in 1826, so it is clear that in describing the Alps Hazlitt is either drawing on or formulating his ideas about Burke's style. The recalcitrance of matter in the process of prose composition is savoured in those verbs 'drags' and 'splits', and from 'splits' to 'pitchy' is not far to go in terms of expressive action and texture. Hazlitt works words, cadences, pauses, assonantal or dissonant clusters, like paint in his prose, so that time and again we get smaller or greater moments, which stand on their own uniquely, like inscapes:

We had a fine passage in the steam-boat (Sept. 1, 1824). Not a cloud, scarce a breath of air; a moon, and then star-light, till the dawn, with rosy fingers, ushered us into Dieppe.

This, as he may have intended, is like a Turner painting, while the cadence of the deliberate cliché 'rosy fingers' oils its conversational lyricism. Hazlitt will soon complain that the French have 'no idea of *cadence* in any of the arts', and it is his rejection of what in the same passage he calls 'dry and systematic prosing for the benefit of others', which makes his prose so continuously interesting.

He is wholly reticent about his personal life, but it is clear from *Notes of a Journey* that this was a period of great personal happiness for him. He is a most companionable writer, and after his arrival at Turin there is this heartfelt moment:

My arrival at Turin was the first and only moment of intoxication I have found in Italy. It is a city of palaces. After a change of dress (which, at the end of a long journey, is a great luxury) I walked out, and traversing several clean, spacious streets, came to a promenade outside the town, from which I saw the chain of Alps we had left behind us, rising like a range of marble pillars in the evening sky. Monte Viso and Mount Cenis resembled two pointed cones of ice, shooting up above all the rest. I could distinguish the broad and rapid Po, winding along at the other extremity of the walk, through vineyards and meadow grounds. The trees had on that deep sad foliage, which takes a mellower tinge from being prolonged into the midst of winter, and which I had only seen in pictures. A Monk was walking in a solitary grove at a little distance from the common path. The air was soft and balmy, and I felt transported to another climate – another earth – another sky. The winter was suddenly changed to spring. It was as if I had to begin my life anew. Several young Italian women were walking on the terrace, in English dresses, and with graceful downcast looks, in which you might fancy that you read the soul of the Decameron. It was a fine, serious grace, equally remote from French levity and English sullenness, but it was the last I saw of it.

This is a beautiful prose lyric – it reads as if Hazlitt has become a child again, starting to be happy. For a moment, he has put aside all his very intelligent and discerning exasperations, and if I have suggested that he is unrelenting in his criticisms of the French, I should add that he does at times stand back from his anger at them for losing the Battle of Waterloo. He portrays them as a nation of serious and discerning readers, remarking that there is 'a transparency in their intellects as in their atmosphere, which makes the communication of thought or sound more rapid and general'. He states that the face 'of the French soldiery is a face of great humanity – it is manly, sedate, thoughtful – it is equally free from fierceness and stupidity; and it seems to bear in its eye defeat and victory, the eagle and the lilies!' He concludes this chapter by saying: 'They over-ran Europe like tigers, and defended their own territory like deer. They are a nation of heroes – on this side of martyrdom!' Praise and exasperation mix here as in dramatic speech, and it is the drama of Hazlitt's puritan consciousness that makes this neglected text so exciting to read.

The Shaggy, the Rude, the Awkard: John Clare

In 1865, a year after John Clare's death in the Northampton General Lunatic Asylum, Frederick Martin, a former amanuensis of Thomas Carlyle, published the first biography of the 'peasant poet'. It laid the foundations, Jonathan Bate says in *John Clare: A Biography* (2003), 'for both the enduring myths and some of the key truths about Clare'. Though there have been other biographies since Martin's, Bate's should finally disprove Dickens's dismissal of it as a 'preposterous exaggeration of small claims', and consolidate Clare's reputation as a major Romantic poet (it's strange to remember that he was much more successful in his lifetime than Keats, with whom he shared a publisher).

Clare was discovered in 1819, when Edward Drury, a young Stamford bookseller, wrote to his cousin John Taylor, who was also a bookseller – what we would now call a publisher – and told him that he had discovered a wholly untutored genius:

> Your hopes of good grammar and correct verse, depend on the inspiration of the mind; for Clare cannot *reason*; he writes and can give no reason for his using a fine expression, or a beautiful idea: if you read Poetry to him, he'll exclaim at each delicate expression 'beautiful! fine!' but can give no reason: yet is *always* correct and just in his remarks. He is low in stature – long visage – light hair – coarse features – ungaitly – awkward – is a fiddler – loves ale – likes the *girls* – somewhat idle, – hates work.

As Bate says, this is condescending, but it also shows real enthusiasm for Clare. The last sentence of Drury's letter, like a moment from Clare's prose – or, I would imagine, his conversation – catches him, pinning on him the adjective 'awkward', which (in the spelling 'awkard') Clare uses obsessively in his writings.

Clare left nearly ten thousand pages of manuscript writings – poems, autobiography, journals, letters, essays and natural history writings, as well as a substantial number of traditional songs, which he transcribed and collected. Four collections of poems – less than a quarter of his output – appeared in print during his lifetime: *Poems, Descriptive of Rural Life and Scenery* (published in 1820, when he was 26), *The Village Minstrel and Other Poems* (1821), *The Shepherd's Calendar; with Village Stories, and Other Poems* (1827) and *The Rural Muse* (1835). For a short time, he was celebrated as the English Burns, but his work hasn't had Burns's lasting popularity. One result of this neglect is that the circumstances of his life are not widely known.

Clare's paternal grandmother, Alice Clare, was the daughter of the senior parish clerk at Helpston in Northamptonshire. In the early 1760s, she had a relationship with John Donald Parker, an itinerant Scottish fiddler and teacher who was working in the village school. On discovering she was pregnant, he disappeared and was never heard of again. Her son was christened for the absent father, and became a talented traditional singer, a gift he passed on to his own son, John, who also became an adept fiddler, like his grandfather. Clare felt an affinity with Robert Burns, collected songs as Burns did, and during his asylum years wrote a number of songs in the Scottish vernacular. Clare says in his autobiography that both his parents were 'illiterate to the last degree'. Concerned to dispel the myths, Bate points out that the Clares, who formed a line of parish clerks, would have been among the most literate people in their village: Parker Clare could certainly read, although his wife, Ann Stimson, did not know a single letter of the alphabet and, like many country people, regarded printed texts as a form of witchcraft. At this time, Bate notes, *illiterate* meant not 'unable to read' but 'ignorant of polite letters'.

Clare and a twin sister were born on 13 July 1793, in a thatched tenement on Helpston High Street, next door to the Blue Bell public house. There were two bedrooms and two downstairs rooms: in Clare's words, his childhood home was 'as roomy and comfortable as any of our neighbours'. There was an apple tree in the garden, which, Clare says in his autobiography, 'stood' his father's 'friend many a year in the days of adversity by producing an abundance of fruit which always met with ready sale and paid his rent'. (His first biographer, Frederick Martin, doesn't mention the apple tree in his biography and describes the thatched cottage as a 'narrow, wretched hut'.) Clare was baptized on 11 August 1793, by which time his sister was dead. Bate suggests that the search for something lost – 'something innocent, female, and associated with childhood' – was bound into Clare's mental state and at the heart of his poetry. The family remembered his sister as Bessy, and talked enough about her to 'ingrain' her in Clare's memory.

When times were hard his father withdrew him from school to save on fees; but, encouraged by two teachers, he read the Bible, the prayer book, penny chapbooks, an agricultural manual and an old book of essays that had lost its title page. He acquainted himself with 'Mathematics Particularly Navigation and Algebra, Dialling, Use of the Globes, Botany, Natural History, Short Hand, with History of all Kinds, Drawing, Music'. He never studied 'Grammer', and always expressed a dislike of its 'tyranny', but he was good at maths, something which helped him in negotiations with publishers. The formative texts of his childhood and early youth were, inevitably, *Pilgrim's Progress* and *Robinson Crusoe*, both of which he echoed in 'To the Snipe', a lyric whose isolated, islanded atmosphere and slough-like, 'rude, desolate' marshes build a distinctive form of Puritan anguish.

Bate begins his third chapter with an account of the most profound experience of Clare's childhood. One morning he went to gather rotten sticks from the wood, then decided 'to wander about the fields'. He gazed over the yellow furze of Emmonsales Heath, and imagined, he says in his autobiography, 'that the world's end was at the edge of the horizon and that a day's journey was able to find it'. He thought that when he reached the brink of the world he would find a large pit, and would be able to look down and see the secrets of the universe. He spent the whole day rambling among the furze, 'till I got out of my knowledge when the very wild flowers and birds seemed to forget me and I imagined they were the inhabitants of new countries'. Before morning seemed over, it was dark, and when by chance he found the right track and got back to his own fields everything appeared different. When he reached home he found his parents distressed and half the village out searching for him – a woodman had been killed by a falling tree and they feared he too had been hurt. This experience – analogous to Wordsworth's childhood need to touch external objects in order to prove they weren't mental and ideal – is behind one of Clare's greatest poems, 'Birds Nesting':

> To the worlds end I thought I'd go
> And o'er the brink just peep adown
> To see the mighty depths below.

Clare is thought of as a marginal, provincial poet, who inhabited a remote green world of heath, woodland, riverbank and marshland, but Bate draws attention to the richness of the cultural life around him. Stamford, to the north-west of Helpston, just over the county border into Lincolnshire, was no backwater. Books were published there; it had a theatre, musical evenings and a newspaper, the *Stamford Mercury*, 'the articulate voice of eastern England'. In 1809 John Drakard established a rival newspaper, the *Stamford News*, edited by the radical journalist John Scott, who was later to edit the *London Magazine*. The village of Helpston itself was caught between two landed and political interests: Burghley Park was the seat of the Exeters, who were Tories, while the Milton Estate belonged to the Fitzwilliams, who were Whigs.

Clare's horizon was set by the parishes that surround Helpston: Maxey, Etton, Glinton, Bainton, Northborough and Ufford. During his childhood, most of these villages had open fields, but in 1799 Bainton was enclosed. Ten years later, when he was sixteen, a Parliamentary Act was passed for 'Inclosing Lands in the Parishes of Maxey with Deepingate, Northborough, Glinton with Peakirk, Etton, and Helpstone in the County of Northampton'. The principal purpose of enclosure was to increase profits, but the price of 'Improvement' was the loss of the commons and waste grounds, which according to the Act 'yield but little Profit'. It took until 1820 to bring the enclosure fully into effect (nearby Castor stayed unenclosed until 1898). Laxton in Nottinghamshire remains as an example of how the English landscape used to look: wide open, unhedged, its spaciousness pushing beyond the horizon.

Clare was devastated by this violation of his natural and social environment. As Bate shows, the open-field system fostered a sense of community, the fields spread out in a wheel with the village at its hub. Enclosure thwarted Clare's 'open-field sense of space', as John Barrell calls it in *The Idea of Landscape and the Sense of Place* (1972), his seminal study of the poems, and imposed a more linear sense. Fences, gates and 'no trespassing' signs went up. Trees were felled and streams diverted so that ditches could follow a straight line:

> Inclosure like a Buonaparte let not a thing remain,
> It levelled every bush and tree, and levelled every hill
> And hung the moles for traitors – though the brook is
>   running still,
> It runs a naked stream, cold and chill.

'Remembrances' is printed without punctuation in the nine-volume Oxford edition, as are all the other poems, but Bate adopts light punctuation where the sense requires 'some form of pointing'. In the last line of this passage the addition of the comma foregrounds the pause after 'stream', as Clare's vernacular voice pushes honestly and severely against the metre and the couplet form (it would have been helpful if Bate had noted the way punctuation can alter cadence and rhythm, but like many biographers he usually employs quotations from the poems simply as narrative illustrations).

Bate follows E. P. Thompson in describing Clare as a poet of 'ecological protest', as well as a political poet angered by the destruction of 'an ancient birthright based on co-operation and common rights'. A local farming family, the Turnhills, with whom Clare and his father were friendly and for whom they did labouring work, were forced from their home without compensation at the time of enclosure, and Clare also identified with the plight of the Gypsies who camped on the common and margins – the 'waste' grounds which became private property. Although use of the commons had been technically restricted to those who occupied certain properties, the unenclosed spaces were perceived as belonging to everyone. Controversially, Bate says that analysis of land-tax assessments and expenditure on parish relief suggests that more smallholders and tenant farmers in Helpston lost their land in the years immediately before the enclosure than in its aftermath, and that the labouring poor may have been 'marginally better off' as a result of enclosure.

There were other changes. Festival days – Plough Monday, for example – were abolished by those whom Clare termed the 'vulgar tyrants of the soil'. Enclosure also infringed the right to roam, creating a claustrophobic environment, marked and ribbed by power and wealth. But Clare, unlike Burns, opposed those he called 'the French Levellers' – he saw the Revolutionaries as analogous to rapacious English enclosers – and in 1808 he joined the Eastern regiment of the Northampton militia. His military service involved only a few weeks of training, but he remained technically an enlisted man, and could have been called up between 1812 and 1816. He worked irregularly in these years with fencing and hedging gangs engaged in enclosure. The Clares' cottage had been divided, and they now had only two rooms. Clare's father wasn't well, and from 1814 was in receipt of Parish Poor Relief. A few years later, the apple tree failed to bear fruit and they were unable to pay the rent. Around this time, Clare fell in love with Martha Turner ('Patty'), who lived in a secluded cottage between Casterton and Pickworth and whose parents were socially a bit above the Clares.

Clare was already writing poetry, inspired by Thomson's *The Seasons*, which he had first read as a thirteen-year-old in a battered, fragmentary copy lent him by a Helpston weaver. Overwhelmed by Thomson's Whig pastoral, Clare nagged his father for some money, and bought his own copy for the bargain price of a shilling. He didn't want to be seen reading on a working day, so he climbed over the high wall round Burghley Park. Like the young Blake seeing a tree full of angels in the fields at Peckham Rye, this moment is part of literary folklore: 'What with reading the book,' Clare wrote in his autobiography, 'and beholding the beauties of artful nature in the park, I got into a strain of descriptive rhyming on my journey home.' He wrote a poem called 'The Morning Walk'; a companion piece called 'The Evening Walk' followed soon after. He began to write poems in secret and to hide them in an old cupboard. One of the poets he admired was Robert Bloomfield, another 'peasant poet', who in 1800 had published a poem called *The Farmer's Boy*, which sold 26,000 copies in three years and made its author £4000.

In 1818, Clare resolved to try to get his work published. It was a low point for him: he was lime-burning at Casterton, very short of money, concerned about his parents' ill health and poverty, and in love with Patty Turner, but without the prospect of marriage. His only contact with the publishing world was J. B. Henson, a printer and bookseller in nearby Market Deeping. He showed Henson two of his earliest sonnets, 'The Setting Sun' and 'To a Primrose', together with a poem on the death of Chatterton. Henson agreed to get in touch with his London bookseller, but claimed the only viable means of publication would be by subscription. In order to get up a subscription list, there would have to be a prospectus with a specimen of Clare's poetry. To print three hundred copies of the proposal, Henson would charge a pound. By working day and night at the limekiln, Clare saved the money. He then wrote the prospectus on a sheet of paper that was 'crumpled and grizzled' with lying in his pocket. He described his poems as a mixture of juvenile productions and the 'offsprings of those leisure intervals which the short remittance from hard and manual labour sparingly afforded to compose them'. Henson demanded not just the agreed pound, but an extra five shillings for expenses. He said he would print the book as soon as a hundred subscribers had been signed up, but demanded an advance of £15 from Clare, who had, he said, 'not 15 pence nor 15 farthings' to call his own. It was then that Clare received a bill for 15 shillings from a Mr Thompson who kept a bookshop in Stamford High Street. He was selling up and wanted to settle his accounts. Clare now had a lucky break. The new owner of the bookstore was a young man called Edward Drury, whose father was a printer in Lincoln. Drury read Clare's prospectus and saw an opportunity. He paid off Clare's bill and went to see him. Clare had been about to go to Yorkshire in search of work – the family was two years behind with the rent and on the point of eviction – but Drury now began to send him advances on a volume of poems. Clare wrote through the winter and into the spring, sending Drury new poems and corrections to earlier ones. On 8 April 1819 'To the Glow-worm' appeared in the *Macclesfield Courier*, a clumsy sonnet that began: 'Tasteful Illuminations of the night'.

Drury gave Clare's poems to his cousin John Taylor, who had worked for the booksellers who published Bloomfield's *Farmer's Boy* and had himself published *Endymion* in 1818. Taylor launched Clare in the *London Magazine*, which he founded. The first issue (1 January 1820) contained an article about Clare by Octavius Gilchrist: 'Some Account of John Clare, an Agricultural Labourer and Poet'. It was at this time that fears about Clare's mental health began to surface. Drury wrote to Taylor that he feared Clare would be 'afflicted with insanity if his talent continues to be forced as it has been these 4 months past'. Drury noted how sensitive Clare was to criticism, and how even a small amount of alcohol left him with terrible hangovers, which in turn made him 'melancholy and completely hypochondriac'.

On 15 January 1820, Clare's first book appeared under the title *Poems, Descriptive of Rural Life and Scenery*. He was described as 'A Northamptonshire Peasant'. The edition of 1000 copies sold out within two months. A second edition of 2000 sold out before the year was over, and two more followed soon after. Taylor's introduction, Bate argues, set the tone for the critical response to the volume. In it, Taylor told the story of Clare saving his shilling to buy *The Seasons*, and praised his distinctive use of a vernacular style and regional dialect. He presented Clare as a poet of immediate impressions and a child of nature, which, as Bate says, failed to honour his 'breadth of reading and depth of formal artfulness'. *Poems, Descriptive* was well received: both the *Eclectic Review* – a radical journal – and the reactionary *Anti-Jacobin Review* praised it.

Clare was received at Milton Hall by the Fitzwilliams, who gave him money and advice, as well as blankets and other comforts for his parents. The family would provide Clare with financial assistance for the rest of his life. He also visited Burghley House, where he was kindly received by the Marquess of Exeter's family. The Marquess immediately gave him an annuity of £15 a year. Clare also found patrons in Baron Radstock and Eliza Emmerson. In March he made his first visit to London, where his portrait was painted by William Hilton. Taylor and his business partner James Hessey gave a dinner for him, at which Clare met and became friends with Henry Cary, whose translation of Dante he draws on in 'To the Snipe'. A week after returning to Helpston, he married Patty Turner, who was pregnant. An announcement of the wedding was placed in the *London Magazine*, and Hessey sent Clare a Cremona violin. When their first daughter, Anna Maria, was born, Clare and his wife moved into the tenement next door to his parents.

Despite the money that was beginning to come to Clare from the annuities, gifts from patrons, and remittances from Taylor and Hessey, he had to take up manual labouring in the summer of 1820. Among the stresses of literary fame was the postage he had to pay on the unwanted fan letters he received, not to mention the visits from well-wishers who turned up as he worked in the fields and lost him valuable hours. Others took him to the Blue Bell and got him drunk.

Clare and Taylor came under pressure from Baron Radstock and Eliza Emmerson to remove lines from *Poems, Descriptive* which expressed radical sentiments. (This episode is described by Alan Vardy in *John Clare, Politics and Poetry*. He also gives a detailed and in the main convincing account of Clare's relationship with his other patrons, and with Taylor and Hessey.) Taylor wrote to Clare that he was 'inclined to remain obstinate', and told Emmerson that since 2000 copies of the third edition of *Poems, Descriptive* had already been printed, it was too late to make any alterations. Taylor did, however, drop some poems which were thought indelicate. Though Clare was annoyed by this 'medlars *false delicacy*', Taylor treated him, Bate says, with exemplary fairness, offering a half-share of the profits and refusing to let Clare bind himself to the publishing firm in perpetuity. Arguing convincingly against those critics and scholars who see Taylor as an interfering editor, Bate defends his changes to Clare's unpunctuated, irregularly spelled texts, and argues that Clare expected his editors to insert punctuation and correct his spelling. Bate persuades me that I was mistaken many years ago in criticizing Taylor's editing. He had to transcribe, correct, regularize and improve Clare's manuscripts, whose 'clutter, insertions and erasures', as Bate notes, are an editor's nightmare. It has taken the editors of the Oxford edition forty years to decipher, transcribe and publish Clare's surviving manuscripts. (They opt to print the poems without punctuation.) Bate also addresses the question of the copyright to Clare's manuscripts, which is claimed by his Oxford editor, Eric Robinson, who bought them for £1 in 1965.

Bate's account of Clare's relationship with Taylor convincingly shows that Clare often needed the stimulus of his publisher's urgings: 'If I cannot hear from John Taylor now and then I cannot rhyme.' Taylor's health was fragile and he could be distracted by the demands of his business, so this support wasn't always forthcoming. Sometimes Clare wrote furiously day and night, at other times he was unable to put pen to paper. Bate suggests that he suffered from manic depression – he frequently wrote in his letters of 'blue devils'. He felt alienated from his community, and his first son died while he was working on his second volume, *The Village Minstrel*. In a letter of 1822 to Taylor he complained:

> I live here among the ignorant like a lost man in fact like one whom the rest seems careless of having anything to do with – they hardly dare talk in my company for fear I shoud mention them in my writings & I find more pleasure in wandering the fields then in musing among my silent neighbours who are insensible to every thing but toiling & talking of it & that to no purpose.

Clare was also, as he told Eliza Emmerson, 'love-sick' – he had had an affair – and worried about money.

On a visit to London in 1824 he watched Byron's funeral moving up Oxford Street, and noted that it was the common people who were mourning him. Byron's death marked the waning of the enormous popularity of poetry in England – a reaction was setting in. There was a severe commercial recession in which publishing was affected, and Taylor and Hessey ceased trading, though Taylor published *The Shepherd's Calendar* in 1827.

While Clare was working on *The Shepherd's Calendar*, which Bate rightly calls one of the great poems of the nineteenth century, he and Taylor became exasperated with each other. Towards the end of January 1826, Clare wrote to tell Taylor that he couldn't cope with further delays and cross-purposes. Taylor wrote back saying that no progress could be made because the 'July' poem was 'unfit for Insertion' and the next day wrote:

> Heretofore I have submitted, and apologized, and taken Blame to myself, – because I was resolved, if possible, to complete my Undertaking, whatever Pains it cost me: but your frank Censure has at last relieved me from my irksome Situation, and I must now as frankly tell you, that for the principal part of the Delay and for the present total Stop again, you are alone responsible – Look at the Vol. of MS. poems which I now send you, and show it where you will, and let any of your Friends say whether they can even read it. – I can find *noone* here who can perform the Task besides myself. Copying it therefore is a Farce for not three Words in a Line on the Average are put down right, and the number omitted, by those whom I have got to transcribe it, are so great, that it is easier for me at once to sit down and write it fairly out myself – But suppose I attempt to do this; here I encounter another Difficulty: – The Poems are not only slovenly written, but as slovenly *composed*, and to make Good Poems out of some of them is a greater Difficulty than I ever had to engage with in your former Works, – while in others it is a complete Impossibility.

The letter ended: 'Farewell, dear Clare, I am not less your Friend for speaking so freely.' Vardy calls this letter 'cruelly haranguing', and says that 'to lash out at Clare was cruel and dishonest', arguing that the arbitrariness of Taylor's editorial decisions points to 'the incompetence of a desperate and shattered man'. Five days later Taylor apologized for his tone. Clare wrote a new and much shorter poem for 'July', and *The Shepherd's Calendar; with Village Stories, and Other Poems* was published at the end of April 1827 (Vardy says that Taylor made a 'mess' of the text when he edited the manuscript, though he cites no evidence). It was a poor season for new books, Taylor complained, and the new *Calendar* had 'comparatively no sale'. It received some substantial and laudatory reviews, however, and the anonymous reviewer in the *Literary Chronicle* claimed that Clare had now made good his early promise to be the English equal of Burns. But Clare felt lonely, depressed and alienated. Echoing Exodus, a favourite biblical book, he wrote, 'I am but as an alien in a strange land', and compared himself to Sisyphus, 'the poor purgatorial convict of Grecian mythology'. He was becoming more and more obsessed with the memory of an early love, Mary Joyce. He wrote poems to her and she became a symbolic figure who incorporated other lost girls he may have known much more intimately than he ever knew her. The notion of Mary Joyce as his one true desire was a 'convenient fiction' of his poetry and his first biographers.

In the spring of 1829, the land steward at Burghley Park noted that Ford and Trigg were thrashing, Stanger minding the pigs, Henson and Isaac bringing in the malt and 'Clare cutting a hedge'. In his letters we catch glimpses of him harvesting, and 'revelling afterwards in Stamford'. We also glimpse his practical gifts when he responds to the long overdue accounts Taylor and Hessey sent him in August 1829. He had been busy with the harvest, and was not able to look at them in detail until November. There were six accounts, whose net result showed that Clare was in debt to Taylor and Hessey to the sum of just over £141 – the equivalent of three and a half years' worth of his regular annuity and dividend payments, or nearly six years' income from agricultural labour. Clare noticed several errors or sleights of hand. He pointed to these and to a number of other problems, and they were able to reach an agreement. At the beginning of January 1830, Taylor sent Clare a £10 note, which more than accounted for the half-yearly annuity due to him. It was a gesture of reconciliation, and the question of the money Clare owed was quietly dropped. But, Bate points out, one of the enduring myths about Clare has been that he was a victim of sharp financial practice on Taylor's part.

Clare was always short of paper, which was very expensive: a blank folio notebook cost a week's wages. Bate notes that whatever hardships the Clares had to endure, they ensured that their children had sixpenny chapbooks for Christmas. In the chaos of Clare's papers, this little note survives:

Christmas Boxes promised my childern

Anna Valentine and Ornson
Eliza Cock Robin
Frederic Peacock at Home and Butterflyes Ball
John Dame Trott and her Cat
William Mother Hubard and her Dog
Sophy House that Jack Built.

The Reform Bill of 1832 achieved nothing for the rural poor and riots in the countryside were brutally suppressed by executions, imprisonment and transportations. The Clares' financial difficulties were symptomatic of a widespread economic crisis.

Then they had what looked like a stroke of good fortune. A cottage belonging to the Milton estate was available for rent in the village of Northborough, three miles from Helpston, and through the intervention of the local clergyman it was offered to Clare. It had a large garden, an established orchard and a grazing pasture, but the rent was £13 a year, several times what he was paying at Helpston. Northborough was an isolated, gossipy, introverted community, and the move desolated Clare, whose poem 'The Flitting' represents his sense of loss and bereavement at leaving 'mine own old home of homes' (Bate does not include this major poem in his selection).

Three years later, in July 1835, he published his fourth and last volume, *The Rural Muse*. Sales were slow, but reviews were uniformly favourable. As Bate points out, the volume was distinguished by a run of 86 sonnets, several of which used 'a hitherto unattempted rhyme scheme' ('Evening Schoolboys' rhymes *abababcbcbcdcd*, and 'The Crab Tree' rhymes *ababacdcdefeff* – Bate remarks that he knows of 'no precedent for either scheme'). It was during this period that Clare wrote 'To the Snipe'. In Taylor's letters we catch glimpses of Patty Clare, his 'comely', tough wife, whom Taylor describes as 'a very clever active woman', who keeps 'them all very respectable and comfortable, but she cannot manage to control her husband at times'. Taylor says in a letter to his sister (9 December 1835) that Clare's mind 'is sadly enfeebled', and that he is 'very violent, I dare say, occasionally'. In July 1837, he was committed to Allen's private asylum in Epping Forest, 'by authority of his wife'.

*

It was Clare's particular gift to develop the anxieties that had faced the late-Augustan poets, and to understand what Gray meant when he wrote:

Those invasions of effeminate Southern nations by the warlike Northern people seem, (in spite of all the terror, mischief, and ignorance which they brought with them) to be necessary evils; in order to revive the spirit of mankind, softened and broken by the arts of commerce, to restore them to their native liberty and equality, and to give them again the power of supporting danger and hardship; so a comet, with all the horrors that attend it as it passes through our system, brings a supply of warmth and light to the sun, and of moisture to the air.

Attempting to state the opposite point of view, the opening paragraph of Gibbon's *Decline and Fall* moves from confident polysyllables – 'comprehensive', 'civilized', 'constitution', 'luxury' – to tough Germanic monosyllables like 'fall', 'felt', 'earth', which anticipate the overthrow of Roman civilization. William Collins takes Gibbon's side in 'Ode to Liberty', where he says:

> No, *Freedom*, no, I will not tell,
> How *Rome*, before thy weeping Face,
> With heaviest Sound, a Giant-statue, fell,
> Push'd by a wild and artless Race,
> From off its wide ambitious Base,
> When Time his Northern Sons of Spoil awoke,
>   And all the blended Work of Strength and Grace,
>   With many a rude repeated Stroke
> And many a barb'rous Yell, to thousand Fragments broke.

The nodal word here is 'rude', which Collins draws from Milton's 'rude axe with heaved stroke', and which he uses elsewhere in his verse. Gray gives a less pejorative sense in 'the rude and moss-grown beech', which canopies the glade in 'Ode to Spring', where 'rude' picks up 'glade' and 'rushy' in the lines that follow to draw in the idea of the Greenwood, and by implication English liberty. A couplet in Goldsmith's 'The Deserted Village': 'A time there was, ere England's griefs began, / When every rood of ground maintained its man', suggests that 'rood' both in the sense of 'unit of measure' and 'cross' must also inform 'rude', which is one of Clare's favourite, and in Empson's sense most complex, words (he uses it at least 265 times in his poetry, far more than any other Romantic-period poet). As Clare would have noticed, 'rude' associates in Gray and Collins with 'runic', 'Druid', 'ruddy', 'Muse', 'ruin', and 'uncouth', and represents a developing interest in Anglo-Saxon, Old Norse, tradi-tional ballads, orality – an interest that issues from an anxiety about the assumptions and values embodied in polished Augustan diction, as well as from the social pressures of the age. Both Gray and Collins knew that the artificial and the artless were moving into intimate confrontation.

That anxiety is evident in a more radical manner in Gray's poetry, where a line like 'The untaught harmony of spring' expresses his interest in the 'unletter'd muse', as he terms it in the *Elegy*. Clare must have felt, as he read the English poets and composed his early verse, that Gray's poem was addressed personally to him (as a young farm labourer he read Thompson's *The Seasons* in the same way), and he would have known that beyond the social struggle to get published and favourably reviewed, there was an aesthetic problem of finding not a balance – the term is old-fashioned, Augustan – but a means of giving his readers the pastoral felicities they expected, while keeping something of the naivety, roughness and spontaneity of what Gray terms 'uncouth rhymes'. As his devoted editors show in a long appendix which covers corrections and additional versions for the previous five volumes, when Clare's 'To the Rural Muse' was published in *The Morning Post* (31 August 1821) it was preceded by this puff: 'We have been favoured with the following further Extracts from the forthcoming volume of beautiful Poems by our own sweet Peasant Poet, John Clare.'

Clare often plays to this image of being England's sweet peasant poet, as for example in these lines, included in this volume's appendix, which are additional to another early poem *The Village Minstrel*:

> He loved the brook that rambling did proceed
> Along its pasture path with dimpling stride
> & well he might for it was sweet indeed
> With many a thorn & willow by its side
> & smooth & easy did its curdle glide
> Checked by the polished pebbles – it did run
> Soft as a lovers speed who by its side
> Leads his love homeward when their toils are done
> Neath summers leisure hour or summers evening sun.

The smooth, sweet, easy brook with its polished pebbles is an obvious image of poet, language and pastoral subject ('dimpled', 'curdle' and 'checked' offer a slightly roughened counter-texture), and in another manuscript version he writes of aiming at 'sweeter & more polished lays'. But as Clare became more confident and more angry, he began to draw deeply on the sometimes populist emotions in Gray's verse, and on popular ballads, which he sang and collected. He left the Church of England for the Wesleyan Methodists in 1819 or earlier, then moved to the Primitive Methodists or Ranters, then hid his tracks. In Gray's 'Hymn to Adversity', there is a counter-movement to smoothness and sweetness: adversity is hailed as a stern 'rugged Nurse'. In his translation from Propertius, the moon controls the 'sandy bounds' of the 'rude surge', and in the *Elegy* he exclaims: 'How bow'd the woods beneath their sturdy stroke!' – the stroke of the rude forefathers' axes. 'Rude' is ghosted in 'woods' and 'sturdy', while the woods then bow like courtiers to the axe-wielding peasants, who are like northern invaders, except they are native.

Throughout his work, Clare draws on these seminal lines from the *Elegy*:

> Save that from yonder ivy-mantled tow'r
> The mopeing owl does to the moon complain
> Of such, as wand'ring near her secret bow'r,
> Molest her ancient solitary reign.
>
> Beneath those rugged elms, that yew-tree's shade,
> Where heaves the turf in many a mould'ring heap,

> Each in his narrow cell for ever laid,
> The rude forefathers of the hamlet sleep.

If this was a Yeats poem, the word 'ancient' would both signify and ratify a type of traditional ethnic nationalism, sometimes with an eldritch cadence, and there is here a slightly Gothic, deliberately spooky English patriotism, which then reaches beyond the Norman ruin to the freedom of the Greenwood, before slipping back into the graveyard where the ancestors sleep like King Arthur in his cave. The fused sounds 'rugged', 'yew' and 'rude', with the implicit image of a taut bow, help design a distinctively English image of the robustly heaving, popular will and the cultural memory joined to it by the internal rhyme on 'heap', whose defining adjective 'mouldering' in turn picks up 'mopeing' and 'molest', which are keyed to the four *o* sounds in the opening stanza – 't*o*lls', 'l*o*wing', 'sl*o*wly', 'h*o*meward'. That image of the village graveyard, and especially the much more vigorous *oo* sounds in 'rude' and its cousins, spoke to Clare, who draws on them throughout his work, most especially in one of his greatest poems 'To the Snipe', which is included in volume four of this edition.

The word 'rude' appears, for example, in one of the Northborough sonnets, where Clare wishes for 'the quiet of a humble mind', and then says:

> A light not dull nor glaring falls around
> That seems to say the peace of life is found
> The rude formed table & still ruder chair
> Seats for simplicity & none for care
> & O how weariness with heavy eye
> Upon that mossy couch will love to lie

The repeated use of 'rude', like the 'rude letters on the snow', which the schoolboy loves to make in a sonnet Clare wrote a year later, points to his class anxiety and the fear that his poems won't last, but it is also an allusion to Gray's use of the adjective, so its literariness plays against the primary meaning, flicking its more complicated sense back at the middle-class reader. Clare was writing a few miles from his native Helpstone in the village of Northborough, a place where, as Bate shows, he never felt at home and where he became mentally ill. The fenland there has a chill, exposed quality, and his sense of desolation is evident throughout these poems, where ugly images of pollarded or 'dotchel trees', 'bulky dotterel trees' and an 'old squatty oak' embody his sense of loss and dislocation. In 'Wandering by the rivers edge', a characteristically untitled poem, he employs the form of *L'Allegro* and *Il Penseroso* lovingly to represent reeds, kingfishers, osiers, and a sinister hissing snake coiling in the flood, before describing trees 'to stumpy dotterels lopt' and then: 'Oer treeless fens of many miles / Spring comes & goes & comes again / & all is nakedness & fen'. The social isolation, the pressure of his celebrity, the loss of a familiar, unenclosed landscape culminate in these alienated lines:

> A scene that makes the cold achill
> Large grounds bethronged with thistles brown
> Shivering & madding up & down
> Was but a bramble in the place
> Twould be a sort of living grace
> A shape of shelter in the wind
> For stock to chew their cuds behind
> But all is level cold & dull
> & osier swamps with water full

The blasted bareness, the 'cold achill', 'cold & dull' and repeated 'acold' elsewhere in the poem pick up 'Tom's acold' on the heath with Lear and the Fool, while the earlier image of 'dithering' thistles that 'crowd the lane' alludes to the violent disturbances of the early 1830s, when Clare wrote this poem. Just before the lines quoted, he writes of 'dunghills hiding snake & toad', meaning the rich farmers, placemen and recipients of clerical tithes he discusses in a letter to his publisher, John Taylor, on 1 February 1830, where he recounts political meetings in the locality.

That final hard *uh* sound in 'full' brings 'dull' back with added emphasis, striking a dank, hollow reverberation. The mention of the snake and the toad, and Clare's use elsewhere in the poem of the word 'puddock', or kite, make it anti-pastoral, as does the Crabbean coldness and use of 'dreary', and the obsessive use of 'rude'. Words such as 'awkard', 'rawky', 'crizzled', 'clumbsy', 'crimped', 'chafe', 'grubbing', 'slur', 'prog' (celebrated by Seamus Heaney), as well as 'ragged', 'shabby', 'sour', 'stroked harls' and the reference to the 'muck that clouts a ploughman's shoe', are also markers of this significant aesthetic category. When Clare says in an untitled poem beginning 'Good morning to ye honest swain' that he goes 'to dinner with the lark / Behind a stubble shock', he is deliberately roughening the conventional lyric image. (Keats beautifully and subtly employs this strategy in 'To Autumn', where the clammy, bloody or deliberately mawkish images and effects code a republican politics, although this is still not accepted by many scholars. Clare, who knew Keats and shared a publisher with him and Hazlitt, objected to Keats's ignorance of wildlife and the countryside, but he learnt from his poetry, most especially in the use of unsettling textures.)

In such poems Clare draws on Hazlitt's essay 'On Thomson and Cowper', which he read in *Lectures on the English Poets*. Clare had met and admired Hazlitt, and would have been taken by his praise of Robert Bloomfield, who Hazlitt says 'gives the simple appearance of nature, but he gives it naked, shivering, and unclothed with the drapery of a moral imagination'. The shivering thistles are a version of that unclothed imagination. Hazlitt also praises Bloomfield as an 'ingenious and self-taught' poet, whose verse is distinguished for 'delicacy, fruitfulness and naïveté' – this last quality is also present in the gravestone texts designed by what Gray calls the 'unletter'd muse'. This primitivism is cherished by Clare, but alongside it is the anxiety that because the ploughman's shoe fits him, he will be seen as forever plodding homeward, not as a poet with a soodling, sauntering, rambling gait that makes him wholly, uniquely and confidently part of his habitat. Clare's images of walking, as with Hazlitt, are often a means of representing the act of writing and thinking. In forming his aesthetic, Clare would have drawn both confidence and inspiration from Hazlitt's remarks that it is not the 'beautiful and magnificent alone' that we admire in nature: 'the most insignificant and rudest objects are often found connected with the strongest emotions.' Clare's 'rude formed table & still ruder chair' belong to this aesthetic of the naif, or what Hazlitt calls 'the most common and familiar images', which we become attached to, as we do to the face of a very old friend. The line also draws on *Robinson Crusoe*, a seminal text for him, and on *Pilgrim's Progress*, another founding work, and one which employs 'rude' in the verse apology which prefaces it. Milton's modesty topos at the opening of *Lycidas* – 'forced fingers rude' – also informs Clare's use of the adjective, but from Langland onwards it would be possible to write a history of English poetry and culture centred on the word. Obsessive, layered, it goes right to the contradictory heart of the country's identity. As recent Hazlitt scholars such as Zachary Leader and Mina Gorji have shown, Clare is a highly allusive, self-consciously literary author, not the simple, natural and authentic vernacular poet some of us earlier attempted to describe. He submitted poems written in the style of earlier poets – Marvell, Suckling, Harrington – to newspapers and journals, and as Vardy shows, Mina Gorji argues in a 'provocative article' that these imitations of the 'old poets' mark not an effort at anonymity, but at sociability. Here he was following in the tracks of his friend Charles Lamb and other writers associated with the *London Magazine*, who wanted to challenge the rhetoric of the isolated genius with a 'poetics of sociability and conviviality'.

We can see his imagination working on a passage from Cowper, which Hazlitt quotes in his essay: the wind blowing through a snowfall is described 'intercepting in their silent fall / The frequent flakes'. Clare picks up that Augustan, rather gravid adjective 'frequent' in a poem that begins 'Agen the homestead hedge with brambles green', and ends:

> Right heavy hangs the wet & beaded flower
> & trees that patter long behind the shower
> Puddles the lane & prints the beaten ground
> By frequent fall of dropples pattering round

Many times in his verse, Clare offers the image of strinkled or sprinkled dropples as an image for poetry – more accurately for counting syllables, which are more conventionally imaged as polished pebbles in a stream. It's what I've called an ontic image, and it's one that suggests that his poetry is a natural phenomenon – it grows as simply as leaves on a tree, is as natural as wild birds' eggs, or water drops falling from the leaves on a tree. But the adjective 'frequent' reminds the reader that Clare has read the educated English poets, and can write like them when he wants to (he has delicate fun with the adjectives 'gelid' and 'trepid' in 'To the Snipe'). Nature is doubly a printed text in these lines, and when he remarks earlier in the poem that the hedgerow trees 'to red & yellow turn / & in their bright excesses seem to burn', we are not very far from Gray's lines on Milton in 'The Progress of Poesy', where the too reckless bard sees the heavenly republic, then 'blasted with excess of light, / Closed his eyes in endless night'.

Clare's allusiveness is evident in his use of the adjective 'shaggy', which appears five times in this volume, along with 'shagged' and 'shag', and which he associates with 'tattered', 'ragged', an 'old smoked blanket', and with the marvellous bad taste moment in his sonnet sequence 'Turkeys':

> The turkey gobbles loud & drops his rag
> & struts & sprunts his tail & drags
> His wing on ground & makes a huzzing noise

The rough, deliberately rebarbative texture, the relished ugliness and love of dissonance are also present in the opening of 'The Badger':

> The badger grunting on his woodland track
> With shaggy hide & sharp nose scrowed with black
> Roots in the bushes & the woods & makes
> A great hugh burrow in the ferns & brakes
> With nose on ground he runs a awkard pace
> & anything will beat him in the race

'Shaggy' was used by Milton, Gray and others to abrade the Latinate, full-vowelled melody of their verse and, particularly in the late Augustan period, it was employed to signify the rude, northern barbarity Gray was drawn to. Scott uses it many times, and Thomson is remembering his native speech when he describes a hill in 'Spring' which is 'shag'd with mossy Rocks'. In *De Vulgari Eloquentia*, Dante speaks of moulding Italian into the language of his epic, and uses the image of four different knaps of cloth to describe different kinds of word: *pexa* ('combed-out'), *lubrica* ('glossy'), *yrsuta* ('shaggy') and *reburra* ('rumpled'). In Clare's friend Henry Cary's translation of the *Inferno*, the forest, which represents the Italian language in its unmoulded, variously provincial state, is described as 'savage wild . . . robust and rough' ('selva selvaggia e aspra e forte'). This idea of savage shagginess, or vigorous dialect, is picked up when the badger is referred to in another Northborough poem about the marten, which has 'badger hair long shagged'. It is a heroic emblem of Clare's feelings as a poet in a rural community where he was the victim of jealousy and backbiting, the result of his fame and the sometimes patronizing attentions of his aristocratic, middle-class or episcopal patrons. He also identified strongly with persecuted people like the Gypsies, as well as with mistreated animals, trees, plants, and the English earth itself ('The Lament of Swordy Well', is one of his finest, most passionate political poems, a deep chthonic cry of rage).

The badger's 'awkard pace', like his shaggy hide, expresses Clare's sense of being an ungainly peasant poet, who lacks the confidence of a university education and a knowledge of the classics, and who speaks a rough, provincial dialect. But when he says of badgers 'The frequent stone is hurled where ere they go', he is again demonstrating that he can pitch a heavy, neoclassical, unhairy adjective along with Cowper, Gray, Thomson and the others. It looks out of place, as though it's wearing a dinner jacket or is simply a random chunk of marble, which may be Clare's point.

In a draft of a preface to *The Shepherd's Calendar*, which is included in an appendix, Clare says 'To the Public also I return my hearty acknowledgments & however awkardly I may write them here I feel them at heart as sincerely as any one can do'. His aim is to make 'awkardness' carry some of the more enabling qualities that 'rude' does in the phrase 'rude good health', or in that admiring phrase in contemporary black speech 'rude boy'. By confessing it, by calling the alphabet a 'regiment of letters / This awkard squad of odds & ends', by identifying it with the badger, he draws on the associations with integrity, and the refusal of a servile conformity, which the popular phrase 'the awkward squad' represents. This type of apparent gaucheness can become that deftness of gesture, which naif or primitive art aims at, and may be regarded as a prized, traditional English characteristic.

Associated with the critical category of 'awkardness' is the adjective 'grotesque', which Clare uses twice in these poems. In a fragment, where his thoughts were probably running with Gray's moping owl, he says 'The winking owl in grotesque plumage dight / Roosts in the barn & hollows all the night'. Then in a sonnet he wrote at the same period, he returns to that adjective, which he places very close to the centre of its seven casual rhyming couplets:

> I found a ball of grass among the hay
> & proged it as I passed & went away
> & when I looked I fancied something stirred
> & turned agen & hoped to catch the bird
> When out an old mouse bolted in the wheat
> With all her young ones hanging at her teats
> She looked so odd & so grotesque to me
> I ran & wondered what the thing could be
> & pushed the knapweed bunches where I stood
> When the mouse hurried from the crawling brood
> The young ones squeaked & when I went away
> She found her nest again among the hay
> The water oer the pebbles scare could run
> & broad old sexpools glittered in the sun

This is also Burns's 'Wee, sleekit, cow'rin, tim'rous beastie', so there is an allusiveness in the choice of subject, as well as a playfulness in the poem's 'mixed language', as Zachary Leader has termed it.

If we take 'grotesque', with its double gutturals, as the nodal or vanishing point of the poem, its most complex word, we can see that it takes on an added emphasis by the way it assonates with 'proged', 'hanging', 'teats', 'odd', 'crawling', 'squeaked', and that culminating phrase 'old sexpools'. Clare's editors write interestingly of Clare's fondness for puns, and his refusal to inscribe the already vulgar word 'cesspools' is curious ('sexpools' does not appear to be a dialect word). We are back with those polished pebbles and that smooth and easy stream, as Clare offers a perfectly modulated iambic pentameter in the penultimate line before dropping a clatter of strong stresses into the last line: '& bróad | óld séxpóols | glíttered | ín the sún'. By employing an iamb, a molossus, a trochee, and a cretic foot, he shows his mastery of metrics, designing a line which has both dis-sonance and that 'living grace' he discerns in a possible fenland bramble bush. The clashing kiss of 'broad old' with 'odd' and 'bolted' earlier makes all the difference between smooth and rubbed pebbles, as 'glittered' takes an extra jagged edge because of its subliminal ghosting of 'grotesque'. The penultimate image of a lack of fluency is both extended and dispelled by the closing stagnant sexpools, which are yet female like the mouse. Typically, fear and anxiety are at the heart of this poem, Clare being one of the great poets of aesthetic and ontological angst, but he compensates for it by giving this epiphany a confidently shaggy surface.

Again and again, my ear is drawn to the delicacy of his acoustic texture, and the wit of his linguistic and literary self-consciousness. He writes about ornithology better than anyone, and is attracted by the yellowhammer or 'writing lark', which is so called because the irregular zigzag lines on its eggs resemble writing. Wild birds' eggs are among his primary images of poems, they are always wonderingly discovered, and they are also tiny unique images of world and being, or being-in-the-world, as we can see in the deliberately named 'Bumbarrels Nest', where the little oval nest contains:

> Ten eggs & often twelve with dusts of red
> Soft frittered & full soon the little lanes
> Screen the young crowd & hear the twittring song
> Of the old birds who call them to be fed
> While down the hedge they hang & hide along

The dusty, earthy, little eggs in their mossy nest tied with grey cobwebs have a 'Soft frittered' appearance, and that phrase is echoed in the old birds' 'twittring song'.

*

In July 1841, after four years in the asylum, Clare made an escape – the journey out of Essex, which has entered literary folklore. Over four days, he walked the hundred miles back to Northborough. Still obsessed with Mary Joyce, he wrote two songs for her on his first night home. Patty was at first glad to have him back, and though Allen sent a man to persuade him to return to High Beech, she thought him so much better 'that she wished to try him for a while'. Poem fragments from this period describe meadow lands which are 'blea' (exposed) and 'flags' (irises) that are 'bleached and brown' near more 'dotterel' trees. In December 1841, two local doctors certified his insanity for the second time, and he was admitted to the Northampton General Lunatic Asylum. He was placed among the 'fifth class', or 'harmless patients', and was allowed considerable freedom. He could walk into Northampton alone and became a well-known figure in the town. He chewed tobacco and smoked a clay pipe all the time, and had an 'agreeableness of disposition' which contrasted with the aggressiveness of many of the other inmates. Patty, as far as we know, never visited him during his twenty-three years in the asylum. In letters home, Clare refers to being in captivity 'among the Babylonians', and in conversation he claimed several identities – Byron, Shakespeare, Lord Nelson, various prizefighters. To an American visitor he claimed to have visited the United States and to have called on a New England poet called Corduroy who 'dwelt in a beautiful cottage – a poet's cottage, encircled by trees and flower-gardens. Hundreds of gentlemen and ladies, in their splendid carriages, came to see the poet's cottage.' Bate has tried without success to trace this American poet called Corduroy – a wild goose chase, because he is a projection of Clare's own experience. In his poems, Clare uses that rough, ribbed, then relatively new material as an image for ploughed fields or trees (maple bark is 'ribb'd like corderoy in seamy screed') and for his identity as a peasant poet.

During the asylum years, Clare wrote some of his finest poems, among them 'I Am' ('I Am – Yet what I am, none cares or knows; / My friends forsake me like a memory lost'), and 'A Vision':

I lost the love of heaven above,
I spurn'd the lust of earth below,
I felt the sweets of fancied love
And hell itself my only foe.

Clare never went home again, and, it seems, never tried to. He died during a heatwave in May 1864, 'very helpless and quite childish'. He was ready to die, often saying in his last years, 'I have lived for too long' and 'I want to go home.' As he expresses it in the last stanzas of 'A Vision':

I lost earth's joys, but felt the glow
Of heaven's flame abound in me
'Till loveliness and I did grow
The bard of immortality.

I loved but woman fell away
I hid me from her faded fame,
I snatch'd the sun's eternal ray
And wrote till earth was but a name.

In every language upon earth,
On every shore, o'er every sea,
I gave my name immortal birth
And kept my spirit with the free.

Clare's quietly triumphant voice was heard by many poets – F. T. Palgrave, Edward Thomas, Edmund Blunden, Geoffrey Grigson. A number of Irish poets beginning with Patrick Kavanagh, and followed by Michael Longley and Seamus Heaney, have sustained and cherished Clare's reputation as, in Sidney Keyes's phrase, 'the simple timeless poet'.

Gently and Pauseably: Christina Rossetti

It could be argued that Germaine Greer's 1975 edition of Christina Rossetti's masterpiece, *Goblin Market*, initiated the rediscovery of her poetry. Published in the United States by Stonehill, Greer's edition had a publisher's blurb which described the poem as a 'haunting classic of Repressed Victorian Eroticism', and among the puffs on the jacket was a quotation from a 1973 issue of *Playboy* which read, 'Born out of a storm of guilt and emotion . . . It is a lewd goblin that rises dripping out of the dark depths of the Victorian psyche.' In her powerful introductory essay, Greer argued that Rossetti's work is devalued by listing her among the lesser religious poets, and she lamented the absence of a current edition of Rossetti's collected poems. Four years later, R. W. Crump published the first volume of her edition of the collected poems, and when Geoffrey Grigson welcomed it in the *TLS* (11 April 1980), he noted that Rossetti had been 'neglected and undervalued'. Referring to Christina Rossetti's brother William's 1904 edition, *The Poetical Works of Christina Georgina Rossetti*, Grigson observed that her poems had only been available 'cramped and crowded, poorly printed, meanly published, two columns to a small page'. Crump went on to publish a second volume in 1986, and a third in 1990. That expensive hardback edition was published in 2002 as a single volume, *The Complete Poems*, by Penguin, who have added useful notes and an introduction by Betty Flowers. This is the first fully annotated edition of her poems. Twenty-seven years after Greer's essay, Rossetti may be said to have entered the literary canon. It was embarrassingly late, but at least she made it. Future critics may discover the reasons for the neglect of this poet who, as Flowers comments, is remarkable for 'the perfect pitch and clarity of her line'.

In his *TLS* review, Grigson stated that in Rossetti's poetry, 'it is the ear that speaks . . . in a music delicate, subtle and exceptional, yet not too separate from speech'. The astringent delicacy of her acoustic imagination makes her a poet's poet (Hopkins and Swinburne were early admirers, Larkin was devoted to her work), and in my view it was her reading of George Herbert and her deeply held Anglican beliefs which structured her verse. It is worth considering how she absorbs Herbert's influence.

There are a number of poems where Rossetti too closely resembles Herbert in language and cadence:

> So I did win a kingdom, – share My crown;
> A harvest, – come and reap.
> ('The Love of Christ Which Passeth Knowledge')

> Yet all my loveliness is born
> Upon a thorn.
> ('Consider the Lilies of the Field')

> Thou who didst hang upon a barren tree,
> My God, for me;
> ('Long Barren')

> Consider
> The birds that have no barn nor harvest-weeks;
> God gives them food:–
> Much more our Father seeks
> To do us good.
> ('Consider')

> Am I a stone and not a sheep
> That I can stand, O Christ, beneath Thy Cross,
> To number drop by drop Thy Blood's slow loss,
> And yet not weep?
> ('Good Friday')

Here Rossetti is echoing Herbert too earnestly – characteristically he uses a short last line, or a short final phrase to spring a direct, clinching statement of faith on his reader – a statement that appears to jettison the rest of the poem and release a moment of pure spirituality. The most winning and decisive example of this is Herbert's sonnet 'Prayer', in which the sestet, with deliberate over-insistence, continues a series of images for prayer:

> Softness, and peace, and joy, and love, and bliss,
> Exalted manna, gladness of the best,
> Heaven in ordinary, man well dressed,
> The milky way, the bird of Paradise,
>
> Church-bells beyond the stars heard, the soul's blood,
> The land of spices; something understood.

Herbert's physical sensuous images are suddenly cancelled – kicked away like a ladder – by the two abstract words which follow the semi-colon in the last line. This pause is mirrored by the slighter pause after the spondaic 'something', and this use of pauses is a central effect Rossetti noticed and was inspired by.

In *A Priest to the Temple*, Herbert insists on simplicity, recommending that a preacher should employ 'earnestness of speech'. In this devotional prose work, he says that the character of a sermon is 'holiness', and that everything should be 'natural, and sweet, and grave'. There should be 'directness and open plainness' in all things. The furniture of his house 'is very plain, but clean, whole and sweet'. That sweetness and clean-swept plainness is evident also in Rossetti's aesthetic, where it helps design a language which Jerome McGann has called 'paradisal'. But that deceptively simple language, as Betty Flowers shows, is freighted with biblical allusions. Flowers argues that while the secular reader might experience Rossetti's 'I Will Lift Up Mine Eyes unto the Hills' as a kind of 'flat piety', its many biblical allusions turn it into what she terms 'a richly shaded emotional journey'. The last stanza contains allusions to some well-known phrases in Isaiah, the first book of John and the first book of Corinthians, as well as Revelation:

> Then the new Heavens and Earth shall be
> Where righteousness shall dwell indeed;
> There shall be no more blight, nor need,

> Nor barrier of the sea;
> No sun and moon alternating,
> For God shall be the Light thereof;
> No sorrow more, no death, no sting,
> For God Who reigns is Love.

Although it is helpful to know the biblical sources of these lines, I do not think that they, and indeed most of Rossetti's religious poetry, are helped by that knowledge. Rossetti weaves her sources in what for her was probably a therapeutic process, but the lines are sterile, like most of the poems in the last 300 pages of this edition. It is these poems which have helped to diminish her reputation.

There is, however, a difference between an inflexible and unresponsive piety, and the embodiment of the deep inspiration she drew from Herbert's verse. In the chapter entitled 'The Parson Praying' in *A Priest to the Temple*, Herbert says that everyone in church should voice 'Amen' and all other responses 'gently and pauseably'. That phrase 'gently and pauseably' is curious and interesting; it makes the pause between the two syllables long, drawn out, strangely vibrant like a kind of Anglican *Aum*, and it is this humming pause which is such a distinctive feature of the Anglican liturgy. Rossetti builds it into the structure and cadence of her poems to embody both her religious faith and that particular mild-mannered English toughness and resilience which she celebrates in her poems (notably in 'Enrica', with its contrast between the trim correctness but freeborn strength of Englishwomen and the natural warmth and grace of their Italian cousin). Take these lines from Rossetti's 'Winter Rain', where every line scans differently:

> But miles of barren sand,
> With never a son or daughter,
> Not a lily on the land,
> Or lily on the water.

The first line consists of three iambic feet, the second line is an amphibrach (three syllables, middle one stressed), followed by an iamb and an amphibrach, the third line is trochaic. When we reach the comma at the end of the third line, we pause slightly more than we pause at the previous two commas. The reason for this, I think, is that the last line does not follow the expected, because insistent, trochaic meter of the previous line. 'Or lily' is an amphibrach, like 'With never' at the start of the second line. Because it begins unexpectedly with an unstressed syllable, a pause is enforced before the trochaic rhythm of the previous line is picked up by 'on the water'. That pause has an invisible but very firm authority, and it is one example of Rossetti's subtly stringent ear, an acoustic imagination that is uninsistently perfect. The postures or contours of her spirit express themselves pauseably, in Herbert's phrase.

Here we perhaps enter into a kind of metrical mysticism, but we also catch the accent of autonomy – the silent accent, which is what a pause is. This is firmly evident in the famous last line of 'No, Thank You, John', where she begins 'I never said I loved you, John' and finishes by saying: 'Here's friendship for you if you like; but love, – / No thank you, John.' Perhaps her characteristic syntactic marker is the combined comma and dash which she uses to mark the pause before 'No thank you, John'. That pause is the expression both of her principled female power and her Anglican faith.

Other instances of this pausal inflection are:

> Her breath was sweet as May
> And light danced in her eyes.
> ('Goblin Market')

> Then she was silent, and I too.
> ('The Iniquity of the Fathers Upon the Children')

> An opal holds a fiery spark:
> But a flint holds fire.
> (from *Sing-Song*)

> No more change or death, no more
> Salt sea-shore.
> ('Luscious and Sorrowful')

Trilled her song and swelled her song
With maiden coy caprice
In a labyrinth of throbs,
Pauses, cadences.
('Maiden-Song')

The last example shows how Rossetti was conscious of her deployment of pauses, and in the third example we can see how the pause after 'flint' serves to throw an extra shade of stress on 'fire', which, because it alliterates with 'flint' retroactively, puts a little more stress on 'flint' to make the line tougher than the conventional iambic tetrameter which precedes it.

These resilient cadences inform the second example, which is from a remarkable and neglected poem in which Margaret the speaker discovers intuitively that she is the illegitimate daughter of the unmarried lady of the manor. They first become friendly when 'my Lady' sometimes stops at the house she shares with her nurse. Leaning from her horse, the lady will 'stoop and pat my cheek':

And I was always ready
To hold the field-gate wide
For my Lady to go thro';
My Lady in her veil
So seldom put aside,
My Lady grave and pale.

Later Margaret says:

I turned and stared at her:
Her cheek showed hollow-pale;
A wonderful fall of hair
That screened her like a veil;
But her height was statelier,
Her eyes had depth more deep;
I think they must have had
Always a something sad,
Unless they were asleep.

This is a poignant poem on an emotional and psychological level, but the veiled lady is possibly a feminist inversion of the Patient Griselda story – the Lady is God; Margaret the human soul suffering on earth.

Rossetti did not warm to the idea of an omnipotent God the Father, and it is interesting to note that when she published a book of prayers, *Annus Domini*, in 1874, the Anglican clergyman who wrote the preface was careful to point out that 'all the prayers are addressed to the Second Person in the Blessed Trinity, and are therefore intended only to be used as supplementary to other devotions'. She could not address God the Father, it was always Christ she prayed to, so the Lady in 'The Iniquity of the Fathers' may be a female Christ, or she may be the Virgin Mary and Margaret a female Christ. Although the poem is wanly resigned and quietist at the end, it is one of her masterpieces, instinct with her faith and mastery of pause and cadence.

If we take the last long line of this passage about death from 'A Ballad of Boding', we can see how central the pause is to her metric:

> With a hoof it swayed the waves;
> They opened here and there,
> Till I spied deep ocean graves
> Full of skeletons
> That were men and women once
> Foul or fair;
> Full of things that creep
> And fester in the deep
> And never breathe the clean life-nurturing air.

What is so powerful about the last line is the way the pause after 'clean' releases the uplifting phrase 'life-nurturing air'. The emphasis which the pause adds to 'clean' foregrounds the internal rhyme with 'breathe', a rhyme that cleanses the negative *ee* sounds in 'creep' and 'deep' before reinforcing the noun 'air' in terms of sense, not sound.

One of her most arresting and moving uses of the pause occurs in the first stanza of 'Grown and Flown':

> I loved my love from green of Spring
> Until sere Autumn's fall;
> But now that leaves are withering
> How should one love at all?
> One heart's too small
> For hunger, cold, love, everything.

There is a pause after the amphibrach which begins the last line, then there is a spondee or two monosyllabic feet divided by a pause, then a longer pause before the cretic foot 'everything'. The last two letters of 'love' are turned round to become the opening letters of 'everything' – a ghostly reversed assonance bridges the pause, but only just. That pause puts huge weight on to that last big trisyllabic word, which rhymes with 'withering' and becomes tragic in its quiet intensity. It resounds almost silently, like the preceding pause which launches it – we catch the drop in the voice as it turns bleak and frail here.

The effect of this use of richly significant pauses is to place an elevating emphasis on the word which follows. Thus 'light danced' in the first of the earlier examples, gives the verb more stress than the noun it follows, and 'life' has more stress than 'clean' in 'And never breathe the clean life-nurturing air'. This is also true of these lines from 'Spring':

> Young grass springs on the plain;
> Young leaves clothe early hedgerow trees.

Technically, the first three feet of both lines form a foot called a molossus, though here each syllable has a different degree of stress. Herbert too sometimes likes to place three strong stresses together:

> *Wherefore be cheered, and praise him to the full*
> *Each day, each hour, each moment of the week,*
> *Who fain would have you be new, tender, quick.*
> ('Love Unknown')

Following Herbert, Rossetti delights in creating a soaring effect by placing a monosyllabic verb after a monosyllabic noun. This can be paradoxical, as in 'Song', where the sense of 'died' in the fourth line is challenged by the strong stress on the verb which gives it a buoyant tightness and lift:

> I wept for memory;
> She sang for hope that is so fair;
> My tears were swallowed by the sea;
> Her songs died on the air.

Something similar happens in 'Christian and Jew: A Dialogue', where the verb in 'Of mother-dove clad in a rainbow's dyes' is so strongly stressed that it exists as a monosyllabic foot followed by a pyrrhic foot 'in a', whose two unstressed syllables create space for the molossus 'rainbow's dyes'. Those three strong stresses seem to concentrate in the *d* sound which works to intensify 'clad' – this sensitivity to retroactive stress is something she again learnt from Herbert. Also, this use of the molossus is another stylistic device which she absorbed from her devoted and devotional reading of his work. This is important in one of the most important sections of *Goblin Market*:

> White and golden Lizzie stood,
> Like a lily in a flood, –
> Like a rock of blue-veined stone
> Lashed by tides obstreperously, –
> Like a beacon left alone
> In hoary roaring sea,
> Sending up a golden fire, –
> Like a fruit-crowned orange tree
> White with blossoms honey-sweet
> Sore beset by wasp and bee, –
> Like a royal virgin town
> Topped with gilded dome and spire
> Close beleaguered by a fleet
> Mad to tug her standard down.

White, gold and blue are the Virgin Mary's colours, but I can't help thinking that the arresting image of *lapis lazuli* – 'Blue as a vein o'er the Madonna's breast' – in Robert Browning's 'The Bishop Orders His Tomb in St Praxed's Church' is somewhere in her imagination. The beacon left alone in a hoary sea (the obvious pun follows the sensual thread) is a version of Milton's lonely tower, and therefore a Protestant symbol of individual conscience given a strongly female identity. The phrase 'blue-veined stone' is a molossus, and this pairs it with 'fruit-crowned orange tree', an image that may draw on Herbert's 'Employment': 'O that I were an Orange-tree / That busie plant.' But the word 'orange' must surely also be associated with William of Orange – the Marian blue and Williamite orange become in their conjoined, their metrically consonant state, a representation of the Church of England, which is the *via media* between extremes. Blue and orange were regarded as complementary colours in the nineteenth century, so there is a vibrant pairing of opposites here.

The sea imagery releases an atavistic memory of the Spanish Armada, with perhaps a recall of another royal virgin's famous speech at Tilbury: 'I know I have the body of a weak and feeble woman, but I have the heart and stomach of a king, and a king of England too.' This patriotic imagery is there in the closing stanzas of 'Enrica' where 'we' chill, northern, rigid Englishwomen win out over Enrica's southern charms:

> But if she found us like our sea,
> Of aspect colourless and chill,
> Rock-girt; like it she found us still
> Deep at our deepest, strong and free.

They are proud daughters of Britannia, who are both welcoming and repelling a later Italian invader, whose country is not a free sovereign nation.

In 'Enrica', there is an image of blossom and a glance at Botticelli's *The Birth of Venus*, and in the passage just quoted from *Goblin Market*, Rossetti draws on Botticelli's *La Primavera*, as well as again designing an image of the eternally inviolable English spirit. She rhymes 'sea / free' in 'Enrica' and 'sea / tree / bee' in this passage. For all its assertion of spiritual strength, it is hard not to read a coarse, no doubt unconscious, *double entendre* into the last line, and this sense of sexual threat is caught in one of the most remarkable verses in *Sing-Song, a Nursery Rhyme Book*:

> Margaret has a milking-pail,
> And she rises early;
> Thomas has a threshing-flail,
> And he's up betimes.
>
> Sometimes crossing through the grass
> Where the dew lies pearly,
> They say 'Good morrow' as they pass
> By the leafy limes.

A flail is a weapon and it rhymes with 'pail', then Rossetti's ear catches the labial in 'pearly' – the foggy, foggy dew is a sexual image in traditional song and like its more polite equivalent image, the string of pearls, it sets up the possibility of sexual intimacy. The symbolism and the 'flail / pail' rhyme are a version of Jack and Jill going up the hill to fetch a pail of water. That intimacy is shadowed in a both erotic and delicately sinister fashion by the two *l*'s in the last line.

The leafy limes belong by association with her insistent imagery of fruit in *Goblin Market* and in other poems, and here they become tempting and troubling through her use of the dominant *l* sound which also suggests the word 'lover' as well as 'lips'. Rossetti runs with labials again in 'Last Night':

> Where were you last night? I watched at the gate;
> I went down early, I stayed down late.
> Were you snug at home, I should like to know,
> Or were you in the coppice wheedling Kate?

That unexpected, insinuating, cold verb 'wheedling' is perfect in the way it catches a particular kind of uncaressing, seductive voice – 'weed' and 'needle' must be associated with it.

It is surprising that a verbal imagination of this fineness should have been so long neglected. The *DNB*'s original verdict has stood for generations: it states that Rossetti never approaches Dante Gabriel's 'imaginative or descriptive power', and suggests that she is 'like most poetesses, purely subjective and in no sense creative'. This is grotesquely dated, but it did contribute to the neglect of her work. The new Penguin edition will stimulate more interest and appreciation. In one of her weakest religious poems, 'Young Death', she looks forward to eternity:

> Then shall be no more weeping,
> Or fear or sorrow,
> Or waking more, or sleeping,
> Or night, or morrow
> Or cadence in the song
> Of songs, or thirst, or hunger.

It is the waking cadence in the song that makes her work remarkable – to read her is to participate in the exercise of pure style, to witness a genius in complete confident control of the language.

A Juicy and Jostling Shock: Hopkins's Poems and Poems in Prose

On the 9 April 1874, Hopkins went to an exhibition of modern Japanese art at the Kensington Museum, now the Victoria and Albert. He commented in his journal:

> There was a shew of beautiful Japanese work, modern, from which one gathers that their art is very flourishing: there was a capital fight between a night-hawk and a dragon on a gilded platter; ivory relief, I don't know how to call the work, but it was, I think, by cutting out certain beds or fields and in them relieving the figures (incised work?), which gives rather precision to the whole than simple relief and then further heightening, on one side only, the edges of the figures within the fields or dies or else the edges, cliffs of these dies with Indian ink, which gives great finish; also there were complete soldiers' accoutrements with masks for the face, which shewed the type of features and that was ugly.

It's likely that this exhibition began his interest in Japanese art, because in a letter to his mother two years later he remarked that: 'There is a lamentable account in the *Graphic* of the sweeping away of the old civilisation in Japan' (26 / 28 June 1876). Twelve years later, he writes to thank his mother for the gift of a Japanese pocket book, and then mentions the various books he's read on Japan, saying that he's become a little knowledgeable in things Japanese (24 December 1888).

In between these prose moments, he wrote what he calls a 'long sonnet', which he mentions in a letter to Robert Bridges (11 December 1886). In 'Spelt from Sibyl's Leaves', occur these lines:

> Óur évening is over us; óur night | whélms, whélms, ánd will end us.
> Only the beakleaved boughs dragonish | damask the tool-smooth
> bleak light; black,
> Ever so black on it.

These lines anticipate by more than twenty years the best and most famous Imagist poem:

> The apparition of these faces in the crowd:
> Petals on a wet, black, bough.

Pound's 'In a Station of the Metro' sees the pale faces in the crowd in terms of a Japanese print, and like Hopkins he relishes a hard, terse, monosyllabic texture which affirms a wholly unsentimental warrior aesthetic. Perhaps in these almost over-deliberate apocalyptic lines, Hopkins is thinking of the sweeping away of the 'old civilization' in Japan. (I have searched the *Graphic* for the article he mentions but haven't found it.) But he is also fascinated by the antithesis of form in the poem, a subject represented by the word 'throughther', which is his spelling of the word 'throughother', which in Irish English is used often to describe an untidy room or occasion (it derives from the Irish *trina cheile*). Against formlessness he sets the black dragonish boughs which in the 'tool-smooth' light carry the sense of military hardware which has been polished by machine tools. War and revolution – political as well as industrial revolution – are deeply and uncomfortably present in Hopkins's imagination. He may even be remembering that early Jesuit mission to Japan, now a new industrial nation that Britain will one day fight a very cruel war with.

Hopkins the proto-modernist artist speaks in these lines, as he subjects his lines to maximum punitive stress on *beak boughs bleak black black*. To adapt Yeats, he has brought his sword downstairs, and is imagining the end of civilization, as well as doubting the nature of western civilization. His notebook entry on the Japanese exhibition is clearly a preparation for these lines – it is their seed. Similarly, if we consider the theme of collapsing civilization in Hopkins, we can adduce one of his seminal letters – the so-called Red Letter to Bridges in which he admits: 'Horrible to say, in a manner I am a Communist' (2 August 1871). In that letter he states that England's civilization is 'founded on wrecking', and so looks forward to a poem he was to write four years later, 'The Wreck of the Deutschland'.

We naturally look to Hopkins's prose for clues, omens, light travelling from stars which have yet to be born. Take this little remark in the notebooks: 'The Battle of Dorking and the fear of the Revolution make me sad now' (24 July 1871). This is Hopkins the devout English patriot responding to an anonymous article which had appeared in *Blackwood's Magazine* the previous month. Entitled 'The Battle of Dorking: Reminiscences of a Volunteer', it gave an account of the defeat of an English – not a British – army by invading Prussian forces. Ostensibly written fifty years after this defeat, the pamphlet exposed the weakness of the army and the unstable nature of the economy. *The Battle of Dorking* was written by Lieutenant-Colonel Sir George Tomkyns-Chesney, and ran through many editions. It touched Hopkins deeply, and is, I believe, one of the sources of 'The Wreck of the Deutschland'. Tomkyns-Chesney writes of the degradation of Old England, a rising in India, an imminent Fenian invasion of Ireland and an attack by the USA on Canada (a few years earlier, there had been a farcical attempt to invade Canada by a group of Fenians). The lieutenant-colonel is clearly worried by the strength of the German state: he notes that 'our neighbours' are now the leading military power in Europe and 'are driving a good trade too'. He then says that this prosperity was before 'their foolish communism had ruined the rich without benefiting the poor'. This prophecy of disaster was prompted by Bismarck's success in uniting Germany in January 1871. Gladstone described it as alarmist, but it is clear that Tomkyns-Chesney had caught a mood of public anxiety: Britain felt threatened, and as the Germans had recently defeated France in the Franco-Prussian War many British citizens feared their country would be next.

In *The Battle of Dorking* there is an interesting description of a big naval battle, which anticipates our experience of live coverage of warfare. A submarine cable is laid just before the battle, and this gives 'continuous communication' to newspaper readers on shore. There are newspaper special editions every few minutes – the Victorian equivalent of video cameras in Afghanistan or Iraq. This idea of continuous, virtually live, communication is a central part of Hopkins's inspiration in 'The Wreck of the Deutschland', whose source was a series of stories in *The Times* in December 1875, which Hopkins read and which are often reprinted in editions of the poem.

Tomkyns-Chesney's narrator describes how England is taken by surprise, and says, 'happy are those whose bones whitened the fields of Surrey. They at least were spared the disgrace we lived to endure'. And he remarks that 'we must give place to a new naval power stripped of our colonies'. In a moment that's like a passage from early Auden, the narrator looks at England:

> its trade gone, its factories silent, its harbours empty, a prey to pauperism and decay. France recovered but our people couldn't be got to see how artificial our prosperity was. All rested on foreign trade and financial credit. Power was passing away from the class which had been used to use it into the hands of the lower classes, uneducated, untrained to the use of political rights, and swayed by demagogues.

A reply to this vision of a decayed and powerless England appeared in *Macmillan's Magazine* two months later, in July 1871. It was called 'Der Ruhm or the Wreck of German Unity', and was ostensibly the narrative of a 'Brandenburger Hauptmann'. In it the old soldier describes a big naval battle between Germany and Britain which resulted in the defeat of Germany. The description is like a prophecy of the First World War, with Britain, Russia and France fighting Germany. It's possible that Hopkins read the article – like Whitman, he was fascinated by wrecks and his eye would have caught the word 'wreck' in the title of the reply to *The Battle of Dorking*. We need to read his poem as a great European historical vision, as a prophetic poem which was inspired by Bismarck's actions and policies. Hopkins's deepest feelings are devoted to the five powerless nuns who are being deported by legislation enacted by Adalbert Falk, the Prussian minister of public worship. Beyond this, Hopkins identifies with the poor, the dispossessed, the exploited, but he also admires sheer power and authority: brute beauty, beak-leaved boughs dragonish, the master of the tides' growl. There are intense, passionate contradictions in his work, which were deepened by his unhappy years in Dublin.

When Falk was appointed, he asked Bismarck what he wished him to do, and Bismarck replied that he should 'restore the rights of the state over to the church and to do it with the least possible fuss'. What was called a war against the priests then took place in many Prussian towns. A law forbidding the establishment of Jesuit institutions in Germany was passed, and a deputy in the Reichstag coined the phrase *Kulturkampf* – culture struggle – to describe the attacks on the Roman Catholic Church. According to the Reichstag deputy, the struggle was assuming more and more 'the character of a great struggle for civilization in the interest of humanity'. A law passed in May 1874 gave the Prussian government the power to expel all clerics who persisted in practising their religious functions without having satisfied state requirements, and in 1875, in response to a papal encyclical declaring all government measures invalid, the government banned all monastic orders in Prussia, except those engaged in medical service. By 1876, a third of all Catholic parishes in Prussia – 1,400 – were without incumbents.

These events – for an English Catholic like a rerun of the Reformation – moved Hopkins deeply, and imagining 'the call of the tall nun' carrying over 'the storm's brawling' he cries out in sympathy:

> She was first of a five and came
> Of a coifèd sisterhood.
> (O Deutschland, double a desperate name!
> O world wide of its good!
> But Gertrude, lily, and Luther, are two of a town,
> Christ's lily and beast of the waste wood:
> From life's dawn it is drawn down,
> Abel is Cain's brother and breasts they have sucked the same.)

The 'beast of the waste wood' I take to be a glance at Sir Satyrane, Spenser's symbol for Henry VIII. Hopkins is reliving the Reformation here, and in the reference to the fact that both Luther and Saint Gertrude were born in Eisleben. By implication, Bismarck, the Chancellor of the new united German state, is the reincarnation of Luther:

Loathed for a love men knew in them,
Banned by the land of their birth,
Rhine refused them. Thames would ruin them;
Surf, snow, river and earth
Gnashed: but thou art above, thou Orion of light;
Thy unchancelling pòising palms were weighing the worth,
Thou martyr-master: in thy sight
Storm flakes were scroll-leaved flowers, lily showers – sweet
heaven was astrew in them.

Echoing the doubly desperate name 'Deutschland', he echoes the trumpet-call of German militarism in the second line's brash, internal rhyme. His ear is also running on *n* sounds – *Rhine, ruin, snow, gnashed* – till he elevates that hard, gnarled negative into 'Orion of light', which has the effect of transcending the previous harshness because it contains two *o*'s and what for Hopkins was the crucial *i* sound in the word 'Christ', which is also repeated. In both stanzas, especially the first, his ear is attracted also to the *st* sound, which in 'astrew' is elevated by the long *oo* sound.

But this is a dense and difficult stanza. God the 'martyr-master' – a kind of ringmaster? – has 'unchancelling poising palms'. Does this mean that God, like the Chancellor of Germany, 'unchancells'? – i.e. dismantles chancels, churches, religious houses? The idea may be that Bismarck is executing God's purpose by creating martyrs. He is merely the expression of God's purpose in history and will one day be unchancelled.

There is much in Hopkins's political thinking that is intensely authoritarian, but here he is confronting the authoritarian spectre of Bismarck and expressing his fear of all that the Iron Chancellor is doing. The *n* sound that has so caught Hopkins's ear is there in that phrase, and in the phrase 'blood and iron', with which he is most famously associated (in 1862 Bismarck said 'the great questions of the day will not be settled by speeches and majority decisions – that was the great mistake of 1848 and 1849 – but by blood and iron'.)

Hopkins wants to take us out of history's heavy gunge, its blood and iron, and he does so by first returning to an emphatic double *n* in 'unchancelling', then moving to the cognate but softer *m* sound in 'palms' and 'martyr-master'. The softer sounds elsewhere in the lines and the sense of the word 'heaven', as well as its softening *vuh*, work to redeem the gnashing quality of *n*, though the close of the stanza is one of Hopkins's less successful bad taste moments. The baroque lily showers appear almost to belong in a William Morris wallpaper, or in some mushy and embarrassing Crashaw poem. Notice that 'sweet heaven' is astrew *in* the storm flakes. The storm has become God's mercy – or God's mercy is instressed by the storm. By using 'in' rather than 'with', Hopkins insists on his harsh and uncompromising theodicy.

But why does Hopkins address God as 'thou Orion of light'? In Greek mythology Orion received the gift of being able to walk on the sea from Poseidon. For the Christian this makes him a precursor of Christ, but Orion is also and primarily the great hunter who was blinded as a punishment for sexually assaulting Merope. Then Orion came to Lemnos, set his face to the rising sun and recovered his sight. His image is set among the stars, where, followed by Sirius the Dog Star, he forever pursues the Pleiades, the seven daughters of Atlas and Pleione. But Orion is a dangerous figure: for Hazlitt he is the 'classical Nimrod', a symbol of Napoleon in his account of Poussin's *Paysage avec Orion aveugle*. Hazlitt remarks that Poussin, like 'his own Orion . . . overlooks the surrounding scene' and appears to ' "take up the isles as a very little thing, and to lay the earth in a balance" '. Hazlitt is quoting Isaiah: 'Behold the nations are as a drop of a bucket, and are counted as the small dust of a balance: behold, he taketh up the isles as a very little thing' (40.15). A few verses earlier the prophet asks: 'Who hath measured the waters in the hollow of his hand, and meted out heaven with the span, and comprehended the dust of the earth in a measure, and weighed the mountains in scales, and the hills in a balance?' But it may be that Hopkins is remembering the mention of Orion in the Old Testament, where God says to Job:

Which alone spreadeth out the heavens, and treadeth upon the waves of the sea.
Which maketh Arcturus, Orion, and Pleiades, and the chambers of the south.

It may be that Hopkins is recalling Amos:

Seek him that maketh the seven stars and Orion, and turneth the shadow of death into the morning, and maketh the day dark with night: that calleth for the waters of the sea, and poureth them out upon the face of the earth: the Lord is his name.

Here, Orion turns the shadow of death into morning, which is Hopkins's theme, as is the waters of the sea pouring upon the earth.

In the storm passage which opens 'The Wreck of the Deutschland', Hopkins says, 'The swoon of a heart that the sweep and the hurl of thee trod'. He is meditating on nation states and power, and in rhyming 'trod' with 'God' and 'rod' in the second stanza, his subconscious is somewhere with the phallic Whitman, whose sexual explicitness is lodged among Hopkins's guilty secrets.

Hopkins is also thinking of the constellation Libra when he writes of 'poising palms weighing the worth'. Libra is sometimes identified with Astraea, the Roman goddess of justice, so this image works to extend Hopkins's theodicy and so help justify the ways of God to man. Even so, that 'Orion of light' is somehow unexpected and not quite resolvable. At one level, this is a work which boldly and intricately puts forward the incredible argument that the shipwreck was planned by God as a way of making martyrs for Holy Church.

Going with the hardnosed, the hardline boldness of this imaginative conception is Hopkins's deployment of crowd theory in the poem. He was fascinated by crowds, and in a letter to his mother ten years after he wrote 'The Wreck of the Deutschland', he describes attending a monster meeting in Phoenix Park, which was addressed by the MP William O'Brien, who was a member of Parnell's party. Hopkins went to the vast outdoor meeting with a French priest, Father Mallac, and he tells his mother:

Fr. Mallac, who in Paris witnessed the revolution of '48, said that there the motions of the crowd were themselves majestic and that they organized themselves as with a military instinct.

(2 March 1888)

In political theory, there are several studies of crowd theory – Elias Canetti was the most famous crowd theorist of the twentieth century, and in his study *The Crowd and the Mob from Plato to Canetti*, J. S. McClelland says that the mid-nineteenth century 'perhaps 1848, more probably 1871, is the turning point in the history of the crowd', because from that time onwards the crowd becomes central to social and political theorizing. Or, McClelland suggests, any exercise in social theorizing, which did not make room for the crowd at its centre 'looked makeshift, mistaken, or wilfully obtuse'.

I would suggest that somewhere near the centre of Hopkins's poem – I read it as the first modernist poem – is the organized crowd. In his famous Red Letter, he observed:

I am afraid some great revolution is not far off. Horrible to say, in a manner I am a Communist. Their ideal bating some things is nobler than that professed by any secular statesman I know of (I must own I live in bat-light and shoot at a venture). Besides it is just. – I do not mean the means of getting to it are. But it is a dreadful thing for the greatest and most necessary part of a very rich nation to live a hard life without dignity, knowledge, comforts, delight, or hopes in the midst of plenty – which plenty they make. They profess that they do not care what they wreck and burn, the old civilisation and order must be destroyed. This is a dreadful look out but what has the old civilization done for them? As it at present stands in England it is itself in great measure founded on wrecking. But they got none of the spoils, they came in for nothing but harm from it then and thereafter. England has grown hugely wealthy but this wealth has not reached the working classes; I expect it has made their condition worse. Besides this iniquitous order the old civilisation embodies another order mostly old and what is new in direct entail from the old, the old religion, learning, law, art, etc and all the history that is preserved in standing monuments. But as the working classes have not been educated they know next to nothing of all this and cannot be expected to care if they destroy it. The more I look the more black and deservedly black the future looks, so I will write no more.

(2 August 1871)

Again we have that almost Burkean phrase 'the old civilization', which he uses five years later in the letter to his mother about the Japanese exhibition. He is preoccupied, rather as Yeats would be, with social violence and culture. That preoccupation is present in the beautiful image – almost out of George Herbert – which subliminally and proleptically converts the sandbank on which the ship is wrecked into what is at first an ordinary domestic image:

I am soft sift
In an hourglass – at the wall
Fast, but mined with a motion, a drift,
And it crowds and it combs to the fall;
I steady as a water in a well, to a poise, to a pane,
But roped with, always, all the way down from the tall
Fells or flanks of the voel, a vein
Of the gospel proffer, a pressure, a principle, Christ's gift.

Hopkins probably wrote *planks* not *flanks*, an odd choice of noun but one which is consistent with the run of *p* sounds. The run of *f* sounds take up the three *f* sounds that occur in the previous stanza's last line, a line that in turn picks up 'frown', 'face', 'fled', 'fling'. The mining motion of the unstable sand suggests military action, even coalmines, while the verb 'crowds' suggests the idea of the active, organized crowd. Canetti gives a list of crowd symbols: sea, rain, rivers, forests, corn, wind, sand, heaps and treasure. Hopkins's poem includes sea, rain, wind, sand and heaps, while the lily-showers 'astrew' is also a treasure image.

A later image in the poem – 'the storm's brawling' – is also a crowd, more particularly a mob image. In crowd theory, crowds are shown to organize themselves with a highly sophisticated military instinct (the overthrow of Ceausescu in Romania would be an example). In Thomas Jefferson's political thinking, riot and sedi-tion are the means to hold free government true to its republican principles. They cleanse corrupt government and are necessary to the health of a society. There is an element here of this neoclassical republicanism, which goes back to Machiavelli, as Hopkins imagines a primitive cleansing of what Clough in 1848 called a 'wicked artificial civilization'.

The opening of 'That Nature is a Heraclitean Fire', a poem set in County Dublin, is a complex crowd image:

> Cloud-puffball, torn tufts, tossed pillows ¦ flaunt forth, then chevy on an air-
> built thoroughfare: heaven-roysterers, in gay-gangs ¦ they throng; they glitter in marches.
> Down roughcast, down dazzling whitewash, ¦ wherever an elm arches,
> Shivelights and shadowtackle in long ¦ lashes lace, lance, and pair.
> Delightfully the bright wind boisterous ¦ ropes, wrestles, beats earth bare
> Of yestertempest's creases.

Many years ago, I realized that this great – I can only call it expressionist – poem had its source in a letter to Robert Bridges (30 July 1887), in which Hopkins asks Bridges to recognize that Home Rule is likely to come: he uses imagery of flood and says Gladstone 'the Grand Old Mischiefmaker' is loose 'like the Devil'.

Writing to another poet friend, Canon Dixon, he exclaims:

> What a preposterous summer! It is raining now: when is it not? However there was one windy bright day between floods last week: fearing for my eyes, with my other rain of papers, I put work aside and went out for the day, and conceived a sonnet.
>
> (29 July 1888)

The imagery of fluctuation, storm, wind, bright light fills the stretched sonnet, which he wrote on 26 July 1888.

There is a white fungus called the devil's puffball – step on it and a puff of black spore bursts out. The clouds, which must be white mixed with black stormclouds, are addressed as 'cloud-puffball'. They are devilish like Gladstone, or like the crowd / sea in 'The Wreck of the Deutschland'. Placing the letter beside the poem we gain a greater insight into Hopkins's imaginative intention, but my anxiety is that in treating his prose like this – letters and notebooks both – we devalue the prose in the interests of discovering more about the complexities of his imagination. Supposing, however, we were to treat the prose as something valuable in its own right: I don't mean by this looking at prose passages as effectively prose poems – in English, unlike French, the prose poem is an overly self-conscious form. Rather, I would want to approach prose passages as poems in prose.

Take this entry from Hopkins's journal for 1868:

Aug. 3. Fine and hot.

Spiculation in a dry blot in a smooth inkstand.

Aug. 4. Fine and hot.

Saw Edgell and sat talking with him in Regent's Park.

Aug. 5. Sunlight dim; radiations in the sky at night.

Aug. 6. Rain at last.

Aug. 7. Dull morning; threatening afternoon, with some rain.

An owl has come even to Oak Hill and I saw it wheeling through the moonlight in front and presently there were scuffling sounds in the bushes.

Aug. 8. Fine.

A letter from Maples which made me go to see him at his curacy in Soho.

Aug. 9. Fine.

Aug. 10. Fine but dim.

It is said the swifts have flown unusually early.

Aug. 11. Sultry dim morning; dark afternoon; then hard rain; fine nightfall.

Aug. 12. Fine.

Aug. 13. A downpour till evening.

Aug. 14. Fine. There were the travelling stack clouds with straight-cut under-sides but yet later the sky was somewhat overcast and a little rain fell.

Aug. 15. Fine.

Aug. 16. Rain.

Aug. 17. Dark, soft, and wet.

Saw Garrett.

Aug. 18. Morning and night wet; fine afternoon with snow-white flying scarf-ends in the clouds.

Balloons seen at Willesden.

Aug. 19. Dark, with wet.

In Devonshire *wants* = moles. – Aunt Annie told me that a lady who knew that country had told her of a field near Chester with a tumulus in it, where a figure in gold armour was said to stand at midnight: some years before a man had seen it. The owner to lay the ghost had the mound opened and a beautiful suit of golden Roman-British armour was found in it. She quotes it to shew the persistency of tradition.

Aug. 20. Dull, with wet.

Of course, in the culmination of this passage – really the point where I've simply terminated the quotation – in the culmination lies the seed of the end of 'The Wreck of the Deutschland', because that golden Romano-British armour stayed in Hopkins's imagination:

> Dame, at our door
> Drowned, and among our shoals,
> Remember us in the roads, the heaven-haven of the reward:
> Our King back, Oh, upon English souls!
> Let him easter in us, be a dayspring to the dimness of us, be a crimson-cresseted east,
> More brightening her, rare-dear Britain, as his reign rolls,
> Pride, rose, prince, hero of us, high-priest,
> Our hearts' charity's hearth's fire, our thoughts' chivalry's throng's Lord.

But I don't want to follow the parallel up and dwell on Hopkins's vision of Roman Britain, his glance at *Idylls of the King*, his interest in Arnold's epic essay 'On the Celtic Element in Literature'.

Rather, I want to say that this prose passage is about the imagination observing, lying indolent, recognizing the quotidian, remembering what did (to paraphrase Larkin), then pouncing with that worked sentence: 'Sultry dim morning; dark afternoon; then hard rain; fine nightfall.' This is like two lines of verse, breaking at 'afternoon', and it shows Hopkins searching for form and subject. He has a painter's eye, as in:

> Laus Deo – the river today and yesterday. Yesterday it was a sallow glassy gold at Hodder Roughs and by watching hard the banks began to sail upstream, the scaping unfolded, the river was all in tumult but not running, only the lateral motions were perceived, and the curls of froth where the waves overlap shaped and turned easily and idly. – I meant to have written more. – Today the river was wild, very full, glossy brown with mud, furrowed in permanent billows through which from head to head the water swung with a great down and up again. These heads were scalped with rags of jumping foam. But at the Roughs the sight was the burly water-backs which heave after heave kept tumbling up from the broken foam and their plump heap turning open in ropes of velvet.
>
> (20 October 1870)

There is a beautifully unified image in 'sallow glassy gold', the *o*'s and the *g*'s and the *l*'s welding together and echoing the opening 'Laus Deo'. But Hopkins typically can't resist a yuck, a bad taste moment in the 'rags of jumping foam'. His subconscious is already coming into view in the phrase 'a great down and up again', for when we know that Hopkins was both attracted to and repelled by rough working men, the repeated word 'Roughs' – a favourite word of Whitman's – begins to function as an erotic invitation. It's not too far from this moment to the grotesque image of the drowned sailor 'dandled' on the cobbled foam-fleece, but I don't want to see this passage as leading to that and to linked moments in 'The Wreck of the Deutschland' and in other poems. My hunch is that this passage has something to do with male bonding, and that those 'ropes of velvet' are intentionally rebarbative, even monkish. Or perhaps more to the point, this is the bathing place for Stonyhurst schoolboys in the summer.

There are more insistently rebarbative moments in this passage:

> A little before 7 in the evening a wonderful Aurora, the same that was seen at Rome (shortly after its seizure by the Italian government) and taken as a sign of God's anger. It gathered a little below the zenith, to the S.E. I think – a knot or crown, not a true circle, of dull blood-coloured horns and dropped long red beams down the sky on every side, each impaling its lot of stars. An hour or so later its colour was gone but there was still a pale crown in the same place: the skies were then clear and ashy and fresh with stars and there were flashes of or like sheet-lightning. The day had been very bright and clear, distances smart, herds of towering pillow clouds, one great stack in particular over Pendle was knoppled all over in fine snowy tufts and pencilled with bloom-shadow of the greatest delicacy. In the sunset all was big and there was a world of swollen cloud holding the yellow-rose light like a lamp while a few sad milky blue slips passed below it. At night violent hailstorms and hail again next day, and a solar halo. Worth noticing too perhaps the water-runs were then mulled and less beautiful than usual.
>
> (25 October 1870)

But it may be that I am resisting the Catholic design which is so visible in this passage of dedicated and arresting observation of nature. The assonantal run of 'ashy', 'fresh' and 'flashes' is subtle, and it aids the argument from design which also informs this passage:

I was looking at high waves. The breakers always are parallel to the coast and shape themselves to it except where the curve is sharp however the wind blows. They are rolled out by the shallowing shore just as a piece of putty between the palms whatever its shape runs into a long roll. The slant ruck or crease one sees in them shows the way of the wind. The regularity of the barrels surprised and charmed the eye; the edge behind the comb or crest was as smooth and bright as glass. It may be noticed to be green behind and silver white in front: the silver marks where the air begins, the pure white is foam, the green solid water. Then looked at to the right or left they are scrolled over like mouldboards or feathers or jibsails seen by the edge. It is pretty to see the hollow of the barrel disappearing as the white combs on each side run along the wave gaining ground till the two meet at a pitch and crush and overlap each other.

(10 August 1872)

The image of the lumps of putty rolled between the palms immediately joins nature with human labour to communicate a sense of being-in-the-world, which also in democratic, practical fashion quite effortlessly naturalizes the argument from design. Barrels and glass, of course, are formed by human, technological processes which the natural process either illustrates or is illustrated by. Both sides of the divide between nature and technology are bridged by 'mouldboards or feathers or jibsails'. Reading this, I catch an early Cubist imagination at work, as Hopkins shows how perception is dynamic like nature – it discovers and imposes order, and at times has difficulty in making sense of the phenomena it is entwined with:

About all the turns of the scaping from the break and flooding of wave to its run out again I have not yet satisfied myself. The shores are swimming and the eyes have before them a region of milky surf but it is hard for them to unpack the huddling and gnarls of the water and law out the shapes and the sequence of the running: I catch however the looped or forked wisp made by every big pebble the backwater runs over – if it were clear and smooth there would be a network from their overlapping, such as can in fact be seen on smooth sand after the tide is out – ; then I saw it run browner, the foam dwindling and twitched into long chains of suds, while the strength of the backdraught shrugged the stones together and clocked them one against another.

That verb 'unpack' has unfortunately lost its freshness and innocence in recent years, but it beautifully catches the physical texture of perception in Hopkins, the way it is embodied in the noun 'gnarls' that he invents to represent water in motion – a motion whose 'huddling' takes us back to his interest in crowds.

Looking at this passage, I feel the draw again of making a connection with his verse, because there is a recognition in 'the foam dwindling and twitched into long chains of suds'. Years later Hopkins was to remember this passage:

> A windpuff-bonnet of fáwn-fróth
> Turns and twindles over the broth
> Of a pool so pitchblack, féll-frówning,
> It rounds and rounds Despair to drowning.

In this stanza from 'Inversnaid' the phrase 'dwindling and twitched' becomes the neologism 'twindles'. The crowd is on the farthest fringes of the prose, which is Cézanne-like in its strictness, but that 'windpuff-bonnet of fáwn-fróth' takes us back to an armed crowd, as Hopkins remembers the Jacobite rebellions. The foam becomes a Highlander's bonnet, and reminds him of the last attempt to restore a Catholic monarch to the British throne. The roaring burn reminds him of an armed crowd of rebels hurtling down the brae, as he contemplates the final extinction of the Stuart cause.

I imagine Hopkins in our time would have interested himself in chaos theory:

> All the world is full of inscape and chance left free to act falls into an order as well as purpose: looking out of my window I caught it in the random clods and broken heaps of snow made by the cast of a broom.
>
> (24 February 1873)

Examining this statement, I notice how the *oo* in 'looking' is echoed in the last word 'broom', how the gutturals in 'looking', 'caught', 'clods', 'broken' and 'cast' all chime, just as 'broken' and 'snow' chime too. The *m*'s also reverberate in this part of the sentence, which is also picking up the *k* sounds in 'inscape' and 'act' in the first half.

The visionary strictness of Hopkins's prose, his profound joy in perception, in the phenomena he describes, fill his notebooks and journals with an exacting heavenly light. He completes his description of the random heaps of snow by saying:

> The sun was bright, the broken brambles and all boughs and banks limed and cloyed with white, the brook down the clough pulling its way by drops and by bubbles in turn under a shell of ice.

Once again Hopkins's beloved *i* sound structures the sentence, which seems to father itself in that perfect, entirely unexpected verb 'cloyed', before finishing in that strange 'shell of ice' which reflects 'bright' at the beginning.

Observing pigeons, Hopkins says:

> I looked at the pigeons down in the kitchen yard and so on. They look like little gay jugs by shape when they walk, strutting and jod-jodding with their heads. The two young ones are all white and the pins of the folded wings, quill pleated over quill, are like crisp and shapely cuttleshells found on the shore. The others are dull thundercolour or black-grape-colour except in the white pieings, the quills and tail, and in the shot of the neck. I saw one up on the eaves of the roof: as it moved its head a crush of satin green came and went, a wet or soft flaming of the light.
>
> (16 June 1873)

The jug image makes them anthropomorphic, but the shapely cuttleshells bring nature and God's design into the picture, as Hopkins characteristically tries to unite human, divine and natural processes. It is motion, process, which fascinates him endlessly: those 'jod-jodding' pigeons seem to nod a new verb into the language, while that 'crush of satin green', coming and going, has a sensuous delicacy that culminates in the discriminating perception of the 'wet or soft flaming of the light'. The notes in my edition point properly to relevant poems – the phrase 'dull thundercolour' is aligned with the 'thunder-purple seabeach' in 'Henry Purcell' – and although this attention is necessary, it does subordinate the genius of Hopkins's prose to his finished poems. The prose becomes part of the process, and so it twindles and dwindles. Really I want to argue – or assert – the autarkic, the autonomous, nature of these prose passages. Each in its own right is a perfect inscape, which needs as it were to be exhibited and displayed for the object it so uniquely is, rather than being treated as the occasion for a poem, which did or did not get written.

Immediately after the note on the pigeons, we find a passage which is obviously the jumping off point for this beautiful fragment:

Repeat that, repeat,
Cuckoo, bird, and open ear wells, heart-springs, delightfully sweet,
With a ballad, with a ballad, a rebound
Off trundled timber and scoops of the hillside ground, hollow
hollow hollow ground:
The whole landscape flushes on a sudden at a sound.

The beautiful tenor climb of that pauseless, because comma-less, 'hollow hollow hollow ground' carols out like a song by Dowland, and that softly dominating 'flushes' has a Keatsian richness and suggestiveness, which concentrates the *l* sounds in the previous lines and is lingering, softly tactile and intense, as well as visual. But the prose which began it has its own perfectly distinctive character:

Sometimes I hear the cuckoo with wonderful clear and plump and fluty notes: it is when the hollow of a rising ground conceives them and palms them up and throws them out, like blowing into a big humming ewer – for instance under Saddle Hill one beautiful day and another time from Hodder wood when we walked on the other side of the river.

That piece of putty between the palms is reworked in this sentence, so that the cuckoo becomes like a ball being bounced up into the air – the so very apt adjective 'plump' carries 'up' inside it, just as the *oo* in 'fluty' echoes 'cuckoo'. Hopkins's eye is also on the shape of that *u*, which appears again in the surprising, revelatory image of the 'big humming ewer' (an image as domestic and man-made as the pigeon jugs). Again a human artefact clinches this perception of a natural phenomenon. The ewer carries within it the *oo* in 'cuckoo', while the run of 'wonderful', 'hollow', 'throws', 'blowing', and 'ewer' designs an inscape based on *w*. Returning to the sentence, I notice that there is a delayed repetition of the double *oo* at the beginning in 'beautiful'.

The intensity of Hopkins's being-in-the-world means that he dwells within the here-and-now of his perceptions with a cleansing eagerness that works on the reader like redemption. There is an arresting, even, at times, overwhelming, immediacy in his encounters with nature that is utterly individual:

> The bluebells in your hand baffle you with their inscape, made to every sense: if you draw your fingers through them they are lodged and struggle with a shock of wet heads; the long stalks rub and click and flatten to a fan on one another like your fingers themselves would when you passed the palms hard across one another, making a brittle rub and jostle like the noise of a hurdle strained by leaning against; then there is the faint honey smell and in the mouth the sweet gum when you bite them. But this is easy, it is the eye they baffle. They give one a fancy of panpipes and of some wind instrument with stops – a trombone perhaps. The overhung necks – for growing they are little more than a staff with a simple crook but in water, where they stiffen, they take stronger turns, in the head like sheephooks or, when more waved throughout, like the waves riding through a whip that is being smacked – what with these overhung necks and what with the crisped ruffled bells dropping mostly on one side and the gloss these have at their footstalks they have an air of the knights at chess. Then the knot or 'knoop' of buds some shut, some just gaping, which makes the pencil of the whole spike, should be noticed: the inscape of the flower most finely carried out in the siding of the axes, each striking a greater and greater slant, is finished in these clustered buds, which for the most part are not straightened but rise to the end like a tongue and this and their tapering and a little flattening they have make them look like the heads of snakes.
>
> (9 May 1871)

Again the tactile fascination with palms occurs, perhaps because Hopkins, like Vermeer, wants to communicate a tingling, tactile sensation that is intimate and personal. This passage always reminds me of Stanley Spencer, perhaps because the movement from bluebells and fingers to the much larger straining hurdle introduces a gigantesque, slightly homely moment typical of his paintings.

We can glimpse Hopkins's subconscious here (Spencer's is out in the open, hugely), and the note ends with the bluebells looking 'like the heads of snakes'. Observantly, the editor's note points us to the homoerotic lyric 'The furl of fresh-leaved dogrose down', where the man's locks are first compared to a 'ravel-rope's-end', 'hempen strands in spray', 'foam-fallow, hanks', and then to:

a juicy and jostling shock
Of bluebells sheaved in May
Or wind-long fleeces on the flock
A day off shearing day.

Hopkins may be describing bluebells in the prose, but he is also figuring the erotic, as he is in 'Harry Ploughman':

Hard as hurdle arms, with a broth of goldish flue
Breathed round; the rack of ribs; the scooped flank; lank
Rope-over thigh; knee-nave; and barrelled shank –
Head and foot, shoulder and shank –

Once again I've allowed the poems to pull me away from giving the prose my undivided attention. I don't want to hear the creak of a bed in that noise of a hurdle strained by leaning against, rather the idea of safety, a sheepfold – Milton's image of Christianity – is possibly in his mind. But perhaps Hopkins is both holy and profane, and this is the cause of his devotion to tender-as-a-pushed-peach bad taste.

An Indian Child: Rudyard Kipling

Shortly before his death on 17 January 1936, an American newspaper said that Rudyard Kipling had become so secluded and remote that to most Englishmen – Kipling would have preferred the term 'British citizens' – he had become part of 'the folk-lore of his country – a silent, shadowy figure of the past'. Already he was regarded as 'a dead Classic', and his reputation has diminished with time. The appearance of three biographies in as many years – Harry Ricketts, *The Unforgiving Minute: A Life of Rudyard Kipling* (1999) and Andrew Lycett, *Rudyard Kipling* (1999) and David Gilmour, *The Long Recessional: The Imperial Life of Rudyard Kipling* (2002) – would suggest that a fascination with Kipling the man lives on. But anyone who teaches Kipling (as I have for the past thirty years) is bound to wonder why students in a post-imperial country should be interested in his work. Why should they care about the way some of us were enthralled in our ancient British childhoods by his sights, cadences and smells? I can still remember the moment in 'Rikki-Tikki-Tavi' when the cobra eggs are shown not to have shells but skins, as they nestle in the melon patch under the warm mud wall. Like the cadence of the 'great, grey-green, greasy Limpopo River', the sensuous particularity of that moment spoke out like an epiphany.

Kipling, as David Gilmour shows in *The Long Recessional*, was devoted to children, and loved entertaining them. He is a children's writer of unsurpassed genius, and as a literary primitivist is never quite adult or fully or seriously mature, in that there is always a togetherness, at times forced, in his relationship with his audience. He loves to talk shop, is often a know-all, and so does not quite possess the lonely voice of the classic masters of the short story.

Though he speaks for the British Imperial tribe, he does so with an anxiety which knows deep down that the Empire cannot last. A driven, vigilant, unresting writer, he is also a national avatar. In a moving moment, Gilmour shows that the seals in *The Jungle Book* are invoked in Churchill's great Dunkirk speech. The seals 'fought in the breakers, they fought in the sand, and they fought in the smooth-worn basalt rocks of the nurseries'. Churchill, who loved Kipling's work, said: 'we shall fight on the beaches, we shall fight on the landing grounds, we shall fight in the fields and the streets'.

Kipling was fiercely hostile to Churchill, whom he regarded as a prostituted politician. He loathed Radical and Liberal politicians for their criticisms of the Empire and their support for Irish Home Rule, yet as Ashis Nandy has shown in his study, *The Intimate Enemy: The Loss and Recovery of Self under Colonialism* (1983, 1988), Kipling was 'culturally an Indian child' who became 'an ideologue' of Western moral and political superiority. One of his voices belonged to his martial, violent, self-righteous self; the other was full of awe for the culture and mind of India.

Kipling was born in Bombay in 1865, and like many Anglo-Indian children spent most of his time with servants and spoke Hindi as his first language. The servants spoilt him to such an extent that his English relatives hated him when he and his parents visited England for the birth of his sister in 1868. Two years later, he and his sister were sent to England, where they were lodged in the grim boarding-house in Southsea which in his memoirs he called the House of Desolation. The experience was partly responsible for his most endearing quality – 'his deep understanding of the vulnerabilities of children'. Kipling's father, Lockwood, to whom he was devoted, was a teacher at the School of Art and Industry in Bombay, and from him Kipling acquired a love of craft skills and a belief that craftsmanship is the essential basis of all great art.

The boarding-school he attended from the age of twelve was not a typical mid-Victorian establishment – it had no uniforms, no cadet corps and no school chapel. Its teachers were not in holy orders, and its headmaster, Cornell Price, was a reluctant and intermittent flogger. Price was a liberal and a friend of Kipling's uncle, the painter Edward Burne-Jones, and of William Morris. Oddly, in a speech delivered at the headmaster's retirement, Kipling said that Price had had only one aim: 'to make men able to make and keep empires'.

Kipling's parents couldn't afford to send him to university, so he returned to India to work as a journalist on the *Civil and Military Gazette* in Lahore, the capital of the recently annexed province of Punjab. He was sixteen, with a 'protruding cleft chin out-thrust, as though it were leading him', a friend recalled, and his skin was sufficiently dark to provoke a rumour that his real father was an Indian. In his fine essay on Kipling, Orwell noted that his contemporaries in India didn't approve of him. He mixed with the wrong people and had a dark complexion. Orwell, who had been a colonial police officer in Burma, was drawing on conversations with British colonialists who had known Kipling, and in his devoted biography Charles Carrington quotes a French writer, Joseph-Renaud, who describes Kipling stroking 'his bald head with a hand so brown that you might have thought him a Hindu (he was so dark that some people put about a rumour – quite false – that he was a half-caste)'.

Orwell's testimony is backed by Nandy's analysis of Kipling as a tragic figure seeking 'to disown in self-hatred' an aspect of himself identified with Indianness. Gilmour draws on other remarks Orwell makes in his essay, but as a historian he is, I would guess, sceptical of a psychological approach to his subject. He recounts how, when Kipling became assistant editor of the *Civil and Military Gazette*, he was fascinated by Lahore, 'that wonderful, dirty, mysterious ant hill' with its bazaars, opium and gambling dens and brothels. He was very hard-working, and contributed a lot of hack journalism to the *Gazette*, but soon he was also publishing poems, stories and comic sketches in the paper. He spent the summers in the hill station, Simla, where the government retired in the hot season (the Viceroy, Lord Dufferin, liked Kipling's mother and often dropped in for tea).

Among the stories he published was 'The Man Who Would Be King', which describes how two adventurers create a kingdom in the mountains of Kafiristan. One of the adventurers, Dravot, says of the natives: 'these men aren't niggers, they're English'. His decision to take a native woman as his wife causes their downfall, and he is beheaded by the rebellious natives. Early in the story, Kipling says that Indian Native States are 'the dark places of the earth, full of unimaginable cruelty, touching the Railway and the Telegraph on one side, and, on the other, the days of Harun-al-Raschid'. Kipling's story was published in his collection *Wee Willie Winkie* (1890), and Conrad must be alluding to it, when in *Heart of Darkness* (published in *Blackwood's Magazine* in 1899) the Thames at the time of the Roman invasion is called 'one of the dark places of the earth'.

In 'Little Foxes' (1909), a satire on anti-Imperialism, an interfering English Liberal MP, who is visiting Egypt, says 'Good God! What callous oppression! The dark places of the earth are full of cruelty.' Kipling's story makes the case for Imperialism as a sort of feudal cooperation between whites and natives, cemented by fox-hunting. It is a weak story, with an attack on 'Demah-Kerazi, which is a devil inhabiting crowds and assemblies', wisely ignored by Gilmour.

Kipling was regarded by his Anglo-Indian contemporaries as bumptious and opinionated, sometimes as a cad, a bounder and a 'subversive pamphleteer given to criticize his betters'. As Gilmour shows, he was able to experience much more of native India than most British people did. He had a 'sensory receptiveness' which enabled him to 'watch and listen and not condemn', as he absorbed impressions from the bazaars, the hill stations, the Grand Trunk Road that stretches all the way from present-day Pakistan to Calcutta. He had an enormous knowledge of local habits, language and ways of thought, and could communicate with everyone. To this day, Indian writers respect and admire his work, praising *Kim* as (still) the outstanding Anglo-Indian novel. Years ago, after travelling from Jullundur Cantonment to the tiny station at Simla, I looked at the bare-assed monkeys on the corrugated iron roof of the Anglican church with its sandstone walls and the snowy slopes of the Tibetan foothills beyond, and wondered at its craziness. That surreal feeling suffuses Kipling's imagination and makes every scene unstable. Near the end of the novel, Kim throws a basket belonging to the Russian spies over a huge cliff below the mountain village of Shamlegh:

> The wheeling basket vomited its contents as it dropped. The theodolite hit a jutting cliff-ledge and exploded like a shell; the books, inkstands, paint-boxes, compasses and rulers showed for a few seconds like a swarm of bees. Then they vanished; and, though Kim, hanging half out of the window, strained his young ears, never a sound came up from the gulf.

The objects which fall are Russian, but they could just as well be British, and Kipling, who was proud of his membership of a Masonic Lodge in Lahore, where all races met as equals, has added the compasses and rulers from freemasonry to underline his anxiety about the future of Western ideas in India. Yet, paradoxically, there is a sense of freedom in this cinematic moment, because Kim, who has suffered a crisis of identity about whether he is Indian or British, is now experiencing a sense of relief, of liberation, of visionary freedom.

In *Plain Tales from the Hills* and subsequent stories, Kipling displays, as Gilmour shows, his essential sympathy for the peoples among whom he lived. A different and much wider kind of sympathy, he rightly suggests, infuses *Kim*, though when he suggests that Edward Said and others have detected blemishes of Orientalism in the novel, he omits to mention Said's argument in his fine edition of *Kim* that it is a work of 'great aesthetic force', which cannot be dismissed simply as the racist imagining of one fairly disturbed and ultra-reactionary imperialist. Like Said, but unlike the more facile forms of postcolonial theory, Gilmour is concerned to demonstrate that Kipling was a complex figure with a remarkable historical prescience. In 1897, he predicted a 'big smash' with the Germans. After the Boer War, he predicted the apartheid regime of Dr Malan, saying 'We put them [the Boers] in a position to uphold and expand their primitive lust for racial domination.' He admired multiracial Brazil, and (his occasional anti-Semitism notwithstanding) detested Hitler. He was so disgusted by the Nazis and the sight of their flag that he removed the swastika, the symbol of good luck and prosperity used by Hindus, Jains and Buddhists, from his book-bindings.

It had been his trademark for nearly forty years, but it was now 'defiled beyond redemption'.

Kipling's favourite child, Josephine, died at the age of six, and his son John was killed in the First World War. John failed the medical examination because he had inherited his father's bad eyesight, but Kipling pulled strings and got him commissioned in the Irish Guards. He was killed at the Battle of Loos, but as there was no corpse or definite evidence of death, Kipling and his wife Carrie continued to hope that he was alive in Germany. He commemorated John movingly in 'My Boy Jack':

> 'Have you any news of my boy Jack?'
> *Not this tide.*
> 'When d'you think that he'll come back?'
> *Not with this wind blowing, and this tide . . .*

Kipling also wrote an icily clever short story, 'Mary Postgate', in which a repressed English spinster refuses to help a dying airman whom she believes is German, though he speaks to her in French. In a notorious scene, she gives herself an orgasm by leaning on a poker while he dies. Though the story is prefaced with a poem that begins:

> It was not part of their blood,
> It came to them very late
> With long arrears to make good,
> When the English began to hate

and though Kipling's cousin, Oliver Baldwin, called 'Mary Postgate' 'the wickedest story ever told', there is another way of reading the story which contradicts its apparently hardline and unforgiving nationalism. The airman may not have been German, and the bomb he is supposed to have dropped and killed a child with may also belong to the poor, limited woman's imagination. The story, Gilmour suggests, is a masterpiece where a repressed woman is racked by love and hate.

The Kipling who emerges from *The Long Recessional* is a driven, rootless figure who refused all honours, was not interested in his ancestry, and refused payment for the 'national' poems, such as 'Recessional', which he published regularly in *The Times*. Here, Gilmour challenges Carrington, who in his biography contrasts Kipling with what he terms 'deracinated intellectuals'. Gilmour perceptively links Kipling's political and national verse with Bunyan, 'his most direct spiritual ancestor', whom he celebrates in 'The Holy War' as a soldier and minister who would have 'thoroughly . . . understood the Hun and the Pacifist mind'. With his Methodist background on both sides (his grandfathers were Methodist ministers), Kipling represents that core Nonconformism in the national character, but one which can express itself in a bold, resolute, martial, hyperbolic, yet somehow sensitive manner, that owes something to his admiration for Pathan frontiersmen (Mahbub Ali in *Kim* is one example), and I think also to his admiration for Sikhs, whom he encountered in the Punjab. In 'A Sahib's War', he writes a story about what would have happened if the British had had the sense to deploy Sikh regiments in the Boer War, and creates a boastful, proudly loyal, very convincing Sikh trooper, Umr Singh.

Kipling wrote 300,000 words of propaganda during the First World War. He often criticized British officials and generals for their incompetence and corruption, particularly over the defeat at Ctesiphon in Mesopotamia. He did not take part in the celebrations after the Armistice – like many bereaved parents, he and his wife realized that the loss of their son was even harder to bear in peacetime. He believed that the Versailles Peace Treaty was too lenient, and remained paranoid about Germany. He contributed to a fund for General Dyer, the officer condemned by the House of Commons for the massacre of more than 300 Indians at Amritsar in April 1919. He believed the Irish Free State was the precursor of 'Free States of Evil' throughout the Empire, and described Irish nationalism fatuously as 'Bolshevism in Erse'. He broke with Beaverbrook over Ireland, and became increasingly isolated, though he was a close friend of King George V and was for many years on good terms with his cousin Stanley Baldwin, who first became Prime Minister in 1923.

As Gilmour shows, Kipling's most memorable war work was done at the end of the struggle and in the early years of the peace, through his literary epitaphs, his inscriptions for memorials and gravestones, and his service with the Imperial War Graves Commission.

He attended meetings of the Commission, contributed to its booklets and visited the cemeteries as they were formed along the line of the Front. He also argued strenuously for 'equality of treatment' for the fallen, knowing that the richer the bereaved were, the more likely it was that they would want something ornate and imposing to distinguish their graves from the others. The wealthy, he argued, should not be permitted to 'proclaim their grief above other people's grief' simply because they had larger bank accounts. 'Lord knows I'm no democrat', he said, but everyone's sons had died for a common cause; the movement for special graves was unacceptable because it was a demand for 'privilege in the face of death'. The Commission was attacked by Lord Hugh Cecil for employing Kipling, 'not a known religious man', to choose its inscriptions.

It is here that we can see Kipling as an architect of the British national memory – or British and Commonwealth memory – as he chose terse, moving and appropriate inscriptions. On the stones of remembrance, he chose five words from Ecclesiastes – 'Their Name Liveth for Evermore'. He selected seven more from the same source for those whose burial places had been destroyed by shelling: 'Their Glory Shall Not Be Blotted Out'. And in those graves for which a name could not be found, he chose nine of his own: 'A Soldier of the Great War Known unto God'.

During the last twenty years of his life, when he was often ill, Kipling became more and more of a francophile, even liking Poincaré, the most fractious and unsympathetic of French leaders. He also admired Clemenceau, whom he fawned on and addressed as 'Master' in their correspondence. An international campaign to malign the French must, he assumed, have had 'an enormous amount of Hebrew and Hun money behind it'. Although the French may justly be seen as responsible for the Carthaginian Peace of the Versailles settlement, and, therefore, largely responsible for the Second World War, Kipling was unable to see this. Though he argued that Liberalism was 'the mother of Destruction the world over', he was not a Fascist; his limited and temporary admiration for Mussolini was based on his belief that the Duce was a strong man who got things done. He called Mosley 'a bounder and an arriviste', and by the mid-1930s he had come to regard Mussolini as a crazy and irrational megalomaniac. One of his solaces late in life was his friendship with the King, who invited him to Balmoral and to dinner at Buckingham Palace. In 1932, he agreed to write the King's first Christmas message for the wireless, and wept as he heard his own words broadcast to the Empire.

The Long Recessional is an important act of cultural reclamation, which ought to bring readers back to the Kipling canon. Gilmour is sensitive to the aesthetic sophistication of Kipling's late stories, though at one point he remarks that they are not 'alas relevant' to the themes of his study. We need as readers to integrate his historical approach with Ashis Nandy's postcolonial view of Kipling as a type of self-hating babu and imperialist, who is trying to disown the Indian aspect of himself. In his masterpiece, *Kim*, he uses a series of contradictions to construct his endearing central character, Kimball O'Hara, who is variously described as 'English', a 'poor white of the very poorest', and who is also Irish as well as being 'burned black as any native'. Kim's father was an Irish colour-sergeant. The 'half-caste' woman – Kipling's phrase – who looks after Kim claims she is the sister of Kim's mother, but Kipling says 'his mother had been nursemaid in a Colonel's regiment and had married Kimball O'Hara'. This does not prove that young Kim is white, and it is curious that Kipling should raise the idea of Kim's being of mixed race only to dispel it. In an odd non-sequitur, we are told that the lama was Kim's 'trove, and he purposed to take possession. Kim's mother had been Irish too.'

Kipling, Gilmour shows, did not like anyone drawing attention to the Celtic side of his ancestry (he had Scottish Jacobite and Ulster ancestors on his mother's side), but he is presenting Kim as belonging to the 'other' in a favourable manner here. He frequently uses racial and cultural stereotypes – Kim hates cobras, and Kipling says 'no native training can quench the white man's horror of the serpent'. But Kim sits cross-legged in native fashion; he ensures that Mahbub Ali whips the English drummer boy who refers to 'niggers', and he also forgets what Kipling calls 'his white blood' by having his face dyed in a brothel, so that he looks 'like a low-caste Hindu boy'. Later, Kim dresses 'like a Mohammedan' and longs for the vernacular – for Hindi. His craving for the spoken language is linked to his craving for 'the saffron-tinted rice, garlic and onions, and the forbidden greasy sweetmeats of the bazaar'. This is one example of a favourite allusion of Kipling's to that moment in Exodus when the Israelites crossing the desert long for 'the garlic and onions of Egypt'. Kim asks 'What am I? Mussalman, Hindu, Jain, or Buddhist?' Huree Babu tells him 'this half-year of leave is to make you de-Englishized'. Kim thinks and dreams in the vernacular. He squats, Kipling says, as only natives can, despite the abominable clinging trousers he is forced to wear. At one point, the 'Irish' and the 'Oriental' in his soul are 'tickled'. Kim's Irishness is a questionable form of whiteness, and Kipling may have heard of the theory that the Irish are descended from primeval Dravidian Indians.

The point Kipling is making or exploring is that these identities are not polar opposites. Kim has a shifting, ambiguous, protean identity – an identity that expresses so much that is essential to the experience of the colonized, a cunning personality which often takes on or mirrors the identity of the colonizer. Kim's complexity perhaps expresses Kipling's impatience with what we now term cultural essentialism, and with the racist ideology that, on another level of his mind, he held to.

On the other hand, Kipling works subtly to integrate British imperialism with Indian culture; this is the theme of his short story 'The Bridge Builders', which mixes heavy British engineering with a hashish-induced vision of the Hindu gods. In *Kim*, there are similar moments of visionary liberation, like the kilta spilling its contents down the cliff, or like this moment where Kipling says of the lama:

> the thin air refreshed him, and he sat on the precipice with the best of them, and, when talk languished, flung pebbles into the void. Thirty miles away, as the eagle flies, lay the next range, seamed and channelled and pitted with little patches of brush-forests, each a day's dark march. Behind the village, Shamlegh hill itself cut off all view to southward. It was like sitting in a swallow's nest under the eaves of the roof of the world.

The concluding anapaestic lilt gives poetic closure, but we should note that it picks up the novel's opening image of Kim sitting on the cannon outside the Lahore Museum. Kipling is drawn to images of his characters sitting in perilous places, because he aims to communicate a liminal anxiety about identity and imperial history. Like *Huckleberry Finn*, *Kim* belongs to what Hazlitt termed the feeling of immortality in youth. It is also, as Gilmour rightly argues, part of the inspiration which enabled the British people to defeat the Nazis: from Churchill to the non-commissioned officers and the ranks, 'he remained an inspiration'. Quoting Namier, he says it was the Kipling imperialists who 'were called in to bring back to us the creed of an older generation'. And in 1985, Kipling's imperial theme was again visible when loyalist shipyard workers in Belfast painted these lines from his 'Ulster 1912' on a placard outside the gates of Harland and Wolff:

> Before an Empire's eyes
> The traitor claims her price.
> What need of further lies?
> We are the sacrifice.

Kipling foresaw the Anglo-Irish Agreement, too. Like Rikki-Tikki, he kept the garden 'with tooth and jump and spring and bite, till never a cobra dared show its head inside the walls'.

Synge and Irish History

I first studied Synge at school in Belfast in the mid-1960s. It seemed to me then that *Riders to the Sea* was a timeless drama about the Aran Islanders whom I also read about in *The Aran Journal* – one of those texts like *On the Road* which appealed so strongly to my generation (the poet Andrew McNeillie read it as a sixth-former and went to live on Inishmore for a year, an experience he describes in *An Aran Keening*). Over the years I began to see – or to think I saw – a different pattern in the play. The perception of that pattern was shaped by reading a lot of Irish history – the deepening of the Troubles in the North of Ireland meant that many people went back to Irish history in search of a way of understanding what, if anything, the historical situation we were living through meant. From teaching the play as a beautifully constructed miniature classical tragedy, I turned to teaching it as a coded historical drama that represented Irish history in both a tragic and a revisionist manner – one associates revisionism with various forms of irony, from the laidback to the savage, but a revisionist tragedy is, I believe, an appropriate oxymoron. I made a set model in order to communicate to my students how the stage props work to build the shadow of the gallows which falls across this play, as it also obsessively falls across *The Playboy of the Western World*.

This is meant to be an informal account of the play – I find it very difficult to write about drama, and because this play has changed for me over the nearly forty years I've known it, I find it difficult to fix my response to it. For me, it is part of the dreamtime that was Belfast in the mid-sixties, but this drama has also taken on other resonances as the Troubles in the North of Ireland have affected my response to it. It stimulated Lawrence, a great admirer of Synge, to write 'The Odour of Chrysanthemums', and then to adapt that story into his fine play *The Widowing of Mrs Holroyd*.

In 1998, the bicentenary of the 1798 Uprising, I imagined how a theatre group might tour Ireland presenting a triple bill. First they would stage Yeats's[1] *Cathleen Ni Houlihan* and the audience would see Bridget, Michael's mother, in the opening scene undoing a parcel while the noise of cheering comes in from outside. That noise of cheering they would hear recur in the company's third play, *The Playboy of the Western World*, while the parcel recurs in the second play, *Riders to the Sea*.

The noise in *Cathleen ni Houlihan*, the audience would remember, is that of the French army landing at Killala, but early in the play Patrick says, 'they are cheering again down in the town. Maybe they are landing horses from Enniscrone. They do be cheering when the horses take the water well.' When Christy is victorious in the racing on the strand in *Playboy* we remember this moment. Just after Michael in *Cathleen* says, 'I see an old woman coming up the path,' Peter goes over to a large box in the corner, opens it and puts the bag in and fumbles at the lock. When Nora and Cathleen in *Riders* put the bundle of clothes in a hole in the chimney corner we remember this action.

Then in 1993, during the commemorations of the bicentenary of Robert Emmet's trial and execution, I began to see that this play, which was produced the year after the first centenary commemorations, draws on that myth – here we watch a young man going out to die, though the irony is he doesn't know it.

The actor playing the old woman in *Cathleen* in my imaginary production plays the widow Quinn in *Playboy* and Maurya in *Riders* – this means that the spooky moment when she looks through the window at Michael in *Cathleen* will reverberate and complicate the part of Maurya. The song the old woman sings:

[1] I say 'Yeats's' but really, as scholars now agree, it is Lady Gregory's work.

I will go cry with the woman,
For yellow-haired Donough is dead
With a hempen rope for a neckcloth,
And a white cloth on his head,–

that song and the reference to Donough who was hanged in Galway as well as the gallows in the next song the old woman sings are picked up in the frequent references to hanging in *Playboy of the Western World*, and in the very subtle use of stage props in *Riders* – the four new boards and the rope.

Similarly the old woman's historical narrative is caught up in *Riders*. She says:

there was a red man of the O'Donnells from the north, and a man of the O'Sullivans from the south, and there was one Brian that lost his life at Clontarf by the sea, and there were a great many in the west, some that died hundreds of years ago, and there are some that will die tomorrow.

Maurya in *Riders* says: 'there were Stephen and Shawn were lost in the great wind, and found after in the Bay of Gregory of the Golden Mouth, and carried up the two of them on one plank, and in by the door.' They are like Roman heroes brought out of battle on a shield. What seems to be a natural disaster is in fact a historical disaster. It is towards a historical disaster that Michael moves in *Cathleen* when he drops the bundle of his new clothes, his wedding clothes, and rushes out of the cottage following the old woman's voice. In *Riders*, we realize, the name of the young man who once wore the clothes in the bundle is also Michael. Synge turns the moment round when he has Bartley going out and refusing to heed the old woman, his mother's injunction to remain in the cottage. On one level he is a rebel going out to join a rebel army just as Michael does, on another he is a pragmatic forward-looking businessman who is refusing to stay by the superstitious backward-looking hearth. If poetic images can convey contradictory movements of thought and feeling, so can dramatic scenes.

In the opening scene of this imaginary production of *Riders* the set designer has added the halter, the bit of new rope Bartley asks for when he comes in. The audience see that:

the new boards and the new rope chime
beside the fire there is a hole where the bundle is put later
the bundle consists of a shirt and one stocking – as audience we think of baby clothes, so the hole by the chimney is a womb – on the other hand we think of a dead body and a grave
the spinning wheel makes the three women into the three fates
the pot over on the fire makes them into the three witches in *Macbeth* who are wreckers – 'though his bark can not be lost, / Yet it shall be tempest-tossed.'

For the audience, superstition is aroused when Nora and Cathleen put the ladder against the gable – we are most of us scared of walking under ladders – I don't know why, but the associations with executions are strong. The United Irish general Hugh Munro, I recall, was hanged from the lamp bracket outside his house in Lisburn. He mounted the ladder placed against the wall, said, 'I die for my country,' and leapt to his death. Patriotic woodcuts sometimes show ladders with the hangman leading a noosed rebel up to his death.

Synge, being a Protestant, knew that the ladder had another symbolic significance – it is Jacob's ladder, a masonic symbol. Maybe it's meant to communicate two opposite things here. Superstition and a mindset that is for freedom, equality, and which is opposed to superstition (I am conscious, though, that there is an essay by Roy Foster which argues convincingly that Irish Protestants have been and remain actually deeply superstitious). What I hope this production would communicate is an ironic doubleness of intention. The play is written in prose, but it reads like a verse play: 'Is the sea bad by the white rocks, Nora?' Ten syllables, six stresses, not an iambic pentameter, but a perfect line of verse, a beautifully poised sentence sound, to use Robert Frost's phrase for the vernacular in poetry.

Maurya says to her son, her only surviving son, 'You'd do right to leave that rope, Bartley, hanging by the boards.' We hear that word 'hanging' again (it runs so much through *Playboy of the Western World*), but Bartley ignores his mother and takes the rope. Maurya says, 'It will be wanting in this place, I'm telling you, if Michael is washed up tomorrow morning, or the next morning, or any morning in the week; for it's a deep grave we'll make him, by the grace of God.'

Maurya is trying to restrain Bartley from going on the sea, but he is moving, he thinks, towards life and activity; she is dedicated to memory and the dead. We remember that the actor playing her in *Cathleen Ni Houlihan* draws Michael towards death in battle or by hanging. We remember too that the old woman in *Cathleen* – Cathleen ni Houlihan herself – was played by Maud Gonne in the first production. Maud / Maurya / Cathleen would commemorate a bicentenary; Bartley wouldn't – he is Craig the would-be pragmatist and modernizer to her backward-looking De Valera. (There is a famous story that when Craig and De Valera met in 1921 to try to reach a compromise, Craig was frustrated at having to listen to De Valera's long account of 700 years of Irish history, a subject Craig judged irrelevant to the business of the meeting.) This pragmatism exists on one level; on another Bartley is like young Michael in Yeats's play going out to die, and his mother is trying to prevent him.

Then Maurya says: 'It's hard set we'll be surely the day you're drowned with the rest.' Dramatically this functions as a kind of curse. Bartley lays down the halter, takes off his old coat and puts on a newer one of the same flannel – we remember the new wedding clothes in *Cathleen Ni Houlihan* – we remember the hidden bundle in this play. We also remember the general's uniform Emmet designed for himself, and which he wore during the rebellion. Now we see that the new boards, the new rope, the new or newer coat chime with each other and create a sense of danger. The old woman in the Yeats play has the walk of a young woman at the end, while in *The Playboy of the Western World* the Widow Quinn and Pegeen are contrasted – youth and age, birth and death are brought together. In John Crowley's production some years ago the whole cast of *Riders* had a hooley at the end – in a subtle echo of the end of Behan's *The Hostage*, there was dancing and music as Bartley came back to life.

Now Cathleen says to her mother: 'Why didn't you give him your blessing – sending him out with an unlucky word behind him and a hard word in his ear?' This makes Maurya responsible, like the old woman in Yeats's play. Then Cathleen realizes they've forgotten to give Bartley the bread – another bundle, for the bread will be wrapped in cloth. Now the bread is taken out of the black pot oven – out of another hole. As she takes it out of the oven Cathleen says, 'It's destroyed he'll be, surely' – the colloquialism 'destroyed' has an ominous literal meaning. Maurya is sent out to give Bartley the bread and to break the 'dark word' and say, 'God speed you.' Cathleen says, 'Give her the stick' – 'What stick?' asks Nora – 'The stick Michael brought from Connemara,' Cathleen says – the introduction of the name of the drowned Michael is deliberate here, it increases the ominousness of the scene, it works against the idea of care and comfort and the blessing of a traveller on the road – like the ladder which Nora immediately goes over to, it is a symbol of bad luck.

Now the two young women take the bundle from the loft and Nora gets a knife to cut the string – they are the Fates slitting the thin-spun life. Nora should stand by the wheel – at this very moment Bartley must be drowning.

When Christy is tied up with ropes in *Playboy* we remember this scene – his father loosens the ropes and he escapes. In a sense he is like a rebel who escapes execution or like a rebel escaping through death from history into eternity and myth. The boards in *Riders* aren't simply coffin boards – one of them represents the boards which a condemned man walked on to carrying a handkerchief. The noose was placed round his neck. When the condemned man dropped the handkerchief, the hangman kicked the board away. 'Are you ready, sir?' said the hangman to Emmet. 'Not yet, not yet.' In a sense the stage in *Riders* is a scaffold – its horizontal wooden boards are what Prospero means by 'this bare island'.

When Maurya re-enters keening, she tells us that something choked the words in her throat and stopped her saying 'God speed you.' Bartley says, 'the blessing of God on you,' but she can say nothing. As Declan Kiberd has shown, this is like the scene Macbeth recounts just before he murders Duncan and the two grooms:

MACBETH: One cried 'God bless us' and 'Amen' the other,
As they had seen me with these hangman's hands.
List'ning their fear I could not say 'Amen'
When they did say 'God bless us.'
LADY MACBETH: Consider it not so deeply.
MACBETH: But wherefore could not I pronounce 'Amen'?
I had most need of blessing, and 'Amen'
Stuck in my throat.

The effect of this is to make Maurya a guilty party, so that when she remembers that when her son Patch was drowned – 'I was sitting here with Bartley and he a baby lying on my two knees' – the bundle and the drowning theme, birth and death are joined.

When Bartley's body is brought in on a plank with a bit of sail over it, the bundle is again present, but there is a comic moment later when the bread bundle is given to one of the men to eat while he is making the coffin.

For all its apparent naturalism, for all its transcendental tragic effect, this play is a dream vision of Irish history, of repetitive cycles of death and suffering. As I write, a coffin containing the body of Eamon Molloy, one of the disappeared, is being taken from an ancient, disused graveyard in County Louth. There is a purple cloth – an alb – over it.

The Poetry of the Present: D. H. Lawrence

Near the end of his life, Lawrence typed up a preface to a volume of poems *Chariot of the Sun* by an American friend, Harry Crosby. Poetry, Lawrence remarks, 'is a stringing together of words into a ripple and jingle and a run of colours'. He is thinking of his own free verse, not Crosby's attempts, and in an interesting passage he remarks:

> Man fixes some wonderful erection of his own between himself and the wild chaos, and gradually goes bleached and stifled under his parasol. Then comes a poet, enemy of convention, and makes a slit in the umbrella; and lo! the glimpse of chaos is a vision, a window to the sun.

This acts as a gloss on 'Bat' – 'Wings like bits of umbrella' – and implies that the bat flying is a slit in an umbrella, a glimpse of the creative chaos, which Lawrence describes later in the preface:

> The poetry of conceit is a dead-sea fruit. The poetry of sunless chaos is already a bore. The poetry of a regulated cosmos is nothing but a wire bird-cage. Because in all living poetry the living chaos stirs, sun-suffused and sun-impulsive, and most subtly chaotic. All true poetry is most subtly and sensitively chaotic, outlawed. But it is the impulse of the sun in chaos, not conceit.

These remarks are the culmination of Lawrence's thinking about the nature of poetry, and they extend the images of the chaotic, poetic act which he offers in his first successful poems, and which, dying, he affirms.

Every so often in his early verse, Lawrence chucks out an example – concrete, *en passant* – of his presentist, class-driven, aesthetic. In 'The Wild Common', he says, 'Now see, when I / Lift my arms, the hill bursts and heaves under their spurting kick!' In the next poem,

'Dog-Tired', the sky loses its 'active sheen'; in 'End of Another Home Holiday', he hears 'the sharp clean trot of a pony down the road, / Succeeding sharp little sounds dropping into silence'. Towards the end of the poem, he picks these sounds up in 'The wild young heifer, glancing distraught, / With a strange new knocking of life at her side'. And the sound pattern, which has included 'the long-drawn hoarseness of a train across the valley', is still there in the corncrake's call at the end of the poem. His imagination is stirred by such fresh, sudden moments, what he calls 'a crisis, a meeting, a spasm and throb of delight' ('Guards').

In 'Piano', the best-loved of his early poems, his crisp, exact delight in unique sounds is beautifully present:

Softly, in the dusk, a woman is singing to me;
Taking me back down the vista of years, till I see
A child sitting under the piano, in the boom of the tingling
  strings
And pressing the small, poised feet of a mother who smiles as she
  sings.

The way the piano's *p* sound is repeated in 'pressing' and 'poised' and the way those three strong stresses on 'small, poised feet' run against the iambic and anapaestic rhythm, isolate both the notes and his beloved mother's feet. The three stresses are a version of the pony's 'sharp clean trot'. They are reprised in the clever disclaimer at the beginning of the third stanza, where he says:

> So now it is vain for the singer to burst into clamour
> With the great black piano appassionato.

Three strong stresses, then the extra burst of 'appassionato' as it draws 'clamour' and 'piano' into itself. The effect carries into what follows:

The glamour
Of childish days is upon me, my manhood is cast
Down in the flood of remembrance, I weep like a child for the
  past.

The word 'glamour' still registers the shock of 'appassionato', while 'upon' is steady like the piano in the middle of the next line before passing its plosive and the *ee* sounds in 'me', 'see', 'feet' on to 'weep', with a final heightened plosive at the last moment.

This is his most successful rhyming poem, which is not to say much, as he's uncomfortable with rhymes, and rejects them in his arresting manifesto, 'Poetry of the Present', which he wrote as the introduction for the American edition of his poems in 1918.

Lawrence's sometimes argumentative engagement with Whitman shapes the impassioned prose of this essay, an essay which breaks the boundaries between critical and imaginative writing, just as the prose of *Kangaroo* and *The Boy in the Bush* break those boundaries from the other direction.

Lawrence, at the end of the First World War, is intent on saying goodbye to the nineteenth century, and this was in effect the message of Hopkins's poems, which draw deeply on Whitman, and were published in the same year. Lawrence rejects perfection, finality, exquisite form, perfect symmetry, rhythm that aims always at 'the supreme moment of the end'. He rejects perfected 'bygone moments', and in a glance at Pater's hard, gem-like flame, says such moments are 'the treasured gem-like lyrics' of Keats and Shelley. Like the 'spurting kick' of those rabbits in 'The Wild Common', 'the very white quick of nascent creation' is what he seeks and identifies with. He wants nothing crystal, permanent, eternal or changeless, nothing fixed or static, no unfading, timeless gems. Instead, he seeks the 'source, the issue, the creative quick':

> This is the unrestful, ungraspable poetry of the sheer present, poetry whose very permanency lies in its wind-like transit. Whitman's is the best poetry of this kind. Without beginning and without end, without any base and pediment, it sweeps past for ever, like a wind that is forever in passage and unchainable.

This is how free verse works, he insists; in it we look for 'the insurgent naked throb of the instant moment'. Free verse has its own nature; it is neither star nor pearl, and is 'instantaneous like plasm'.

In his search for this 'immediate, instant self', Lawrence is drawn to process, sudden critical collisions, movement, with only temporary rest or respite. This is the iconoclastic Protestant conscience, endlessly reshaping an always plastic reality, and using metaphors drawn from biology and heavy industry to figure it. As Lawrence states in an early, unrhyming poem, 'Moonrise', 'That perfect, bright experience never falls / To nothingness'. He believes that passing, ephemeral, present experience is somewhat eternal in its own right, but perhaps vital would be more accurate. This is the subject of 'Craving for Spring':

I wish it were spring
cunningly blowing on the fallen sparks, odds and ends of the old, scattered fire,
and kindling shapely little conflagrations
curious long-legged foals, and wide-eared calves, and naked sparrow-bubs.

I wish that spring
would start the thundering traffic of feet
new feet on the earth, beating with impatience.

This reworks the pony's 'sharp clean trot' and the wild young heifer in 'End of Another Home Holiday'. Sound and a vital pulsing fertility are identified for Lawrence, who earlier in 'Craving for Spring' reworks his aesthetic antipathy to bygone poems:

I trample on the snowdrops, it gives me pleasures to tread down the jonquils,
to destroy the chill Lent lilies;
for I am sick of them, their faint-bloodedness,
slow-blooded, icy-fleshed, portentous.

Jonquils he probably substitutes for daffodils, because the Wordsworth reference would be too obvious, but that poet will be numbered among 'these exquisite, ghastly first-flowers, which are rather last-flowers!' These are 'jets of exquisite finality', a phrase close to the 'exquisite form' he perceives in old-fashioned, traditional poems.

For all his hatred of technology, Lawrence is able to invoke it as he designs his vitalist aesthetic: white-hot molten steel in a blast furnace is behind the white-hot seething in 'Poetry of the Present', and electricity powers this image:

> Oh, yes, the gush of spring is strong enough
> to toss the globe of earth like a ball on a water-jet
> dancing sportfully;
> as you see a tiny celluloid ball tossing on a squirt of water
> for men to shoot at, penny-a-time, in a booth at a fair.

Lawrence's lines are autotelic, which means that his free verse poems, as well as being about birds, beasts, flowers and other subjects, are also risky, dynamic celebrations of themselves, often with a fairground bravado and a jostling, crowded, precarious element of pure fun.

When he'd written his best poems, he offered a development of his poetics in *Kangaroo* and *The Boy in the Bush*, where often the descriptive passages are really about imaginative process, about the actual act of creation Lawrence aims to perform every time he puts pen to paper. In the opening pages of *Kangaroo*, he says the ground is 'almost asking for tin cans', the bungalows are built on an 'improvized road'. In 'Tortoise Family Connections', a baby tortoise 'scuffles tinily past her as if she were an old rusty tin'. Often Lawrence compares natural creatures to metal, an effect which foregrounds his perception of them and neutralizes while simultaneously subverting that relationship. His bat is a 'twitch, a twitter, an elastic shudder in flight', its wings are 'like bits of umbrella'. The disgusted anthropomorphic vision bounces back on Lawrence, till eventually the bat escapes it. This process issues from what Lawrence calls 'come-and-go, not fixity' and its essence is that the poem should look as though it is being improvised in front of our eyes, rather as if Lawrence is a dressmaker suddenly cutting and sewing a piece of cloth in front of our eyes: running up a poem like a piece of material. When in *Kangaroo* he admires 'bungalows and tin cans scattered for miles, this Englishness all crumbled out in formlessness and chaos', he is recalling or remarking what in his manifesto he calls 'inconclusiveness, immediacy, the quality of life itself, without denouement or close'.

This improvised immediacy is the real subject of his best poems, and it works as an energy against the forward struggle of his own writing:

> Fig-trees, weird fig-trees
> Made of thick smooth silver,
> Made of sweet, untarnished silver in the sea-southern air –
> I say untarnished, but I mean opaque.

The first three lines certainly struggle – Lawrence can't quite get them off the ground. One adjective, then two, then two more, then another – they weigh the lines, drag them down like recycled Swinburne. Swinburne can write in an automatic chant like this:

> From the depth of the dreamy decline of the dawn through a
> notable nimbus of nebulous noonshine,
> Pallid and pink as the palm of the flag-flower that flickers with
> fear of the flies as they float.

Lawrence knows he is being pulled back to one of his early masters, so he suddenly turns on what he's just written and interjects in a perfect iambic pentameter:

x / x / x / x / x /
I say untarnished, but I mean opaque.

The natural exasperated speaking voice, as Frost would say, does it. He's writing against the fixed, the final, 'the crystalline, pearl-hard jewels, the poems of the eternities'. Lawrence's poetic is a puritan anti-poetic which delights in what in *Kangaroo* he calls 'a raw, loose world' which is 'mostly fringe', a 'raggle-taggle of amorphous white settlements' with, beyond them, the 'brightly-burning bush of consciousness' – an Old Testament and Presbyterian image, which again insists on the puritan cast of his imagination. Describing a deserted jetty, he sees 'spurts of activity, when steamer after steamer came blorting and hanging miserably round, like cows to the cowshed on a winter afternoon'.

Like the rabbits with their 'spurting kick' in 'The Wild Common', the steamers embody life and motion, even if they do so heavily and uncomfortably. Lawrence is fascinated in his descriptions of the Australian outback by bushiness, shagginess, tangled branches and mosses, all of which figure vigorous dialect in opposition to Standard English. When he says:

> tree-ferns rose on their notchy little trunks,
> and great mosses tangled in with more
> ordinary bushes. Overhead rose the gum-trees,
> sometimes with great stark, dead limbs
> thrown up. Sometimes handsome like pine trees

he is figuring the wildness and fecundity of free verse. Similarly the sea which 'talked and talked all the time in its disintegrative, elemental language' is a figure for the poetry of the present.

In one extraordinary moment, Lawrence designs what is effectively a poem in prose, which fuses nature, art, technology in the way all his most accomplished free verse poems do:

> The sea had thrown up, all along the surf-line, queer glittery creatures that looked like thin blown glass. They were bright transparent bladders of the most delicate ink-blue, with a long crest of deeper blue, and blind ends of translucent purple. And they had bunches of blue, blue strings, and one long blue string that trailed almost a yard across the sand, straight and blue and translucent. They must have been some sort of little octopus, with the bright glass bladder, big as smallish narrow pears with a blue frill along the top, to float them, and the strings to feed with – and perhaps the long string to anchor by. Who knows. Yet there they were, soft, brilliant, like pouches of frailest sea-glass. It reminded Somers of the glass they blow at Murano, at Venice. But there they never get the lovely soft texture and the colour.

Ruskin's reflections on Venetian glassblowing in 'The Nature of Gothic' chapter in *The Stones of Venice* are present here, and behind Ruskin's use of the image is Hazlitt's image of blown glass as a figure for journalism or writing to the moment. This passage is required at the end of the novel, where in what is termed 'the pale, white, unwritten atmosphere of Australia', we are shown 'the big bladder-weed thrown up, the little sponges like short clubs rolling in the wind, and once, only, those fairy blue wind-bags like bags of rainbow with long blue strings'. Free verse poems, like prose being written in the unwritten continent, are wind-bags, rainbow bags, sudden, unexpected arguments for design.

In a reminiscence of 'Bat', Lawrence says: 'A queer bird sat hunched on a bough a few yards away, just below; a bird like a bunch of old rag.' (From *Kangaroo*, ch. 10.) In 'Bat', bats 'hang themselves up like an old rag, to sleep', they are like 'rows of disgusting old rags'. At the end of this cinematic prose passage, the bat makes an effort, spreads 'quite big wings and whirred in a queer, flickering flight to a bough a dozen yards farther off. And there it clotted again'. It clots like an ink-blot – from rag, old cloth, to clot, the movement is again autotelic. In a moment, the bat will unclot and another poem of the present will happen in what Somers sees as 'the *uncreatedness* of the new country, the rawness, the slovenliness'.

Lawrence responds to Australia with a disgusted fascination: at night the township is full of the sound of frogs, 'rattling, screeching, whirring like a whole fairy factory going at full speed in the marshy-creek bottom'. At the end, Somers realizes that he 'had been thankful for the amorphous scrappy scattering of foundationless shacks and bungalows . . . the bungalows perched precariously on the knolls, like Japanese paper-houses, below the ridge of wire-and-tuft trees'.

This is a version of the Venetian glass, and it reads like an anticipation of Elizabeth Bishop's 'Jerónimo's House', that fragile, papery shack which is her alternative to Yeats's Norman tower, though a tower which is also a piece of recycled bricolage. This is Amit Chaudhuri's central conception of the way Lawrence's poetry works (in *D. H. Lawrence and 'Difference'*, 2003). Chaudhuri takes Picasso's sculpture 'The She-Goat', which is made from a wicker basket, palm leaves, scraps of iron, ceramic pots, and shows how Lawrence's fascination with debris and raw material infiltrates and shapes his poems. Chaudhuri shows that even in the 'finished' poem, the materials of creation, the process of construction and making, the 'peculiar pathos and joy of gradual creation are left open to view'. In their incompleteness, gaps, silences, ragged false starts, Lawrence's poems are not unlike the 'southern swarming milky way' he describes in *Kangaroo*, 'all bushy with stars and yet with black gaps, holes in the white star-road'. This 'strange, ragged southern sky' – ragged like a kookaburra bird or a bat – is evoked again in *The Boy in the Bush* where, in a witty reprise of clay and wattle cabins in 'The Lake Isle of Innisfree', Jack wants 'the empty, timeless Australia, with nooks like this, of flimsy wooden cabins by a river with wattle bush'.

Jack wants this new culture and aesthetic because he has a momentary dread of 'solid homes of brick and stone and permanence'. Echoing the ragged Southern sky, Lawrence describes a 'scraggy', 'greasy' and 'unkempt' world where ugly shacks have 'fly-dirts and lamp-black on the ceiling'. Yet this, the implication is, has to be preferable to 'a melancholy room' where 'the calico ceiling drooped, the window and front door were hermetically sealed, an ornate glass lamp shone in murky, lonely splendour upon a wool mat on a rickety, round table'.

This is a form of the bygone poem, of Pater's pure, gem-like flame, but at the same time it is a rickety, improvised structure, both conventional and displaced, like a sentence shrilled by Dame Edna. Lawrence responds to what might be termed the 'decentred' nature of Australian culture: 'Life seemed unhinged in Australia. In England there was a strong central pivot to all living, but here the centre-pin was gone, and the lives seemed to spin in weird confusion.' He admires this and what he calls 'this looseness and carelessness of Australia', and he responds to 'a pure Westralian air that was like a clean beginning of everything'. Constantly, Lawrence is sketching his persistent aesthetic as he rewrites Molly Skinner's prose (her manuscript has disappeared) and responds to the 'great hinterland country' where there is 'nothing but the moment, the instantaneous moment', a 'great hot desolation'. Whitman and Yeats are in his mind as he embraces the imaginative freedom Australia offers, and in the passage in *The Boy in the Bush* which culminates in the glance at 'The Lake Isle of Innisfree', he describes:

> The mushroom settlement, a string of slab cabins with shingle roofs and calico window-panes – or else shuttered-up windows. The stoves were outside the chimneyless cabins, under brush shelters. One such 'kitchen', a fore-runner, and already a roof of flattened-out, rusty tin cans.
>
> But it was a cosy, canny nook, homely, nestling down in a golden corner of the earth, the mimosa in bloom by the river. And it was beautifully ephemeral. As transient, as casual as the bushes themselves.

Like the eaten peach in 'Peach', this is a version of ephemeral beauty which is the alternative to Jack's dread of solid houses and permanence. What he affirms time and again is an improvised beauty, which the scattering of *o* sounds in *cosy*, *homely*, *golden*, *mimosa,* braces like the corner posts of the shack.

This is his subject in the home Jack and Tom make, which

> seemed to be a matter of forked sticks. If you wanted an upright of any sort, drive a forked stick into the ground, or dig it in, fork-end up. If you wanted a cross-bar, lay a stick or a pole across two forks. Down the sides of your house you wove brush-wood. For the roof you plaited the long stringy strips of gum-bark. With a couple of axes and a jack-knife they built a house fit for a – savage – king.

Perhaps there's a glance at Kurtz in *Heart of Darkness* here, but Lawrence is unable to accommodate aboriginal experience in the two novels – the aborigines are ghosts at the edge of his fiction. It is weird, vast emptiness and improvisation he responds to, even as he resists democracy in favour of 'the aristocratic principle, the innate difference between people'. Australia is a country with 'no consecutive thread', the 'friendliest country – but without a core'. Every time he describes a tree we catch a poem happening: the cabbage-palms in the sea wind are 'there like old mops', the great 'gum-trees ran up their white limbs into the air like quicksilver, plumed at the tips with dark tufts'. Reading this, we realize that the silver branches of the fig trees are also quicksilvery, mercurial figures for the loose, unpindownable strategies of Lawrence's imagination, an imagination that one moment is drawn to Venetian glass blowing, in another he says Venice is an

> Abhorrent, green, slippery city
> Whose Doges were old, and had ancient eyes.

Perhaps Yeats, who admired *Lady Chatterley*, is picking up 'ancient eyes' in *Lapis Lazuli* – certainly in the first stanza of 'Sailing to Byzantium' Lawrence and Whitman are the poets who are making Yeats anxious. There is more than a trace of Melville's suspicion of old Europe's republican corruption – the Venetian slippers and blinds mentioned in *Moby Dick* – but what is lovely about these lines is that Lawrence allows a complex series of assonances to unfurl. He remarks:

> In the dense foliage of the inner garden
> Pomegranates like bright green stone,
> And barbed, barbed with a crown.
> Oh, crown of spiked green metal
> Actually growing!

Lawrence's ear insistently repeats the *n* in Venice. Then the *s* sound in Venice retrospectively picks up the susurrus in that naffly archaic word 'Whereas' and rubs it into 'slippery city', then spaces it out in 'Doges', 'ancient' and 'eyes'. The *o* in 'Doges' is then repeated in 'old', 'foliage', 'stone' and 'growing'. The *stone / growing* assonance is particularly effective, because it enacts stone becoming organic, but the effect is also a kind of visual pun: the *ow* is picked up in 'crown' and 'growing', which then summons the *on* in 'stone'. But we also notice that 'Doges', 'foliage' and 'pomegranates' are also interconnected by *o*'s and *g*'s – *g*'s that culminate in 'growing'. Much later in the poem the word 'integument' will summon those words. But Lawrence is also stroking the *k* sound, which is a harder version of *g* – *guh*, that is. It's there in 'crown' and 'spiked' and in 'Now in Tuscany', in the later words 'kingly' and 'skin', and in the last lines:

> For my part, I prefer my heart to be broken.
> It is so lovely, dawn-kaleidoscopic within the crack.

The last line picks up the fourth line of the poem: 'In Syracuse, rock left bare by the viciousness of Greek women', whose three *k*'s are repeated at the end, insisting on the cracked skin. The 'crack' is iconoclastic, a rejection of all that's gone before.

There is a similar effect in 'Peach':

Would you like to throw a stone at me?
Here, take all that's left of my peach.

Blood-red, deep;
Heaven knows how it came to pass.
Somebody's pound of flesh rendered up.

Wrinkled with secrets
And hard with the intention to keep them.

Why, from silvery peach-bloom,
From that shallow-silvery wine-glass on a short stem
This rolling, dropping, heavy globule?

I am thinking, of course, of the peach before I ate it.

Why so velvety, why so voluptuous heavy?
Why so hanging with such inordinate weight?
Why so indented?

Why the groove?
Why the lovely, bivalve roundnesses?
Why the ripple down the sphere?
Why the suggestion of incision?

Why was not my peach round and finished like a billiard ball?
It would have been if man had made it.
Though I've eaten it now.

But it wasn't round and finished like a billiard ball.
And because I say so, you would like to throw something at me.

Here, you can have my peach stone.

Right at the end, there's a cheeky buttonholing questioning voice that accosts the reader – so the poem is instant and natural. The language is meant to be so spontaneously natural that it seems to fit the peach exactly to give us a realistic description of a peach – this type of realism, as we can see from *Robinson Crusoe*, is a distinctive and important part of the Puritan aesthetic. Realism seems to give us the thing itself, exactly and authentically, without linguistic frills, without similes, metaphors and images – without the decorative, as Lawrence says in his essay on Whitman. But as we know from painting, realism is just a particular style of imagining – like Cubism or Impressionism.

Lawrence's realism in this poem isn't something fixed and photographic – that would be anathema to him – he wants to give his image animate sensuous qualities, and he does this partly in the movement from 'silvery peach-bloom' to 'shallow-silvery wine-glass' to the more arresting movement of 'This rolling motion, dropping, heavy globule'. Then follows the velvety voluptuousness which is a Miltonic movement in the poem. This fruit belongs to Eden before the Fall, to a pure primal utopian reality which is Milton's vision of England as a perfect republic – perfect because it has expelled royalty. This is the smiling, delicious, cool-breathed earth Whitman celebrates.

But we have to notice that this is a poem that is insouciantly and cheekily about consumption. Comparing the peach to a raindrop forming on a branch, Lawrence says: 'I am thinking, of course, of the peach before I ate it.' Part of Lawrence's problem is that he must avoid making the peach appear to be a slightly exotic consumer object. He wants his poems to consume themselves in the moment, in a distinctively Puritan manner to happen now and be complete and perfect in the present, but he doesn't want the peach to be a fixed object with a price tag on it. He wants his poem to avoid resembling these lines by one of the poets – Keats – whose gem-like lyrics he aimed to replace with a new type of poetry:

he from forth the closet brought a heap
Of candied apple, quince, and plum, and gourd,
With jellies smoother than the creamy curd,
And lucent syrops, tinct with cinnamon;
Manna and dates, in argosy transferr'd
From Fez; and spiced dainties, every one,
From silken Samarcand to cedared Lebanon.

This type of language Lawrence deeply dislikes – its cloying prurience, the voyeurism of the scene, the polished, Latinate, over-literary writing – he wants to replace this consumerist language with a natural vernacular flow. So he chucks a series of questions at us, his readers. This keeps us on our toes and at the same time lets those questions create a sense of instant and complete familiarity with the peach so that it appears to be a warm, living, organic thing – even though the peach doesn't actually exist – he's eaten it before the poem even started. Though paradoxically the peach is words, a voice speaking, it attains such presence in the poem that we seem to be contemplating perfect peachness – the absolute nature of the peach. But Lawrence and the peach are one step ahead of us, for we remember that Lawrence has rejected the gem-like poem, the poem of finality and 'perfected bygone moments'. This type of fixed and polished poem is really what he is glancing at when he asks:

> Why was not my peach round and finished like a billiard ball?
> It would have been if man had made it.
> Though I've eaten it now.

Lawrence's hatred of industrial civilization can be felt here, but he is also using the mechanical billiard ball as a symbol for the fixed, gem-like poem. This is just the type of poem that you want, he is saying – you readers who want to criticize me – throw things at me.

This is one, very succinct expression of the polemical, feisty cast of Lawrence's mind – he likes to argue with his readers, to unsettle them – and this unsettled and unsettling quality is also a significant trait in the Puritan imagination. We can see this in Emily Dickinson's poetry, in fluid, unfixed, restless homeless quality of her imagination.

Then in the very last line Lawrence picks up his opening line and leaves us with the peach stone – the poem is written, the peach is eaten, all that remains is the parabola of a peach stone as it were in flight between writer and reader. What an intense and direct type of communication this is! Just like the communication – the epistle written in the heart – that St Paul calls for, instead of the dead letter. We can see, then, that this type of imagination places great stress and value upon communication, personal communication.

It might be stretching it to accuse the poem of covert anti-Semitism, but we must note that deep down for Lawrence the peach stone is a symbol of Judaic law – 'Somebody's pound of flesh rendered up' – the allusion is to Shylock in *The Merchant of Venice* and the Ten Commandments carved on the tablet of stone. His eating of the peach expresses a new consciousness – that of the New Testament, the spirit that gives life – as against the dead letter of the law. The peach stone is the Mosaic law and it is also the letters on the printed page – the voice, perhaps more of a lemony than a peachy voice, is meant to transcend those fixities. It catches us off guard and we're left with both hands held out in the inferior posture of catching something that is even now travelling towards us. The peach and the poem have been eaten, only the words remain.

The Mosaic reference is present again in one of Lawrence's marvellous sequence of tortoise poems, 'Tortoise-Shell':

> It needed Pythagoras to see life playing with counters on the
> living back
> Of the baby tortoise;
> Life establishing the first eternal mathematical tablet,
> Not in stone, like the Judean Lord, or bronze, but in life-clouded,
> life-rosy tortoise shell.

For Lawrence the hardness of the tortoise shell is not of a fixed and dead hardness like stone – it is 'life-clouded, life-rosy' and therefore suffused with the living spirit. We see that redemptive living voice at work in the lines that immediately follow:

> The first little mathematical gentleman
> Stepping, wee mite, in his loose trousers
> Under all the eternal dome of mathematical law.

The phrase 'wee mite' like 'sprottling' or 'Wee, sleekit, cow'rin, tim'rous beastie' is the dialect voice at work – the life-rosy, tender, intimate and loving voice which suffuses the mathematical rigidity of the text.

Lawrence sprinkles his texts with dialect words and expressions: 'They are beyond me, are fishes' ('Fish'); 'Nay, tiny shell-bird'

('Baby Tortoise'); 'his feet are still nesh' ('The Risen Lord'). Always he catches perfectly the cadences of the intimate, speaking voice:

> Does the sun need steam of blood do you think
> In America, still,
> Old eagle?
>
> ('Eagle in New Mexico')

With this goes his adjectival insistence, as he pushes adjectives to the limit: 'a glittering, rosy, moist, honied, heavy-petalled four-petalled flower' ('Figs'). First *t* then *s*, then *st*, then *h h* with *ee ee*, then back to *t* with *ih* summoned from 'glittering', then *f* summoning *v* from 'heavy', till finally 'flower' seems inevitable, its *l* strong and permanent.

From far back, that 'sharp clean trot' of the pony in 'End of Another Home Holiday', where it signifies 'a strange new knocking of life', is being summoned in 'Autumn at Taos':

> Trot-trot to the mottled foot-hills, cedar-mottled and piñon;
> Did you ever see an otter?
> Silvery-sided, fish-fanged, fierce-faced, whiskered, mottled.

Lawrence runs with *ot ot* to the point of over-saturation, then switches to hyphenated, softer adjectives before, at the very last moment, reverting to 'mottled', in a witty, almost for badness manner that decisively turns the sound up.

This isn't simply a handy metaphor for Lawrence's technique – his Puritan upbringing insists that he communicates as clearly and emphatically as he can, even in 'Bare Almond-Trees' turning the trees into a combination of a radio and a radio transmitter:

> Almond tree, beneath the terrace-rail,
> Black, rusted, iron trunk,
> You have welded your thin stems finer,
> Like steel, like sensitive steel in the air,
> Grey, lavender, sensitive steel, curving thinly and brittly up in a parabola.

It's as if the almond tree and the terrace rail fuse, and then become a delicate steel aerial, which is what a few pages earlier, in 'Grapes', he calls an 'active, / Audile, tactile sensitiveness as of a tendril which orientates and reaches out'. Here, as in 'Bare Almond-Trees', he flexes the *l* sounds before throwing a series of questions at the braced parabola he has just designed:

> What are you doing in the December rain?
> Have you a strange electric sensitiveness in your steel tips?
> Do you feel the air for electric influences
> Like some strange magnetic apparatus?

And when he asks, 'Do you telephone the roar of the waters over the earth?' we almost get the image of a radiotelephone.

Modern communications are images for the poetry of the present, and they are part of his willed desire to break with traditional poetry and create a wholly new and contemporary type of verse. This is the subject of his most famous poem, 'Snake', where the snake is seen in slow, sluggish motion as he

> Proceeded to draw his slow length curving round
> And climb again the broken bank of my wall-face.

This is picked up in the next poem 'Baby Tortoise': 'And set forward, slow-dragging, on your four-pinned toes', and a few pages later in 'Lui et Elle' the tortoise 'pulls herself free, and rows her dull mound along'.

Lawrence proudly repeats versions of the same moment because he is wittily reprising a well-known couplet in Alexander Pope's 'An Essay on Criticism': 'A needless alexandrine ends the song / That like a wounded snake drags its slow length along'. For a moment the snake and the tortoise are like this example of dreary, dragging bygone verse, except they, especially the snake, are examples of free verse, the new poetic consciousness he associates with Whitman. The snake is the molten lava, a psychic energy which should not be repressed. It is also reminiscent of the miners he saw going down into the pit, of Duncan entering Macbeth's castle, of Aeneas going down into the underworld. Here, Lawrence dramatizes his split,

Cartesian consciousness, as he invokes Coleridge's and Baudelaire's albatross to figure the snake as both poetry and the poet.

In a sense, once Lawrence has established that his subject is the momentaneous instant of poetry, all he does is to seek occasions to affirm it. He does this with a grotesque, bad taste brilliance in 'Tortoise Shout', which evokes the copulation of tortoises:

Long neck, and long vulnerable limbs extruded, spread-eagle over
  her house-roof,
And the deep, secret, all-penetrating tail curved beneath her walls,
Reaching and gripping tense, more reaching anguish in uttermost
  tension
Till suddenly, in the spasm of coition, tupping like a jerking leap,
  and oh!
Opening its clenched face from his outstretched neck
And giving that fragile yell, that scream,
Super-audible,
From his pink, cleft, old-man's mouth,
Giving up the ghost,
Or screaming in Pentecost, receiving the ghost.

The tortoise's 'fragile yell' becomes an image for talking in tongues, giving up the ghost – dying in both senses – and for the poem itself. And lest we've missed this point, Lawrence underlines it a few lines later: 'till the last plasm of my body was melted back / To the primeval rudiments of life, and the secret'. Here, he is recalling his assertion in 'Poetry of the Present' that free verse is 'instantaneous like plasm'. This is of course a version of Whitman's semen theme, as we see two sentences later: 'It is the instant; the quick; the very jetting source of all will-be and has-been.' Whitman's 'jetting masculine republics' is invoked here. Lawrence however differs from Whitman in not being an insistently phallic poet. This is apparent in his repeated word 'fissure' in 'Pomegranate', where

The end cracks open with the beginning:
Rosy, tender, glittering within the fissure.

In 'Figs' he develops the theme:

> The Italians vulgarly say, it stands from the female part; the fig-fruit:
> The fissure, the yoni,
> The wonderful moist conductivity towards the centre.

The 'earth-lipped fissure' in 'Snake' is another version of the theme, which in turn is a version of the theme of beginning, the dawn of creation, the poem of the present coming into being. Repeating 'fissure' in 'Pomegranate' we hear *fizz-yure*, loudly, with a firm pause, and register what he calls 'dawn-kaleidoscopic within the crack', as the *you* sound puts each of us, as readers, inside the poem. Lawrence's buttonholing questions, his abrupt exclamations, dramatic shifts of vocal tones all involve the reader and make us sensuously complicit in the subject.

It's as if these poems came down the sheen of wet ink on paper – hence the bat in 'Man and Bat' is 'a clot' with 'bead-berry eyes, black', and the mosquito's 'long thin shanks' – three stresses, a molossus – becomes in the last line 'a dim, dark, smudge' of Lawrence's blood which is much larger than the infinitesimal 'smear of you'. This is the culmination of the process theme, the 'sudden curved scissors' of the tortoise mouth, the 'queer dress shawl' of steel slag on the turkey's wattles, which in turn expresses the brindled, mottled, rusty, shaggy, tactile, gawky, splintery, braying subject or subjects.

Lawrence is in dialogue with Whitman, and I think he and Yeats are in conversation too, but his essential argument is with the United States, where in a sense he is anticipating Jackson Pollock's 'I don't paint nature, I am nature'. This argument is there in 'Turkey-Cock' where Lawrence characteristically opens up the bad taste theme which is one of his strategies for developing tone and intimacy:

> Your wattles drip down like a shawl to your breast
> And the point of your mantilla drops across your nose, unpleasantly.

This is part of the unfinished, the process theme:

Or perhaps it is something unfinished
A bit of slag still adhering after your firing in the furnace of
creation.

Beyond this autotelic image, is Melville's theme of the power and direction of the puritan republic:

The over-drip of a great passion hanging in the balance.
Only yours would be a raw, unsmelted passion, that will not
quite fuse from the dross.

The pitch of the lines isolates 'melt' in 'unsmelted' to make it run free as the *d's* in 'drip', 'unsmelted' and 'dross' shape and brace the movement of the verse like the sides of a mould, while the *oo* in 'fuse' passes into the next line: 'You contract yourself.' Then, noticing how the turkey-cock's 'brittle, super-sensual arrogance' tosses its 'crape of red' – cape of red – across its brow, he moves into the language of the American Enlightenment:

It is a declaration of such tension in will
As time has not dared to avouch, nor eternity been able to
unbend
Do what it may.
A raw American will, that has never been tempered by life;
You brittle, will-tense bird with a foolish eye.

Partly Lawrence is thinking of Benjamin Franklin, who suggested the turkey should be the national bird (he lacerates Franklin in *Studies in Classic American Literature*), but he is also trying to distance himself from his own tensile, tactile language by using a polite, academic or philosophical register, which sits slightly uncomfortably with the bird's raw American will. 'Are you the bird of the next dawn?' he asks, knowing that it is, knowing 'The East a dead letter, and Europe moribund'. Then he sees the Americans as the next Aztecs in all 'the sinister splendour of their red blood-sacrifices', before uttering this prophecy:

Or must you go through the fire once more, till you're smelted
pure,

Slag-wattled turkey-cock.
Dross-jabot?

The smelting image, which he uses in 'Poetry of the Present', is repeated here, but Lawrence's use of the French word 'jabot', which means a frill of lace, worn in front of a woman's dress or on a man's shirt-front, asserts old Europe at the very last moment and so visits the turkey-cock's dominance in a dismissive phrase that is also ugly, jokey, slagging or jabbering.

Here, Lawrence the anti-colonial prophet takes his stand. His verse is rough-and-tumble, eloquent, passionate, delicate – it invites us to rub our tongues all over it, even as it gives what Hazlitt terms 'hard blows'.

Pick, Pack, Pock, Puck: Joyce's Dislike of Aquacity

Bloom, waterlover, drawer of water, watercarrier, admires water for, among many other qualities, its 'universality: its democratic equality and constancy to its nature in seeking its own level'. Bloom returns to the stillflowing tap, washes his soiled hands with the tablet of Barrington's lemon-flavoured soap which has accompanied him on his odyssey. He asks, the catechistic narrator implies, if Stephen wants to wash his hands:

What reason did Stephen give for declining Bloom's offer?
That he was hydrophobe, hating partial contact by immersion or total by submersion in cold water (his last bath having taken place in the month of October of the preceding year), disliking the aqueous substances of glass and crystal, distrusting aquacities of thought and language.

The narrator, evidently pleased by his use of that pompous, uncomfortable word 'aquacities', returns to it in the next reply where he, in his overwhelmingly male voice, cites 'The incompatibility of aquacity with the erratic originality of genius'.

The English language, at this late moment in the narrative, is in a state of heavy-metal exhaustion, but inside the intense and devoted facticity of his prose here, Joyce wants us to consider the water theme in the novel, and the theme which counterpoints it, which the *k* sound in 'aquacity' represents. In Joyce's imagination *k* means fact, while water represents the romantic idealism he scorned. 'What makes people's lives unhappy,' he told Arthur Power, 'is some disappointed romanticism, some unrealised or misconceived ideal.' This rejection of romanticism is expressed by Stephen in *Portrait*, where he formulates his classical aesthetic in a series of epiphanies. For Joyce, the classical artist's 'constant' state of mind contrasts with the inconstancy of water, and the formlessness of the romantic imagination. As Stephen explains in *Portrait*, the aesthetic emotion is static: the mind is 'arrested and raised above desire and loathing'.

There is a crucially important passage in *Stephen Hero*, which Joyce chose not to include in *Portrait*, where Stephen writes an essay on the classical style, arguing that

> Classicism is not the manner of any fixed age or of any fixed country: it is a constant state of the artistic mind. It is a temper of security and satisfaction and patience. The romantic temper, so often and so grievously misinterpreted and not more by others than by its own, is an insecure, unsatisfied, impatient temper which sees no fit abode here for its ideals and chooses therefore to behold them under insensible figures. As a result of this choice it comes to disregard certain limitations. Its figures are blown to wild adventures, lacking the gravity of solid bodies, and the mind that has conceived them ends by disowning them. The classical temper on the other hand, ever mindful of limitations, chooses rather to bend upon these present things and so to work upon them and fashion them that the quick intelligence may go beyond them to their meaning which is still unuttered. In this method the sane and joyful spirit issues forth and achieves imperishable perfection, nature assisting with her goodwill and thanks.

The classical temper is both stringently intelligent and sensuous, while the romantic temper is formless, anxious and lacking 'the gravity of solid bodies'. Later, in *Stephen Hero* Joyce describes how Stephen, in 'a stupor of powerlessness' reviews 'the plague of Catholicism'. A paragraph later, Stephen

> gazed wearily out of the window, across the mist-laden gardens. The air was webbed with water vapours and all the flower-beds and walks confronted the grey of the sky with a truculent sodden brown. Mackintoshes and overcoats came along the walks or down the steps of the monument under their umbrellas or surmounted by a muffled human head. The footpaths inside the chains where Stephen had so often walked with his friends at night glistened like a grey mirror.

Like a moment out of Sartre's *La Nausée*, this watery scene expresses Stephen's disgust and alienation – it isn't simply descriptive because the water imagery carries a whole attitude of mind which is set out in the distinction between the classical and romantic tempers. Those chained footpaths belong in Minotaur's labyrinth, a labyrinth which is symbolized by the iron railing at the end of 'Eveline', and by the priest's 'black cavernous nostrils' in 'The Sisters'.

As a schoolboy, Stephen has a crucial epiphany in which he recognizes this distinction:

> The fellows were practising long shies and bowling lobs and slow twisters. In the soft grey silence he could hear the bump of the balls: and from here and from there through the quiet air the sound of the cricket bats: pick, pack, pock, puck: like drops of water in a fountain falling softly in the brimming bowl.

In this crucial passage, we recognize the gravity of solid bodies as cricket balls clock cricket bats. Joyce, typically, makes the image of water dripping carry a series of hard sounds, each with a *k* at the end: *pick, pack, pock, puck*. He deploys this sequence of sounds to challenge the sentimental, dead cadences that precede it: 'and from here and from there through the quiet air'. The anapaestic rhythm and the preening *there / air* rhyme, as well as the facile alliteration 'fountain falling' at the close of the sentence, and the *soft / softly* repetition, are briefly broken up by the slow, measured, precise and acoustically ineluctable consonantal density of the cricket balls. They and the bats that hit them make an expression of the classical temper, which knows that art, like any game, is based on rules. Hopkins has a lovely phrase for this effect – 'each tucked string tells' – an effect in the Joyce passage that is like someone thrumming the taut strings of a violin or cello. In the last sentence of 'The Dead', Joyce describes flakes of frozen water falling in a deliberately over-cadenced prose:

> His soul swooned slowly as he heard the snow falling faintly through the universe and faintly falling, like the descent of their last end, upon all the living and the dead.

Gabriel is a romantic who as he falls asleep imagines 'the solid world itself . . . dissolving'. He is a self-regarding provincial intellectual, whose imagination in the closing paragraphs is a mixture of Shelleyan, Yeatsian and Catholic imagery: his swooning soul is Shelleyan, the 'vast hosts of the dead' and the west of Ireland location are Yeatsian, even Syngian, while the crosses, spears and 'barren thorns' are Catholic. This is the romantic temper self-consciously watching itself fade out.

The sound of the water drops embodies Joyce's realist aesthetic. As he told Arthur Power, 'in realism, you are down to facts on which the world is based: that sudden reality which smashes romanticism into a pulp.' The sound of cricket balls becoming water drops, and the way that sound wrecks the vocabulary and the rhythm of the prose which contains it, is an example of romanticism being smashed to a pulp.

In *Ulysses* it is in the deployment of sound, in the acoustic imagery and texture of the epic, that we can observe Joyce's realism, his devotion to hard fact, at work. He told Power, in a laconically punning phrase, that a novelist's work must have 'a sound basis in fact', and he went on to describe how essential to him noise was when he was working. He showed Power Valéry Larbaud's Paris apartment where he had stayed and worked in a room that was soundproof, compared with the rooms in most flats, and he said:

> I don't like being shut up . . . When I am working I like to hear noise going on around me – the noise of life; there it was like writing in a tomb. I suppose I would have got used to it, but I didn't want to because then I might have lost my ability to work wherever I happen to be, in a lodging-house, or in a hotel room, and silence might have become a necessity to me as it was, for example, to Proust.

This communicates both the democratic nature of Joyce's imagination – he calls writing 'work', and like a *Luftmensch* he writes in whatever lodging house or hotel room he happens to be temporarily staying in. He doesn't like being shut up, in the other sense of not being allowed to communicate, and he must have the noise of life going on around him.

At the centre of his imagination is the most important meal of the day, breakfast, where Bloom in the beloved opening sentence of 'Calypso' eats 'with relish the inner organs of beasts and fowls. He liked thick giblet soup, nutty gizzards, a stuffed roast heart, liverslices fried with crustcrumbs, fried hencod's roes.' The pattern of guttural *k*'s texture the otherwise dominant softness of the inner organs. The effect of Joyce's prose is apparently realistic, and this fits Bloom's 'solid pragmatic presence', as Jeri Johnson terms it. This realism is partly a tribute to Defoe, whom Joyce revered, and whose imaginative presence can be felt throughout *Ulysses*.

Much earlier, Joyce alludes to *Robinson Crusoe*, when he describes the Conroys' hotel room at the end of 'The Dead': 'A petticoat string dangled to the floor. One boot stood upright, its limp upper fallen down: the fellow of it lay upon its side.' This picks up one of the seminal moments in the history of Western realism, when Crusoe, newly landed on the island, laments his drowned comrades (Defoe is thinking of Sedgemoor, so doesn't use 'shipmates') and says 'I never saw them afterwards, or any sign of them, except three of their hats, one cap, and two shoes that were not fellows.' Joyce called *Robinson Crusoe* 'the English *Ulysses*', and he has Bloom think of the novel as he stands by Paddy Dignam's open grave. But Joyce is also thinking as Bloom prepares breakfast of another great Dissenting English writer, William Blake, whom he also revered and whom he alludes to frequently.

In March 1912, in Trieste, Joyce gave a lecture on Defoe and a lecture on Blake under the title 'Realism and Idealism in English Literature'. In the lecture on Blake, he says:

> Elementary beings and the spirits of deceased great men would often enter the poet's room at night to speak to him about art and the imagination. Blake would then bounce out of bed and, grabbing his pencil, stay up through the long hours of the London night drawing the features and limbs of the visions while his wife crouched next to his armchair, lovingly holding his hand and staying quiet so as not to disturb the ecstasy of the seer. When the visions disappeared towards dawn, the wife would get back under the covers while Blake, radiant with joy and benevolence, would hurriedly set about lighting the fire and making breakfast for them both. Ought we to be amazed that the symbolic beings Los, Urizen, Vala, Tiriel, and Enitharmon and the shades of Homer and Milton should come from their ideal world into a poor room in London, or that the incense that greeted their coming was the smell of Indian tea and eggs fried in lard?

Those symbolic beings are present in Bloom's kitchen, as he makes tea and fries kidneys, because Bloom is a version of Blake in that 'poor room in London'. His wife doesn't hold his hand like Catherine Blake, but Joyce's admiration for Blake finds a radical and democratic expression in Bloom in the kitchen.

It's here that Joyce reintroduces a pattern of acoustic images which will come to dominate the novel, and which is made up of the sometimes separate, sometimes linked sounds of creaking and jingling. This happens early in 'Calypso' where Bloom goes up the staircase on 'quietly creaky boots'. Then, when he brings Molly a cup of tea and says, 'You don't want anything for breakfast?' she grunts and turns over in the bed so that 'the loose brass quoits of the bedstead jingled'. This introduces the jingling theme – or it seems to. A few pages later, when Bloom sets the tray on the chair by the bedhead: 'She set the brasses jingling as she raised herself briskly.' This theme, which is more major than its cousin, the creaking theme, will journey through the narrative like the tablet of lemon-flavoured soap, until in their last appearances they will have a similar partially used quality. The creaking theme begins in *Portrait* in the famous scene where Stephen encounters the Dean of Studies:

> A smell of molten tallow came up from the dean's candle-butts and fused itself in Stephen's consciousness with the jingle of the words, bucket and lamp and lamp and bucket. The priest's voice too had a hard jingling tone. Stephen's mind halted by instinct, checked by the strange tone and the imagery and by the priest's face which seemed like an unlit lamp or a reflector hung in a false focus. What lay behind it or within it? A dull torpor of the soul or the dullness of the thundercloud, charged with intellection and capable of the gloom of God?

The jingling sound must have been fixed forever in Joyce's mind as signifying power, dominance, sterility. The priest's English accent, his 'pale loveless eyes', are present in the sound.

In *Ulysses*, the jingling sound is a reprise of Mr Deasy's conversation with Stephen twenty pages earlier, where Deasy proudly informs Stephen that he is descended from Sir John Blackwood who put on his topboots to ride from the Ards of Down to vote for the Union. In fact, Blackwood died in the act of putting his topboots on to go to Dublin to vote against the Union, but it suited Joyce's imaginative strategy to give the Unionist Deasy a wholly Unionist pedigree. What stuck in his mind were those topboots, which become in Stephen's mind 'Two topboots jog dangling on to Dublin'. In effect, this is an acoustic poem, where a jangling noise is added to, or played over, the visual image. The jangling noise is created by superimposing the *j* of 'jog' on the *d* of 'dangling'. The jangling sound is played over the motion of the boots, like added soundtrack. In *Paradise Lost*, Milton's ear is also drawn to 'jangling' sounds, and to what he terms 'barbarous dissonance'. Epics need noise to convince us of their gigantic form and scope, and they need to insist that we are in the presence of serious historical action. Such action, for Joyce, can be found in any noise. Both he and Milton use grating, often rebarbative sound to purge their styles of any type of magniloquence or preciousness – all that Joyce meant by aquacity, and Milton by a cloistered, and therefore silent, virtue. Although Milton identifies barbarous dissonance with Satan, he needs erratic noise – needs error – because the unexpectedness of its sudden interventions are an expression of 'the erratic originality of genius'. By seeming to break form, they reintegrate it and give it greater force and authority. When a gavel bangs, we know that we are compelled to listen, but in epic the authority of sudden noise appears not to derive from the author, but from life itself, which is that 'sound basis in fact' that Joyce insists on.

In *Ulysses*, it is the noise of Irish history, which is implicit in the phrase 'Jingle jingle jaunted jingling' in the musical overture to 'Sirens' which reprises phrases from later in the episode. Thus we get:

Jingle jaunty jingle

jingle jaunty blazes boy

Jingling on supple rubbers it jaunted

Jingle jaunted by the curb and stopped

Jingle a tinkle jaunted

By Bachelor's walk jogjaunty jingled Blazes Boylan

Jiggedy jingle jaunty jaunty

jingle jogged

Jingle jaunty

Jingle by monuments

Jingle into Dorset street

This is the jingle that joggled and jingled

Joy jig jogged stopped

After 'Jingle a tinkle jaunted', Joyce writes:

Bloom heard a jing, a little sound. He's off. Light sob of breath Bloom sighed on the silent bluehued flowers. Jingling. He's gone. Jingle. Hear.

Like salt in a wound, the sound of his bed reverberates in Bloom's mind. The repeated sound is counterpointed by the *knock / cock* sound and by the imperious and imperial 'Imperthnthn thnthnthn' of the vice-regal coach, so that the lord lieutenant in his coach and Boylan in his jingling jaunting car are identified, as we hear 'the viceregal hoofs go by, ringing steel'. Time and again, Joyce varies and repeats the jingling theme, the idea being that even before Molly and Boylan have sex, the bed's jingling sounds are all over Dublin. Molly is embarrassed by the sound and in the early hours of the morning remembers 'this damned old bed too jingling like the dickens I suppose they could hear us away over the other side of the park till I suggested to put the quilt on the floor with the pillow under my bottom'.

The jingling noise of the bed is inside Bloom's head throughout much of the narrative (there are two harness jingles at the end of 'Circe', where, so far as I can tell, Joyce lays the theme to rest before it is briefly recapitulated as Molly lies in bed, half asleep on the current of her consciousness). This theme, as I've suggested, is linked to the creaking theme, which is first introduced by Bloom's quietly creaky boots. This acoustic theme draws on an early passage at the beginning of 'Proteus', where Joyce deliberately avoids evoking the sea, which Stephen has already dismissed as 'snotgreen'. Instead, he has Stephen walk over 'seaspawn and seawrack'. Stephen closes his eyes in order to hear his boots 'crush crackling wrack and shells'. The reiterated *k* sounds are versions of *pick, pack, pock, puck*, and they are pitched against aquacity, or what Stephen terms his 'weak watery blood'. That aqueous formlessness is present in the deliberately kitschy 1890s paragraph which follows Mulligan's booming recitation of these lines from Yeats's song 'Who Goes with Fergus', from his play *The Countess Cathleen*:

And no more turn aside and brood
Upon love's bitter mystery
For Fergus rules the brazen cars.

Joyce does not quote the next three lines, which end the poem:

And rules the shadow of the wood,
And the white breast of the dim sea
And all dishevelled wandering stars.

Instead, he makes Stephen's mind compose a prose variation on them:

Woodshadows floated silently by through the morning peace from the stairhead seaward where he gazed. Inshore and farther out the mirror of water whitened, spurned by lightshod hurrying feet. White breast of the dim sea. The twining stresses, two by two. A hand plucking the harpstrings merging their twining chords. Wavewhite wedded words shimmering on the dim tide.

Twenty-eight pages later the 'Crush, crack, crick, crick' of seawrack and seashells under Stephen's boots act as a repudiation of this watery rhetoric.

But that rhetoric will not leave Stephen alone:

Under the upswelling tide he saw the writhing weeds lift languidly and sway reluctant arms, hising up their petticoats, in whispering water swaying and upturning coy silver fronds.

This weedy theme is picked up again at the end of 'Lotus Eaters', where Bloom foresees his body lying naked in the bath and imagines the 'dark tangled curls of his bush floating, floating hair of the stream around the limp father of thousands, a languid floating flower'.

This in turn picks up a phrase of Bloom's from the opening of 'Lotus Eaters': 'Sensitive plants. Waterlilies', which looks forward to the 'wideleaved flowers' of porter froth on a 'lazy pooling swirl of liquor', which Bloom – alias Henry Flower – imagines 'winding through mudflats all over the level land'. These moments are reprised, when Bloom looks out of the coach in Paddy Dignam's funeral cortege and sees a man standing 'on his dropping barge between clamps of turf', as water 'rushed roaring through the sluices'. This is an unstable moment, one that acts as a prolepsis for the lowering of Dignam's coffin into the grave, which Bloom and the other mourners will very soon witness. And it is the instability of water that is to blame for this.

Bloom, lover of water, reacts romantically to the sight of the bargeman as he stands on the disappearing barge:

> On the slow weedy waterway he had floated on his raft coastward over Ireland drawn by a haulage rope past beds of reeds.

This, like the languid floating flower, is an image of the baby Moses from the Book of Exodus. Its weedy wateriness is toughened or rejected by the chunky factual phrases which follow: 'over slime, mudchoked bottles, carrion dogs'. It's as though Joyce must take back any freefloating, unanchored lyrical moment and smash it to pulp. Inventing a new verb, he says that the 'felly harshed against the curbstone' as the carriage came to a halt, a rebarbative noise that drowns out any facile sentiment. A similar effect occurs when Bloom waits for the *kran, kran, kran* of an approaching tram to reach a crescendo, so that its *Krandlkrankran* will conceal the sound of his imminent fart, an acoustic *pick, pock* moment, which is also meant to drown out the sentimental engraving of Robert Emmet above the text of his last words from the dock.

In one passage in 'Sirens', Joyce shows that Bloom has a technical interest in acoustics:

> Jog jig jogged stopped. Dandy tan shoe of dandy Boylan socks skyblue clocks came light to earth.
>
> O, look we are so! Chamber music. Could make a kind of pun on that. It is a kind of music I often thought when she. Acoustics that is. Tinkling. Empty vessels make most noise. Because the acoustics, the resonance changes according as the weight of water is equal to the law of falling water. Like those rhapsodies of Liszt's, Hungarian, gipsyeyed. Pearls. Drops. Rain. Diddle idle addle addle oodle oodle. Hiss. Now. Maybe now. Before.

Bloom, lover of water, considers its acoustics here, as Joyce makes a mocking reference to his first book of poems, *Chamber Music*. If we trace this noise theme back to *Portrait*, we can see that it is deep in Joyce's early struggle towards complete aesthetic freedom and independence. As an undergraduate, the young Stephen – Stephen is forever young – watches birds flying round the 'jutting shoulder' of a house in Molesworth Street. They fly high and low in straight and curving lines, 'circling about a temple of air'. Then Joyce says:

> He listened to their cries: like the squeak of mice behind the wainscot: a shrill twofold note. But the notes were long and shrill and whirring, unlike the cry of vermin, falling a third or a fourth and trilled as the flying beaks clove the air. Their cry was shrill and clear and fine and falling like threads of silken light unwound from whirring spools.

This is the thread that will lead him out of the Minotaur's labyrinth, which is here, ever so faintly, also Macbeth's castle, where the 'temple-haunting martlet' flies before Duncan's murder. He imagines 'the hawklike man whose name he bore soaring out of his captivity on osierwoven wings', and immediately he imagines Thoth, the god of writers, 'writing with a reed upon a tablet'. Stephen is about to leave for ever 'the house of prayer and prudence into which he had been born and the order of life out of which he had come'. It's then that Joyce returns to the flying birds: 'They came back with shrill cries over the jutting shoulder of the house, flying darkly against the fading air.' They must be swallows, he thinks, 'ever going and coming, building ever an unlasting home under the eaves of men's houses and ever leaving the homes they had built to wander'.

The prose here is too watery, too selfconscious, and to heighten this Joyce has Stephen remember four lines from *Countess Cathleen*:

> *Bend down your faces, Oona and Aleel,*
> *I gaze upon them as the swallow gazes*
> *Upon the nest under the eave before*
> *He wander the loud waters.*

Yeats's 'She' becomes 'He', as Stephen allows a fantasy to overwhelm his imagination. Then:

> A soft liquid joy like the noise of many waters flowed over his memory and he felt in his heart the soft peace of silent spaces of fading tenuous sky above the waters, of oceanic silence, of swallows flying through the seadusk over the flowing waters.

This is a false epiphany – a point Joyce underlines by immediately repeating the opening lines of the paragraph:

> A soft liquid joy flowed through the words where the soft long vowels hurtled noiselessly and fell away, lapping and flowing back and ever shaking the white bells of their waves in mute chime and mute peal and soft low swooning cry.

A key adjective here is 'soft' – we remember it from the *pick*, *pack pock*, *puck* passage earlier – and to Joyce its rebarbative texture is heightened by the noiselessness and muteness of the fantasy, which gives way to Stephen's memory of the audience at the play, their 'catcalls and hisses and mocking cries' that ran in 'rude gusts' round the hall. These noisy cries and the sweating 'burly policeman' are moments of reality which crush the fantasy. Joyce's use of *The Countess Cathleen* here and in *Ulysses* suggests, I think, that his quarrel with aquacity is partly a quarrel with Yeats's early style – his ear refuses to be charmed by 'lake water lapping with low sounds by the shore'. By not taking a bath for nearly a year, Stephen is asserting his independence against Yeats's 'aquacities of thought and language'.

In *Ulysses*, Joyce designs variations on what he terms a 'black crack of noise in the street', and he sets up a cognate or related leitmotif in the persistent image of creaking shoes. In the first example I gave, the sound of Bloom's shoes creaking on the stairs is innocent and domestic. At another moment, the sound has the poignancy of a banal and irrelevant detail as he remembers his father and the hotel in Ennis where he committed suicide, then sees rain dotting the pavement and then adds, 'My boots were creaking I remember now.' It is this sound that helps to quicken the scene into actuality. This extra and particular, as well as otiose memory of the creaking sound his shoes made underwrites Bloom's recall of his father telling him to be good to his dog, Athos.

Creaking shoes reappear at the beginning of 'Scylla and Charybdis', where the librarian moves forward 'on neatsleather creaking', and then corantos off 'Twicreakingly'. The librarian is also 'softcreakfooted'. A few pages later the sound is mentioned again 'rectly creaking rectly rectly he was rectly gone'. Later in 'Sirens' Lenehan follows Boylan's 'hasty creaking shoes'. Then in a pedantic narrative moment: 'Blazes Boylan's smart tan shoes creaked on the barfloor, said before.' When he first describes the shoes in 'Wandering Rocks', Joyce simply says that Boylan walked up and down the greengrocer's shop 'in new tan shoes'. Then the shoes creak on the bar floor, and a few pages later Bloom thinks 'There's music everywhere. Ruttledge's door: ee creaking. No, that's noise.' This creaking sound, like the more dominant jingling sound, is meant to represent Boylan. In 'Murder Considered As One of the Fine Arts', De Quincey is fascinated by the fact that the murderer Williams wears creaking shoes, and although Joyce parodies De Quincey's prose in 'The Oxen of the Sun' the coincidence is too tenuous to suggest an allusion. The creaking sound, like the *tap tap tap* of the blind stripling's cane, is a way of representing pure fact, and is one example of the way in which Joyce's ear is obsessively drawn to words that either contain a *k* or a *kuh* sound. In the poignant passage where Paddy Dignam's young son remembers his father's death, the screws are screwed into the coffin with a 'scrunch', and in 'Nausica' there is a run of words that appear to advertise this guttural consciously. Gerty MacDowell is dreaming and thinking:

every morning they would both have brekky . . .

there wasn't a brack on them . . .

the little kinnatt.

Bloom is watching and thinking:

Up like a rocket, down like a stick.

And the episode concludes with the cuckoo clock in the priest's house going

Cuckoo.

Cuckoo.

Cuckoo.

Especially in the words 'brekky' and 'kinnat', Joyce is recalling his hopeless infatuation with Gertrude Kaempffer, whom he met in Locarno in 1917. It's almost as though he is running his tongue over the *k* that begins her surname.

There are a number of other moments where Joyce delights in a run of guttural *k*'s that texture his sentences with an irrefutable reality:

Stuck on the pane two flies buzzed, stuck.

At Duke lane a ravenous terrier choked up a sick knuckly cud on the cobblestones and lapped it with new zest.

A monkey puzzle rocket burst, spluttering in darting crackles.

Joyce almost overemphasizes the sound in order to signal his delight in its solidity and to rub our noses in its facticity. It's there in Bloom's passing glimpse: 'An illgirt server gathered sticky clattering plates', where the two cognate *guh* sounds intensify the two *k*'s and smear them with grease. And those clattery *k* sounds are there in his belief that Molly would sooner 'have me as I am than some poet chap with bearsgrease plastery hair, lovelock over his dexter optic', where the target is again the young Yeats. Earlier, in 'Sirens', the butt of the barmaids' hysterical mockery has become 'greaseabloom', the wanderer or the gleam on the slippery sea, a moment that is implicit in the image of the 'sticky clattering plates', which is like a shot that is held to give it extra significance. This means, I think, that Joyce is introducing a grease theme similar to the sacral and rebarbative grease theme which Dickens explores in *Great Expectations*, where many objects, like the condemned coiner's hat, are greasy with use. What I'm suggesting here is that some novels need to be read in the way we have to look at pictures and films – i.e. in terms of visual and acoustic leitmotifs, which are organizing principles, ends in themselves, not necessarily thematic vehicles.

In 'Eumaeus' Joyce pays an ironic tribute to Dickens in his portrait of the tedious English sailor, who produces 'a blunt hornhandled ordinary knife', which is an allusion to Magwitch's 'great horn-handled jack-knife'. The Dickensian reference is signalled in the next sentence, when Bloom observes 'Our mutual friend's stories are like himself'. There is also a reference to the circumlocution office and in 'Penelope' Molly refers to 'that lame sailor for England home and beauty'. There is a Dickensian allusion here, as he quotes 'For England, home, and beauty' from the song 'The Death of Nelson', which Micawber quotes at the end of his letter in Chapter 52 of *David Copperfield.* (Molly also encounters the sailor and quotes the phrase – a phrase which Joyce probably saw as shorthand for Dickens's novels and for British imperialism.) The word 'knife', of course, has a silent *k* (it is called a 'dangerouslooking claspknife' earlier), but it belongs as much as *kran, kran, kran* and 'A black crack of noise in the street here, alack, bawled back' to Joyce's insistence on the superiority of hard fact to watery formlessness. This is the music of fact, the noise of time in Mandelstam's phrase, and it means that when the 'jingle of harnesses' are twice mentioned in 'Lestrygonians' within a few sentences of 'creaking beds', we need to hear this as the introduction of a theme which culminates in Bloom's hope in 'Penelope' that the old press doesn't creak and his reference four lines later to 'the lumpy old jingly bed'. As readers our pleasure lies not in the interpretation of this moment, but in the completion of a theme.

Our pleasure, too, lies in our recognition that Joyce loved fact, and delighted to chuck noisy dollops of it at the soppy and the sentimental. Knowing this, and knowing that he used the 1904 edition of Thom's *Dublin Directory*, these bare facts become marvellous, like a passage from an epic:

1 W.–Eccles-street.

From Dorset-street Lower, to Royal Circus, P. St. George.–Inns-quay W.

A PILLAR LETTER-BOX *corner of Nelson street.*

1 Clarke, Mrs. 25*l.*
2 Verdon, Mr. Christopher 27*l.*
3 Bermingham, William, stucco plasterer, 26*l.*
" Dickie, James, esq. solicitor, and Seatown house, Swords
" M'Donnell & Brogan, house and land agents
4 Lynch, Mrs. 27*l.*
5 Molloy, Mr. George F. 27*l.*
6 Smith, Miss Rose, music teacher 28*l.*
7 Vacant, 28*l.*
8 Woods, Mr. R. 30*l.*
9 Hayes, John, esq. 26*l.*
10 Daly, Ulick J. esq. 30*l.*
11 *The Bertrand Protestant Female Orphan School* – Miss Kathleen Andrews, matron & head teacher; Thos.Gick, esq. secretary 35*l.*
12 Booker, Mrs. 25*l.*
13 Frith, Mrs. James, 30*l.*

" Frith, Charles W. journalist
14 Browne, Mrs. W. 37*l.*
15 Flynn, Miss E. 37*l.*
16 O'Ferrall Doran, Miss 35*l.*
17 Fetherston Haugh, Albany, B.A. solr. & 21 Wellington-quay, 40*l.*
18 to 21 *Dominican Convent of Our Lady of Sion* – Mrs. Mary Augustine Clinchy, prioress, 98*l.* exempt from rating
22 Reynell, Rev. Wm. C.J. 55*l.*
23 *University College*, connected with Dominican Convent
24 Conry, Mrs. Annie 42*l.*
25 O'Connor-Morris, Mrs 37*l.*
26 Byrne, J. G. esq. 40*l.*
" *University College*, connected with Dominican convent,
27 Watson, Lecky W. esq. 48*l.*
28 Bowden, Samuel, esq. 32*l.*
29 Shaw, Mrs. 40*l*
30 Northbridge, Rev. John, B.D., Rector St. Thomas's Church, 45*l.*
31 Hanson, James, esq. 30*l.*
32 and 33 *Nurses' Home*
34 to 36 *Mater Misericordiæ Hosp. training home for nurses*, 48*l.*, 15*l.*
37 Aux. Hos. for *Mater Misericordiæ Hospital* 56*l.*
.... *here Eccles-lane, Lower, intersects*....
38 *St. Mary's Private Hospital* connected with the *Mater Misericordiæ Hospital*, under the care of the Sisters of Charity
.... *here Berkeley-road intersects* ....
39 Brennan, Rev. Joseph, C.C. 42*l.*
" O'Callaghan, Rev. Joseph, C.C.
40 Garry, James, esq. 42*l.*
41 Segrave, James, esq. 30*l.*
42 Bermingham, Mrs. 30*l.*
43 Wright, Mrs. 24*l.*
" Wright, A. G. esq.
44 Vacant, 29*l.*
45 Hehir, Mr. F. 29*l.*
46 *St Brigid's Orphanage* – Mrs. M. A. Vickers, superioress, 18*l.*
47 Berney, Mrs. 30*l.*
48 Kennedy, Mrs. 34*l.*
49 Kelly, Charles, painter and contractor 30*l.*
50 Edge, Mrs. 25*l.*
51 Maher, Mrs. 23*l.*
.... *here Nelson-street intersects* ....
52 Beers, Mrs. 24*l.*
53 Derencourt, Mrs. 22*l.*
54 Griffith, Mrs. Nora, 30*l.*
55 Chambers, Mrs. 34*l.*
56 MacLarney, Miss, professor of music and languages 34*l.*
57 Gallagher, John, esq. 27*l.*
58 Seymour, Mrs. 30*l.*
59 Downing, Rev. Daniel, P.P. 64*l.*
" Ryan, Rev. Patrick, C.C.
60 Young, Peter, financial assis. sec. Board of National Education, 50*l.*
61 Vacant, 58*l.*
62 Patchell, John R., B.L. 33*l.*
63 Moore, Joseph H. esq. county surveyor of Meath, 40*l.*
64 *Albert Retreat – Home for Aged Females* – Mrs. Dormer, matron, 60*l.*
65 Whelan, Mrs. Mary Jane, hotel proprietress, 45*l.*
66 Gaffney, Thomas B. esq. I.S.O. Valuation Office, 50*l.*
67 Freeman, Denis, esq. M.A. M.B. 33*l.*
" Freeman, Joseph Kelly, architect, M.B.I.A.I.
68 Barden, Mrs. 29*l.*
69 O'Donnell, Wm. H. esq. 30*l.*
" O'Donnell, Charles Wm. esq.
70 Carroll, Mrs. 35*l.*
" Smyth, Mrs.
71 Mollan, William, esq. and Inisfallen house, Howth, 35*l.*
72 Molloy, Edmund P. esq. 32*l.*
73 Middleton, Mrs. 32*l.*
74 O'Farrell, Mr. James, 30*l.*
75 O'Conor, P. J. esq. 25*l.*
" O'Conor, Mrs.
76 Smyth, Thos. esq. 25*l.*
77 Moriarty, M. esq. 22*l.*
78 Rice, Mrs. 28*l.*
79 Murray, John, barrister, 25*l.*
80 M'Keon, Mr. Timothy, 17*l.*
81 Mathews, Mrs. 25*l.*
" Wilson, Mr. WIlliam

The Waste Land: A Keynsian Epic?

In *The Idea of a Christian Society*, published in 1939, T. S. Eliot remarks: 'But totalitarianism can retain the terms "freedom" and "democracy" and give them its own meaning: and its right to them is not so easily disproved as minds inflamed by passion suppose.' In the notes appended to the essay, he observes:

A letter appeared in *The Times* (April 23, 1939) from General J. F. C. Fuller, who, as *The Times* had previously stated, was one of the two British visitors invited to Herr Hitler's birthday celebrations. General Fuller states that he is 'a firm believer in the democracy of Mazzini, because he places duty to the nation before individual rights.' General Fuller calls himself a 'British Fascist', and believes that Britain 'must swim with the out-flowing tide of this great political change' (ie to a fascist system of government).

From my point of view, General Fuller has as good a title to call himself a 'believer in democracy' as anyone else.

Fuller was a retired major-general and a key figure in the Policy Directorate of the British Union of Fascists. Nazi archives show that from 1935 he was writing secret intelligence reports for Goebbels and Himmler. Later in the paragraph which he is glossing, Eliot remarks that 'a compost of newspaper sensations and prejudice' can make us reject 'possible improvements' to our society, simply because they are practised in totalitarian systems, or it can 'lead us to be mere imitators *à rebours*, in making us adopt uncritically almost any attitude which a foreign nation rejects'.

Eliot was obviously a keen reader of newspapers. In support of his point he writes:

A column in the *Evening Standard* of May 10, 1939, headed 'Back to the Kitchen Creed Denounced', reported the annual conference of the Civil Service Clerical Association.

'Miss Bower of the Ministry of Transport, who moved that the association should take steps to obtain the removal of the ban (ie against married women Civil Servants) said it was wise to abolish an institution which embodied one of the main tenets of the Nazi creed – the relegation of women to the sphere of the kitchen, the children and the church.'

The report, by its abbreviation, may do less than justice to Miss Bower, but I do not think I am unfair to the report, in finding the implication that what is Nazi is wrong, and need not be discussed on its own merits. Incidentally, the term 'relegation of women' prejudices the issue. Might one suggest that the kitchen, the children and the church could be considered to have a claim on the attention of married women? Or that no normal married woman would prefer to be a wage-earner if she could help it? What is miserable is a system that makes the dual wage necessary.

These remarks are germane to Eliot's attack on liberalism, and they also reveal something of the attention he gave to 'the compost of newspaper sensations and prejudice' – a compost he himself added to from time to time.

Perhaps the most shocking example is the letter he wrote to the *Daily Mail* in January 1923 in which he congratulated that newspaper for a series of laudatory articles by Sir Percival Philips on the rise of Mussolini, and then turned to the *Mail*'s coverage of the notorious Ilford murder. Edith Thompson and her young lover, Frederick Bywaters, had been sentenced to death for the murder of her husband. (Bywaters, who admitted having fatally stabbed his rival, tried to protest his mistress's innocence, and to some extent she seems to have been convicted on the strength of her unashamed sexuality, as revealed by her letters to her lover and her taste in romantic fiction.) There had been a public outcry at the prospect of hanging a woman and a very young man, but Eliot disapproved of this liberal distress and praised the paper's firm line: 'On the Ilford murder your attitude has been in striking contrast with the flaccid sentimentality of other papers I have seen.'

Both the letters to the press and the notes to *The Idea of a Christian Society* tell us something about Eliot's politics, and they show how closely he attended to current events. That attention is in turn part of the fabric of *The Waste Land*, which aims at the immediacy of journalism (Hegel remarks that the daily newspaper is 'the realist's morning prayer').

Painted Shadow, Carole Seymour-Jones's biography of Eliot's first wife, Vivienne, shows the extent to which that poem is, among other things, an elegy for Jean Verdenal, the French friend of Eliot's pre-war sojourn in Paris, who was killed at Gallipoli. A memory of Verdenal is present in the opening lines of the poem:

> April is the cruellest month, breeding
> Lilacs out of the dead land, mixing
> Memory and desire, stirring
> Dull roots with spring rain.

In the April 1934 issue of the *Criterion*, Eliot wrote: 'I am willing to admit that my own retrospect is touched by a sentimental sunset, the memory of a friend coming across the Luxembourg Gardens in the late afternoon, waving a branch of lilac, a friend who was later (so far as I could find out) to be mixed with the mud of Gallipoli.' Also present here is one of the greatest American poems – Whitman's tenderly erotic elegy 'When Lilacs Last in the Dooryard Bloom'd':

> When lilacs last in the dooryard bloom'd,
> And the great star early droop'd in the western sky in the night,
> I mourn'd, and yet shall mourn with ever-returning spring.
>
> Ever-returning spring, trinity sure to me you bring,
> Lilac blooming perennial and drooping star in the west,
> And thought of him I love.

We know that Whitman is behind *The Dry Salvages* – 'the rank ailanthus in the April dooryard' – but his presence in the opening lines of Eliot's anti-epic of Europe's first civil war is less well known (though S. Musgrove's short study, *T. S. Eliot and Walt Whitman*, 1952, details Eliot's very substantial debt to Whitman). Walter Allen remarked in a brief article in the *New Statesman* in 1959 that *The Waste Land* and Whitman's *Song of Myself* and 'When Lilacs Last in the Dooryard Bloom'd' are attempts 'to seize and recapitulate history in an eternal present'. That present is a type of stretched, eternal beginning – like a huge morning newspaper.

The link to Whitman is made even clearer if we consider the confessional poem Eliot published in a volume entitled *Ara Vos Prec* ('I Pray You') in February 1920. Only 264 copies were printed and he later suppressed the volume. The poem has a Whitmanesque title 'Ode on Independence Day, July 4 1918', and in it he recalls his honeymoon three years earlier:

To you particularly, and to all the Volscians
Great hurt and mischief.

Tired.
Subterrene laughter synchronous
With silence from the sacred wood
And bubbling of the uninspired
Mephitic river.
Misunderstood
The accents of the now retired
Profession of the calamus.

Tortured.
When the bridegroom smoothed his hair
There was blood upon the bed.
Morning was already late.
Children singing in the orchard
(Io Hymen, Hymenae)
Succuba eviscerate.

Tortuous.
By arrangement with Perseus
The fooled resentment of the dragon
Sailing before the wind at dawn.
Golden apocalypse. Indignant
At the cheap extinction of his taking-off.
Now lies he there
Tip to tip washed beneath Charles' Wagon.

This is not a successful poem, but it alludes to Whitman's *Calamus* volume, in particular I think to 'These I Singing in Spring' where Whitman calls himself 'the poet of comrades', is embraced by 'the spirits of dear friends, dead or alive', where he repeats the word 'lilac' and calls the calamus-root 'the token of comrades'. Whitman's phrase 'stems of currants, and plum-blows' may be associated with Mr Eugenides in 'The Fire Sermon' – 'the Smyrna merchant / Unshaven, with a pocket full of currants'. This memorializes a sexual proposition made to Eliot. It is a Tiresias-like moment in which an apparently female voice is in fact a male voice which also happens to be the author's.

The opening of *The Waste Land*, has another Whitmanesque characteristic in the slightly overdone present participles, but it also recalls the first lines of Chaucer's General Prologue to *The Canterbury Tales*:

> Whan that Aprille with his shoures soote
> The droghte of March hath perced to the roote,
> And bathed every veyne in swich licour
> Of which vertu engenderd is the flour.

Considering those lines in relation to Eliot's memory of Verdenal, one realizes that the phallic and orgasmic image in Chaucer must also be present in Eliot's subconscious, and his allusion to Chaucer, the father of English poetry, subtly proclaims that this poem is a new beginning, with Eliot as a new and different type of founding father.

In the context of Eliot's poem, 'the droghte of March' – the god of war's month – must be aligned with the images of aridity and desert which suffuse Eliot's poem. Those parched images represent the devastation caused by the war, and they are also linked to similar images of Europe as a desert which John Maynard Keynes uses in his great polemic against the Versailles Treaty, *The Economic Consequences of the Peace*. (After realizing the connection between Eliot and Keynes, I read an interesting article by Eleanor Cook in *English Literary History*, 1979, which also made the link, though Cooke admits she can't prove that Eliot read Keynes.) In

The Economic Consequences, a work as urgent and concentrated as the best journalism, Keynes discusses the damage done to the earth by the war and invokes drought as a symbol of lack of economic investment. The 'dead land' at the opening of Eliot's poem is the landscape Keynes surveys in his book, where he describes how in Paris in 1919 'those connected with the Supreme Economic Council received almost hourly reports of the misery, disorder, and decaying organization of all Central and Eastern Europe'.

This remark follows a passage from Hardy's *The Dynasts* in which the Spirit of the Years and the Spirit of the Pities discuss how 'throngs' of people are 'driven to demonry / By the Immanent Unrecking'. In quoting from *The Dynasts* to evoke the political forces shaping history at the Peace Conference (Hardy's epic is saturated in Schopenhauer's determinism), Keynes emphasizes a vision of the Conference as an unfolding Greek tragedy. Hardy's work turns the Napoleonic Wars into a prophecy of the First World War, while Keynes's polemic is a prophecy of the Second. By imposing humiliating economic reparations on Germany, the Treaty created the conditions which led to the rise of Nazism. Keynes was a representative of the British Treasury at the Paris Peace Conference, and when it became evident that there was no hope of making substantial changes to the Draft Terms of Peace, he resigned.

Eliot, the corporate raider of English poetry, was stimulated to furnish Keynes's argument with poetry superior to Hardy's worthy but claggy lines. On 6 November 1920, he wrote to his mother:

> I wonder if America realizes how terrible the condition of Central Europe is . . . people [are] most pessimistic about the future, not only of Germany, but of the world. They say there is no hope unless the treaty is revised. I believe by the way that J. M. Keynes *The Economic Consequences of the Peace* is an important book, if you can get hold of it.

The Waste Land can be understood as a Keynesian poem which arises out of the economic as well as the cultural disintegration of Europe in the immediate post-war period. Eliot was working in Lloyds Bank when he wrote the poem, and he mentions in one letter that he had to handle transactions between his bank and

German banks. He had close links with the Bloomsbury circle, of which Keynes and the Woolfs were members. In 1923, Virginia Woolf asked Keynes to back Eliot for the editorship of the *Nation* (Keynes was on the board of directors). Hugh Kenner has argued that there is a reference to the Treaty of Versailles – to the Hall of Mirrors where the Treaty was signed – in 'Gerontion', which was first published in 1920:

> After such knowledge, what forgiveness? Think now
> History has many cunning passages, contrived corridors
> And issues, deceives with whispering ambitions,
> Guides us by vanities.

The draughty, empty house in Eliot's poem is Europe – ruined by a colossal war and a punitive peace. Its vicious aftermath can be felt in the speaker's bitterness, his senescent prejudices. Keynes was himself fascinated by Clemenceau, who suffered from psoriasis and wore silk gloves throughout the proceedings, and whom Keynes describes 'in his grey gloves, dry in soul and empty of hope, very old and tired, but surveying the scene with a cynical and almost impish air'. Clemenceau's nickname was 'the Tiger' – his Jacobin ancestry was important to him (he grew up with portraits of Saint Just and Robespierre in the family house in the Vendée). Christ the tiger in 'Gerontion' ('In the juvescence of the year / Came Christ the tiger') is, I believe, a reference to Clemenceau's famously hardline and vindictive personality, although it is only fair to say that the French public thought Clemenceau hadn't been tough enough in the terms that were forced on Germany, and that he had been an uncompromising Dreyfusard.

But the little old man – Gerontion himself – is surely also a version of Clemenceau, and perhaps that is why Eliot uses 'merds' instead of 'turds' ('The goat coughs at night in the field overhead; / Rocks, moss, stonecrop, iron, merds'). Eliot is also drawing on Blake's 'The Tiger', a poem which employs the image, common in British journalism during the 1790s, of the Revolutionary Paris crowd as tigers.

Keynes writes with feeling and severity as he attacks:

> The policy of reducing Germany to servitude for a generation, of degrading the lives of millions of human beings, and of depriving a whole nation of happiness should be abhorrent and detestable, – abhorrent and detestable, even if it were possible, even if it enriched ourselves, even if [it] did not sow the decay of the whole civilized life of Europe. Some preach it in the name of Justice. In the great events of man's history Justice is not so simple. And if it were, nations are not authorized, by religion or by natural morals, to visit on the children of their enemies the misdoings of parents or of rulers.

It is this spectre of Justice – Christ the tiger, not the lamb – that dominates Eliot's imagination, and that 'one strong figure Clemenceau', as Eliot called him, stands behind the imaginative despair and bitterness of 'Gerontion' and *The Waste Land*.

The atmosphere of the post-war period is caught by Keynes in a series of powerful vignettes – really dramatic images – which illustrate his argument in *The Economic Consequences of the Peace*. In a passage which must have touched Eliot deeply, he says:

> Paris was a nightmare, and every one there was morbid. A sense of impending catastrophe overhung the frivolous scene; the futility and smallness of man before the great events confronting him; the mingled significance and unreality of the decisions; levity, blindness, insolence, confused cries from without, – all the elements of ancient tragedy were there. Seated indeed amid the theatrical trappings of the French Saloons of State, one could wonder if the extraordinary visages of Wilson and of Clemenceau, with their fixed hue and unchanging characterization, were really faces at all and not the tragi-comic masks of some strange drama or puppet-show.

This evocation of the scene anticipates the confused cries, the nervous anxiety, the mingling of the banal, the sublime and the futile in *The Waste Land*. Keynes speaks of 'the terrible exhaustion' of Germany and Austria, and says that 'an occasional visit to the hot, dry room in the President's house, where the Four fulfilled their destiny in arid and empty intrigue, only added to the sense of nightmare'. Eliot aims to dramatize that nightmare, and the desert aridity evoked in *The Waste Land* embodies the atmosphere in Clemenceau's residence as well as Keynes's theme of the 'exhaustion of the soil'. Commenting on the winter of 1918–19 in the battle zones, Keynes remarks on the 'extraordinary scale of blasted grandeur. The completeness of the destruction was evident. For mile after mile nothing was left. No building was habitable and no field fit for plough.' Such scenes and the human misery that underlies them are part of the blasted fabric both of 'Gerontion' and of Eliot's later, visionary European poem, with its ruins, empty chapels, exhausted wells, falling towers and phantasmagoric cities. And like Keynes, Eliot imagines his fragmentary scenes in terms of quotations.

Writing to his mother on 2 October 1919, Eliot commented on the Paris Peace Conference:

> But it is certain that at the Peace Conference the one strong figure was Clemenceau, who knew just what he wanted, and that Wilson went down utterly before European diplomacy. It is obviously a bad peace, in which the major European powers tried to get as much as they could, and appease or ingratiate as far as possible the various puppet nationalities which they have constituted and will try to dominate. That is exactly what we expected. And I believe that Wilson made a grave mistake in coming to Europe.

Although it would be two months before Keynes's polemic was published, Eliot is speaking from inside knowledge. He tells his mother that he has just been asked to write the occasional leading article for the *Times Literary Supplement*, and he calls this 'the highest honour possible in the critical world of literature'. He is reaching the centre of the English establishment, and he articulates the wisdom and the ideas of its most gifted and cultured members.

Of the Allied policy of Making Germany Pay, as the newspaper headlines termed it, Keynes says this is 'one of the most serious acts of unwisdom our statesmen have ever been responsible for'; and 'As I write the flames of Russian Bolshevism seem, for the moment at least, to have burnt themselves out, and the peoples of Central and Eastern Europe are held in a dreadful torpor.' That phrase 'a dreadful torpor' might well be applied to the atmosphere Eliot designs in *The Waste Land*.

Keynes also suggests that a victory of the revolutionary Spartacists in Germany might well be the prelude to revolution elsewhere. Then he imagines:

> A new military power establishing itself in the east, with its spiritual home in Brandenburg drawing to itself all the military talent and all the military adventurers – all those who regret emperors and hate democracy . . . a new Napoleonic domination rising as a phoenix from the ashes of cosmopolitan militarism.

This is a prophecy of the rise of Hitler and Nazism, and it again invokes Napoleon, the puppet of history in Hardy's *The Dynasts*. Although Eliot belonged in many respects with those who, in Keynes's terse phrase, 'regret emperors and hate democracy', his great poem testifies to his agonized response to the disintegration of Europe. Keynes's book radically illuminates the disenchantment of the post-war years. C. E. Montague published a book on a similar theme – called simply *Disenchantment* – in 1920. As Raymond Sontag points out in his historical study, *A Broken World*, the war and the peace which followed reduced Austria to an impoverished landlocked state with a population of 6.5 million, of whom nearly two million lived in the derelict capital, Vienna. There is an echo of this in the final section of Eliot's poem:

> Who are those hooded hordes swarming
> Over endless plains, stumbling in cracked earth
> Ringed by the flat horizon only
> What is that city over the mountains
> Cracks and reforms and bursts in the violet air
> Falling towers
> Jerusalem Athens Alexandria
> Vienna London
> Unreal

Britain felt strengthened after the war, but there was unrest in India, Ireland and Egypt, and a growing public outcry against British action in the colonies. The government started to retreat and an economic depression began in 1920.

A. J. P. Taylor states that in 1918 Europe ceased to be the centre of the world – the legacy of the narrow Allied victory was Bolshevism and American intervention in Europe (for the defeat of Germany was achieved only with American backing). Europe was superseded, and in January 1918 there began, Taylor says, 'a competition between communism and liberal democracy which has lasted to the present day'. (Taylor was writing in 1954, and could not anticipate – who could? – the break-up of the Soviet Union and the end of Communism in Europe.) Those 'hooded hordes', I think, refer to the failed Soviet attempt to invade Poland (one of Stalin's early failures). Here, Eliot has shifted back to Europe after the earlier 'mountains of rock without water passage', where the setting is South American:

> There is not even silence in the mountains
> But dry sterile thunder without rain
> There is not even solitude in the mountains
> But red sullen faces sneer and snarl
> From doors of mudcracked houses

Eliot may be drawing on Conrad's *Nostromo*, where the description in the third paragraph of the 'wild chaos' of the peninsula of Azuera, which is 'utterly waterless, for the rainfall runs off at once on all sides into the sea, it has not soil enough – it is said – to grow a single blade of grass, as if it were blighted by a curse'. Also the phrase 'waste land' occurs in *Nostromo*. Eliot wanted to use a quotation from Conrad's *Heart of Darkness* as epigraph to *The Waste Land* – 'Did he live his life again in every detail of desire, temptation, and surrender during that supreme moment of complete knowledge? He cried in a whisper at some image, at some vision, – he cried out twice, a cry that was no more than a breath – "the horror! the horror!" ' Pound wrongly advised against using this quotation.

The poem is full of images of drought and famine – 'Dead mountain mouth of carious teeth that cannot spit' – that reflect Keynes's anger at the spectacle of Europe starving. 'It is an extraordinary fact', Keynes says, that the 'fundamental economic fact of a Europe starving and disintegrating before their eyes' was the one question in which it was impossible to arouse the interest of the Council of Four. Warning of the consequences of starvation, he writes:

> The danger confronting us, therefore, is the rapid depression of the standard of life of the European populations to a point which will mean actual starvation for some (a point already reached in Russia and approximately

reached in Austria). Men will not always die quietly. For starvation, which brings to some lethargy and a helpless despair, drives other temperaments to the nervous instability of hysteria and to a mad despair. And these in their distress may overturn the remnants of organization, and submerge civilization itself in their attempts to satisfy desperately the overwhelming needs of the individual. This is the anger against which all our resources and courage and idealism must now cooperate.

Eliot harnesses lethargy and nervous instability (which was also a painful fact of his personal life at the time, as his first marriage to Vivienne Haigh-Wood began to cause deep unhappiness to both partners), and he also expresses despair and anger, courage and idealism in what is really the greatest poem of the First World War. The poem also catches the hysterical gaiety Keynes describes during the holiday season in Paris in 1919 – so hysterical that the french government imposed a curfew on New Year's Eve to prevent a repetition of the bacchanal of Christmas Eve. Eliot transposes this to a flapper's English voice:

> O O O O that Shakespeherian Rag –
> It's so elegant
> So intelligent

Eliot did not possess the classical temperament, though he wanted his readers to think he did. Rather, Eliot is a writer like Dostoevsky or Yeats, impelled by the currents and extremities of the social moment, pushed and pulled by history. There is a profound liberal humanism in Keynes – a balanced, compassionate power of judgement and analysis – which inspired Eliot to try, at times, to reach beyond his miserable and disgusting anti-Semitism (Keynes, though, admired *After Strange Gods*, so this may be too generous). The voice at this moment in the poem occupies a decayed hole among the mountains, like 'Gerontion' he stiffens in the natural equivalent of a rented house – but in his agony of hatred and self-hatred, he says:

> I sat upon the shore
> Fishing, with the arid plain behind me.
> Shall I at least set my lands in order?

In submitting to the destructive energies of post-war Europe, Eliot exposes his naked shivering self to his readers' judgement, and seeks to embody Keynes's stark wisdom in poetry much greater than the lines of *The Dynasts* or *Prometheus Unbound*, which Keynes quotes to add force and eloquence to his statistics.

Keynes opposes Clemenceau's primitive and vindictive harshness. He also opposes, in an echo of Burke on the French Revolutionaries, what he calls 'the bloodthirsty philosophers of Russia'. This absolute sense of an enduring core of civilized values is what Eliot is communicating at the end of *The Waste Land*, with the prayer for peace after madness and war with which the poem closes – 'Shantih shantih shantih'. This echoes the heavily ironic, negative force of the word 'Peace' in Keynes's title, but it does so in a gentle, caressing manner that expresses mercy. At the same time, both writers see death approaching:

> The lately gathered harvest keeps off the worst privations, and Peace was declared at Paris. But winter approaches. Men will have nothing to look forward to or to nourish hopes on. There will be little fuel to moderate the rigours of the season or to comfort the starved bodies of the town-dwellers. But who can say how much is endurable, or in what direction men will seek to escape from their misfortunes?

He mentions the devastating poverty of Vienna, and Eliot echoes this in the last section:

> What is the city over mountains
> Cracks and reforms and bursts in the violet air
> Falling towers
> Jerusalem Athens Alexandria
> Vienna London
> Unreal

The 'violet air' is a pun on 'violent', and it occurs again a few lines later:

> And bats with baby faces in the violet light
> Whistled and beat their wings
> And crawled head downward down a blackened wall

Here, Eliot is remembering this passage near the beginning of *Dracula*:

As I leaned from the window my eye was caught by something moving a storey below me, and somewhat to my left, where I imagined, from the lie of the rooms, that the windows of the Count's own room would look out. The window at which I stood was tall and deep, stone-mullioned, and though weather-worn, was still complete; but it was evidently many a day since the case had been there. I drew back behind the stonework, and looked carefully out.

What I saw was the Count's head coming out from the window. I did not see the face, but I knew the man by the neck and the movement of his back and arms. In any case, I could not mistake the hands which I had had so many opportunities of studying. I was first interested and somewhat amused, for it is wonderful how small a matter will interest and amuse a man when he is a prisoner. But my very feelings changed to repulsion and terror when I saw the whole man slowly emerge from the window and begin to crawl down the castle wall over that dreadful abyss, *face down*, with his cloak spreading out around him like great wings. At first I could not believe my eyes. I thought it was some trick of the moonlight, some weird effect of shadow; but I kept looking, and it could be no delusion. I saw the fingers and toes grasp the corners of the stones, worn clear of the mortar by the stress of years, and by thus using every projection and inequality move downwards with considerable speed, just as a lizard moves along a wall.

What manner of man is this, or what manner of creature is it in the semblance of man? I feel the dread of this horrible place overpowering me; I am in fear – in awful fear – and there is no escape for me; I am encompassed about with terrors that I dare not think of.

The wolves in the novel, the phrase 'the whirlpool of European races', and the nightmare of Lucy with 'pointed teeth' and 'blood-stained voluptuous mouth' must have spoken to Eliot's deepest fears and anxieties – his 'Ode' with its 'succuba eviscerate' is a moment from *Dracula*.

'If we aim deliberately,' Keynes says, turning to *Mittel-Europa*, 'at the impoverishment of Central Europe, vengeance, I dare predict, will not limp. Nothing can delay for very long that final civil war between the forces of Reaction and the despairing convulsions of Revolution, before which the horrors of the late German war will fade into nothing, and which will destroy, whoever is the victor, the civilization and progress of our generation.' Keynes's sense that

Germany will exact a terrible revenge for its treatment by the Allies rings out like a prophecy in the wilderness.

Keynes is remembered by Eliot in the obituary tribute he published in the *New English Weekly* (16 May 1946). Here he praises Keynes's intelligence, cultivated mind and 'powerful and original intellect'. He remarks that the two men first met twenty-five or more years before – shortly before *The Waste Land* was published, it would seem – and he also mentions that *The Economic Consequences of the Peace* is the 'only one of his books I have ever read'. To return to Eliot's poem after reading Keynes is to realize that in it Eliot is anatomizing that 'dry sterile', punitive intellect he shared with Clemenceau in order to reach out like Raskolnikov to an ethic of mercy and forgiveness, and so pass, as Dostoevsky phrases it, from one world to another.

Your Roundy Face: Hughes and Hopkins

Dialect, or vernacular language, and Dissent can express each other in tender, surprising, sometimes challenging ways. Ted Hughes now and again draws on Hopkins to reach back into the depths of the English language, and also to touch on the energies of the 'old religion' to which Hopkins converted (the success of the English Reformation turned Catholicism into a form of Dissent). Nourished in Yorkshire Nonconformism, Hughes was fascinated by Shakespeare's Catholic background, and spent ten years working on a long study, *Shakespeare and the Goddess of Complete Being*, which has at its heart his agonized perception that Protestant England's national poet and prime cultural icon is a poet and dramatist whom he believes was a deep, secret, committed Catholic, who didn't believe – or didn't believe wholly – in the reformed state's purpose.

Part of the excitement of reading Ted Hughes's poetry and prose is the sense that he is in urgent conversation with a whole series of authors. Reading '18 Rugby Street' in *Birthday Letters*, I was struck by these lines:

> And now at last I got a good look at you.
> Your roundy face, that your friends, being objective,
> Called 'rubbery' and you, crueller, 'boneless'.

The adjective 'roundy' stayed with me. I remembered a story I once heard Seamus Heaney tell: how a pupil at a primary school in County Cork began an essay on the swallow by writing, 'The swallow is a migratory bird. He have a roundy head.' The move between best-behaviour, Standard English and intimate spoken dialect – between the official and the warmly oral – is touching. Hopkins uses the word in 'As Kingfishers Catch Fire':

As kingfishers catch fire, dragonflies dráw fláme;
As tumbled over rim in roundy wells
Stones ring; like each tucked string tells, each hung bell's
Bow swung finds tongue to fling out broad its name.

Linking the two poems means that a void also opens up – stones are falling down the roundy well, and with a sound that's like plucked catgut, a hard, tight, tough sound knocking against the serried stones that rise up from the darkness. Auden is catching a similar moment when he speaks of 'the pluck / And knock of the tide' in 'Look, Stranger'. The scrambling shingle in Auden's poem goes back beyond the 'grating roar / Of pebbles' in 'Dover Beach' to Edgar's mendacious description of a shingle beach near Dover, where 'The murmuring surge, / That on th'unnumb'red idle pebble chafes, / Cannot be heard so high'. Cliff, stone, well, littoral – we are peering into the depths of the English language here, and catching its ontic, crowded, consonantal clatter. For Hughes 'roundy' is both a tender dialect word, and a word which carries hardness and an image of falling – there is danger as well as love and a certain gaucheness in the word.

Interestingly at the close of the sonnet, Hopkins uses the word 'faces':

Chríst – for Christ plays in ten thousand places,
Lovely in limbs, and lovely in eyes not his
To the Father through the features of men's faces.

I like to think that in a certain type of heightened imagination, individual words or phrases in particular poems aren't simply being alluded to, but the whole poem. Hopkins's triumphantly religious sonnet, which has 'roundy' in its second line and 'faces' in its last, is compressed into the 'roundy face', which triumphs over the pejorative alternatives – 'rubbery' and 'boneless'. The phrase is redemptive and unique:

Each mortal thing does one thing and the same:
Deals out that being indoors each one dwells;
Selves – goes its self; *myself* it speaks and spells,
Crying *What I do is me: for that I came.*

This valuation of the individual is there in Hopkins's remark to Bridges: 'Every poet, I thought, must be original and originality a condition of poetic genius; so that each poet is like a species in nature (not an *individuum genericum* or *specificum*) and can never recur.' Thus there is a great tribute to Plath's genius concealed in that tender phrase, 'roundy face'. And the tenderness of the adjective is there in this couplet from John Clare's *The Village Minstrel*:

> Welcome red and roundy sun
> Dropping lowley in the west

The word belongs to dialect, to the spoken language that so inspired Hopkins, and which informs everything Ted Hughes has written.

I catch another moment from Hopkins in these lines from 'Daffodils':

> We worked at selling them
> As if employed on somebody else's
> Flower-farm. You bent at it
> In the rain of that April – your last April.
> We bent there together, among the soft shrieks
> Of their jostled stems, the wet shocks shaken
> Of their girlish dance-frocks –
> Fresh-opened dragonflies, wet and flimsy,
> Opened too early.

Before the tense, stretched Degas-image – physically tortured young ballerinas – there is a reminiscence, I think, of this passage I've quoted from Hopkins's journals:

> The bluebells in your hand baffle you with their inscape, made to every sense: if you draw your fingers through them they are lodged and struggle with a shock of wet heads; the long stalks rub and click and flatten to a fan on one another like your fingers themselves would when you passed the palms hard across one another, making a brittle rub and jostle like the noise of a hurdle strained by leaning against; then there is the faint honey smell and in the mouth the sweet gum when you bite them.

Both poem and prose involve flower stalks and jostling shocks – they remind me of Stanley Spencer, for this is an intensely English vision with a clear, cold, quietly redemptive light. Read in its entirety, behind the Hopkins passage there is an almost subliminal religious iconography – hurdle, sheephooks, crook – and this informs the glistening sense of transience in the Hughes lines to give a sense of tough, flexible permanence like a hurdle being leant against.

The third citing – or sighting – of Hopkins occurs in 'The Beach', where

> The sea moved near, stunned after the rain,
> Unperforming. Above it
> The blue-black heap of the West collapsed slowly,
> Comfortless as a cold iron stove
> Standing among dead cinders
> In some roofless ruin.

At the end of 'The Windhover', Hopkins shrugs his shoulders:

> No wónder of it: shéer plód makes plough down síllion
> Shíne, and blue-bleak embers, ah my dear,
> Fall, gáll themsélves, and gásh góld-vermílion.

Here, apparently dead cinders break open and reveal a glowing heart that is given a painterly inscape that is meant to remind us of an Italian painting of Christ crucified. Significantly, Hopkins uses the word 'dangerous' in 'To What Serves Mortal Beauty':

> To what serves mortal beauty ˈ – dangerous; does set danc-
> Ing blood – the O-seal-that-so ˈ feature, flung prouder form
> Than Purcell tune lets tread to? ˈ See, it does this: keeps warm
> Men's wits to the things that are; ˈ what good means – where
> a glance
> Master more may than gaze, ˈ gaze out of countenance.
> Those lovely lads once, wet-fresh ˈ windfalls of war's storm,
> How then should Gregory, a father, ˈ have gleanèd else from
> swarm-
> Èd Rome? But God to a nation ˈ dealt that day's dear chance.

Danger and sexual desire are fused here in this almost Bloomian stream-of-consciousness reflection on the beautiful blond slave boys who should, in Pope Gregory's pun, be called not Angles but angels. For Hughes, danger is a strong part of his desire for Plath.

A Hopkins scholar, Charles Lock, has suggested that in the combination of 'sillion' and blood, Hopkins is recalling the 'Marseillaise': 'Aux armes, citoyens, formez vos bataillons! / Marchons! / Qu'un sang impur abreuve nos sillons!' He is also recalling Gray's ploughman plodding homeward his weary way – a democratic populist moment, which chimes with the possible allusion to the 'Marseillaise', and with his famous admission that 'in a manner' he is one with the Paris Communards.

Another Hopkins scholar has noticed an allusion in the earlier part of the sonnet:

I caught this mórning morning's mínion, king-
　dom of daylight's dauphin, dapple-dáwn-drawn Falcon, in his
　　riding
　Of the rólling level úndernéath him steady aír, and stríding
Hígh there, how he rung upon the rein of a wimpling wing
In his écstasy! then off, off forth on swing,
　As a skate's heel sweeps smooth on a bow-bend: the hurl and
　　gliding
　Rebuffed the bíg wínd. My heart in hiding
Stírred for a bird, – the achieve of, the mástery of the thing!

Brute beauty and valour and act, oh, air, pride, plúme here
　Buckle! AND the fire that breaks from thee then, a billion
Tímes told lovelier, more dangerous, O my chevalier!

Hopkins is drawing on this passage in *Macbeth*:

ROSS: Ha, good father,
Thou seest the heavens, as troubled with man's act,
Threatens his bloody stage. By th'clock 'tis day,
And yet dark night strangles the travelling lamp.
Is't night's predominance or the day's shame
That darkness does the face of earth entomb
When living light should kiss it?

OLD MAN: 'Tis unnatural,
Even like the deed that's done. On Tuesday last
A falcon, tow'ring in her pride of place,
Was by a mousing owl hawked at and killed.
ROSS: And Duncan's horses – a thing most strange and certain–
Beauteous and swift, the minions of their race,
Turned wild in nature, broke their stalls, flung out,
Contending 'gainst obedience, as they would
Make war with mankind.
OLD MAN: 'Tis said they eat each other.

The opening of Hopkins's sonnet is a breathless assertion of the beauty of aristocratic 'virtu', but deep in his guilt-ridden subconscious, the word 'minion' is troubling him. In French it is 'mignon', a darling, a loved one, but in English there is a disgusted, pejorative sense to the word. It is used ten times in Marlowe's *Edward II*:

and at thy wanton head,
The glozing head of thy base minion thrown.

And let him stollick with his minion.

Were he a peasant, being my minion,
I'll make the proudest of ye stoop to him.

The king is love-sick for his minion.

Fear ye not Madam, now his minion's gone.

Hark how he harps upon his minion.

The mightiest kings have had their minions.

And still his mind runs on his minion.

Your minion Gaveston hath taught you this.

He turns away, and smiles upon his minion.

I've written elsewhere of the allusions to Whitman in this and other poems of Hopkins's – the allusion to Marlowe reinforces the homoerotic subject. Shakespeare uses the word twice in *Henry IV, Part 1* –

'A son who is . . . sweet Fortune's minion and her pride'; '"gentlemen of the shade", "minions of the moon"'. And he uses it once in the sonnets: 'Yet fear her, O thou minion of her pleasure' (126).

In French there is a 'pêche mignonne', a particular kind of attractive peach, but there is also a 'péché mignon', a darling sin. Notice how in 'To What Serves Mortal Beauty', the 'lovely lads' are 'wet-fresh ꞁ windfalls of war's storm'. They are fallen apples, shining with dew – water, especially running water, is a significant erotic image in Hopkins, as it is in Hockney.

The *pêche / péché* pun may be relevant to Hopkins's stanza in 'The Bugler's First Communion', which is one of his riskiest bad taste moments, instinct with sin and desire:

> How it dóes my heart good, visiting at that bleak hill,
> When limber liquid youth, that to all I teach
>   Yields ténder as a púshed péach,
> Hies headstrong to its wellbeing of a self-wise self-will!

In an essay, 'Hopkins and the Pushed Peach', Peter Swaab quotes Hopkins's confessional notes, from Martin's biography, which, crossed out but not effaced, record his attraction to men: 'temptation in meeting man at Godstow', 'looking at temptations, esp. at E. Geldart naked'. In 'The Windhover', the Old Man in *Macbeth*'s ''Tis unnatural' is somewhere deep in his guilty conscience, playing against the word 'pride'. In early Shakespeare texts, 'dolphin' is often used for 'dauphin' so, subliminally, there is a phallic symbol here.

Hopkins's deployment of bad taste is there, too, in 'My heart in hiding / Stírred for a bird', where the double – to my ear triple – assonance on the ugly *ur* sound digs a vocal pit of the kind we sometimes stumble into during conversation. He immediately recovers and flies up and out of it as he exclaims: 'the achieve of, the mástery of the thing!' But he cannot resist a final risky, bad taste moment in 'gásh gold-vermílion'. His editor suggests this ends the sonnet with 'the glories of sunset', but Christ's body on the cross, the many maimed male bodies in Whitman, are there too. Italian paintings of the crucifixion are present in the too pigmenty phrase, which suddenly aestheticizes the suffering in the rest of the line and the two previous lines.

But if we look at the 'blue-black' in Hughes, we see that in Hopkins's line the idea of falling is again present. Hughes's lines are even more ominous than they appear: physical pain and harm, as well as falling, are all there, with an artistic and religious triumph beyond them. The pain is there in the Hughes lines, but invisibly the uplift which is also present in Hopkins is there too.

What we find is a kind of allusiveness that has a fresh-peeled, sappy, present-moment directness, as a line, a phrase, a whole poem, is caught up in the current of Hughes's imagination, so that it both lives again and imparts energy to the verse. What Hughes says of Keith Douglas is also true of his own imagination:

> There is nothing studied about this new language. Its air of improvisation is a vital part of its purity. It has the trenchancy of an inspired jotting, yet leaves no doubt about the completeness and subtlety of his impressions, or the thoroughness of his artistic conscience.

Hughes's introduction to his 1964 selection of Keith Douglas brings out, I think, how the dead speak with tongues of fire in his own poetry. His inspired tribute to Douglas makes us realize that, like Hopkins, that young, hugely gifted poet lives on in Hughes, and that his writing is an invocation and a celebration which exalts a whole community of writers and readers – past, present, and to come.

Crusoe Revisited: Elizabeth Bishop

When the *New Yorker* sent Elizabeth Bishop the proof of 'Crusoe in England' it came with a fact checker's note, 'anachronism', next to her quotation from Wordsworth's 'Daffodils'. Mentioning this in an interview with George Starbuck, she says, 'I told them it was on purpose. But the snail shells, the blue snail shells, are true.' Her remark about the snail shells is a perfectly cadenced iambic pentameter: the voice of the sad, lyric, puritan realist, whom she reinvented is still running in her mind. For her, Crusoe is a type of early postmodern anachronism, whose nostalgia is both for the future – the Wordsworth quotation, the binoculars at the beginning of the poem – and for the past. The voice she parodies is less Defoe's Crusoe and more Larkin's: 'Beautiful, yes, but not much company' plays on 'Vers de Société', while Crusoe's beer – 'awful, fizzy, stinging stuff' – is close to the 'awful pie' Larkin eats at Sheffield station in 'Dockery and Son'. Crusoe playing his flute, and whooping and dancing among his goats is rather like Larkin dancing round his bachelor flat to jazz records.

With wry affection, Bishop is writing an elegy for an idea – Englishness – which was soon to become a topic in numerous books, essays, television programmes, and newspaper articles. This happened as what Unionists tend to call 'the British archipelago' began to shift. The island being born in the poem (based on an actual occurrence off Iceland, I think) might be a figure for the new English – i.e. not British – nation.

Bishop on a trip to London in 1964 became exasperated by the poets she met there, and told Lowell:

Oh so many poets – all the names at the bottoms of columns in those reviews, or at the bottoms of reviews – and most of whose poetry I can't tell apart. And all I'm afraid not terribly interesting. – I'm afraid you're the only poet I find very interesting, to tell the truth! There is a deadness there – what is it – hopelessness . . . that kind of defiant English rottenness – too strong a word – but a sort of piggish-ness! As if they have thrown off Victorianism, Georgianism, Radicalism of the '30s – and now let's all give up together. Even Larkin's poetry is a bit too severely resigned don't you think? – Oh I am all for grimness and horrors of every sort – but you can't have them, either, by shortcuts – by just saying it.

(30 July 1964)

Of visiting England, she remarked it was rather like seeing the film when you'd read the book. In her poem, Crusoe represents a curatorial culture and a more sympathetically inflected hopelessness than that which she describes in her letter. He is a tired naif – 'Home-made, home-made! But aren't we all!' – whose flute, knife, 'shrivelled shoes' and parasol are destined for the local museum. Just before it began to happen, Bishop has anticipated the heritage culture that weighs on contemporary Britain. Crusoe's nightmares of islands spawning islands 'like frogs' eggs turning into polliwogs' is like a moment from a Kipling short story reinvented by Edward Lear. Bishop knows the place of whimsy in English culture, and she also recognizes a claustrophobic insularity, which is most strongly expressed in Crusoe's 'I'd heard of cattle getting island-sick'.

There is a particularly subtle moment when Crusoe says 'the turtles lumbered by, high-domed, / hissing like teakettles'. This might almost be Betjeman or Tennyson (there is a 'fluttering' tea urn in *In Memoriam*), but that compound adjective 'high-domed' ghosts the word 'home', which appears about twenty lines later in the Larkinesque aphorism ' "Pity should begin at home." So the more / pity I felt, the more I felt at home'.

Home, dwelling-in-the-world, is Bishop's theme, and one she balances and explores through the theme of travel. Here, she gives it a melancholy pitch, as she also ironizes realism in this passage near the end:

> The knife there on the shelf –
> it reeked of meaning, like a crucifix.

It lived. How many years did I
beg it, implore it, not to break?
I knew each nick and scratch by heart,
the bluish blade, the broken tip,
the lines of wood-grain on the handle . . .
Now it won't look at me at all.
The living soul has dribbled away.
My eyes rest on it and pass on.

She then moves to the closing passage, which begins 'The local museum's asked me to / leave everything to them'. The used and worn knife is a dead object, which lacks what Heidegger calls the 'transparency' of an object in working use.

Defoe was one of the chief architects of the Act of Union; now, more than two and a half centuries later, Bishop is writing an elegy for the British. Ironically, it was under Margaret Thatcher, who described herself as an English nationalist, and who was the child of provincial Dissent, that the break-up of Britain began. Bishop offers a lasting image for this process, and she finds in Crusoe's loneliness a series of visual and vocal images for her own sense of homelessness.

Bishop had an unhappy childhood. She was born in Worcester, Massachusetts, on 8 February 1911. Her mother was from Nova Scotia, her father, who was half Canadian, half American, died in 1911, eight months after she was born. Her mother became deeply disorientated over the next five years, was diagnosed as permanently insane in 1916 and died in a public sanatorium in Nova Scotia in 1934. Bishop lived alternately with one set of grandparents in Nova Scotia and the other in New England, and later with an aunt. She started school in Nova Scotia, but had poor health and hadn't much formal education until she was fifteen. She attended public and private schools in New England, and in 1930 went to Vassar College.

Bishop impressed everyone she met – she was also a gifted amateur artist, with an abiding interest in naive art, which she collected and sometimes imitated in her paintings (her paintings have been collected and published in *Exchanging Hats: Elizabeth Bishop Paintings*, ed. William Benton). She was a compulsive traveller, and this need to be always on the move can be felt in an extraordinary piece of prose which she contributed to the Vassar *Journal of Undergraduate Studies* in 1933:

One afternoon last fall I was studying very hard, bending over my book with my back to the light of the high double windows. Concentration was so difficult that I had dug myself a sort of little black cave into the subject I was reading, and there I burrowed and scratched, like the Count of Monte Cristo, expecting Heaven knows what sudden revelation. My own thoughts, conflicting with those of the book, were making such a wordy racket that I heard and saw nothing – until the page before my eyes blushed pink. I was startled, then realized there must be a sunset at my back, and waited a minute trying to guess the color of it from the color of the little reflection. As I waited I heard a multitude of small sounds, and knew simultaneously that I had been hearing them all along, – sounds high in the air, of a faintly rhythmic irregularity, yet resembling the retreat of innumerable small waves, lake-waves, rustling on sand.

Of course it was the birds going South. They were very high up, a fairly large sort of bird, I couldn't tell what, but almost speck-like, paying no attention to even the highest trees or steeples. They spread across a wide swath of sky, each rather alone, and at first their wings seemed all to be beating perfectly together. But by watching one bird, then another, I saw that some flew a little slower than others, some were trying to get ahead and some flew at an individual rubato; each seemed a variation, and yet altogether my eyes were deceived into thinking them perfectly precise and regular. I watched closely the spaces between the birds. It was as if there were an invisible thread joining all the outside birds and within this fragile net-work they possessed the sky; it was down among them, of a paler color, moving with them. The interspaces moved in pulsation too, catching up and continuing the motion of the wings in wakes, carrying it on, as the rest in music does – not a blankness but a space as musical as all the sound.

The birds came in groups, each taking four or five minutes to fly over; then a pause of two or three minutes and the next group appeared. I must have watched them for almost an hour before I realized that the same relationships of birds and spaces I had noticed in the small groups were true of the whole migration at once. The next morning when I got up and went to the window they were still going over, and all that day and part of the next whenever I remembered to listen or look up they were still there.

It came to me that the flying birds were setting up, far over my head, a sort of time-pattern, or rather patterns, all closely related, all minutely varied, and yet all together forming the *migration*, which probably in the date of its flight and its actual flying time was as mathematically regular as the planets. There was the individual rate of each bird, its rate in relation to all the other birds, the speed of the various groups, and then that mysterious swath they made through the sky, leaving it somehow emptied and stilled, slowly assuming its usual coloring and far-away look. Yet all this motion with its effect of precision, of *passing* the time along, as the clock passes it along from minute to minute, was to result in the end in a thing so inevitable, so absolute, as to mean nothing connected with the passage of time at all – a static fact of the world, the birds here or there, always; a fact that may hurry the seasons along for us, but as far as bird migration goes, stands still and infinite.

This is like an extended epiphany from her unwritten *A Portrait of the Artist as a Young Woman*, and her mention of the Count of Monte Cristo picks up the young Stephen's fascination with that romantic figure. That 'sort of little black cave' she dips into begins the theme of dwelling, of being-in-the-world, which in her poems acts as a counter-theme to migration and travel. We can also see her beginning to work out the relation of regular form and timing to irregular or distorted rhythm. This is written prose, but it has a finely spoken texture, as in that little spontaneous addition 'lake-waves', which blocks what would have otherwise been the ordinary rhythm of 'yet resembling the retreat of innumerable small waves rustling on sand'. In 'Cape Breton', the weaving 'silken water' is offset by 'hackmatack' (a hard American spruce), by the 'irregular nervous saw-tooth edge', and by the 'rough-adzed pole'. Bishop's personal life was often unhappy – two lovers committed suicide – and she became an alcoholic as a young woman. Behind the formal facade of her poems, there is a homeless, orphaned imagination, whose loneliness was expressed in her insatiable letter-writing and in late-night phone calls to friends.

Her fascination with complicated poetic rhythms right from the beginning of her career shows in a note on timing in Hopkins's poetry, which she contributed to the *Vassar Review* the following year, and where she says '*sense* is the quality which permits mechanical irregularities while preserving the unique feeling of timeliness in the poem.' The migrating – we assume – Canada geese design an intricate and complex pattern of sounds, which marries mathematical form with process and with dissonant irregularity.

It was at this time that Bishop read an essay by the distinguished scholar M. W. Croll called 'The Baroque Style in Prose'. She quotes it in an unpublished letter to Donald E. Stanford (20 November 1933), and links baroque style to Hopkins, whom, with George Herbert, she revered, saying that the baroque style's purpose was to portray ' "not a thought, but a mind thinking . . . They knew that an idea separated from the act of experiencing it is not the idea that was experienced." ' What, typically, she admires is the 'ardour' of an idea's conception in the mind. The result is a poetry of intense visual and vocal power, where the play of rhythm, rhyme, spoken inflection and carefully composed, sometimes abraded images, have a spontaneity and deft authority whose perfect cadences create that 'unique feeling of timeliness' which she sought and admired in poetry. That feeling of timeliness must, she said, be combined with 'mechanical irregularities', and both qualities are present in her account of the bird migration in that early piece of prose, where she recognizes and embraces her vocation as poet. So in 'Cape Breton' she places against the rapid movement of the song-sparrows' songs as they float upward 'freely, dispassionately, through the mist', the sudden short, heavily stressed line 'in brown-wet, fine, torn fish-nets'.

We can see her delight in the Baroque in 'Seascape', which is one of her wittiest and most painterly poems:

> This celestial seascape, with white herons got up as angels,
> flying as high as they want and as far as they want sidewise
> in tiers and tiers of immaculate reflections;
> the whole region, from the highest heron
> down to the weightless mangrove island
> with bright green leaves edged neatly with bird-droppings
> like illumination in silver,
> and down to the suggestively Gothic arches of the mangrove
> roots

and the beautiful pea-green back-pasture
where occasionally a fish jumps, like a wild-flower
in an ornamental spray of spray;
this cartoon by Raphael for a tapestry for a Pope:
it does look like heaven.
But a skeletal lighthouse standing there
in black and white clerical dress,
who lives on his nerves, thinks he knows better.
He thinks that hell rages below his iron feet,
that that is why the shallow water is so warm,
and he knows that heaven is not like this.
Heaven is not like flying or swimming,
but has something to do with blackness and a strong glare
and when it gets dark he will remember something
strongly worded to say on the subject.

The first thirteen lines are all one sentence, with an energetic vocal emphasis on 'does' in line 13, an emphasis which underlines the ardour of her conception. The white herons are versions of the migrating birds in the early prose poem, and their angelic and baroque immaculate reflections are counterpoised by the 'bright green leaves' that are 'edged neatly with bird-droppings'. Bishop allows this bad-taste moment ever so slightly to disturb the polished surface of her lines, just as she breaks the long *ee* sounds in 'green leaves' with the adze-like 'edged' before picking up the dominant *ee* sound again in 'neatly', then letting the *d* in 'edged' come back in 'bird-droppings', before transforming their faecal randomness into 'illumination in silver'. This effect is one expression of her Puritan upbringing – it introduces an anxiety into the delineation of a beautiful image, and this discomfiting effect then serves to strengthen and make more flexible the particular aesthetic moment.

But her ear is running with that *ee* sound, and she brings it back in 'pea-green', an adjective that carries an ironic inflection as it tips towards the familiar territory of the owl and the pussycat in their beautiful pea-green boat. In doing so, she introduces a note of whimsy and nonsense that prepares us for the change of subject in the poem, as well as subtly ironizing the otherwise rather precious 'cartoon by Raphael for a tapestry for a Pope'. She then returns to the sound in the opening line of the next sentence: 'But a skeletal lighthouse standing there'. The American long *ee* in the second syllable of 'skeletal' is rammed up against the hard dental *t*, while that word's guttural *k* sound picks up the two *k*'s in the previous line and passes the rough sound on to 'black' and 'clerical' in the second line of the new sentence. The second word in the poem 'celestial' is also echoed by 'skeletal' as Bishop makes the transition from the Baroque south to the moral north of children's or naive art. That clerical lighthouse is masculine, but it comes as a relief. Bishop, who described her ancestry as 'Scotch Irish', plays it gently back against the sensuous, sophisticated, Catholicism of what feels like the octet of a stretched, largely unrhymed sonnet, which is dominated by *k* and *t* sounds, set up by 'celestial seascape' right at the beginning.

In 'Seascape' Bishop's subject isn't nature, but art, hence the campy tone she can, always very tightly, adopt. This subject she outlines in a very important letter to Donald Stanford which she wrote on 1 December 1933. In it she says:

> I think what I was saying about subject matter was something like this: All the primary poetic sources have been made use of and we're in possession of a world made up of poetry, the natural world. Now for people like myself the things to write poems about are in a way second-degree things – removed once more from this natural world. It's like Holland being built up out of the sea – and I think that I am attempting to put some further small structures on top of Holland. But from the poems of yours I've read so far, I'd say that you are rather making use of the primary sources. If you have any idea what it is I'm talking about I wish you'd tell me what you think, because I find it very interesting to speculate on such things.

In 'Seascape' she is writing of 'second-degree things' – a Baroque painting, Gothic architecture, naive painting. But in order to prevent the poem from taking in the precious or fixed style of a self-conscious aficionado, she introduces that emphatic vocal tone in 'does' and in the last line's 'strongly worded', which asks to be voiced in the tone of someone imitating the official gravitas of a humourless and philistine preacher. Bishop the youthful story-teller, singer and musician is present here, and this means that her persona is often that of a performer. Here, she is true to Croll's essay on Baroque prose style – this is not a fixed thought, but a mind thinking.

We can see this type of reflective inflection in the early, rather laboured poem 'The Monument', which ends:

> It is the beginning of a painting,
> a piece of sculpture, or poem, or monument,
> and all of wood. Watch it closely.

That final injunction – 'Watch it closely' – breaks with the woodiness of the earlier lines and frees us from their rigidity and claustrophobia, while making a bridge over the caesura through the alliterating *w*'s, while using the liquid *s* sound and the two labial *l*'s to lubricate its dry woodiness.

What she admires is the temporary, the flexible, the flimsy, values she sets against those masculine values represented by the 'gun-metal blue dark' at the beginning of 'Roosters'. Carefully she places 'Jerónimo's House' before 'Roosters' and populates it with second-degree things: a wasps' nest made of chewed-up paper, a wicker table, blue chairs, big beads, palm leaf fans, a calendar, fried fish, tissue-paper roses, an old French horn, writing paper, radio voices, flamenco songs, lottery numbers. With its short, then even shorter alternating lines, this poem has a throwaway, improvised, song-like quality, which in the first stanza is braced by its plosives:

> My house, my fairy
>   palace, is
> of perishable
>   clapboards with
> three rooms in all,
>   my gray wasps' nest
> of chewed-up paper
>   glued with spit.

The word 'fairy' contains 'airy', for this is the palace of the imagination, whose medium like the radio's is air. It is a female building, the work of a *bricoleuse*, who assumes a man's voice, but a delicate, drifting, uninsistent voice that builds the equivalent of Yeats's tower, without asserting power and mastery. In 'To be Carved on a Stone at Thoor Ballylee', Yeats, too, is a *bricoleur*, a collector of secondhand objects which he recycles:

> I, the poet William Yeats,
> With old mill boards and sea-green slates,
> And smithy work from the Gort forge,
> Restored this tower for my wife George;
> And may these characters remain
> When all is ruin once again.

Where Yeats ends his otherwise dissonant verse with a perfectly regular couplet, Bishop risks repeating 'from' in the last three lines of her answering poem in order to leave us with a vulnerable, naive ending.

The 'uncontrolled, traditional cries' of the roosters in the next poem glance back at all the phallic rhetoric, which 'Jerónimo's House' refuses to suggest. A subject Bishop is glancing at here is the terminal nature of a particular and influential type of male personality. This is the subject of 'Crusoe in England', where with a tender and gentle irony she confronts the solitary dissenter, who has left one island kingdom for another. This is the autonomous, traditional male displaced to another time, an anachronism like his allusion to Wordsworth:

> Why didn't I know enough of something?
> Greek drama or astronomy? The books
> I'd read were full of blanks;
> the poems – well, I tried
> reciting to my iris-beds,
> 'They flash upon that inward eye,
> which is the bliss . . .' The bliss of what?
> One of the first things that I did
> when I got back was look it up.

In her letter to Donald Stanford about her subject matter being 'second-degree things', Bishop talks about how their distance from the natural world resembles 'Holland being built up out of the sea'. This is the subject of one of her most assured poems, 'The Bight', which begins with a muddy tidal basin:

> At low tide like this how sheer the water is.
> White, crumbling ribs of marl protrude and glare
> and the boats are dry, the pilings dry as matches.

The third line has the spoken, repetitive form of 'small waves, lake-waves, rustling on sand' in that early prose description of birds migrating. The repeated *i* sounds emphasize the dryness of the bight, while the colour of the gas flame – also 'low' like the tide – changes nature into technology, cultural artefact, second-degree object. She is also drawing on the most famous passage in Crabbe's poetry, the description of low tide in 'Peter Grimes', which begins 'When tides were neap, and, in the sultry day'. The effect she is aiming for is a Dutch, a Protestant realism, with a WASPish colour scheme – blue and white, which, as Auden would say, is the too too truly Aryan. This she immediately cancels by shifting to Baudelaire and the deliberately slightly affected, because repeated, 'one', which lifts the lines away from the North American vernacular, which I hear particularly in 'protrude', pronounced 'pro-tood' in American speech. The reference to marimba music in 'if one were Baudelaire / one could probably hear it turning to marimba music', develops what is a miscegenating theme, because that music is African-Mexican.

Bishop then introduces dissonant sound when she shows the 'little ocher dredge' working off the edge of the dock and always making a noise she compares to 'dry perfectly off-beat claves'. This reintroduces the dry sound and theme, as well as extending the multiracial theme, because a clave is a round stick made from a special kind of hard wood found in Cuba. Work is being done by the dredge, and both that process and the boat with the ugly, utile name introduce a Whitman-like moment: 'I see the procession of steam ships, / The gigantic dredging machines' ('Passage to India'). This modulates into the naif as she remarks that the birds are 'outsize'. She then says:

Pelicans crash
into this peculiar gas unnecessarily hard,
it seems to me, like pickaxes,
rarely coming up with anything to show for it.

The half-rhyme *crash / gas* emphasizes the unnecessarily hard force of the birds, but it also introduces the idea of an air battle over the sea.

The next line is deliberately slightly lame, echoing the pelican's failure. The theme of failure, which the subtitle 'On my birthday' introduces, and which the theme of dryness develops, is glanced at in this line, as it is when she remarks of the little white boats that they lie

on their sides, stove in,
and not yet salvaged, if they ever will be, from the last bad storm.

The second, slightly lame line gives the illusion of being the poem's final line. It has an air of over-emphatic finality, but Bishop turns it with a comma, and closes the sentence with:

like torn-open, unanswered letters.

She then wittily reintroduces the Baudelaire theme, remarking in a terse single line:

The bight is littered with old correspondences.

Here, she picks up Baudelaire's 'Correspondances,' where he states:

La Nature est un temple où de vivants piliers
Laissent parfois sortir de confuses paroles;
L'homme y passe à travers des forêts de symboles
Qui l'observent avec des regards familiers.

(Nature is a temple whose living pillars sometimes utter confused words; we cross it through forests of symbols that watch us with knowing eyes.)

She is also drawing on a passage in a recent letter to Robert Lowell:

The water looks like blue gas – the harbour is always a mess, here, junky little boats all piled up, some hung with sponges and always a few half sunk or splintered up from the most recent hurricane. It reminds me a little of my desk. (1 January 1948)

This passage is sometimes cited by critics as a dummy run for the poem (it is also close to '12 O' Clock News'), but this is to misread Bishop's letters, a selection of which are published in *One Art*, edited by Robert Giroux. Bishop belongs with Keats and Hopkins as one of the greatest masters of the art of letter writing. Her prose sentence isn't simply a staging-post to the poem: notice how the half-rhyme *gas / mess* helps structure the sentence, while the nimble rapidity of 'junky little boats all piled up', and the complex of chiming sounds – *junky*, *hung*, *sponges*, *sunk* – tense the poem into an exact expressive arc. Bishop was also a gifted short-story writer, and her stories are included in *The Collected Prose*, also edited by Robert Giroux.

The 'impalpable drafts' on which the man-of-war birds soar make a pun on written drafts, for this is a poem about air and imagination like 'Jerónimo's House'. But the line about old correspondences stops the poem dead in its tracks. This forces us to identify and assess what those correspondences are: dry colour, dry sound, dry textures, water turning to gas to marimba music. There is also a visual V theme – pickaxes, scissor-like tails, chicken wire (double *V*'s – that is, diamond shapes), wishbones and shark tails. This gives a provisional or improvised cubist shape to the composition, a formal structure which is challenged by:

> The frowsy sponge boats keep coming in
> with the obliging air of retrievers,
> bristling with jackstraw gaffs and hooks
> and decorated with bobbles of sponges.

This is a moment from a child's painting, which also in 'frowsy' puts the bad-taste theme back in play. It also develops the nature / consumption or 'second-degree' theme, which is present in the next lines:

> There is a fence of chicken wire along the dock
> where, glinting like little plowshares,

> the blue-gray shark tails are hung up to dry
> for the Chinese-restaurant trade.

The blue-gray shark tails and the Chinese-restaurant trade pick up and play against what I've suggested are the WASPish blue and white of the opening lines. When I first read the poem, I thought it was set in New England, until the sponge boats took me south, but I've no doubt Bishop intended to begin with a cold effect, which would help emphasize the skeletal image in 'crumbling ribs of marl'. We are meant to see random half-buried ribs here, as if the tide has uncovered a graveyard.

The word 'correspondences' carries a scrambled 'end' in it and, as I've suggested, acts as a false closure. Then Bishop picks up the dry ringing claves:

> Click. Click. Goes the dredge,
> and brings up a dripping jawful of marl.
> All the untidy activity continues,
> awful but cheerful.

Like a metal dinosaur, the dredge lifts up the marl it bites into – another pun. Then Bishop allows the ugly, untidy, quotidian, utile activity to continue before making it dulce in the final line which rhymes with 'jawful of marl' and at the very last moment draws everything into perfect form. And at the final moment she interpolates the Yankee Whitman into the poem, and silently subsumes Stevens's 'The Idea of Order at Key West'. His velvety rhetoric – 'ghostlier demarcations, keener sounds' – is banished by the dry clicks, the busy boats, and their machines and engines.

Bishop, who was friendly with Billie Holiday, was fascinated by black speech and resists the temptation of Stevens's elevated aesthetic dedication. In poetry classes, her favourite example of iambic pentameter was the first line of the Blues song, which begins 'I hate to see that evenin' sun go down', and she pays tribute to that speech in 'Songs for a Colored Singer':

> The neighbours got a radio with an aerial;
> we got a little portable.

They got a lot of closet space;
we got a suitcase.

It's this type of vocal deftness that we see again in her poems, where it is the equivalent of what Frost terms 'sentence sound', but with an unselfconscious naturalness that is spontaneous and unforced:

From narrow provinces
of fish and bread and tea,
home of the long tides
where the bay leaves the sea
twice a day and takes
the herrings long rides.
('The Moose')

The first line moves briskly because a trisyllabic word follows a bisyllabic one. It scans 'From nárrow próvinces': an amphibrach followed by a dactyl. The next line is slow, monosyballic, iambic: 'of físh and bréad and téa'. The parable of the loaves and fishes is in here somewhere, so the line first expands and is then stilled, after the relative speed of the first line. That stilled, reflective, and awed quality is there in the next line – 'hóme of the lóng tídes' – where the rhythm changes again. The word 'home', which is crucial to the theme of dwelling in the world in her poems, picks up the *o* in 'narrow' and holds it to itself like a ball. Then there is a movement out of stasis – 'where the bay leaves the sea'– a line whose double *ee* sound is free, sensuous, beautiful, as it is in 'Seascape'. Then in 'twice a day and takes' the echoing *a* sound seems to pull 'day' forward, pull it north, as she switches meter yet again: 'the hérrings lóng rídes'. An amphibrach followed by a spondee, which far from arresting the flow increases it because it carries 'tides' as if it were on its back, and pushes over and on into the next stanza. Partly this effect is produced by the initial labials in *long, leaves, long*, which help almost physically to voice the lines, like pursing one's lips.

The stringent, or astringent, fineness of Bishop's acoustic texture can be seen in her brilliance as a translator. My favourite is 'Sonnet of Intimacy' by Vinícius de Moraes, which in a literal translation from the Portuguese reads:

I go sometimes I follow by the pasture now
chewing a straw my chest nude sticking out
in unreal pyjamas from three years back
I go down to the river where are little streams
in order to go to drink at the fountain with water cold and
  sonorous
and if I meet or come across a spot of red in a blackberry
  bush
I spit blood at the corral rail

I breathe the good odour of manure
between the cows and oxen that look at me without envy
and when by chance a piss sounds out
followed by a look not without jealousy
we all of us animals without commotion
piss all in common in a feast of foam.

Bishop renders the poem like this:

Farm afternoons, there's much too much blue air.
I go out sometimes, follow the pasture track,
Chewing a blade of sticky grass, chest bare,
In threadbare pajamas of three summers back,

To the little rivulets in the river-bed
For a drink of water, cold and musical,
And if I spot in the brush a glow of red,
A raspberry, spit its blood at the corral.

The smell of cow manure is delicious.
The cattle look at me unenviously
And when there comes a sudden stream and hiss

Accompanied by a look not unmalicious,
All of us, animals, unemotionally
Partake together of a pleasant piss.

As in 'The Bight', she puts blueness under pressure. She wants *s* sounds, susurrus, always a danger in a line of verse, because so easily overdone, but every line she sets down, including the title, has at least one *s*. The first two are businesslike, slightly grouchy, then Bishop introduces what with hindsight we'll discover is the nodal phrase 'a blade of sticky grass'. Two *s*'s there, and a bad-taste discomfort, which is developed by the 'threadbare pajamas'. Perhaps we're back at the bight on the dried-up river-bed, but it's musical, its coldness emphasized by the way the *k* sound picks up 'drin*k*'. Then Bishop puts the dominant *s* sound with the plosive *p*: *spot* and *spit*. The internal near-rhyme draws attention to the verbs – they acquire even more energy. Then Bishop builds through the next five lines toward the final, arresting and releasing line where the first two plosives seem to combine in 'piss', which gives the last plosive even more force, just as the last two *s*'s seem to sound a double susurrus that rhymes back through 'unmalicious' and 'his' to 'delicious', which in the very last word catches the ecstasy and relief of full and complete micturation. In the original, de Moraes writes 'festa de espuma' ('festival of spray'), but Bishop's closing phrase improves on it.

'Sonnet of Intimacy' is one of the results of her fifteen-year stay in Brazil. She moved there in 1952 to live with Lota de Macedo Soares, moving back to New York in 1967. Lota committed suicide in New York that year, and Bishop briefly returned to Brazil two years later, before returning to the USA the following year. Though she continued to travel, she based herself in the United States, and died in Boston on 6 October 1979. She is one of the greatest American poets of the last century, and a subtle and persistent critic of her country's power. Blue and white are not her favourite colours.

Political Anxiety and Allusion: Seamus Heaney

In his Nobel lecture 'Crediting Poetry', Seamus Heaney celebrates the poets who were seminal for him in his youth. After expressing his love as a schoolboy for Keats's ode 'To Autumn', he says: 'as an adolescent, I loved Gerard Manley Hopkins for the intensity of his exclamations which were also equations for a rapture and an ache I didn't fully know I knew until I read him.' Hopkins is celebrated earlier in 'Fosterage', the penultimate poem in the sequence 'Singing School', which completes *North*, and also in an essay, 'The Fire i' the Flint', which was given as a lecture the year before that volume was published. 'Fosterage' is dedicated to the novelist and short-story writer Michael McLaverty, who was head of St Joseph's Secondary School, where Heaney taught after graduating from Queen's University:

> 'Description is revelation!' Royal
> Avenue, Belfast, 1962,
> A Saturday afternoon, glad to meet
> Me, newly cubbed in language, he gripped
> My elbow. 'Listen. Go your own way.
> Do your own work. Remember
> Katherine Mansfield – *I will tell*
> *How the laundry basket squeaked* . . . that note of exile.'
> But to hell with overstating it:
> 'Don't have the veins bulging in your biro.'
> And then, 'Poor Hopkins!' I have the *Journals*
> He gave me, underlined, his buckled self
> Obeisant to their pain. He discerned
> The lineaments of patience everywhere

> And fostered me and sent me out, with words
> Imposing on my tongue like obols.

The last word 'obols' takes us to MacNeice's 'Charon', which was written in 1962 and published by Faber in *The Burning Perch* in 1963. MacNeice compares a London bus conductor to Charon:

> He looked at us coldly
> And his eyes were dead and his hands on the oar
> Were black with obols and varicose veins
> Marbled his calves and he said to us coldly:
> If you want to die you will have to pay for it.

Instead of a communion wafer, Heaney substitutes a small, dirty Greek coin, ugly as a pomona. The encouraging McLaverty, without in any way being compromised by the image, becomes the ghostly ferryman, because language and his love of it is going to take Heaney both to the underworld and into the future. Just as MacNeice's repeated 'coldly' picks up the first long *o* in 'obols', so 'obeisance' is cancelled by 'obols' at the end of 'Fosterage'. In a few years' time the Troubles will begin – those obols anticipate the bullets, and they also point to the danger in the act of writing, the possible price to be paid, because Heaney does not believe that the imagination is necessarily innocent or redemptive – it has to win those virtues against the odds. That phrase 'his buckled self' catches the famous moment in 'The Windhover', where 'air, pride, plúme, here / Buckle!' and resituates the ambiguity of the verb inside the Belfast Catholic community, which was to rise up and riot in 1964 in protest at the seizing of an Irish tricolour from a small republican party's office in Divis Street on the Lower Falls.

In 'Waterfall', placed just before 'Docker' in *Death of a Naturalist*, Heaney responds to Hopkins's deployment of bad taste and human artefacts and technology inside the 'burl', as he called it, of natural energy:

> The burn drowns steadily in its own downpour,
> A helter-skelter of muslin and glass
> That skids to a halt, crashing up suds.

> Simultaneous acceleration
> And sudden braking; water goes over
> Like villains dropped screaming to justice.

The burn becomes the torrent of history, as it does in Hopkins's 'Inversnaid', where the landscape holds the memory of massacred Jacobites:

> This dárksome búrn, hórseback brówn,
> His rollrock highroad roaring down,
> In coop and in comb the fleece of his foam
> Flutes and low to the lake falls home.

The dark pool has a 'wíndpuff-bónnet of fáwn-fróth', is 'pítch-black, féll-frówning', until in the next stanza the metre echoes the skirl of bagpipes as the water becomes an irregular army treading down the hillside:

> Degged with dew, dappled with dew,
> Are the groins of the braes that the brook treads through,
> Wiry heathpacks, flitches of fern,
> And the beadbonny ash that sits over the burn.

Both poems are studies in crowd theory, and both look forwards as well as back to historical chaos and suffering. The poem, 'Docker', which immediately follows 'Waterfall', is a portrait of a bigoted Protestant worker in an East Belfast pub, but by describing him sitting 'strong and blunt as a Celtic cross', Heaney insists the docker is firmly Irish, not a planted settler. Similarly, when Heaney wrote *An Open Letter*, many years later, protesting his inclusion in the *Penguin Book of Contemporary British Poetry*, he cast the poem in the Burns stanza, employed by the Presbyterian rhyming weavers in Down and Antrim during the late-eighteenth and nineteenth centuries.

In the poem which ends *North*, 'Exposure' – it is placed next to 'Fosterage' – Heaney uses the phrase 'diamond absolutes', a phrase he returns to in his Nobel lecture, where he speaks of 'Attending insufficiently to the diamond absolutes, among which must be counted the sufficiency of that which is absolutely imagined.' It has a theological and ideological precision, and I trace the phrase not back to, but back towards the end of Hopkins's 'That Nature is a Heraclitean Fire and of the Comfort of the Resurrection':

I am all at once what Christ is, | since he was what I am, and
Thís Jack, jóke, poor pótsherd, | patch, matchwood, immortal
  diamond,
  Is immortal diamond.

In Heaney's 'Exposure', the diamond absolutes conflate political ideology, catholic theology and the autonomy – or possible autonomy – of the work of art. They represent the hardest and purest of hard lines, above all a complete commitment to art. (I once heard Heaney, when he introduced this poem at a reading, speak of Mandelstam's absolute commitment to poetry, so 'My responsible *tristia*' is a reference both to Ovid's volume written in exile and to Mandelstam's second volume, also called *Tristia*.) Heaney has an anxious fascination with fixed ethical, aesthetic and political principle, and this finds expression in 'Perch', which is placed near the beginning of *Electric Light*, and which gives a coded image of those on the Unionist and Republican side who oppose the Good Friday Agreement:

> Perch on their water-perch hung in the clear Bann River
> Near the clay bank in alder-dapple and waver,
>
> Perch we called 'grunts' little flood-slubs, runty and ready,
> I saw and I see in the river's glorified body
>
> That is passable through, but they're bluntly holding the pass,
> Under the water-roof, over the bottom, adoze,
>
> Guzzling the current, against it, all muscle and slur
> In the finland of perch, the fenland of alder, on air
>
> That is water, on carpets of Bann stream, on hold
> In the everything flows and steady go of the world.

The three *o* sounds in the last couplet create a fixed trinity of sound, like an absolute that challenges the waterflow. The perch are like sentinels holding the pass, and they are 'hung' in the clear river in a manner similar to the static motion of a much more beautiful creature – Hopkins's windhover. Hopkins doesn't use the same verb, but he ghosts it in: 'how he rung upon the rein of a wimpling wing / In his écstasy!' In the present moment of vacillating, liberal gush and consumerism, these flinty fish hold stubbornly to a fixed position, echoing the traditional Unionist catchphrase: What we have, we hold. I can't read this poem without thinking of the Official Unionist politician, Jeffrey Donaldson, who eventually joined Paisley's Democratic Unionist Party. This is a narrow and particular interpretation – they could also be hardline Republicans but it draws on the inescapable nature of the social experience in these poems, the way their textures can one moment be smoothly sensuous, the next rebarbative and unsettling.

The word 'diamond' is used in one of his finest poems, 'Keeping Going', where the IRA gunmen approach the Ulster Defence Regiment reservist as he stands against a wall in the centre of Bellaghy:

> A car came slow down Castle Street, made the halt,
> Crossed the Diamond, slowed again and stopped
> Level with him.

The Orange Order was founded in County Armagh as a secret society after a confrontation between Protestant Peep o' Day Boys, who attacked their Catholic neighbours in what was known as the Battle of the Diamond, so the word carries specific hardline, historical associations in his imagination. Those associations constantly work against the simply beautiful and erotic in the poems. In 'La Toilette', from *Station Island*, he writes 'the stuff I love: slub silk'. This complicates the apparently dismissive 'little flood-slubs' in 'Perch', introducing an erotic depth which is amplified by 'runty and ready', which in turn ghosts 'randy'. The word 'slub' means thick sludgy mud, ooze, mire, a lump on thread.

Tracing these associations starts a memory of the nodal word 'talus' in Frost's 'The Most of It', where that term from the military science of fortification (it means the sloping side of a wall and comes from the Latin for 'ankle') is magnified in the *uh* sounds in the closing image:

> As a great buck it powerfully appeared,
> Pushing the crumpled water up ahead,
> And landed pouring like a waterfall,
> And stumbled through the rocks with horny tread,
> And forced the underbrush – and that was all.

In these lines male sexual desire and military force are identified, and it is from Frost's subtle, mischievous ability to play the social against the natural world that Heaney draws deep inspiration. On some level the 'tread' in Frost is that of a tank, while from 'slub' to metal slug is no distance.

Near the beginning of 'That Nature is a Heraclitean Fire', Hopkins celebrates the volatility of Irish light:

> Down roughcast, down dazzling whitewash, | wherever an elm arches,
> Shivelights and shadowtackle ín long | lashes lace, lance, and pair.

The opening of 'Churning Day', its metric also tuned to Anglo-Saxon alliterative verse, perhaps glances at Hopkins:

> A thick crust, coarse-grained as limestone rough-cast,
> hardened gradually on top of the four crocks
> that stood, large pottery bombs, in the small pantry.

The 'roughcast' in both poems sets Irish vernacular architecture and the spoken language at the autotelic centre of both poems. Hopkins, as the *Journals* show, was fascinated by regional vernaculars. There is one dialect word, 'plumping', in 'Churning Day', but as he develops, Heaney moves, like Hopkins, between an adept spoken standard language and one which draws on dialect, so that each line is tanged and tested by its fidelity to local speech.

Hopkins's Catholicism is closely entangled with Heaney's liberal Catholic imagination, which sometimes recognizes the punitive threat and iconoclasm of Protestant populism. This is subtly apparent in 'Leavings', where the first stanza:

A soft whoosh, the sunset blaze
of straw on blackened stubble,
a thatch-deep, freshening
barbarous crimson burn–

leads to a vision of the Reformation:

Ely's Lady Chapel,
the sweet tenor latin
forever banished,
the sumptuous windows

threshed clear by Thomas Cromwell.

The word 'barbarous' alludes to Hopkins's 'Hurrahing in Harvest':

Summer énds now; now, bárbarous in béauty, the stóoks ríse
Around; up above, what wind-walks! what lovely behaviour
Of sílk-sack clóuds!

From 'silk-sack' to 'slub silk' and 'flood-slubs' is again a short distance – both poets want to complicate and abrade pleasure (in Shelley's phrase for translation: to put the violet in the crucible). By doing this, they place under critical scrutiny the whole process by which the imagination works.

This is the Hopkins whose intense exclamations Heaney discovered as an adolescent, and in 'Leavings' he converts Hopkins's homoerotic pun on 'bearded' into barbarous, crimson stubble, which through the iconoclastic verb 'smashed' in the second stanza's 'smashed tow-coloured barley' leads to the Shakespearean adjective 'sweet', which in context is also choral: 'Bare ruined choirs where late the sweet birds sang.' Heaney is recalling the fourth line of Sonnet 73, and Empson's famous offhand discussion of it in *Seven Types of Ambiguity*. Empson remarked that the simile takes its place in the sonnets 'for various sociological and historical reasons (the Protestant destruction of monasteries; fear of Puritanism), which it would be hard now to trace out in their proportions'. Heaney is remembering, I would guess, Shakespeare through Empson, whose seminal study was the most famous critical text in the 1960s, and was eagerly read in Belfast. Writing in the 1970s, the worst decade of the Troubles, Heaney places Thomas Cromwell in hell – along with, implicitly, another member of the family, Oliver. The historical code points to contemporary preacher politicians such as Ian Paisley, who stood out against the attempts by the Civil Rights Movement to bring about change by peaceful means. Then in a balancing counter-movement, Heaney recalls a famous scene in that Puritan novel, *The Rainbow* – another 1960s text – and starts 'Will Brangwen's ghost'. Lawrence's provincial nonconformism, where Will Brangwen is 'a breaking sheaf of light', moves the poem out of Dante's *Inferno* to an image of beatitude that is 'abroad in the hiss / and clash of stooking', a final image that conflates Anna and Will's marriage with religious and civil conflict, ghosting 'kiss' through the susurrus and gutturals.

In 'From the Canton of Expectation', there is another recall of Hopkins in 'the banked clouds / edged more and more with brassy thunderlight'. This picks up 'The thunder-purple seabeach, plumed purple-of-thunder' in 'Henry Purcell'. Like Hopkins, Heaney responds to the deep tidal pull of the English language: 'I yearn for hammerblows on clinkered planks, / the uncompromised report of driven thole-pins'. In Hopkins's poem, his praise of Purcell's 'abrúpt sélf' that 'so thrusts on, so thróngs the éar' embodies the cleated push of often monosyllabic, Germanic words. In 'The Fire i' the Flint', Heaney quotes these lines from 'Henry Purcell':

> It is the forgèd feature finds me; it is the rehearsal
> Of own, of abrúpt sélf there so thrusts on, so throngs the ear

and he comments that Hopkins's 'own music thrusts and throngs and it is forged'. In 'From the Canton of Expectation', he responds to this monosyllabic abruptness in a manner that rejects the earlier deliberately Latinate, passive translationese at the beginning of the poem: 'We lived deep in a land of optative moods, / under high, banked clouds of resignation.' Though it could be that this land rejects that language of 'assertion or command', which he finds in Hopkins, and which is flinty, fiery, as opposed to the oozy gum, the 'gentle flame', which is the alternative form of the poetic imagination.

However, it's in 'Sunlight', which, with 'The Seed Cutters', opens *North*, that Heaney introduces an oblique allusion to Hopkins, which has taken me more than two decades to recognize:

> There was a sunlit absence.
> The helmeted pump in the yard
> heated its iron,
> water honeyed
>
> in the slung bucket
> and the sun stood
> like a griddle cooling
> against the wall
>
> of each long afternoon.
> So, her hands scuffled
> over the bakeboard,
> the reddening stove
>
> sent its plaque of heat
> against her where she stood
> in a floury apron
> by the window.
>
> Now she dusts the board
> with a goose's wing,
> now sits, broad-lapped,
> with whitened nails
>
> and measling shins:
> here is a space
> again, the scone rising
> to the tick of two clocks.
>
> And here is love
> like a tinsmith's scoop
> sunk past its gleam
> in the meal-bin.

'Sunlight' is an introductory poem, and it looks forward to a later poem in *North*, 'Bone Dreams', where Heaney's search through the forest of language leads him

> to the scop's
> twang, the iron
> flash of consonants
> cleaving the line.

The mealy scoop is plain, utile, concealed, but in one ever so slightly influential way it is associated with 'scop', and so is a possible figure for the poet himself. But the association of the Norse poet is directly with the roots of the English language, with Hopkins's relishing of those roots, and with a weapon, a sword. Consonants are Viking, invasive, and they represent power.

In 'A New Song', Heaney says:

> But now our river tongues must rise
> From licking deep in native haunts
> To flood, with vowelling embrace,
> Demesnes staked out in consonants.

Consonants are associated with English power, vowels with the Irish language: Heaney wants to mix both together, even as he demonstrates his instinctive attraction to monosyllabic words and curt consonants. Characteristically, those consonants 'scoop', 'meal' and 'bin' combine hard and soft textures, with the almost Titanic accent of disaster strongly stressing 'sunk'. It's that *uh* sound which is indelible: 'The Grauballe Man' ends with 'the actual weight / of each hooded victim, / slashed and dumped'. It's a sound that runs through 'Churning Day': 'crust', 'cud', 'udder', 'buttermilk', 'churning', 'churn', 'plumping', 'scrubber', in the first nine lines. It's there in the pen in 'Digging', which is 'snug as a gun'. And just as 'snug' is 'guns' backwards, so 'gleam' and 'meal' are almost the same word. This backwards forwards movement is, I think, a version of that acoustic pattern which co-opts or forecloses sound. It's there in 'the hammered anvil's short-pitched ring' in 'The Forge', and is represented as a visual image in 'the dark drop, the trapped sky' in

'Personal Helicon', where the two plosives also foreclose the image. Many years later, he returns to this image in 'Kinship', where each black, incised turf bank is 'a gallows drop'.

In 'Sunlight' the memory must be that of the family farm in Bellaghy in the late 1940s and early 1950s. This appears to lend a nostalgic, peaceful atmosphere to the poem (there was a small and sporadic IRA campaign at this time, it was called off in 1956). But the first line is unsettling – something or someone is missing because the farmyard is significantly empty. That absence follows immediately upon the first *uh* sound – 'sunlit' – which is repeated in almost every stanza: 'honeyed', 'slung bucket', 'sun', 'griddle', 'scuffled', 'apron', 'dusts'. The penultimate stanza doesn't contain the sound, which serves to foreground it when it occurs twice in the last stanza: 'love' and 'sunk'. Among the memories that 'sunk' carries is the 'helmeted pump', which subliminally ghosts both a soldier and a pump-action shotgun. There is an ontological dwelling-in-the-world here – the word 'in' as a separate word and inside other words like 'shins' and 'tinsmith's'; but there is also a discomfort, an anxiety, which the helmet and hidden guns release. As a relief from the guttural *uh*, Heaney introduces the long *oo* in 'stood', 'cooling', 'afternoon', a repeated, sensuous, gently stretched moment.

The same sound occurs in 'The Wife's Tale', where the slightly Miltonic phrase 'Innumerable and cool' softens the hard monosyllables near it:

> But I ran my hand in the half-filled bags
> Hooked to the slots. It was hard as shot,
> Innumerable and cool. The bags gaped
> Where the chutes ran back to the stilled drum
> And forks were stuck at angles in the ground
> As javelins might mark lost battlefields.

The *oo* sound looks back to the more roughened, because guttural, 'Hooked', and is then repeated in 'cool' and 'chutes', so that it acts pleasurably as an escape from the pragmatic, short, working monosyllables, which are 'hard as shot', and so lead back to guns and to javelins.

There is a similar effect in 'The Point', where the sound is repeated in the first stanza:

> Those were the days –
> booting a leather football
> truer and further
> than you ever expected!

The sound, which suggests freedom, is caught up again at the end:

> Was it you
>
> or the ball that kept going
> beyond you, amazingly
> higher and higher
> and ruefully free?

Just as Heaney calls the sound of split coal blocks in 'Clearances' a 'co-opted and obliterated echo', he calls the impacted thump of the booted football 'a kind of dry, ringing / foreclosure of sound', a phrase that hints at the closed-in, the curtailed, experience of the minority, as he remembers games of Gaelic football far back in County Derry.

In 'Sunlight', the full-voiced, melodious *oo* sounds relax the acoustic ambience for a moment, except that 'griddle' is discomfiting. Though I have been fascinated by this poem for nearly thirty years, it is only recently that an early Hopkins poem, 'The Escorial', surfaced in my memory as a possible allusion:

> They tell its story thus; amidst the heat
> Of battle once upon St. Laurence' day
> Philip took oath, while glory or defeat
> Hung in the swaying of the fierce melée,
> 'So I am victor now, I swear to pay
> The richest gift St. Laurence ever bore,
> When chiefs and monarchs came their gifts to lay
> Upon his altar, and with rarest store
> To deck and make most lordly evermore.'

> For that staunch saint still prais'd his Master's name
> While his crack'd flesh lay hissing on the grate;
> Then fail'd the tongue; the poor collapsing frame,
> Hung like a wreck that flames not billows beat –
> So, grown fantastic in his piety,
> Philip, supposing that the gift most meet,
> The sculptur'd image of such faith would be,
> Uprais'd an emblem of that fiery constancy.

Philip of Spain built the Escorial in the image of a gridiron, as a thanksgiving for his victory.[2] There is an image of torture in that griddle cooling against the wall – a specifically Catholic image, which introduces, subliminally, for this is in many ways an idyllic poem, the idea of being trapped inside one's own community. That griddle cooling against the wall succeeds in being both homely and *unheimlich*, uncanny, because it contains a historical memory of torture. It displaces an Ulster Catholic farmyard into Catholic Spain – somewhere at its far edges I catch a pueblo village in New Mexico, or a memory out of the Spanish Civil War. The distinguished Hispanic scholar and translator, Arthur Terry, was a member of the Belfast Group in the early 1960s, and this as well as the family links Heaney has with Spain, must have influenced him.

The griddle's metal bars also resemble the window of a prison cell. The griddle standing against the wall anticipates Heaney's citing of Goya's *The Third of May* later in the volume – there is a firing squad somewhere in this image. In 'Summer 1969', near the end of *North*, Heaney says:

> While the Constabulary covered the mob
> Firing into the Falls, I was suffering
> Only the bullying sun of Madrid.

[2] A note to Hopkins's poem says: 'St. Laurence is said to have been roasted to death on a gridiron.' Another note says: 'The Escorial was built in the form of a gridiron, – the rectangular convent was the grate, the cloisters the bars, the towers the legs inverted, the palace the handle.

The building contained the royal Mausoleum; and a gate which was opened only to the new-born heir apparent, and to the funeral of a monarch.'

Each afternoon, in the casserole heat
Of the flat, as I sweated my way through
The life of Joyce, stinks from the fishmarket
Rose like the reek off a flax-dam.

This echoes the subliminal smell of Spain in 'Sunlight'. The poem continues:

I retreated to the cool of the Prado.
Goya's 'Shootings of the Third of May'
Covered a wall – the thrown-up arms
And spasm of the rebel, the helmeted
And knapsacked military, the efficient
Rake of the fusillade.

The wall in 'Sunlight' and the cooling griddle are present in these lines, so that we read – or reread – the opening poem through memories of Goya.

The long *oo* sound in 'Sunlight' gives way to 'scuffled', with its rough, violent associations, and then the basic provincial word 'bakeboard', for the board on which bread is kneaded, underlines the *k* sound in 'scuffled'. Its two strong stresses and alliteration make 'bakeboard' stand out like 'plaque', a noun out of Latin that is deliberately slightly jarring ('bake' in the northern Irish vernacular is a rude word for 'mouth', as in 'shut your bake'). The way 'plaque' concentrates an *ack* sound is almost like hearing a whipcrack, or a rifle shot, and the word is also reminiscent of a memorial tablet, so that it carries both death and memory with it. (I'm resisting introducing a Wordsworthian 'ache' here, but there is pain as well as anxiety in the texture of the lines, even a sighing Ulster *ack*, a compassionate, mourning sound.) Perhaps with Camus and Defoe in mind, I misread it momentarily as 'plague', or read it as a pun.

The conjunction of 'griddle' and 'plague' is found again in one of the guard's speeches in *The Burial at Thebes*, where he tells Creon how they watched over Polyneices' corpse:

And all the while there's this fireball of a sun
Going up and up the sky until at midday

> You could hardly bear it. The ground was like a gridiron . . .
> And then what happens? A whirlwind. Out of nowhere.
> Leaves whipped off trees. Flying sand and dust.
> The plain below us disappeared, and the path up,
> And the hills on the horizon – like the sky was
> Vomiting black air. So we closed our eyes
> And braced ourselves for whatever plague it was
> The gods were sending.

In a programme note for the opening production in the Abbey Theatre, Heaney explained that for the choruses he used a version of 'the four-beat, alliterating, Old English line'. That beat is present in the guard's speeches, and it co-exists with the three-beat line of Eibhlín Dhubh Ní Chonaill's famous lament, which begins 'Mo ghrá go daingean thú!' Her husband, Art O'Leary, has died 'at the hands of the English soldiery'.

The word 'plaque' also appears in 'Ancestral Photograph' in *Death of a Naturalist*, where his great-uncle's photograph begins to fade and is taken down:

> Now on the bedroom wall
> There is a faded patch where he has been –
> As if a bandage had been ripped from skin –
> Empty plaque to a house's rise and fall.

This image is present in the later use of 'plaque', and helps to introduce a sense of the photographed into the hot, still farmyard, so that it becomes like a double memorial. The goose's wing is a body part, ever so slightly grotesque or surreal, for I can recall a childhood memory of a Donegal farmer's sister cheerfully spreading flour with a large white goose's wing on her kitchen table, as I wondered at its whiteness and dryness and deadness.

The word 'measling' has on its fringes 'measles' and 'measly', and is another image of discomfort just before the lines move into an upward, buoyant register, except that there is something slightly crazy about the competing tick of two clocks. This isn't placid, bucolic, idyllic time, but hectic time. Then we reach a sense of rest and stillness with 'love', until the heavy molossus 'tinsmith's scoop' rams its three strong stresses together to begin the downward movement to 'sunk', a verb that contains the sun of the first line inside it. Because the last line's 'in' is contained in 'bin', there is another foreshortened effect. The tinsmith's scoop is also homely, good, it embodies love, and has that consoling long *oo* sound, even though it is almost like a concealed weapon.

Irish history infiltrates his observation of the natural world constantly and pervasively, so that a poem entitled 'Mint' in *The Spirit Level* immediately substitutes a clump of 'small dusty nettles' for the expected image, then the clump's location – 'where we dumped our refuse and old bottles' – deepens this anti-pastoral, unverdant theme, which also functions perhaps as a form of Jansenist anti-poetic.

Then in the second stanza, Heaney balances the mint's 'promise' and 'newness' and 'callow yet tenacious' personality against the opening negative view, before drawing the two views together in the assertive but in fact self-incriminating last stanza:

> Let the smells of mint go heady and defenceless
> Like inmates liberated in that yard.
> Like the disregarded ones we turned against
> Because we'd failed them by our disregard.

The way *disregarded / disregard* rhymes and repeats 'yard' calls back the initial dental of 'dusty' in the first line to imply an image of ghostly or dusty prisoners in a prison yard. It's a long way from here to Reading Gaol, or to prisons in Ireland and Europe, but as this is another foreshortening effect, it's no distance at all.

Heaney has a subtle and informed way of making words carry a great weight of emotional and historical baggage, as well as the vocal emphasis that comes with being exactly and patiently chosen. In 'Sandstone Keepsake', he subtly sets up the sequence of poems which gives *Station Island* its title by presenting himself as 'one of the venerators'. The last polysyllabic word has apparent authority – it picks up the reference in the fourth stanza to the 'victim's heart in its casket, long venerated'. Heaney's piety appears to be medieval and classical and traditionally Irish, but the view of the poet as one of the venerators is ascribed to a guard high in a watchtower above Magilligan prison camp across Lough Foyle – Heaney is staring across the Lough from its Donegal shore, as his reference to Inishowen and his 'free state of image and allusion' make clear. He is seen through 'trained binoculars' so 'venerators' echoes back to that rhyme-word and carries a dismissive tone. It also takes us back, through their shared Latin, to 'Phlegethon', an obol-like word, which acts as a rebutting echo of 'Inishowen' at the end of the third line of the previous stanza.

The poem begins:

> It is a kind of chalky russet
> solidified gourd, sedimentary
> and so reliably dense and bricky
> I often clasp it and throw it from hand to hand.

Unlike 'Mint', this is a beginning which doesn't deliberately subvert its subject. Somewhere 'bricky' carries a meaning of 'half-brick' or 'halver', thrown in a riot. On the other hand, 'bricky' looks forward to 'Damson': 'Then the bricks / Jiggled and settled, tocked and tapped in line.' It's as if, magically, the bricks have a life of their own, and when the bricklayer 'washed and lapped' his trowel 'tight in sacking / Like a cult blade that had to be kept hidden', we see that, subtly and sympathetically, the workman is being presented as a freemason whose bloody knuckles call back the Red Hand of Ulster. The way 'lapped' both echoes and softens 'tapped' adds to the ritual magic.

A similar imagery of wounds begins in the second section of 'Sandstone Keepsake', with 'ruddier' and 'contusion', while 'underwater' summons the underworld whose bleeding ghosts are both raised and dispelled in 'Damson':

> Ghosts with their tongues out for a lick of blood
> Are crowding up the ladder, all unhealed.

The ladder is a Masonic symbol – it often appears in Orange arches – but here it is not a symbol of the radical enlightenment, rather it carries a weight of historical memory, the darkness of the underworld.

In the fourth stanza of 'Sandstone Keepsake', his hand smokes like a gun, while the damned Guy de Montfort maintains the descent into the underworld, so that the movement back to the twilit littoral is only momentary, because 'venerators' takes us back, as I've tried to suggest, to 'Phlegethon' and also 'Montfort'. The 'on' in both words is repeated in 'wet red stone', and holding the stone in his hand Heaney might almost be remembering the hangman's 'bloodied hands' in Macbeth (after being half-hanged, traitors had their bowels and heart pulled out). The effect of this clutch of historical memories is to taint 'venerators' and make it stand out almost like 'ventilator' – the death camps are somewhere entangled in the poem, without a parallel being intended between them and Magilligan. The penultimate line, where he says he is 'not about to set times wrong or right', picks up Yeats's refusal to write a war poem:

> I think it better that in times like these
> A poet's mouth be silent, for in truth
> We have no gift to set a statesman right.
> ('On being asked for a War Poem')

The allusion to these lines isn't flourished because it leads to the final image of the poet 'stooping along', followed by that curiously windy and tinny word 'venerators'. In the early poem 'Bait', worms are 'Innocent ventilators of the ground', a phrase which suggests that the noun on its own has never possessed innocent qualities for the poet.

Behind 'Sandstone Keepsake' is an early poem, 'The Barn', in *Death of a Naturalist*, where a feeling of menace is built in the first stanza:

> Threshed corn lay piled like grit of ivory
> Or solid as cement in two-lugged sacks.
> The musty dark hoarded an armoury
> Of farmyard implements, harness, plough-socks.

The abrupt final spondee, the ugly compound adjective 'two-lugged' that chimes with 'musty', and that unsettling 'grit of ivory', are deliberately rebarbative, even as one notes the gentle half-rhymes.

Then the second stanza sets up an echo with Yeats's 'mouse-grey waters' in 'The Pity of Love'. (Yeats uses 'grey' obsessively in his poems, sometimes it's the grey of twilight, sometimes that of dawn.) In this stage the mouse is a prolepsis for the rat at the end:

> The floor was mouse-grey, smooth, chilly concrete.
> There were no windows, just two narrow shafts
> Of gilded motes, crossing, from air-holes slit
> High in each gable.

There are no draughts in the barn, its zinc roof burns like an oven all summer, and a series of bright objects – 'A scythe's edge, a clean spade, a pitch-fork's prongs' – form slowly when you go in. They appear to be simple practical tools, but they double for weapons which is why, recognizing them, 'you felt cobwebs clogging up your lungs / / And scuttled fast into the sunlit yard'. The cobwebs are historical memories, or, rather, they are like historical memories, and they have the effect of sending 'you' scuttling like a guilty person into the sunlight of reason and enlightenment.

However, the sunlit yard, which we will visit again in 'Sunlight', immediately changes to 'nights when bats were on the wing'. The bats are glanced at much later in 'A Bat on the Road' in *Station Island*. The epigraph to the poem is from Joyce's *A Portrait of the Artist as a Young Man*: 'A batlike soul waking to consciousness of itself in darkness and secrecy and loneliness.' Stephen Dedalus forms this image of the Irish peasant mind, and the bats' 'fierce, unblinking' eyes in 'The Barn' represent the agrarian violence rooted in South Derry.

The poem concludes with the child's fear and vulnerability:

> The dark gulfed like a roof-space. I was chaff
> To be pecked up when birds shot through the air-slits.
> I lay face-down to shun the fear above.
> The two-lugged sacks moved in like great blind rats.

Again that *uh* sound in the last line, while the 'great blind rats' mirrors the 'great slime kings' at the end of 'Death of a Naturalist', the poem that precedes it. The last line has eight stresses – 'The twó-lúgged sácks móved ín like greát blínd ráts': iamb, spondee, spondee, iamb spondee – which make the sacks somehow both active and immovable, like inherited, ancestral attitudes, chthonic forces, driven by both communities.

The argument is less between what has sometimes been described as an archaic tribal violence and a progressive rationality, than the failure of rationality and the civic sphere – the daylight gods – *not* to carry the burden of the past. The chilly concrete is mouse-grey because it refers not to the love that is the subject of the lyric from which it is taken, but to Yeats's romantic nationalism. The consequence of possessing such an imagination is to carry a sometimes subconscious, sometimes conscious, anxiety, where blackberries burn like 'a plate of eyes', and his mother's clothes are spattered with 'flabby milk' from the churn. With hindsight, it's impossible not to see this image as prolcptic: body parts after a bomb explosion are what it brings to mind, and bombs are signalled in the poem's third line, where the four crocks in which the milk sits become 'large pottery bombs'.

There is a similar historical wound in 'Oysters':

> Our shells clacked on the plates.
> My tongue was a filling estuary,
> My palate hung with starlight:
> As I tasted the salty Pleiades
> Orion dipped his foot into the water.
>
> Alive and violated
> They lay on their beds of ice:
> Bivalves: the split bulb
> And philandering sigh of ocean.
> Millions of them ripped and shucked and scattered.
>
> We had driven to that coast
> Through flowers and limestone
> And there we were, toasting friendship,
> Laying down a perfect memory
> In the cool of thatch and crockery.

Over the Alps, packed deep in hay and snow,
The Romans hauled their oysters south to Rome:
I saw damp panniers disgorge
The frond-lipped, brine-stung
Glut of privilege

And was angry that my trust could not repose
In the clear light, like poetry or freedom
Leaning in from sea. I ate the day
Deliberately, that its tang
Might quicken me into verb, pure verb.

The vision of millions of oysters, 'ripped and shucked and scattered', can be given historical locations – it's an image of genocide. It calls back the images of the Irish Famine in 'At a Potato Digging', where:

Mouths tightened in, eyes died hard,
faces chilled to a plucked bird.
In a million wicker huts
beaks of famine snipped at guts.

The verb 'shucked' remembers the gutturals in 'plucked', 'wicker', 'beaks', as it picks up 'clacked' in the first line's 'Our shells clacked on the plates', while 'dipped' contains the strong plosive that dominates the first stanza.

In the third stanza, the last word 'crockery' echoes 'shucked', daintily yes, but with a slight rattly sound too, while 'disgorge' in the next stanza – 'I saw damp panniers disgorge' – has two muted gutturals which chime faintly with the stronger earlier *k*'s. Then in the closing lines:

I ate the day
Deliberately, that its tang
Might quicken me into verb, pure verb

the double guttural 'quicken', softened slightly by the preceding *g* in 'tang', has a womb-like silence, which sends the breath of life into, not particular verbs like 'clacked' or 'shucked', but verbs so singularly pure and abstract they belong to a simple general category and are nouns only, but nouns that are active like verbs. The tang, its hard dental edge calling back the scop's 'twang', gives way to the word made flesh. The repeated *v*'s redeem the earlier phrase 'alive and violated', a phrase that lives in the adjacent 'bivalves' and in 'privilege'.

Metal in Heaney's imagination is usually risky, suspect, punitive, though he has a liking for that soft or melted metal, solder, and praises the boortree's 'freckled solder'. He also, in a moving elegy for his mother, shows peeled potatoes in their shared time together 'let fall one by one / Like solder weeping off the soldering iron'. This liking for soft metal is a way of solving the dilemma he faces as he confronts a gentleness and decency, which despite being self-critical, because not wanting to let himself off the hook, at times runs up against the diamond absolutes and then feels downcast. Objectively, he cannot take the view that the unassuageable grief in many of these poems – the grief and the guilt – flexes conscience very finely and deliberately: he has to indict himself. His own loving kindness, compassion and informed wisdom, he refuses to embrace. *Station Island* reads like an account of a nervous breakdown caused by and for the Troubles, but it is more than that – as the final lyric asserts – it is a dark night of the soul, which does not find comfort in Joyce's shade. That ghostly voice may eddy 'with vowels of all rivers', but it is immediately characterized as the opposite of this:

> a voice like a prosecutor's or a singer's,
>
> cunning, narcotic, mimic, definite
> as a steel nib's downstroke, quick and clean,
> and suddenly he hit a litter basket
>
> with his stick?

These four exactly weighted adjectives are accurate and authoritative, but they contain an uncomfortable memory of personal grief, which is detailed in 'The Strand at Lough Beg', his elegy for his cousin Colum McCartney, murdered by Loyalist terrorists. He remembers how his cousin was

scared to find spent cartridges,
Acrid, brassy, genital, ejected,
On your way across the strand to fetch the cows.

These four adjectives are remembered in those that describe Joyce's voice, and this means that it is identified with metal, with weapons. Then in *Station Island* the ghost of Colum McCartney turns on him:

'Now do you remember?
You were with the poets when you got the word
and stayed with them, while your own flesh and blood
was carted to Bellaghy from the Fews.
They showed more agitation at the news
than you did.'

For reasons, I can't account for that place name 'the Fews' sounds both desolate and sinister – the line stops dead with it. It is powerless and unconsoling, partly because, subliminally, it draws in the idea of the minority, as well as anticipating 'news' in the next line (it comes from the Irish 'foraois', meaning 'forest').

The poet then makes this anguished reply to his cousin:

'But they were getting crisis
first-hand, Colum, they had happened in on
live sectarian assassination.
I was dumb, encountering what was destined.'
And so I pleaded with my second cousin.
'I kept seeing a grey stretch of Lough Beg
and the strand empty at daybreak.
I felt like the bottom of a dried-up lake.'

His cousin rebukes him:

'You saw that, and you wrote that – not the fact.
You confused evasion and artistic tact.'

Colum McCartney speaks for Heaney's guilt about writing, his unease at being 'the artful voyeur' ('Punishment'), who could be accused of exploiting political violence and suffering, an accusation that is part of the anxiety all of us who address the Troubles are prone to feel. He says that the poet has 'whitewashed ugliness', drawn the 'lovely blinds of the *Purgatorio* / and saccharined my death with morning dew'.

This self-lacerating grief and guilt is a painful and perpetual scepticism and anxiety that finds one symbol in Philoctete's wound and refusal to fight. Morning is never simply morning – it carries mourning with it always. The alternative to his view that there are two sides to every question is presented at the beginning of the third section of 'Weighing In': 'To refuse the other cheek. To cast the stone.' This is developed in the last line of that section: 'Prophesy, give scandal, cast the stone'.

It is an essential condition of his imagination that it will not allow itself to feel other than anxious and self-doubting. In 'Storm on the Island', which is placed near the end of *Death of a Naturalist*, he says

> We just sit tight while wind dives
> And strafes invisibly. Space is a salvo,
> We are bombarded by the empty air.
> Strange, it is a huge nothing that we fear.

Written in peacetime, these lines take the *o* at the end of 'salvo' and pass it on to 'bombarded' before placing it in the middle of the last line in 'nothing'. In doing so they deepen the unconscious anxiety about an imminent military campaign, though to put it like this is to interpret crudely with hindsight.

From several years before the Troubles happened, Heaney gave voice to the fear that the violence of the early 1920s could return. From an early age, he knew that the northern Irish state was claustrophobic, potentially violent like that zinc-roofed barn. Eliot once remarked that a great writer doesn't write about the experiences he has had, but the experiences he's going to have, yet Heaney never congratulates himself on his foresight. Witnessing three decades of violence and atrocity, he has held always to a tested and rigorous aesthetic, and to the holiness of the heart's affections, and so has helped us to remember the dead by giving lasting and memorable expression to all that happened, and had been about to happen, when peaceful demonstrators were scattered by those twin-lugged sacks.

Himself Alone: David Trimble

David Trimble's ancestors were Scottish Presbyterians, who came to County Longford in the eighteenth century. The first recorded ancestor is Alexander Trimble, his great-great-grandfather, who farmed land in County Longford rented from the Edgeworths. The Trimbles were a minority within a minority, and this may explain Trimble's unease with the Unionist establishment and his resistance to joining the Orange Order, which is closely tied to the Church of Ireland. When a friend tried to persuade him to join, he delivered an eloquent defence of the 'Blackmouth' or cause of the Dissenter. In the 1960s, he had a passionate interest in UDI in Rhodesia, strongly backed the US in Vietnam, and like most Ulster Protestants is strongly pro-Israel. Radical Presbyterians have always been a minority, and so it is easy to feel sentimental about them, but the thrawn, uncomfortable, sometimes angry and explosive figure of David Trimble has to be seen, like his enemy Ian Paisley, as a politician who represents a particular form of radical Ulster conservatism, which in its embattled and anxious isolation cannot be compared with a conservative English outlook.

The title of Dean Godson's biography of David Trimble, *Himself Alone* (2004), is reminiscent of that famous moment in Hazlitt's classic essay 'My First Acquaintance with Poets', where he describes Coleridge giving the biblical text of the sermon he is about to preach in the Unitarian Chapel in Shrewsbury: 'And he went up into the mountain to pray, Himself, Alone.' It is unlikely, though, that Godson has read Hazlitt – his prose has a type of discursive consistency that is uninflected and merely efficient.

Godson's title is also reminiscent of a revealing moment in Henry McDonald's earlier biography (a mere 340 pages, published in 2000), when a friend describes bumping into Trimble in the law courts in Belfast on the day his divorce from his first wife was granted: 'I remember being surprised to see him on his own. He told me this was his divorce day and yet he was there alone.' Godson doesn't quote this anecdote, but he prints as one of his four epigraphs an exchange between Trimble and Sean Farren, a senior Irish Nationalist, at Duisburg in the late 1980s: 'What do you want for your people?' Farren asked. 'To be left alone,' Trimble replied. This statement, and the meaning of 'Sinn Fein', 'Ourselves Alone', reverberate in the title to give weight and momentum to Trimble's courage in signing the Agreement.

The title also picks up the cover of a pamphlet, *What Choice for Ulster?*, which Trimble published in 1985. It was unusually glossy by the 'samizdat-like standards' of Ulster pamphlets, and it reproduced the famous propaganda poster, *Ulster 1914*, with the province personified as a young woman with long, flowing hair, defiantly carrying a rifle against a Union Jack, and proclaiming: 'Deserted! Well – I Can Stand Alone.'

Part of Godson's theme is Unionist or Protestant solitariness, their distrust of the English, and commitment to the two-nations doctrine, which isn't much discussed nowadays but shaped Trimble's early thinking. He believed that Republicans could be integrated into existing (but reformed) state structures because the traditional ideology that drove them was dead or dying – the policy was called 'structural Unionism'. But he was also worried by the increasing difficulty of persuading pro-Union electors to vote, especially in middle-class areas like North Down. As the Protestant middle classes began to withdraw from Unionist politics, the quality of the candidates sank and the party stagnated. Many Protestants were leaving the province to go to university in Britain, and often they did not return.

Trimble's political career began with the prorogation of Stormont by Edward Heath on 24 March 1972 – 'I am,' he says, 'the product of the destruction of Stormont' – but it was fuelled by grief and anger along the way. Grief especially at the murder by the IRA of his close friend and colleague in the Queen's University Law faculty, Edgar Graham, in 1983. (When the murder was announced over the tannoy in the Queen's student union, Republican students cheered.) For those who remember the 1970s and 1980s, Godson's detailed account brings back a number of horrible events – the shock not only of Edgar Graham's murder, for example, but that of Eva Martin, ten years earlier – a young French teacher who was a soldier in the UDR. Martin was murdered by Sean O'Callaghan, who later defected from the IRA and on his release from jail in 1996 was to become a close adviser to Trimble.

When the new Northern Ireland Assembly rejected a motion denouncing power-sharing by 44 votes to 28, on 14 May 1974, the Ulster Workers' Council announced that the Loyalists would reduce electricity output. The next day they called a general strike, and roadblocks appeared everywhere. Trimble played a significant role in the organization of the strike, and appears to have enjoyed the 'almost blitz spirit' of this highly unconstitutional action. Despite Harold Wilson's resentment of the strikers, neither the Northern Ireland Office nor the army wanted to confront them: why risk bloodshed for the sake of a doomed executive? Faced with a complete cessation of electricity supplies, more unburied dead and untreated sewage, the Prime Minister, Brian Faulkner, resigned with the executive on 28 May 1974.

Trimble rose in the Unionist Party, and in 1990 was elected to the House of Commons. He was pro-Europe and was less committed to capital punishment than most Unionist MPs. Though he was the party's youngest and most junior MP, he was already acquiring respect both as its most intellectual member and as a potential counterweight to Ian Paisley, but it was Paisley who helped him win the Unionist leadership, when the two men clasped hands at chest level as they took the salute of the admiring throng, after the Orange Order defied a police ban and marched down the Garvaghy Road on 11 July 1995.

Huge numbers of Orangemen had turned up for the occasion. It was an impressive display of Protestant culture (some of the bands had massive seventeenth-century Lambeg drums, three foot in diameter and weighing 40 pounds – one drum was called 'Earl Kitchener the Avenger') which gave Trimble confidence in his negotiations with the RUC. Both he and the district master of the Portadown Orange Lodge addressed the crowd, and though an RUC officer described Trimble as 'grossly irresponsible', the district master's remarks were of greater significance. 'Be it days, hours or weeks, we will stay until we walk our traditional route,' he had told the crowd.

At this point Godson, who has been chief leader writer for the *Daily Telegraph*, articulates the position that joins the British right to the Unionists: 'It was now to be a fight to the finish to preserve Ulster-British culture. Everything, they felt, had been taken away from them: their parliament, their locally controlled security forces; the right to display pictures of the sovereign; the right to fly Union flags and to wear Glasgow Rangers T-shirts in the workplace; and much else besides.' It was a highly emotional moment: men wept as eight hundred or so Orangemen marched down the hill, past the residents of the Garvaghy Road, who at a given signal removed themselves from the thoroughfare. The RUC had had to decide whether more chaos would result from maintaining the ban than from allowing the Orangemen to march. Some Catholics I know in the area felt the authorities made the right decision: the province was on the brink of disaster.

The first 'siege of Drumcree' confirmed the British government's suspicion that none of the Unionists could be trusted. Even now, Godson says, Patrick Mayhew, Northern Ireland secretary at the time, describes Trimble's performance at Drumcree as 'undoubtedly triumphalist'. He aroused great hostility in nationalist Ireland and among what Godson calls 'mainland progressive opinion', which helped him when James Molyneaux, the elderly, gloomy and ineffective leader of the Unionist Party, resigned at the end of the following month. Trimble's campaign to succeed Molyneaux was well planned and, by Unionist standards, sophisticated: at the time, it looked as though the Unionists had elected a hardliner, but he was to prove the most gifted leader since his hero, Sir James Craig, who in effect founded the state of Northern Ireland with Lord Carson, and became its first Prime Minister.

After the Good Friday Agreement, a paranoid revisionist view set in among certain Unionists, who came to believe that the

British state, in particular elements of the intelligence services, wanted to give Trimble such a victory at Drumcree in order to build him up as an ostensibly hardline Unionist – which would give him the credibility to effect a compromise with Irish nationalism. The *Irish Times* meanwhile criticized Trimble for his 'quick temper' and 'truculent manner' which, the paper believed, would align the Unionist Party more closely with the DUP. Worse, they said, he clearly regarded compromise as surrender, which boded ill for the all-party talks. The situation wasn't simple. Trimble was keen to attract Catholics into the Unionist Party, but, for that to happen, breaking the party's link with the Orange Order was necessary, and he failed to do the preparatory work which would have been required to bring this about.

Then came the second battle of Drumcree. In July 1996, the RUC, at the last minute, again rerouted the Boyne anniversary Orange walk so it would not go down the Garvaghy Road. Ten thousand Orangemen turned up in protest. The RUC was starting to feel stretched: the crowd carried pigs' heads on stakes, and fired ballbearings from catapults. A huge mechanical digger, nicknamed the 'police buster', was positioned at the top of the hill at Drumcree. Trimble went to Drumcree and clambered on to it. There the notorious Loyalist terrorist Billy Wright sat in a deckchair sunning himself. 'What on earth do you think you are doing?' Trimble asked the Loyalists in boiler suits manning the digger. They responded angrily, and one denounced him as an MI5 agent. He was rescued by some Orangemen, and was lucky not to be murdered. He met with Wright once more in an attempt to negotiate a compromise.

The authorities feared that 60,000 loyalists would converge on Drumcree, and that the digger and slurry tankers filled with petrol would be used against the RUC. According to Patrick Mayhew, 'respectable people were turning out in masks who were more normally seen at the golf club.' The Chief Constable of the RUC asked the General Officer Commanding: 'Can you hold the line if we fail?' 'Yes,' the GOC replied, 'provided I can use ball' – live ammunition. 'In the light of that,' the Chief Constable replied, 'the position is untenable.' But had the march not gone down the Garvaghy Road,

Trimble would have been destroyed, and with him any prospect of an inclusive settlement. The march was allowed down its traditional route and nationalist Ireland was furious.

Trimble believes that Drumcree II erased the anger some Unionists had felt towards him for his role in the appointment of the US senator George Mitchell as chairman of the Good Friday Agreement talks. Trimble knew he would have to accept Mitchell, but he played along with Paisley and Robert McCartney, the maverick integrationist Unionist, to use their objections to Mitchell as a bargaining chip when it came to the rules and procedures of the talks. When Mitchell took the chair – Godson describes well the hardline Unionists' rage – a long-time Irish goal was reached: the Ulster conflict had been internationalized. British ministers were delighted that Trimble had faced down tremendous pressures within his own party and from the masked men from the golf clubs.

Godson points to the difference between Blair's approach to Northern Ireland and Kevin McNamara's. McNamara is Old Labour, in some ways an Irish nationalist sympathiser, who was the Labour spokesman on Northern Ireland until Blair sacked him. Perhaps controversially, Godson says that the ties McNamara and Clare Short had to their Irish backgrounds did not touch Blair, who was 'little affected' by his Ulster Protestant ancestry (his mother, a Corscadden, came from Donegal Protestant stock; they had lived in Ballyshannon for many generations). It could be argued that Blair's continual insistence that he is right because he knows he is trustworthy and straight-talking – the narcissistic void at the heart of his political personality – is recognizably Ulster Protestant, as anyone who has studied its distinctive cultural form, the sermon, will realize. He deserves praise, though, for the enormous attention he devoted to Northern Ireland (a senior Cabinet Office civil servant said that Blair spent about 40 per cent of his time on the province, unthinkable for Callaghan or Thatcher).

Godson goes on to detail all that happened in the Northern Assembly, and is interesting about the mistakes Trimble's Unionist Party made in their choice of cabinet posts. Martin McGuinness became Minister of Education, and began the abolition of the notorious eleven-plus examination, or 'qually' as it was called by those of us who took the wretched exam. His budget was £1.243 billion. Sinn Fein's Bairbre De Brun took Health, with a £2.029 billion budget. Michael McGimpsey, a subtle and liberal Unionist, took Culture, Arts and Leisure, with its tiny allocation of £64 million and staff of 350. He chose this post because he wanted to 'defend' Northern Ireland's interests – i.e. Unionist interests – in the face of demands from the cross-border language body. The cabinet allocations left Sinn Fein in charge of 60 per cent of the discretionary budget – a 'debacle', Godson calls it, which came about because Trimble didn't liaise with Paisley and the DUP.

Trimble, Godson says, correctly, became the most respected and prestigious figure 'thrown up' by the Unionist movement since the foundation of Northern Ireland. In becoming that figure, he also brought out the essential weakness of official Unionism, its demoralized passivity, its sentimental traditionalism, its dearth of ideas, its hangdog lack of creative energy. Trimble's Unionist Party lost to the DUP in the last election, and the DUP then became locked in complex secret negotiations with Sinn Fein to reinstate the Assembly.

Both parties are working hard to achieve this: the newspapers report a speech by Gerry Adams saying that the IRA needs to be wound up as a paramilitary force in order to stop the Unionists using its existence as an excuse for not sharing power with Sinn Fein. And among growing signs that positions may be shifting on both sides, Jeffrey Donaldson, who broke with Trimble over the Agreement, ignored police security advice to join a debate in Republican West Belfast. He said that the Unionist community would prefer the IRA to destroy the rest of its arsenal in a single act, but he could live with it being done over a longer period if it was 'within a defined timescale'.

Trimble took great risks in signing the Agreement. He then failed to sell it, just as he failed to modernize his party and failed to create a real sense of civil consensus, but this was due to the inadequacy of his party, starved of intelligent support and with a large number of elderly, very reactionary MPs. Attention has now shifted to the DUP. On 16 August 2004 the *Irish Times* carried a statesmanlike article by the party's deputy leader, Peter Robinson, who concluded:

> If we achieve completion on the key issues of decommissioning, ending criminal and paramilitary activity, and institutions are agreed that are capable of commanding Unionist as well as Nationalist support, the DUP will enthusiastically and robustly commend such an agreement to the wider Unionist community.

This clearly glances at Trimble's failure to promote the Agreement. However, the Leeds Castle talks which happened in September 2004 failed to produce an agreement between the DUP and Sinn Fein and the gulf between them is now even wider. Trimble has resigned as leader of the Ulster Unionist Party, and is now an isolated and lonely figure.

The Critic as Artist: Edward Said

The style of literary critics – if we except Hazlitt – is seldom discussed. Now and then, we might find a glance at the gracelessness of Leavis's prose, or praise of a critic's clarity, but it is unusual to find much discussion of how a critic writes.

Because Edward Said saw the critical act as, centrally, a type of performance, I want to look at his writing in terms of style, gesture, performance. As a critic he resembles Hazlitt, whom he greatly admired, in making disinterested aesthetic pleasure the foundation of the critical act, and in making literary criticism and political essays dramatic, without being in the least showy or theatrical – he was the most magnificent and inspiring lecturer: a lecture by Edward Said was always a unique occasion. Right at the very end of his life, when he knew he was dying, we can see this dramatic quality in the essay 'Humanism's Sphere' which introduces his posthumous volume, *Humanism and Democratic Criticism* (2004).

He mentions that although he admired and studied Swift over the years, it used to be a source of regret for him that Swift's attitude to the past, as exemplified in *The Battle of the Books*, was 'so doctrinaire and unyielding'. Then, following the example of Yeats, it became possible to read Swift in a revisionist manner, as 'demonic and tigerish a writer as has ever lived'. In his 1988 Field Day pamphlet *Nationalism, Colonialism and Literature: Yeats and Decolonization*, Said celebrates Yeats as 'the indisputably great *national* poet who articulates the experiences, the aspirations, and the vision of a people suffering under the dominion of an off-shore power'. Yeats magnanimously envisaged Swift's internal world in a ceaseless conflict with itself, 'unsatisfied, unappeased, unreconciled in an almost Adornian way, rather than as settled into untroubled patterns of tranquillity and unchanging order'.

In the adjective 'unsatisfied', he is echoing Yeats's 'Ego Dominus Tuus', where there is this account of Keats:

> His art is happy, but who knows his mind?
> I see a schoolboy when I think of him,
> With face and nose pressed to a sweet-shop window,
> For certainly he sank into his grave
> His senses and his heart unsatisfied.

These lines are present in that run of adjectives – 'unsatisfied, unappeased, unreconciled' – which rises up to challenge the unchanging order described in the rest of the sentence. These adjectives also remember Yeats's phrase, 'The Unappeasable Host', the title of an early poem in *The Wind among the Reeds*. As Said uses the adjective in this late essay, it carries, impacted within it, the grief and unrelenting commitment of these lines:

> I kiss my wailing child and press it to my breast,
> And hear the narrow graves calling my child and me.
> Desolate winds that cry over the wandering sea;
> Desolate winds that hover in the flaming West;
> Desolate winds that beat the doors of Heaven, and beat
> The doors of Hell and blow there many a whimpering ghost;
> O heart the winds have shaken, the unappeasable host
> Is comelier than candles at Mother Mary's feet.

The young Yeats is here anticipating his late poems, poems which Said's run of adjectives – 'unsatisfied, unappeased, unreconciled' – also summon along with the intransigent Adorno to make a last, proud gesture of defiance, a final refusal to be overwhelmed by history. We catch here that Arabic word *sumud*, which Edward Said uses sometimes to represent Palestinian stubbornness in the face of adversity. The adjectives emphatically break the rhythm of the sentence and bring Blake's revolutionary tiger into the hammer-beat of their *un un un* cadence. And he is also echoing Yeats's 'The Magi':

> Now as at all times I can see in the mind's eye,
> In their stiff, painted clothes, the pale unsatisfied ones
> Appear and disappear in the blue depth of the sky
> With all their ancient faces like rain-beaten stones,
> And all their helms of silver hovering side by side,
> And all their eyes still fixed, hoping to find once more,
> Being by Calvary's turbulence unsatisfied,
> The uncontrollable mystery on the bestial floor.

The adjective 'unreconciled' in this context sounds Yeatsian, but he is in fact recalling a passage in his memoir, *Out of Place* (1998), where he says:

> I was suffering a dissociation myself about Palestine, which I was never able to resolve or fully grasp until quite recently, when I gave up trying. Even now the unreconciled duality I feel about the place, its intricate wrenching, tearing, sorrowful loss as exemplified in so many distorted lives, including mine, and its status as an admirable country for *them* (but of course not for us), always gives me pain and a discouraging sense of being solitary, undefended, open to the assaults of trivial things that seem important and threatening, against which I have no weapons.

That *un un un* cadence I've mentioned is essentially performative as Said rings changes on the lines from which they come and the passage in his own prose.

We can trace this effect back to an early essay 'Beginning Ideas', which is the first chapter of *Beginnings: Intention and Method* (1975), where he says: 'To begin to write, therefore, is to work a set of instruments, to invent a field of play for them, to enable performance. "Every art then and every work of art has its own play and performance," wrote Hopkins in 1885 to his brother.' This is picked up in Chapter 4 where he cites Richard Poirier's *The Performing Self*, and says that an author's role is now more 'the result of a performance', than of 'a personality'. Later in the chapter, he develops this through a quotation from Hopkins:

> Poetry is in fact speech only employed to carry the inscape of speech for the inscape's sake – and therefore the inscape must be dwelt on. Now if this can be done without repeating it *once* of the inscape will be enough for art and beauty and poetry but then at least the inscape must be understood as so

standing by itself that it could be copied and repeated. If not repetition, *oftening, over-and-overing, aftering* of the inscape must take place in order to detach it to the mind and in this light poetry is speech which afters and oftens its inscape, speech couched in a repeating figure and verse is spoken sound having a repeating figure . . . Now there is speech which wholly or partially repeats the same figure of grammar and this may be framed to be heard for its own sake and interest over and above its interest of meaning. Poetry then may be couched in this, and therefore all poetry is not verse but all poetry is either verse or falls under this or some still further development of what verse is, speech wholly or partially repeating some kind of figure which is over and above meaning, at least the grammatical, historical and logical meaning.

This passage clearly spoke to Said's antipathy to the settled, the tranquil, the unchanging, because he comments:

'Oftening, over-and-overing, aftering' are effects that cannot be reduced to our habitual view of things. For they achieve the detachment of sense from the logic of sequential reason, and the delivery of sense into figures or patterns whose chief feature is an individuality remarkable for its own (verbal) sake.

This interest in rhythmic individuality – what Hopkins terms 'inscape' – is discussed later in the same chapter, where he comments on the 'abruptness of the heavily vexed rhythm', which is 'made even more clublike with its repeated *b*'s' in these lines from 'Thou art indeed just, Lord':

birds build – but not I build; no, but strain,
Time's eunuch, and not breed one work that wakes.
Mine, O thou Lord of life, send my roots rain.

In the first two lines, he suggests, Hopkins has lifted the poem to its climax, so that when he writes 'Mine, O thou Lord of life, send my roots rain', it is as if 'the long monosyllable *mine* is exhaling great pain. The line's last four words mash together nature, submission, pleading and the bruised self.' What happens here, I think, is that Said's interest in Hopkins's abrupt, selving style fuses with his own sense of personal and political pain.

Immediately after this, Said discusses Hopkins's sonnet 'To R. B.' where he says the simple internal rhymes *wears, bears, shares* convey 'the stale sameness of a poet missing rapture'. He then says that 'missing from its "lagging lines" is evidence of its seminal beginnings, "the roll, the rise, the carol, the creation".' Hopkins concludes his sonnet by saying:

> Sweet fire, the sire of muse, my soul needs this;
> I want the one rapture of an inspiration.
> O then if in my lagging lines you miss
>
> The roll, the rise, the carol, the creation
> My winter world, that scarcely breathes that bliss
> Now, yields you, with some sighs, our explanation.

In citing Hopkins, we again see Said's antipathy to a settled tranquillity, as he comments:

> The words of the poem, therefore, do not inhabit a 'creative' text, but are rather the lifeless verbal remnants of a course that has turned, through the logic of self-straining poetic performance and sacrifice (in Hopkins's special sense), back to its start in the poet's celibate authority. The intense confusion of verbal creation with sexual procreation finally leaves the writer 'widowed' – which is to say, alone with his voice and little else.

This points, I think, to an anxiety at the heart of his idea of performance as critic and teacher, and it means that he characterizes Hopkins in this manner: 'What he speaks now is an explanation outside the text. His language seems to have lost its connection with his creative male gift and retains only its capacity to address the reader directly, sadly, commemoratively.'

Hopkins meant a great deal to Said, and he returns to the sonnet to Robert Bridges in *The World, the Text, and the Critic*. Early in *Beginnings* he has mentioned Robbe-Grillet's polemical essay, 'Sur quelques notions périmées', and this idea of the outdated is there in that adverb 'commemoratively' that he uses of Hopkins addressing the reader – 'directly, sadly, commemoratively'. In 'Remembrances of Things Played: Presence and Memory in the Pianist's Art', the twentieth essay in *Reflections on Exile* (2000), he says that despite 'the energetic immediacy of their presentation, pianists are conservative, essentially curatorial figures'. This again attaches to the performance of the critic and the lecturer, and at the end of the same essay he remarks that the essay, like the recital, is 'occasional, re-creative, and personal'. This is developed in an essay, 'The Horizon of R. P. Blackmur', which almost immediately follows it, and where he remarks there is usually some unstated, or unstatable, balance 'between critical performance and critical influence' that can be found at the heart of every critic's work.

Blackmur is, with Vico, Auerbach, Adorno and Foucault, a significant influence on Said's writing, and in this essay he suggests that Blackmur is one of a tiny minority of critics, among whom he occupies a position of 'intransigent honour'. This is similar to the unappeased Adornian quality he perceives in Swift, in what are in effect Edward Said's parting words. Interestingly, Blackmur does not use either an actor or a musician as his example of the gestural in the introduction to *Language as Gesture*. Rather he describes the performance of a woman he observed as she moved down a jerky, rapidly accelerating bus:

> . . . she managed by sniffs and snorts, by smiles, by sticking her tongue out very sharp, by batting her very blue eyes about, and generally by cocking her head this way and that, she managed to express fully, and without a single word either uttered or wanted, the whole mixed, flourishing sense of her disconcertment, her discomfiture, her uncertainty, together with a sense of adventure and of gaiety, all of which she wanted to share with her companion behind me.

This is a highly wrought anecdote or observation, which conveys something of what Blackmur means when he says that language is made of words, and gesture is 'made of motion'. There is something Yeatsian in its manner of embodying a principle in a human being, and this is a technique Said uses in his own work.

The persistence of Hopkins in his thinking shows in the opening pages of *The Politics of Dispossession* (1995) where he says that since 1967 the Palestinian has become 'a politicized consciousness with nothing to lose but his refugeedom'. So attenuated has the Arab project become, he says, that the Palestinian has been left with his original starting point, as Gerard Manley Hopkins phrased it, being 'a lonely began'. Here, he quotes from another of

Hopkins's 'terrible' sonnets, 'To seem the stranger lies my lot, my life', where he says

> I am in Ireland now; now I am at a thírd
> Remove. Not but in all removes I can
> Kind love both give and get. Only what word
> Wisest my heart breeds dark heaven's baffling ban
> Bars or hell's spell thwarts. This to hoard unheard
> Heard unheeded, leaves me a lonely began.

Hopkins's exile becomes a figure for the Palestinians' exile, their loneliness, and their isolated – 'unheeded' is Hopkins's adjective – attempts to begin the establishment of a nation state.

In an interview in 1991, Said again cites Hopkins, when one of his interlocutors, Una Chaudhuri, says that she is very interested in the idea he's been developing about inhabiting the time of performance, instead of dominating it, and he replies:

> Trying to ride it. It's a phrase that comes out of Gerard Manley Hopkins who has a very strange relationship with time in his poetry, especially the last part of his first great poem, 'The Wreck of the Deutschland'. There's this whole thing where the question of whether you try to resist the time and erect the structure, or you try to ride time and live inside the time.

Here, he is picking up the stanza in 'The Wreck of the Deutschland' where Hopkins speaks of the stroke and stress that 'rides time like riding a river'. The difference he highlights in this interview is the difference between 'remaking the music and inhabiting it', and 'just dispatching it with efficiency and tremendous technical skill'.

At times, Said appears to be inhabiting in his prose the music of Hopkins's verse, where God's mercy 'outrides / The all of water'. As I've noted, he was drawn to Hopkins's line 'The roll, the rise, the carol, the creation', and we can catch an echo of it at the end of a sentence in *Orientalism*, where he says 'since Egypt and subsequently the other Islamic lands were viewed as the live province, the laboratory, the theater of effective Western knowledge about the Orient'. Here, the performative amplification – 'the live province, the laboratory, the theater' – lifts the movement of the prose and makes sure it's neither lagging nor predictable.

Behind his prose, we can discern another master – William Hazlitt, who will sometimes unleash extremely long sentences which accrue an unchallengeable authority, while at the same time suggesting that the writer is beating his head against an immovable wall. This is the effect of an almost paragraph-long sentence in Chapter 3 of *Orientalism*:

To restore a region from its present barbarism to its former classical greatness; to instruct (for its own benefit) the Orient in the ways of the modern West; to subordinate or underplay military power in order to aggrandize the project of glorious knowledge acquired in the process of political domination of the Orient; to formulate the Orient, to give it shape, identity, definition with full recognition of its place in memory, its importance to imperial strategy, and its 'natural' role as an appendage to Europe; to dignify all the knowledge collected during colonial occupation with the title 'contribution to modern learning' when the natives had neither been consulted nor treated as anything except as pretexts for a text whose usefulness was not to the natives; to feel oneself as a European in command, almost at will, of Oriental history, time, and geography; to institute new areas of specialization; to establish new disciplines; to divide, deploy, schematize, tabulate, index, and record everything in sight (and out of sight); to make out of every observable detail a generalization and out of every generalization an immutable law about the Oriental nature, temperament, mentality, custom, or type; and, above all, to transmute living reality into the stuff of texts, to possess (or think one possesses) actuality mainly because nothing in the Orient seems to resist one's powers: these are the features of Orientalist projection entirely realized in the *Description de l'Égypte*, itself enabled and reinforced by Napoleon's wholly Orientalist engulfment of Egypt by the instruments of Western knowledge and power. Thus Fourier concludes his preface by announcing that history will remember how 'Égypte fut le théâtre de sa [Napoleon's] gloire, et préserve de l'oubli toutes les circonstances de cet évènement extraordinaire.'

The three uses of parentheses introduce a pause and change in vocal rhythm which acts as counterpoint – Said has a strong interest in the contrapuntal – and this effect is extended by the three stressed nouns 'shape, identity, definition', and by the six, again strongly stressed verbs, 'divide, deploy, schematize, tabulate, index, and record'. These instressed, contrapuntal moments push the sentence beyond merely technical mastery and give it a unique texture.

Two paragraphs later, he says, 'the Orient was reconstructed, reassembled, crafted, in short, *born* out of the Orientalist's efforts', where the italicized verb picks up the *or* sound at the beginning of the clause and passes it along to the last two words – 'Orientalist's efforts' – with the effect of making it appear an artificial birth. This stressed structure is also there, when he says 'a representation is *eo ipso* implicated, intertwined, embedded, interwoven with a great many other things besides the "truth".' With this goes a form of dramatic empathy, where the speaking voice of the prose enacts its subject: 'The modern Orientalist was, in his view, a hero rescuing the Orient from the obscurity, alienation, and strangeness which he himself had properly distinguished.' Something of Said's fascination for *Kim* pervades this sentence, but behind it, as in the birth of the Western idea of the Orient, is the idea of a Frankensteinian artificial nature. The Orientalist as hero is described as 'a secular creator, a man who made new worlds as God had once made the old'. The power which shapes Orientalism is captured in prose that is instinct with its living sinews. Thus 'Renan's is a peculiarly ravaged, ragingly masculine world of history and learning', where the alliterating *r*'s reinforce the point. There is a similar drama in the reference to 'the endlessly decomposing, cavernous element which is Nerval's Orient', where the repeated *o*'s and *v*'s help to sink the phrase 'Nerval's Orient'.

Essential to his ambition of making sentences escape the routine, the tranquil, the unchanging is his use of the dash:

> My point is that the metamorphosis of a relatively innocuous philological subspecialty into a capacity for managing political movements, administering colonies, masking nearly apocalyptic statements representing the White Man's difficult civilizing mission – all this is something at work within a purportedly liberal culture, one full of concern for its vaunted norms of catholicity, plurality, and open-mindedness.

Sometimes a dash within a parenthesis adds a double counterpoint: 'What this must lead us to methodologically is to view representations (or misrepresentations – the distinction is at best a matter of degree) as inhabiting a common field of play defined for them'. The quick of this prose works always to assert a passionate intelligence, an intelligence which knows that the often abstract vocabulary it has to use could dull the prose. At the beginning of the next paragraph, he says: 'The representations of Orientalism in European culture amount to what we can call a discursive consistency, one that has not only history but material (and institutional) presence to show for itself.' That phrase 'discursive consistency' has a necessary soupiness, whose dullness is disturbed by '(and institutional)', which breaks against its normalizing tendency.

This tendency is obviously there in Sir Hamilton Gibb's 'quietly heedless but profoundly sequential prose', a style which is similar to Conrad's description (in the words of the character Marlow) of the accountant in *Heart of Darkness*:

> When near the buildings I met a white man, in such an unexpected elegance of get-up that in the first moment I took him for a sort of vision. I saw a high starched collar, white cuffs, a light alpaca jacket, snowy trousers, a clean necktie, and varnished boots. No hat. Hair parted, brushed, oiled, under a green-lined parasol held in a big white hand. He was amazing, and had a pen-holder behind his ear.
>
> I shook hands with this miracle, and I learned he was the Company's chief accountant, and that all the book-keeping was done at this station. He had come out for a moment, he said, 'to get a breath of fresh air.' The expression sounded wonderfully odd, with its suggestion of sedentary desk-life. I wouldn't have mentioned the fellow to you at all, only it was from his lips that I first heard the name of the man who is so indissolubly connected with the memories of that time. Moreover, I respected the fellow. Yes; I respected his collars, his vast cuffs, his brushed hair. His appearance was certainly that of a hairdresser's dummy; but in the great demoralisation of the land he kept up his appearance. That's backbone. His starched collars and got-up shirt-fronts were achievements of character. He had been out nearly three years; and, later, I could not help asking him how he managed to sport such linen. He had just the faintest blush, and said modestly, 'I've been teaching one of the native women about the station. It was difficult. She had a distaste for the work.' Thus this man had verily accomplished something. And he was devoted to his books, which were in apple-pie order.

Conrad's novella is near the centre of Said's imagination, and helps shape his writing. The phrase 'quietly heedless', which he applies to

Gibb summons the European self-regarding inattention to what lies beyond its concerns. When, in the same sentence, he remarks that Louis Massignon has 'the flair of an artist for whom no reference is too extravagant so long as it is governed by an eccentric interpretative gift', we may discern Kurtz behind this characterization of the scholar.

Part of the effectiveness of Said's analysis lies in the attention he pays to Orientalist prose style: quoting Bernard Lewis's statement that the root '*th-w-r* in classical Arabic meant to rise up (e.g. of a camel), to be stirred or excited', he remarks that the entire passage is 'full of condescension and bad faith. Why introduce the idea of a camel rising as an etymological root for modern Arab revolution except as a clever way of discrediting the modern?' Gibb, he notices, speaks of 'the characteristic difference in the Oriental', but what is the meaning of 'difference', he asks, 'when the preposition "from" has dropped from sight altogether?'

Here, Said points to a specific stylistic feature: elsewhere he says that, like Orwell's work and status in England, Camus' 'plain style and unadorned reporting of social situations conceal rivetingly complex contradictions'. Noting that Roland Barthes in *Le Degré zéro de l'écriture* describes Camus' style as '*écriture blanche*', he notes what he terms the 'unaffected clarity' of Camus' and Orwell's political formulations. This suspicion of plain style is of a piece with Said's dislike of 'heedless' prose, and from it he moves to the work of a gifted stylist, Conor Cruise O'Brien, whose 'agile demystification' of Camus in his short study he praises. He quotes a passage from O'Brien where Camus is characterized as 'intensely European' because he belonged 'to the frontier of Europe and was aware of a threat'. Pointing to the contradiction in O'Brien's thinking, he says that having 'shrewdly and even mercilessly exposed the connections between Camus' most famous novels and the colonial situation in Algeria, O'Brien lets him off the hook'. In his 'otherwise tough-minded' analysis of Camus, O'Brien is guilty of 'elision and compression'. This is a version of the phrase 'discursive consistency', and it shows that despite its texture, its distance from plain style, O'Brien's prose is inadequate. O'Brien elevates Camus' difficulties to the symbolic rank of 'Western consciousness', Said argues, and that phrase is 'a receptacle emptied of all but its capacity for sentience and reflection'.

In *Reflections on Exile* (2001), he says that 'the plain reportorial style coerces history, process, knowledge itself into mere events being observed'. Out of this has grown 'the eye-witness, seemingly opinion-less politics' of contemporary Western journalism. The textured cadences of Said's style resist the discursive consistency of plain style, as when he says that the role of the intellectual is 'to say the truth to power, to address the central authority in every society without hypocrisy, and to choose the method, the style, the texture best suited for those purposes'. The critical energy he cites and draws on is that of Swift, whose prose has an 'agitational and unacademic' restlessness which supplies modern criticism with what it has sorely needed since Arnold covered critical writing with 'the mantle of cultural authority and reactionary political quietism'. This energetic restlessness can be felt in his list of possible Swiftian interventions – 'a tract, a tale, a digression or a pamphlet' – where there is a climbing effect, a type of achieved freedom in the phrase, within what are intended as limited, as well as 'shaky and ridiculous' opportunities. He is fascinated by repetition both in Vico and in music, particularly in Bach's *Goldberg Variations* as played by Glenn Gould.

This emphasis on performance is pitched against what he called the 'endemic flaccidity' of English Studies. He was hostile to the 'cult of professional expertise' which defended the classics, the virtues of a liberal education, and 'the precious pleasures' of literature, even as we 'also show ourselves to be silent (perhaps incompetent)' about the social and historical world in which these things take place. The word 'silence' is a nodal term in Said's criticism, and it is a force which his eloquence is directed against. In the *Question of Palestine* (1979), he discusses the 'pernicious influence' of Western and Israeli intellectuals, who have continued to celebrate Israel and Zionism 'unblinkingly' for over thirty years. Calling this 'almost total silence' about Zionism's doctrines for, and treatment of, the native Palestinians, he lists the small handful of critics who have stood out against it – Noam Chomsky, Israel Shahak, I. F. Stone, Elmer Berger, Judah Magnes. Such lists are an important feature of his writing – they affirm the courage of certain figures, and they offer communal solidarity, *asabiyah*, and purpose. He writes their names out in the prose equivalent of a verse and elevates them into a canon of heroic opposition. They become points of light in the historical memory.

The point about silence is made in Chapter Two of *Culture and Imperialism* (1993), where he discusses the moment in *Mansfield Park* when there is 'such a dead silence' after Fanny Price asks Sir Thomas Bertram about the slave trade. Though many reviewers – some became irate – failed to notice it, Said did not then engage in what he terms 'the rhetoric of blame' and attack Austen retrospectively 'for being white, privileged, insensitive, complicit'. Rather, he criticizes what he calls 'subaltern, minority, or disadvantaged voices' for such attacks, and insists that *Mansfield Park* is a 'rich work' whose 'aesthetic intellectual complexity' requires a 'longer and slower' analysis.

This insistence on the primacy of the aesthetic is the central expression of the Hazlittian disinterestedness that he upholds. Because Austen belonged to a slave-owning society, we do not therefore jettison her novels as so many exercises in 'aesthetic frumpery'. This affirmation of aesthetic pleasure can be found in the section of Chapter 2 called 'The Pleasures of Imperialism', where he says that Kipling should not be dismissed as an 'imperialist minstrel'. *Kim*, he insists, is a work 'of great aesthetic merit' and cannot be dismissed as the racist imaginings of one 'disturbed and ultra-reactionary imperialist'. Placing Kipling with Gide's *The Immoralist* and Camus' *The Stranger* in counterpoint with other histories is neither to slight 'their great aesthetic force' nor to treat them reductively as imperialist propaganda. This self-delighting pleasure is the rolling, rising carol of style in performance, in communication, and it is the subject of an important letter that Hopkins wrote to his brother Everard, which Said quotes in *The World, the Text, and the Critic*, where Hopkins says that poetry is the darling child of speech, of lips and spoken utterance: it must be spoken; *till it is spoken it is not performed*, it does not perform, it is not itself. Sprung rhythm gives back to poetry its true soul and self. As poetry is emphatically speech, speech purged of dross like gold in the furnace, so it must have emphatically the essential elements of speech.

Commenting on this passage in Hopkins's letter, which was first published in 1972, Said says:

So close is the identification in Hopkins' mind among world, word, and the utterance, the three coming live together as a moment of performance, that he envisages little need for critical intervention . . . So far from being a document associated with other lifeless, wordless texts, Hopkins' own text was for him his child.

At the beginning of the paragraph from which Said quotes, Hopkins says that every art and every work of art has 'its own play or performance'. Hopkins brings poetry very close to music, and it is this which appeals to Said's imagination. We catch this in his prose – those textured, rhythmic cadences which prevent a lecture, an essay, a chapter from being 'lifeless, wordless texts', and which instress the vocalized prose with the sense of being present at a unique occasion.

In *Musical Elaborations* (1991), he quotes Richard Poirier's essay 'The Performing Self': 'Performance in writing, in painting, or in dance is made up of thousands of tiny movements each made with a calculation that is also its innocence.' Commenting on a theme in Brahms' Symphony No. 2, he remarks that it is 'declamatory, confident, intimate, and yet self-exposing, especially dramatic in the alternation between major and minor modes'. This sense of the shifting layers in performance is exemplified in his introduction to *Moby-Dick*, where he says that the whole, mostly monologic novel is 'in constant motion, shifting from one sort of effect to another with great power and uncommon effect'. He then takes this passage from the novel, where Ishmael says:

My hypothesis is this: that the [Sperm Whale's] spout is nothing but mist. And besides other reasons, to this conclusion I am impelled, by considerations touching the great inherent dignity and sublimity of the Sperm Whale; I account him no common, shallow being, inasmuch as it is an undisputed fact that he is never found on soundings, or near shores; all other whales sometimes are. He is both ponderous and profound. I am convinced that from the heads of all ponderous profound beings, such as Plato, Pyrrho, the Devil, Jupiter, Dante, and so on, there always goes up a certain semi-visible steam, while in the act of thinking deep thoughts. While composing a little treatise on Eternity, I had the curiosity to place a mirror before me; and ere long saw reflected there, a curious involved worming and undulation in the atmosphere over my head.

Looking at the prose as performance, Said says in *Reflections in Exile* (2001):

This almost doesn't work, so great is the movement from the seriousness of the beginning to the sentences where 'ponderous and profound' are jammed together as 'ponderous profound,' after which there follows a *very* miscellaneous laundry list, and a mock heroic simile unfolds between the speaker, as author of a 'little treatise on Eternity' with 'a curious involved worming and undulation' over his head, and the Sperm Whale. One has the sense here of a deflation, from high to low material, but there is also the strong apprehension of uncertainty, as if Melville could not go forward without digression or comic self-consciousness. What we get is a sudden change of site: the orator is displaced from lecture platform to barroom floor. From being a grave scholar or sage he becomes a teller of tall tales. These shifts occur almost nonstop in the novel, but instead of making for exasperation, they provide a good deal of the pleasure, as well as the sensuous excitement of reading *Moby-Dick*.

Again, we notice the emphasis on pleasure, on 'sensuous excitement'. This is part of his belief that the essay, like the recital, was 'occasional, re-creative, and personal'. Essayists, like pianists, concern themselves with 'givens', which are those works of art that are always worth another critical and reflective reading.

Though he travelled widely, indefatigably and courageously right to the very last weeks of his life, Said does not engage in the reportorial. He comments on the utter grimness of Gaza, but he does not wish to be, as he describes Naipaul, a 'sensibility on tour'. Sometimes one catches a glimpse of 'skinny quince trees', or of a long-lost relative who spoke a bizarre combination of 'windswept and tattered old Arabic', with a few dozen American phrases. Following his admired Hopkins, he returns often to the spoken language, noting in *Out of Place*, that the language he loves more than any – the spoken Cairo dialect of Arabic – retains 'its quick, irreverent wit, its incomparable economy of line, its sharp cadences and abrupt rhythms'. This could be a characterization of Hopkins's verse.

I have discussed so far the texture of Said's prose – its spoken and performative qualities – but there is another quality I would like to turn to, and here I want to isolate some particular moments because they point to one of the ambitions in his prose, an ambition I would term Yeatsian. In both his mid-to-late poetry, and in his autobiographical writings, Yeats invokes the memory of dead friends and relatives – Lady Gregory, Synge, George Pollexfen – as lasting and permanent sources of imaginative power. Something similar can be discussed in the portrait of Ignace Tiegerman, which follows Said's comments on the spoken dialect of Cairo. Describing Tiegerman as 'a tiny Polish-Jewish gnome of a man' in *Reflections in Exile*, he says that he:

came to Cairo in 1933, attracted by the city's warmth and possibilities in contrast to what was coming in Europe. He was a great pianist and musician, a wunderkind student of Leschetizky and Ignaz Friedman, a lazy, wonderfully precious and bright-eyed bachelor with secret tastes and unknown pleasures, who ran a Conservatoire de Musique on the rue Champollion just behind the Cairo Museum.

No one played Chopin and Schumann with such grace and unparalleled rhetorical conviction as Tiegerman. He taught piano in Cairo, tying himself to the city's *haute société* – teaching its daughters, playing for its salons, charming its gatherings – in order, I think, to free himself for the lazy indulgence of his own pursuits: conversation, good food, music, and unknown kinds (to me) of human relationships. I was his piano student at the outset and, many years later, his friend. We communicated in an English battered into submission by French and German, languages more congenial to Tiegerman, and after we had abandoned the teacher-student relationship, we would gather together a few stalwarts from Cairo's old days – these were the late 1950s and early 1960s – to play music, talk memory, and put ourselves back in time to when Cairo was more ours – cosmopolitan, free, full of wonderful privileges – than it had become. Although by then I was a Nasserite and a fierce anti-imperialist, it was much easier than supposed to slip back into the style of life represented by Tiegerman's soirées.

Tiegerman died in 1967, a few months after the June War. Although he kept his Polish passport, he was subject to Egyptian residency laws, taxes, and the miscellaneous rigors of Nasser's regime. He chafed under the restrictions but refused to consider moving to Israel. 'Why should I go there?' he said rhetorically. 'Here I am unique; there many people are like me. Besides,' he added, 'I love Cairo.' During the early 1960s I started seeing him in Kitzbühel, Austria, where he had built himself a tiny cottage in which he had installed an old Broadwood grand and a Pleyel upright. By this time our friendship had become almost totally nostalgic and reminiscent; its bases had shifted to an absent Cairo of splendid people, charming clothes, magnificent parties, all of which had disappeared. My own last symbolic memory of Tiegerman was watching him at his conservatoire listening in 1959 to his most gifted student, a stunningly fluent and accomplished young married woman, a mother of four, who played with her head completely enclosed in the pious veil of a devout Muslim.

Neither Tiegerman nor I could understand this amphibious woman, who with a part of her body could dash through the *Appassionata* and with another venerated God by hiding her face. She never said a word in my presence, although I must have heard her play or met her at least a dozen times. Tiegerman entered her in the Munich piano competition, but she didn't do well in that overheated and cutthroat atmosphere.

Like Tiegerman, she was an untransplantable emanation of Cairo's genius; unlike him, her particular branch of the city's history has endured and even triumphed. For a brief moment then, the conjunction of ultra-European and ultra-Islamic Arab cultures brought forth a highlighted image that typified the Cairo of my early years. Where such pictures have since gone I don't know, but part of their poignancy for me is that I am certain they will never recur.

This is a poignant and arresting image – the prose has a joyous but elegiac movement that is cinematic and totally engrossing. In this long passage, the dashes, the snatches of speech, the veiled young woman, taught by the tiny exiled Polish Jew, build an image that is at once cosmopolitan and rooted in tragedy – past, passing and to come. Tiegerman is also celebrated in *Musical Elaborations*, and it is clear that he is seminal, inspirational, and yet time-warped in their later friendship.

To this permanent image I would add the portrait of Charles Malik, the husband of Said's mother's first cousin, Eva. A former ambassador to the United States from Lebanon, he was foreign minister under President Chamoun, and though in many ways a brilliant intellectual and linguist, he was also reactionary, anti-Palestinian and 'the great negative intellectual lesson of my life'.

Another arresting portrait – a brief sketch really – is of his father's cousin, Sbeer Shammas, who fled to Egypt in 1948. A patriarchal figure of 'authority and prosperity' in Jerusalem, he appears in Cairo 'as a much older and frailer man, always wearing the same suit and green sweater, his bent cane bearing his large slow bulk as he lowered it painfully and slowly into the chair where he sat in silence'. His children and his worried, complaining wife are described: 'We visited them in a many-storied, dingy Heliopolis apartment building, with peeling walls and no elevator. I remember being alarmed at the emptiness of the flat, and the air of forlornness it seemed to convey.'

This image of exile speaks for a lost world and a defeated people, and has a tragic quality. Looking at the prose, I notice how *Heliopolis, no elevator, forlornness* chime together to unify the description and take it beyond the merely descriptive. What we want here is a photograph, or a piece of film, and in 2000 Said wrote a series of short prose pieces to accompany Mona Hatoum's photographs collected in *The Entire World as a Foreign Land* (2001), a title derived from one of his favourite quotations from Adorno. He says that in Mona Hatoum's 'relentless catalogue of disaffected, dislocated, oddly deformed objects', there is a sense of focusing on what's there 'without expressing much interest in the ambition to rescue the object from its strangeness or, more importantly, trying to forget or shake off the memory of how nice it once was. This is exile figured and plotted in the objects she creates.'

Part of the Palestinians' exilic suffering are the dislocated objects they retain – house keys, title deeds, photographs – objects which inform those captured in Mona Hartoum's photographs. It is out of the tragic experience of exile that critical performance – the making of music, writing of prose – arises. This experience is touched on in *Parallels and Paradoxes* (2002), where there is this interchange between Said and Daniel Barenboim:

DB: I believe that there comes now, I suppose, the mystical element in music.

EWS: You see, I don't have that. Try it. Try and convince me.

DB: I believe that when all things are right on the stage – when the playing, the expression, everything becomes permanently, constantly interdependent – it becomes indivisible. And this is the mystical, because this is the same idea of religion, of God: that there's suddenly something that you cannot divide anymore. The experience of music-making is that, in a way. It's not religious in the sense that one prays to it, but it's comparable to religion in the sense that it cannot be divided. And when this actually happens, I believe that the active listener, who is sensitive, can communicate with that. This is what I mean by the mystical.

EWS: I agree with that. But I think what you have to include, Daniel, is the element of loss. There's a tragic element to it. You know, Shelley has a wonderful phrase, in which he says that the poetic mind, while it is in the act of creation, is like a fading coal. What you have to include, I think, in what you just said, is the fact that it's a kind of extraordinarily energetic and committed battle to keep something alive which is constantly flagging.

The fading coal – Edward trying to keep it and himself alive through the energy and commitment he speaks of – is an apposite image for what they are discussing, but the implication is, I think, that one can lose the element of loss, can lose the sense of exile.

In *The Last Interview* (which took place in November 2002) he quotes Hopkins's line from 'Pied Beauty': 'All things counter, original, spare, strange', a series of impacted adjectives that speak to the themes of loss, counterpoint and exile in his writing, and at the same time a series of pulsing adjectives which can be felt in those instressed moments I've been discussing in his prose. I catch that particular texture in the run of verbs he uses in *Out of Place* to describe his coming to the United States as a schoolboy in 1951: 'relearning things from scratch, improving, self-inventing, trying and failing, experimenting, cancelling, and restarting in surprising and frequently painful ways'. I catch Hopkins here, and I remember the rest of 'Pied Beauty':

Whatever is fickle, freckled (who knows how?)
With swift, slow; sweet, sour; adazzle, dim;
He fathers-forth whose beauty is past change:
Praise him.